New Testament Foundations

NEW TESTAMENT FOUNDATIONS

A Guide for Christian Students

Volume 1

THE FOUR GOSPELS

by

RALPH P. MARTIN M.A., Ph.D
Professor of New Testament, Fuller Theological Seminary, Pasadena, California

EXETER:
THE PATERNOSTER PRESS LTD

ISBN 085364 178 1
*This British Edition published by The Paternoster Press Ltd.
by arrangement with Wm. B. Eerdmans Publishing Co.*

AUSTRALIA:
*Emu Book Agencies Pty., Ltd.,
63, Berry Street, Granville, N.S.W., 2142*

SOUTH AFRICA:
*Oxford University Press
P.O. Box 1141, Oxford House,
11, Buitencingle Street, Cape Town*

*Made and Printed in Great Britain for
The Paternoster Press Ltd, Paternoster House,
3 Mount Radford Crescent, Exeter, Devon
by Butler and Tanner Ltd, Frome, Somerset*

Contents

Acknowledgments

In chapter one the writer has drawn upon some material which first appeared in his book, *Mark: Evangelist and Theologian* (Paternoster Press, Exeter, 1972; Zondervan, Grand Rapids, 1973). From the same source occasional parts of chapter thirteen on Mark's Gospel have been drawn. In chapter fourteen on Matthew's Gospel some paragraphs are taken from the writer's article, "St. Matthew's Gospel in Recent Study," *Expository Times*, 80 (1968-69), 132-36; and permission to use this material has been given by the editor.

Preface

The book which now appears is offered as a handbook of introduction to the study of the Four Gospels. It is chiefly a student's book, but the author hopes that it will be of interest and service to a wider public. It aims at encouraging a serious and disciplined study of the background and contents of the Christian Gospels, and at laying a foundation on which readers may build.

In due course it will be followed by a second volume which covers the remainder of the New Testament books. The second volume will contain chapters dealing with the canon and will try to say something constructive about the vexed questions of authority and validity.

The author is indebted to several generations of students who in various classrooms have heard the contents of these pages. In particular he would pay tribute to two student assistants, Mr. Tom Provence, who compiled the Exegetical Notes in chapter seventeen, and Mr. Eric Behrens, whose use of the typewritten material which underlies this book did so much, by way of helpful criticism, to make the meaning clearer. Finally, Dr. Glenn W. Barker read the proofs and helped further to make the writing more intelligible. Such errors as remain must of course be debited to the author.

RALPH P. MARTIN

Fuller Theological Seminary
Pasadena, California

Introduction

The present volume, which aims at providing a student's guide to the Four Gospels, represents the fruit of ten years of classroom teaching both in a British university and in several seminaries in the USA. The author has endeavored to achieve certain goals in this course of teaching. It may be well to set down some of the objectives which underlie the publication of this book.

One conviction which is presupposed in the writing of sections one and two is that an understanding of the historical and cultural background of the Gospels is of the first importance. This section does not pretend to be exhaustive or complete. But, the author hopes, it does offer some orientation to the task of setting the life of Jesus in its contemporary framework.

The third section equally makes no claim to be comprehensive. Like the other parts of the book, it aims at laying a foundation on which the student can hopefully build in later years. Not every aspect of the foundation is given equal prominence, partly because some selection has to be made in a course with limited time, but more importantly because experience shows that students need more guidance with (say) the synoptic problem than with the latest trend in redaction criticism. Interest in the latter is stimulated by its obvious relevance to theological training and a pulpit ministry. Students, however, need to be motivated to see how relevant literary criticism can be to the same ends and how needful it is to build on whatever "assured results" are available from a close and comparative study of the Gospel texts themselves, rather than on theories which are contrived out of ideas about the Gospels.

This volume is not an Introduction to the science of New Testament criticism. Along with its future partner which will cover the Acts of the Apostles, the Epistles and the Apocalypse, it tries to show how a study of the biblical books fits into the life and problems and opportunities of the early Christian church communities. There are several excellent handbooks which take up in full the more detailed issues of authority, dating, readership and background of the Gospels.

The course for which this book is designed makes required reading of W. G. Kümmel's *Introduction to the New Testament* (Abingdon; SCM Press, 1965) and D. Guthrie's *New Testament Introduction*[3] (Inter-Varsity, 1970).

Therefore, overlapping with these comprehensive guides has been avoided as far as possible, and the present book has the more limited objective of pinpointing and applying what appear to be the salient issues in the modern discussion. The Four Gospels are regarded primarily as theological handbooks, expressing the church's faith in Jesus as Israel's Messiah and the universal Lord. For that reason, the theological motifs in each Gospel are given pride of place.

In a final section I try to say how all the preceding study relates to the students' handling of the Gospels today. In a word, this part throws light on the most sensitive part of this discipline as far as theological seminarians and college students are concerned, namely, how may the student learn to preach the gospel from the Gospels? Three specimen examples are given of how this question may be answered, and the guiding principle is found in the Gospels' kerygmatic and christological witness. Though the final part does not actually say so, it is really a "how to" application of all that has gone before.

In a volume such as this the temptation is to crowd the page with bibliographical references and footnote pointers to other persons' views and to extraneous discussion. I have tried to resist this temptation by using only such materials as are (1) really germane and (2) readily available in university or seminary libraries. Foreign language matter and the use of Greek have been trimmed to what I believe to be a tolerable level. But the references to New Testament Greek and to books and articles in French and German often act as a stimulus and spur to serious language study for enterprising students, as every teacher knows. Most probably the teacher responded positively to such a challenge in his or her student days.

No apology is needed for the subtitle, "A Guide for Christian Students," since the author's conviction is that while New Testament study is a legitimate branch of historical and religious inquiry, it yields its treasures most readily to those who come to it with an open mind and a teachable spirit. While the New Testament Gospels are historical documents of the first century of our era, they are primarily church books and are so best understood by those who stand within the household of Christian faith. But no exclusive right to interpretation belongs to those so privileged; rather the claim and promises contained in these four little books are freely made to all who will study them with an honest intent. Again, every teacher can recall from his classroom experience those occasions when the academic discipline of Gospel criticism has become an encounter with the living Lord by means of the text opened before him and his students. Paul's words in Romans 10:17, "Faith comes from what is heard. and what is heard comes from the message about Christ," seem to be apposite in this context no less than in a service of worship. If this volume serves that end, it will have achieved the author's intention.

Abbreviations

BJRL	*Bulletin of the John Rylands Library* (Manchester)
CBQ	*Catholic Biblical Quarterly* (Washington)
EQ	*The Evangelical Quarterly* (Exeter)
ExpT	*The Expository Times* (Edinburgh)
HDB	*Hastings' Dictionary of the Bible*, ed. F. C. Grant and H. H. Rowley (1963).
HTR	*Harvard Theological Review* (Cambridge, Mass.)
JBL	*Journal of Biblical Literature* (Philadelphia)
JTS	*Journal of Theological Studies* (Oxford)
NovT	*Novum Testamentum* (Leiden)
NTS	*New Testament Studies* (Cambridge)
RB	*Revue Biblique* (Jerusalem/Paris)
SJT	*Scottish Journal of Theology* (Edinburgh)
Strack-Billerbeck	H. Strack and P. Billerbeck, *Kommentar zum Neuen Testament aus Talmud und Midrasch* (Munich)
TB	*Tyndale Bulletin* (London)
TDNT	*Theological Dictionary of the New Testament* (Grand Rapids)
ThL	*Theologische Literaturzeitung* (Leipzig/Berlin)
ThZ	*Theologische Zeitschrift* (Basel)
TSF Bulletin	*Theological Students' Fellowship Bulletin* (London)
TU	*Texte und Untersuchungen* (Berlin)
VT	*Vetus Testamentum* (Leiden)
ZKTh	*Zeitschrift für katholische Theologie* (Innsbruck)
ZNTW	*Zeitschrift für neutestamentliche Wissenschaft* (Giessen/Berlin)
ZThK	*Zeitschrift für Theologie und Kirche* (Tübingen)

PART ONE

Introducing the Gospels

In the opening two chapters we come to a study of the four books called the Gospels with a desire to know what they are all about. At the outset of a course of Bible study we can make only preliminary and tentative observations, because we cannot expect to be in a position to know what are the leading themes of any book until we have first read and studied it! So we will begin with some guidelines before us, and then, in the closing section, we shall return to this question and test the validity and adequacy of these first conclusions.

At the centennial meetings of the Society of Biblical Literature and Exegesis, held in 1964, one important topic was assigned for discussion under the title, "Kerygma and History."[1] *These two terms are our concern in the first two chapters, though it must be understood that we shall consider the terms in an elementary fashion. Students, however, need something like this initiation. They are to be encouraged, right at the outset of the study of the Gospels, to face the two fundamental questions raised by these documents: What is the message of the Gospels (kerygma)? What kind of history is it that these books claim to be recording for their first readers and for us today? It is to these questions we now seek answers.*

[1] The papers may be read in the volume *The Bible in Modern Scholarship*, ed. J. Philip Hyatt (1965).

CHAPTER ONE

What to Look for in the Gospels

READING THE GOSPELS TODAY

In one way the task of reading the Gospels is easy to accomplish. On the face of it, the four records of Jesus' earthly life are both simple to understand and interesting to read. As we read them, we are already on ground that is familiar, even well-trodden. It follows that we have formed certain impressions about these books even before we begin our studies.

This works in two ways. On the side of advantage, we are not wrestling with a subject which is completely unknown and forbidding; we can all make something of our data at first glance. But there is a serious drawback. Such ideas as we have formed over the years tend to become deeply embedded, and there is resistance to change. We have to take seriously the momentous proposition that our thinking about the Gospels needs a drastic revolution. Can it be that until now we have read the Gospels in the wrong way? Or at least that we have failed to grasp what they are really all about? And can it be that we have put questions to these parts of Scripture which they were never intended or designed to answer?

The first requirement is that we try to begin with a new page, as though we were coming to the Gospels fresh and for the first time. Let us attempt to put ourselves back into a situation in which reading the Gospels comes as a new experience. Suppose we were handed a copy of Mark's Gospel and were encouraged to read it for ourselves as a new book. What kind of book would it seem to us to be? Would its contents justify or disappoint the expectation aroused by our glancing first at the sentence which stands as the frontispiece: "*The beginning of the gospel of Jesus Christ the Son of God*"?

We call these four books Gospels. Before we look at this word in detail, it will be worthwhile to pause and ask: What is the meaning of the title Gospel when applied to these literary pieces? Are the four Gospels accurately described under this caption? Are they equally to be classified in this way because they are sufficiently homogeneous in their grouping, or are there distinguishing features which make the term more or less appropriate in the case of each individual Gospel-book? What other designations for these booklets are possible?

We shall examine three other terms closely connected with what these Gospels are popularly understood to be. In each case it will be apparent that the name suggested is not really appropriate without qualification.

In a chapter "What Kind of a Book is a Gospel?", C. F. Evans addresses our question in an interesting way.[1] He invites us to consider how an imaginary librarian at Alexandria, Egypt, near the end of the second century would have classified Mark's Gospel if a copy of it had been presented to the library.

1. He might have thought of including this book, which superficially looks like an account of the life of Jesus, under the heading of "Lives of Famous Men" (*βίοι*). Ancient biographies were devoted in the main to two classes of men: prominent political figures (whether military men or professional statesmen) and leading intellectuals, chiefly philosophers.

One of the most famous ancient biographies was Plutarch's *Lives*, sketches of Greek and Roman politicians arranged in pairs to illustrate some moral virtue. In the frontispiece of his *Life of Alexander*, Plutarch states succinctly his task as a biographer:

> I am not a writer of histories but of biographies. My readers therefore must excuse me if I do not record all events or describe in detail, but only briefly touch upon, the noblest and the most famous. . . . As painters produce a likeness by the representation of the countenance and the expression of the face, in which the character is revealed, without troubling themselves about the other parts of the body, so I must be allowed to look rather into the signs of a man's character, and by means of these to portray the life of each, leaving to others the description of great events and battles.[2]

What is interesting about Plutarch's understanding of his task is how he is self-consciously selective in his choice of material and desire to focus attention on the ethical issues involved. His characters are chosen to exemplify moral qualities, and are held up for emulation.

In spite of a superficial correspondence with the achievement of the Christian Gospel-writers, there is no real affinity of purpose between them and Plutarch. And it is doubtful that the term "biography" really fits the case when we ask about the scope of the Christian Gospels. Certainly if we give a modern connotation to the term, it becomes inappropriate for several reasons.

The evangelists have not assembled information concerning Jesus' antecedents, culture, and environment. Mark in particular as-

[1] C. F. Evans, in *The New Testament Gospels* (1965), pp. 7ff.

[2] Quoted by S. Neill, *The Interpretation of the New Testament* (1964), p. 260, from Plutarch's *Life of Alexander* 1.1.

sumes that his readers will already know that Jesus was a Jew, born to Jewish parents (6:3) and living in a province of the Roman empire when Tiberius Caesar held the reins of power. Luke (3:1-2) is more informative about the historical setting of the gospel events, and he does provide something of a prologue in his narrative having to do with John's parents (ch. 1). It is partly for that reason that recent scholars have suggested that Luke comes close to a biographical interest in composing a "Life of Jesus."[3]

But no attempt is made by any of the evangelists to delve into Jesus' mental or psychological development in the way that has become familiar in the twentieth-century studies of Jesus' personality. The Gospels offer no material for a psychoanalytic case study of the workings of Jesus' mind. Dramatists like Dennis Potter (in his play *Son of Man*) and librettists like Tim Rice (in his rock opera *Jesus Christ Superstar*) have to rely on their imagination and ingenuity to piece together the material which forms their plot. Again and again, to the interesting modern question, "What made Jesus tick?", the Gospels are remarkably silent and inconclusive.

2. Another possibility would be for our imaginary librarian to place the Gospel-book in a section headed "Acts" (πράξεις). Under this heading would be books containing the narratives of heroic deeds performed by some notable person. A good illustration is Arrian's history of Alexander's campaigns, recorded in his *Anabasis*. But our librarian may well have thought that Jesus, whose life was set in a remote province of the Roman Empire, was too inconspicuous a person on the stage of public life to have "Acts." That word suggests movement and exploits, and there is little movement in Jesus' story. The "mighty deeds" he performed are not the kind that would impress a reader in a sophisticated metropolis like Rome. What would count most against Jesus is simply that his story ends with a trial on charges of sedition and revolution against the Roman *imperium*, and a state execution.

3. A third suggested label for Mark's story is a term translated "Memoirs" (Greek ἀπομνημονεύματα). This was a collection of individual anecdotes about, or sayings of, a famous figure, generally supposed to come from someone who knew him well as his disciple or chronicler. Perhaps the most celebrated of such documents in this category have to do with Socrates (469-399 BC)—the *Memoirs* of the historian Xenophon (*c.* 380 BC) and the Dialogues of Plato, Socrates' disciple (380-350 BC). Indeed, the term "memoirs" is found in a description of church worship at Rome in the mid-second century. Justin Martyr (*c.* AD 150) offers the following picture of what went on when Christians assembled for worship:

[3] E. Käsemann, "The Problem of the Historical Jesus," in *Essays on New Testament Themes* (ET 1964), p. 29.

> And on the day called Sunday there is a meeting in one place of those who live in cities or the country, and the memoirs of the apostles or the writings of the prophets are read as long as time permits (*Apology* 67.3).

Earlier Justin mentions that "the memoirs of the apostles . . . are called Gospels" (*Apology* 66).

Justin's account is part of an apology, an attempt to give a non-Christian readership as attractive a presentation of Christian belief and life as possible. Thus we cannot be sure that by calling the Gospels "memoirs" he is doing anything more than using a term which would be current coin in his readers' vocabulary. That explanation is supported in part by the explanatory gloss he appends and even more by the fact that the title *ἀπομνημονεύματα* is found in no other Christian writing after Justin to designate the church's liturgical books.

It looks, then, as if this label too does not exactly fit. So we come back to the basic question. Are the Gospels biography?

As early as 1915, C. W. Votaw raised this question and replied ambivalently, according to the connotation given the term.[4] Votaw distinguished between biography in the "historical" sense and as a "popular" literary form. He concluded that, for the reasons mentioned above, the Gospels do not fit into the former classification. But he argued that in the "popular" sense of the term, the title was applicable, since this genre of literature aims to make the reader acquainted with a historical person "by giving some account of his deeds and words, sketchily chosen and arranged, even when the motive of the writer is practical and hortatory rather than historical" (p. 49). The examples he drew from the ancient world were the popular biographies of Epictetus, whose teaching was written by Arrian (*c.* AD 125-150), Apollonius of Tyana, whose biography was recorded by Philostratus (*c.* AD 217), and, above all, Socrates. According to Votaw, what unites these literary works is a common effort to "eulogize and idealize their heroes, . . . [to] select their best sayings and interpret them for practical use, . . . [to] give the memorabilia in an atmosphere of appreciation, . . . [to] commend the message to the faith and practice of all."[5]

We may question whether the aim of the Christian evangelists is adequately designated in such language. Our suspicion that Votaw is forcing the Gospels into a predetermined pattern is confirmed by his conclusion, after a lengthy but interesting comparison between the

4 C. W. Votaw, "The Gospels and Contemporary Biographies," *American Journal of Theology*, 19 (1915), 45-71, 217-49. These essays have recently been reprinted and published separately as *The Gospels and Contemporary Biographies in the Greco-Roman World* (1970). For a discussion of the literary genres, see H. J. Cadbury, *The Making of Luke-Acts* (1958 ed.), pp. 127ff., and A. N. Wilder, *Early Christian Rhetoric* (American title, *The Language of the Gospel*) (1964), pp. 35ff.

5 Votaw, *op. cit.*, p. 55.

Socratic writings attributed to Plato and Xenophon and the Gospels. He maintains that the purpose of the two groups of biographical writings was in general the same: "to restore the reputation of a great and good man who had been publicly executed and defamed by the state; to re-establish his influence as a supreme teacher in respect to right living and thinking; and to render available to all the message of truth and duty which each had made it his life-work to promulgate."[6]

Votaw's attempt to correlate the evangelists' purpose with that of their contemporaries (even if they share the same literary domain) must be judged a failure. For one thing, in the history of interpretation, the search for contemporary parallels to the literary type (or *Gattung*) of "Gospel" in the popular literature of the ancient world was not likely to seem very fruitful in the 1920s, when the uniqueness of the Christian message was receiving emphasis from Karl Barth's stress on the gospel's transcendental qualities as the unrivaled Word of God.[7] So Votaw's plea went largely ignored.

But there is a second, more telling reason why this correlation is inadequate. For all the superficial resemblances between Socrates' or Apollonius' life story and that of Jesus, it is clear that no Christian "biographer" thought he was in his literary records preserving a memory which might otherwise lapse. To imagine this is to overlook the Christian claim of the resurrection of Jesus Christ, by which his living presence was assured to the church in every generation. It is true that Christians may well have desired a permanent account of Jesus' earthly life and words, especially as more of his first followers were dying. But it remains a conviction throughout the New Testament literature that the memory of Christ the Lord was a present reality to the people who met to worship in his name, to break bread "in remembrance of" him, and to realize the full extent and depth of his promise to be with them (Matt. 18:20).

All that we can learn about early Christian literary techniques from the discipline of form criticism supports this conclusion and shows that the thoughts and aspirations of the first disciples were not oriented to the past, as though the church were continually harking back to some golden age when Jesus was with them in bodily presence, or seeking to recapture a lost Camelot of spiritual life when Jesus lived on earth. On the contrary, they were conscious of his living presence in the present; and it was this reminder to us that James Denney spotlighted in his epigram, "No apostle, no New Testament writer, ever *remembered* Christ."[8]

For that reason, Amos N. Wilder prefers to regard the Chris-

6 *Ibid.*, p. 245.

7 See J. M. Robinson's discussion, "On the *Gattung* of Mark (and John)," in *Jesus and Man's Hope* (1970), A Perspective Book, I, 104.

8 J. Denney, *Studies in Theology* (1895), p. 154.

tian genre of Gospel (especially in Mark) as reenacted history centered on a faith-story in which Christ is recalled as a pattern of meaning or life-orientation for the believer. The element of reenactment—or mimesis—implies that history is recalled not as a record of the past valuable for its own sake, but in order to contemporize Christ who comes out of the past to greet his people in the present.[9]

THE NAME GOSPEL

We have observed the failure of any of the more obvious terms for biographical writing to convey adequately the evangelists' intention. We have now to inquire how in fact the dilemma was met and overcome. The answer is found in the innovative device of coining a new name for what was, in effect, a new literary genre.

The "stories of Jesus' life" were called among Christians themselves Gospels (εὐαγγέλια). In so doing they were laying claim to the appearance of a new genre of writing for which no current categories would do, a type of literary composition which could not properly be called a biography of Jesus or a chronicle of his exploits or even a set of reminiscences by his friends and followers. Rather, these books were preaching materials, designed to tell the story of God's saving action in the life, ministry, death, and resurrection of Jesus of Nazareth. They were called Gospels because they gave the substance of *the gospel*, declared in Romans 1:16 to be God's power to salvation to all who believe.

This is the first principle of Gospel interpretation. We place such a high value on these four books of the Bible because they contain the essence of the saving events which form the bedrock of the apostolic gospel. These books are historical in the way they root Jesus' life-story in the world of first-century Judaism and Graeco-Roman society, but this is history with a novel twist. The Gospel-writers were not biographers concerned to praise the personal impact of their subject on those who came under his spell in Galilee and Jerusalem (on that showing his life's achievement was more of a disaster than a success story). They were not diarists who kept a day-by-day chronicle of his deeds and movements. They did not try to impress the reader with deeds of power and thus extol the merits of the miracle-worker as a figure of some bygone age.[10]

[9] A. N. Wilder, *op. cit.*, pp. 36f.

[10] The technical expression for literature that recounted the miraculous deeds of a god or hero is *aretalogy*. See J. M. Robinson, *op. cit.*, p. 103; and, for a full discussion of the background in the ancient world, Morton Smith, "Prolegomena to a Discussion of Aretalogies, Divine Men, the Gospels and Jesus," *JBL*, 90, 2 (1971), 174-99. The relevant texts are given in M. Hadas and Morton Smith, *Heroes and Gods. Spiritual Biographies in Antiquity* (1965).

The Christian writers are correctly called evangelists. They report the history of Jesus from a particular perspective in order to highlight the *kerygmatic* or salvation-bringing side of that history. In a word, they are men of faith who write to direct their readers' faith to a living person, once localized in Galilee and Jerusalem but now set free from all earthly limitation and exalted as Lord of heaven, in whom alone salvation is to be found. Yet he is accessible to those who desire him as a present, powerful reality, to be known and trusted in the worshiping congregations of his followers and in a personal faith-experience and "existential" commitment.

We are now ready to tackle the question of the correct nomenclature of these pieces of writing under the proposed caption "Gospel." Let us go back to our illustration of the librarian at Alexandria who has received a copy of Mark's "Life of Jesus." As we have seen, he has no appropriate shelf on which to place it; so he improvises, using as a clue the first phrase of the book. He places it on a shelf labeled descriptively "Gospels."

The title "Gospel" would certainly have seemed strange to our librarian—not because he was unused to the word εὐαγγέλιον, but because it was—without precedent—being applied to a category of literature. Indeed, designating the *written* story of Jesus as the "Gospel according to Mark" must have sounded strange to Christian as well as to pagan ears.

In non-Christian contexts the word "gospel" was applied to good news—whether of victory in battle or of the enthronement of a Roman ruler. In the famous calendar inscription from Priene in Asia Minor, dated 9 BC, the birthday of Emperor Augustus was hailed as "joyful news (εὐαγγέλια) for the world." It is quite a different matter, however, to apply the same word to a book as its title.

To first-century Christians as well, the second-century title "Gospels" would have come as something of a shock. The plural form may well have seemed to contradict Paul's insistence that there is, by definition, only one gospel and that to proclaim any rival message is to incur the apostolic sentence of doom (Gal. 1:8; although this risk was apparently run at Corinth, 2 Cor. 11:4). It would have been just as surprising to the early Christians to see the term "Gospel" applied to a group of written compositions. In the New Testament "gospel" is invariably connected with verbs of speaking and responding, never with verbs of writing or reading.[11]

[11] A linguistic note on "gospel." The Septuagint version of the Old Testament does not contain the noun form εὐαγγέλιον. J. Schniewind, *Euangelion, Ursprung und erste Gestalt des Begriffs Evangelium*, I (1927), 78, states: "The substantive εὐαγγέλιον is absent from the LXX; so is the idea of a messenger of good news. We cannot detect a religious value in the verb. . . . The main result is negative: the Septuagint gives us no help in understanding the origin of the concept of 'Gospel.' " The denial that the

Why then did second-century Christians feel it necessary to use a word which traditionally (to them, at least) had to do with oral communication as a descriptive heading for written accounts of the life of Jesus? Existing titles evidently proved inadequate for conveying all that they understood these brochures to contain, so they chose a term which had strict and long associations with preaching.[12] They felt that these books could be rightly called "Gospels" inasmuch as they stood in close relation to the message of Jesus proclaimed by the apostles. The church believed that what they gave in literary form was not a biographical life of Jesus, not a catalogue of his mighty deeds, not even reminiscences of his contemporary followers, but an account of how the good news of the church's proclamation—the rule of God over human lives exerted through the message of a humiliated and exalted Lord—began in Galilee and Jerusalem.

---

idea of messenger of news is present overlooks such evidence as in *Psalms of Solomon* 11:1, 2:

> Blow ye in Zion on a trumpet
> to summon the saints;
> Proclaim [*κηρύξατε*] in Jerusalem
> the voice of him who brings good news [*εὐαγγελιζομένου*].

This set of evidence, which follows on that in the exilic passages of Isa. 40:9; 52:7-10; 60:6; 61:1, is equally neglected in W. Schneemelcher's discussion in *New Testament Apocrypha*, I (1963), 71ff., in the interest of maintaining an exclusively hellenistic origin of the terminology. But see to the contrary W. K. L. Clarke, "What is the Gospel?", in *Divine Humanity* (1936), pp. 87-100, who writes, "A surprisingly conservative result seems to emerge from our critical study. The originality of Jesus was rooted in a revival of the true meaning of 2 Isaiah. The Gospel begins with John the Baptist, who takes up the opening words of Isa. xl. . . . John therefore is the *m'bhasser*, he-that-bringeth-good tidings, proclaiming salvation, saying to Zion, 'Thy God hath ascended the throne' (Isa. lii.7). When John is arrested, Jesus comes into Galilee 'preaching the Gospel of God, and saying, The time is fulfilled, and the Kingdom of God has drawn near: repent ye and believe in the gospel.' The Gospel then *is* 'the Kingdom of God,' the message, which also is the reality, that God has ascended the throne and the New Age has begun; further, the message and the Messenger are one" (pp. 96f.). This is the conclusion also of G. Friedrich, *TDNT*, II, 708, 728f., but he maintains that the use of the term *εὐαγγέλιον* in the emperor cult is decisive. Divine rulers in the hellenistic world were hailed as miracle-workers and human benefactors. Their birth and rule are celebrated as "joyful news," ushering in a reign of peace and prosperity (see the texts, pp. 724f.). But while there is this link of a common terminology, we should note the vast differences of what is meant by world peace and how it is secured.

The Old Testament influence, in spite of the absence of the noun in the singular, seems more determinative for the gospel-writers, especially if there is a middle term in Galilean Aramaic usages of verb and noun, as J. W. Bowman has argued, "The Term 'Gospel' and its Cognates in the Palestinian Syriac," in *New Testament Essays in Memory of T. W. Manson*, ed. A. J. B. Higgins (1959), pp. 54-67.

12 Especially because of its verbal usage in Isa. 40:9; 52:7; 60:6; 61:1. On these verses, which use the verb *εὐαγγελίζομαι*, see F. F. Bruce, "When is a Gospel not a Gospel?", *BJRL*, 45 (1963), 325ff.

The Gospel-writers were not narrating, as detached historians, "exactly what happened" in a disinterested and impartial way. Unlike modern biographies they do not take the liberty of obtruding their own opinions by introducing a set of value judgments on what they record[13] or by offering an assessment of the character of Jesus, of his friends, and his foes. It is remarkable how restrained the narration is, how lacking it is in vituperative comment on those whose hostility to Jesus might well have occasioned some judgmental remark. The Gospel-writers apparently thought of their task as more objective. Nor are they interested in assembling information on their subject's antecedents, culture, and inner mental development and response to the world such as modern biographers deem needful for a full-orbed presentation. Yet there is no attempt to disguise the motives behind their selection of material. Here the Fourth Evangelist speaks for all: "These are written that you may believe that Jesus the Christ is the Son of God, and that believing, you may have life in his name" (John 20:31). The story of Jesus underlies the preaching of the church, and the preaching has preserved and shaped the record of that history.

In summary, the Gospels may be described as theological handbooks, incorporating a paradigmatic history angled to set forth the fulfilment of God's redeeming motive and activity in Jesus, the Messiah of Israel and the church's Lord. That is why the Gospels are so called.

MARK'S USE OF THE TERM "GOSPEL"

Recent studies of how "gospel" (*εὐαγγέλιον*) is used in the Synoptic Gospels have yielded some interesting results.[14]

1. Mark is the creator of this term, since there is no evidence that the noun was used in any of the pre-Markan traditions (e.g., the sayings-source common to Matthew and Luke; "Proto-Luke," the hypothetical source behind Luke; or alleged Judaean traditions underlying the Fourth Gospel). In fact, John's Gospel lacks the noun altogether, and Luke also avoids the noun *εὐαγγέλιον*.[15]

2. Where the Synoptists record sayings attributed to Jesus

[13] Except in the Fourth Gospel, where the evangelist's role is certainly to do just that, e.g., 2:13-22; 11:51, 52; 12:16; 21:24. "First he states what happened (factually) in the past, then he raises questions and gives hints about the significance of the event, and finally he unveils completely, for people living in the present, the positive message which is contained in the events of the past." X. Léon-Dufour, *The Gospels and the Jesus of History* (ET 1968), pp. 86f.

[14] See especially W. Marxsen, *Mark the Evangelist* (ET 1969), pp. 117-50; and N. Perrin, "The Literary *Gattung* 'Gospel'—Some Observations," *ExpT*, 82,1 (1970), 4-7.

[15] The noun does not appear in his Gospel and in Acts it is rare. See H. Conzelmann, *The Theology of Saint Luke* (ET 1961), p. 221.

differently, Mark apparently has inserted the noun εὐαγγέλιον in order to explain a tradition which was ambiguous, whereas the later evangelists have amplified the text by adding other terms. A case in point is found in Mark 8:35 and 10:29.

> Whoever loses his life for my sake and the gospel's will save it (8:35).
>
> There is no one who has left house or brothers or sisters or mother or father or children or lands, for my sake and for the gospel . . . (10:29).

Regarding the first text, Matthew 16:25 and Luke 9:24 agree with slight variation, but have no amplification of the Markan "for my sake." It is clear that Mark has elaborated the tradition by the insertion of the phrase ἕνεκεν τοῦ εὐαγγελίου (for the sake of the gospel);[16] and the other evangelists have chosen not to follow him in this expansion.

Mark repeats this phrase at 10:29; but Matthew 19:29 has recast it as "for the sake of my name" and Luke 18:29 reads "on account of the kingdom of God." The conclusion again seems clear that Mark has expanded an original, simple statement expressing heroic self-denial for Jesus' sake into a similar renunciation "for the sake of the gospel." Matthew and Luke have altered the Markan tradition, in one case by omitting the term for "gospel," in the other by recasting the wording.[17]

3. The impression to be gained from Mark's use of the word is that for him "gospel" was a favorite expression. He has inserted it into the pre-canonical tradition of which he is the first editor.[18] Similarly, perhaps, in Mark 13 the statement that the disciples will have to stand before governors and kings "for my sake, to bear testimony before them" (vs. 9) has been expanded to include the explanation that this witness is tantamount to a preaching of the gospel to all nations (vs. 10).[19] The common factor is the allusion to the Gentiles, mentioned in verse 9 as "governors and kings" and in verse 10 as "the nations" (ἔθνη). It follows that the evangelist may well have amplified Jesus' traditional saying about the disciples' destiny as his witnesses in order

16 Whether this is to be expressed in terms of non-Markan Q or a dependence on an Ur-Markus need not be debated here. For the former, see C. F. Burney, *The Poetry of Our Lord* (1925), pp. 74f.; for the latter W. R. Farmer, *The Synoptic Problem* (1964), p. 143.

17 Marxsen, *op. cit.*, p. 121; cf. E. C. Hoskyns and N. Davey, *The Riddle of the New Testament*[3] (1947), pp. 92f.

18 So G. Friedrich, *TDNT*, II, 727: "εὐαγγέλιον was not present in these passages [where the word occurs in the Gospel] in the original Mark, i.e. in the earliest stratum of the tradition."

19 The argument for maintaining that 13:10 is an independent logion which breaks the connection between verses 9 and 11 is given by J. Jeremias, *Jesus' Promise to the Nations* (ET 1958), pp. 22f. The verse is absent from the parallels in Mt. 10:17-22; Lk. 12:11f. Cf. Mt. 24:14; Lk. 21:12.

to bring out the significance of this for his church and to underline the fact that faithful testimony in Roman courts (exemplified in the case of Paul who represented the Christian cause before Felix, Festus, Herod Agrippa II, and Nero) was foretold by Jesus as part of the worldwide extension of the gospel ministry. Mark has used his favorite expression "the gospel" in this context.

4. A parallel case where a worldwide proclamation of the gospel is envisaged is Mark 14:9. Marxsen maintains that this verse, too, is to be assigned to the evangelist, but he admits that the argument is not compelling at this point. The most he confesses to is that "it would be strange if it were otherwise at just this point," since the remaining instances of the use of εὐαγγέλιον are editorial.[20]

5. The remaining two Markan references to "gospel" (the verse given in the translations as 16:15 is not authentic) are examples of exactly what we should expect: Mark's use of a Greek term to denote his implicit intention as evangelist. At 1:1 he has placed the noun εὐαγγέλιον at the beginning of his entire composition; and in 1:14, 15 Jesus' reported programmatic announcement at the opening of the Galilean mission is made in terms of the gospel: "Now after John was arrested, Jesus came into Galilee, preaching the gospel of God, and saying, 'The time is fulfilled, and the Kingdom of God is at hand; repent, and believe in the gospel.' "

Clearly Mark intends to epitomize Jesus' message as a preaching of the gospel of God. The debate about the meaning of the genitive "of God" is largely an unreal issue, for whether it means that he brought a message from God or that he proclaimed a message which had God as its content and subject-matter, the two elements of divine authority and a new teaching are inseparable and are subsequently attested as belonging together (1:21-28). The announcement was in terms of a fulfilment of God's prophetic promise and the near arrival of his kingdom. In the light of this, Jesus is seen as the proclaimer of a new age in God's salvation-history, since he embodies in himself all that he announces from God and about him. The only fit response is one of turning to God in repentance and a trustful acceptance of him who thus embodies the message.

The precise form of the wording "believe in the gospel" is problematic, because the preposition "in" (ἐν) is not elsewhere found with this verb in the New Testament, though it does occur in the Greek Old Testament.[21] The choice is to take the preposition as either instrumental (believe "on the basis of" or "through" the gospel) or causal (believe "because of" the gospel, i.e., because of the announcement Jesus just made about God's impending rule). Marxsen favors the view that "believe in" should be retained, and the sense

[20] Marxsen, *op. cit.*, p. 125.
[21] See Arndt-Gingrich, *A Greek-English Lexicon* (ET 1957), p. 666, for the possibilities.

given is that this is a call to faith in the proclaimer.[22] This is an attractive possibility especially if we combine it with the idea which seems complementary to it, as Marxsen suggests: believe *in* the gospel (i.e., in Jesus who announces it) *because of* the gospel (i.e., the record which tells of his proclamation). True, Marxsen gives a specialized interpretation to "believe," and seeks to relate faith to the returning Lord whose parousia (he holds) was awaited in Galilee by Mark's church. This specialized sense is not necessary, but we shall postpone to a later chapter our criticism of Marxsen's overall thesis.

For the present we will follow his lead no further than this. For Mark Jesus' appearance in Galilee precipitated an announcement that God's rule was imminent. A new age was breaking in,[23] since Jesus' public ministry was being inaugurated. He therefore summons his hearers to repentance and faith. Mark's record is written from the vantage point of all that Jesus' ministry accomplished as a past fact; and the evangelist, aware that Jesus as the living one is still at work in the church and in the world, expresses this conviction in terms of its full Christian content by using the generally accepted term "gospel" to denote the blessings of the new age which, as he knows, came with Jesus. The call addressed to readers of his work is to believe in Jesus as the bringer of the new age on the strength of the testimony of the written composition to the Lord of the church.

The final usage of "gospel" in Mark to be considered is the evangelist's first, in his opening verse: "The beginning of the gospel of Jesus Christ, the Son of God." There are some issues to be faced before we can examine the meaning of this verse. First, there is a textual question: does the title "the Son of God" belong to the original manuscript? The claim that it is authentic is well supported by the fact that the title "Son of God" runs through Mark's Gospel and is a leading theme in it. With the title so amply attested (1:11; 3:11; 8:38; 9:7; 12:6; 13:32; 14:36, 61; 15:39), a later scribe may well have chosen to omit the phrase here in order to allow the sentence (apparently lacking a verb) to read more easily.

The genitive construction "of Jesus Christ" allows for two interpretations—good news *brought by* Jesus Christ, and the good news *announced by* Jesus Christ. The choice is not exclusive; and since either is possible and would make good sense we cannot say for sure what Mark's meaning was. In any event, the answer will depend on how the next phrase is taken.

What does the evangelist mean by "the *beginning* of the

[22] Marxsen, *op. cit.*, p. 135.

[23] See W. G. Kümmel, *Promise and Fulfilment* (ET 1957), p. 19, on the verb "to be at hand" in this sense, "to denote an event which is near, but has not yet taken place."

gospel"? C.E.B. Cranfield lists no fewer than ten possible interpretations,[24] of which three seem most likely:

1. If we take the Old Testament citation in verses 2 and 3 as parenthetical, the predicate of the (understood) verb is John the Baptist's preaching, which is explained as being the beginning of the gospel (record). This agrees with the apostolic preaching recorded in Acts 1:21f.; 10:37; and 13:24f. in its assessment of John's activity.

2. Similarly, it could be maintained that verse 1 is a sort of title for the content of verses 2-13. This is Cranfield's own preference.

3. Marxsen urges that the opening verse is a title to the whole composition, deliberately chosen by the evangelist to convey what he as an author is seeking to accomplish.[25] This would make Mark the first Christian to give this well-used word a unique connotation, transferring the noun "gospel" from the sphere of oral proclamation and delivery to that of literary composition. The evangelist does this in full consciousness of the momentous change in application he is making. Therefore, he appends the term "beginning" to show that he proposes to find his authority in God who is the author of, and sanctioning power behind, the striking events at the heart of the Christian proclamation. The term rendered "beginning" (ἀρχή) does not mean in this context "first part" or "opening section," but since it covers the entire work of Mark it should be understood as "origin" or even "principle." It is that to which the human author traces back his work; and in this sense it must imply God himself, as the author and originator of all that is, just as Genesis 1:1 opens the Bible's story on this magisterial note.[26]

This view does justice to the attested usages of εὐαγγέλιον in which Mark has employed the term with deliberate intention; and his frontispiece fits into what seems to be his carefully arranged literary plan. We accept the proposal, therefore, that Mark's opening verse is his chosen title embracing the subsequent narrative. His purpose is to tell the εὐαγγέλιον as the message of good news (already known in his church as God's saving power and life-giving reality), which took historical shape in Jesus of Nazareth. As Marxsen perceptively remarks, it is not that Mark has affixed the term "gospel" to the title of Jesus Christ. Quite the opposite. The evangelist has appended the name of Jesus Christ to the term εὐαγγέλιον.[27] The "gospel" is the known factor. Mark's task as the first evangelist is to spell out the relation between the experienced good news of God's salvation and the theologically interpreted historical facts about Jesus of Nazareth, Messiah of Israel and Son of God.

[24] C.E.B. Cranfield, *The Gospel According to St. Mark* (1963), pp. 34f.
[25] Marxsen, *op. cit.*, p. 125.
[26] So E. Lohmeyer, *Das Evangelium des Markus*[17] (1967), p. 10.
[27] Marxsen, *op. cit.*, p. 138.

CONCLUSION

To say that the Christian Gospels are *evangelical* is a tautology, for by the very name they carry in the church's tradition we should expect them to convey the substance of the gospel, the εὐαγγέλιον. Yet they also claim to be historical documents, telling the story of Jesus as a figure of first-century Palestine.

The decisive event which connects the Jesus of Galilee and Jerusalem with the living word of the church's proclamation and the believer's experience is the resurrection. The Gospels contain history transformed by that mighty event, and all the factual details are seen in the radiant light of that new beginning of the Lord's existence. He is now "Son of God with power," so declared by the resurrection (Rom. 1:4). But he is still the same one who lived in obscurity and humility in Nazareth, taught in Galilee, and died in Jerusalem. Continuity with the past is secured by all that the evangelists portray of him; yet their point of view is inevitably on a different side of Easter from those who saw him in "the days of his flesh" and during the time when he moved in and out among his disciples (Acts 1:21).

If we rightly understand how the church's accounts of Jesus' life and ministry came to be called Gospels, we must conclude that their writers were interested in Jesus not in his own right as a figure of the past only, but emphatically as the center and substance of the preaching ministry, teaching responsibility, and living power of Christians in the church and the world. To approach the Gospels in this spirit is to go right to the heart of their purpose as originally conceived and as actualized today in our experience.

But this statement should be taken to include not simply the historical mooring of Jesus to a particular place and time but equally a concern "to characterize and explain Jesus and thus to provide an element without which the proclamation of his death and resurrection and the summons to faith in him would be meaningless."[28]

Provided we understand how widely early Christian interest in Jesus extended beyond the knowledge of his bare factuality, we may return to a final declaration of the evangelists' chief intention. It is vitally important to have the right questions in mind as we commence our inquiry. Framing the questions which the Gospels were designed to deal with is half the way to reaching satisfying conclusions. And we can only know what the right questions may be if we initially recognize the kind of writers the evangelists professed to be and the type of historical writing they purported to give. J. Dupont's statement provides such a point of view:

[28] I borrow this way of putting it from C.F.D. Moule's essay, "Jesus in New Testament Kerygma," in *Verborum Veritas. Festschrift G. Stählin* (1970), p. 25.

It was not the ambition of Matthew, Mark and Luke to preserve for posterity the minutes of Jesus' speeches or any kind of authentic account of the minutiae of his behaviour. An "evangelist," as the name shows, takes it upon himself to declare the good news; whether he does this by speaking or by writing, he performs the work of a preacher. This preaching, being in the direct line of a still vital tradition, bears the impress of eye-witness recollections. But the preacher's purpose in recapitulating these is not simply historiographic: he aims at the same time to consolidate the incidence of Jesus' words and deeds on the life of the Christians he is addressing. Thus the things recounted do not merely belong to the past that is over and done with: what Jesus says and does remains "topical", full of lessons for everyday life.[29]

29 J. Dupont, *Les Béatitudes*[2] (1958), pp. 10f.; this translation is from E. Haenchen, *The Acts of the Apostles* (ET 1971), p. 107.

CHAPTER TWO

Gospel History and Interpretation in the Light of Recent Study

The modern study of the Gospels makes three widely shared assumptions, which will be stated here in simple form, and taken up in more detail in the later stages of the book.[1]

1. Since the time of B.H. Streeter, whose book *The Four Gospels* appeared in 1924, the accepted results of source criticism have evaluated the chief literary sources of the Synoptic Gospels as Mark, a hypothetical sayings-source labeled Q, special material in Matthew, and special material in Luke. Recently, doubt has been cast on the existence of Q as a written document, and even more uncertainty is shown about complicated theories which involve imponderables like Q, e.g., the so-called proto-Luke hypothesis. The priority of Mark, although assailed, commands a wide acceptance, and recent challenges to the pre-literary history of the Gospels as classically stated by Streeter have not produced any substantial dislocation of the critical position.

2. Form criticism is now established in Gospel research as an attempt to probe beneath the surface of the canonical Gospels to discover the literary forms of the narratives and sayings of the individual sections which make up the records. A burning question is how far its often negative judgments on the historical worth of the material may be taken; but as a working tool in literary analysis it has proved its value.

3. Current debate on the "new quest of the historical Jesus" has highlighted the importance of historiography. There is consensus that the evangelists were not writing as detached historians to describe "what exactly happened" in a disinterested and impartial way. They were not primarily biographers, but evangelists, telling of the incursion of the divine into human life in the person of Jesus of Nazareth. By relating his life to his work, and that work to God's saving purposes in

[1] For a more detailed résumé of the issues involved, see H.K. McArthur, "A Survey of Recent Gospel Research," in *New Theology No. 2*, ed. M.E. Marty and D.G. Peerman (1965), pp. 201-21.

the hope of Israel, they were showing the achievement of the world's salvation. At heart, then, the Gospels are *theological* documents. They incorporate history, but it is *interpreted* history, which sets forth the fulfilment of God's redeeming motive and activity in Jesus, the Messiah and Lord.

As these modern presuppositions lie at the center of contemporary discussion on the life of Jesus, a survey of the historical background is called for. The place to begin is the *Leben-Jesu-Forschung*, the "Life of Jesus" school of mid-nineteenth-century Europe.[2]

THE LIFE OF JESUS MOVEMENT

The aim of the approach of this school to the Gospels was clearly defined: to press back from the credal Christ to the Jesus of history. Albert Schweitzer, who chronicled the chief contributions of those who researched the life of Jesus, expresses their purpose thus:

> They were eager to picture him as truly and purely human, to strip off from him the robes of splendour with which he had been apparelled, and clothe him once more with the coarse garments in which he had walked in Galilee.[3]

There were thus several motives which inspired the members of the Life of Jesus school. They had a genuine devotion to Jesus' humanity, which they felt was obscured and overlaid by the church's credal forms and metaphysical doctrines. The Byzantine Christ in his transcendent majesty seemed remote and inhuman; and they were concerned that the tendency to separate Jesus the man from the Christ of glory would result in Docetism—a denial of his full humanity. But they were equally alive to the danger of a revived Monarchianism, which would exclude Jesus from the Godhead in the interest of stressing the unity of God. Precisely this latter peril surfaced in the theology of Adolf Harnack, for whom the quintessence of Christianity lay in the dictum: "The Gospel, as Jesus proclaimed it, has to do with the Father only and not with the Son."

Other motives may be detected. David F. Strauss and the "mythical school" had earlier sought to show that Jesus was a legendary figure whose historicity was debatable. The various "lives of Jesus" asserted that he was, on the contrary, to be placed within the historical frame of the first-century world. Yet this insistence on the historical Jesus invited the philosophical criticism that "accidental historical truths can never become proofs for the necessary truths of

[2] For a short sketch of the history of criticism before 1863, as it affected the life of Jesus, see Ralph P. Martin, *Mark, Evangelist and Theologian* (1972), pp. 29-36. For some perceptive comments on the significance of the *Leben-Jesu-Forschung*, see Daniel P. Fuller, *Easter Faith and History* (1965), ch. 3.

[3] Schweitzer, *The Quest of the Historical Jesus* (ET 1910), p. 4.

reason."[4] Thus the historians of the Life of Jesus were driven into the arms of "historicism," which admits of no unique cases.

Biblical criticism of the time was hospitable to the writing of these lives of Jesus. Since the work of H. J. Holtzmann, a high evaluation had been placed on Mark's Gospel as the first of the canonical Gospels; and it was assumed that this Gospel describes a purely human Jesus for whom no claims to divinity are made. There is no doubt, as Schweitzer noted, that Holtzmann's statement of the Markan hypothesis (that Mark's Gospel is the foundation-document underlying the other Synoptics and contains a clear, factual, unembellished record of the life and public career of Jesus) had a tremendous influence in the second half of the nineteenth century.[5] Holtzmann's vindication of Mark's priority and historicity held the field until the turn of the century when powerful forces already at work assailed and destroyed it, at least as far as German scholarship was concerned.

Holtzmann was not, however, as he himself conceded in 1863, the first to assert what later became known as the Markan hypothesis: that honor goes to C. H. Weisse, who argued for the originality of Mark's Gospel in his two-volume work on Gospel history published in 1838. As we sketch the background of the Life of Jesus movement, the first landmark begins with him.

THE MARKAN HYPOTHESIS AND ITS BACKGROUND

1. What motivated Weisse seems to have been an ancillary interest in warding off the attacks of some new tendencies in German criticism. In 1835 D. F. Strauss had published his *Life of Jesus*, which aimed its thrusts at two fronts. Strauss sought to denigrate the claims of supernaturalist Christianity, which appealed to the Gospels for evidence of miracles, and he opposed the rationalists who still clung to the idea that the Gospels contain factual history. Strauss tried to reduce all opposition to a vanishing point by arguing that both contenders are espousing lost causes since the Gospels are mythical.[6] He treated the Gospels as H. S. Reimarus (1694-1768) had done, without prior consideration of their sources, order, and relative worth.[7] Weisse expressed appreciation for Strauss's labors but then

4 G. E. Lessing, *Theological Writings*, III, 12.

5 Schweitzer, *op. cit.*, pp. 204ff.

6 This was not Strauss's final statement, as Barth shows in his discussion of Strauss's later (1864) work. Barth, *From Rousseau to Ritschl* (ET 1959), pp. 374ff.

7 Reimarus was the first person to address himself to the problems of writing a life of Jesus. Before him "no one had attempted to form a historical conception of the life of Jesus" (Schweitzer, *op. cit.*, p. 13). Reimarus' attitude to the Gospels, however, was entirely negative and led

took him to task at significant points,[8] thus launching the counter-attack as well.

Of special interest in Weisse's reconstruction of the data are his refusal to recognize the eschatological motifs in Jesus' life (which Strauss stressed) and his recourse to the two basic documents of apostolic Christianity—Mark and the *logia*—which evaded Strauss' suspicion of Matthew and John, which he regarded as highly charged with the miraculous element.

Weisse's claim to fame is that he was the originator of the Markan hypothesis. His overall importance lies in the way he sought to erect bulwarks of historical facts in the Gospels against the inroads of the mythical school. Not that he accepted all of Mark as reliably historical; his task was more modestly conceived. It was to construct an outline of the life of Jesus and assign this to history. He was less willing to grant historical value to the separate sections (or "pericopes") which make up the completed Gospels. It became the work of later continental writers of the Life of Jesus school to fill in the gaps and to reconstruct, sometimes with powerful imagination, what the full-dressed picture of Jesus must have looked like—through the eyes of a Renan and a Keim and a Farrar. At least, as Schweitzer had to admit, Renan "offered his readers a Jesus who was alive"; but his vivacity was more the work of invention than reality. Yet Renan erred less grievously than Strauss.

2. The skepticism of Strauss came to full expression in Bruno Bauer. The 1851 edition of his treatise on the "Criticism of the Gospel History" reached the nadir of all historical assessments: there never was any historical Jesus.[9] A number of factors led Bauer to this negative judgment. Ostensibly, he believed that Mark's Gospel was the work of an inventive genius who has "loosed us from the theological lie" of the dogmatic characterization of Jesus of Chalcedonian proportions which we meet in the Fourth Gospel.[10] It was therefore in Bauer's interest to postulate and supply proofs for the theory that Mark was the first Gospel to be written; and he was the first to do this on the ground of the evidence of the Gospel itself.

3. The spate of lives of Jesus was a natural reaction to the aridity and negativism of the preceding decades. And the hinge on which they turned was the appearance in 1863 of H. J. Holtzmann's seminal work, *Die synoptischen Evangelien.*

Holtzmann's achievement was considerable. He took Weisse's

---

to the conclusion that the records are historically worthless, since they are the product of men guilty of manufacturing a pious fraud. See the new edition of *Reimarus: Fragments,* ed. C. H. Talbert (1970).

8 Schweitzer's chapter "The Marcan Hypothesis" is mainly devoted to Weisse in his relations with Strauss's views (*op. cit.*, pp. 121-36).

9 Cf. J. M. Robinson, *The Problem of History in Mark* (1957), pp. 10-12.

10 Cited by Schweitzer, *op. cit.*, p. 153.

statement of the two-document hypothesis (that Mark and the *logia* were foundation-documents) and pressed it into the service of a developed theory of Mark as the "original document" or *Grundschrift* on which the later Gospels drew. In this way he replaced the unknown quantity of Lessing's "original Gospel" (or *Urevangelium*) by a known document—or rather, the antecedent (known as *Ur-Markus*, or first edition of Mark) of our canonical Mark. Just how far Holtzmann was prepared to go in attributing historical credibility to Mark is not clear. What is important is that he was seen by the composers of a succession of lives of Jesus as providing with Mark the framework of a well-attested, early, reliable tradition, which could be used both to counter the extreme skepticism of Strauss and Bauer and to yield the ground-plan for a fuller description of Jesus' life on earth uninhibited by the figure of a virgin-born, miracle-working Byzantine Christ who at length is raised from the dead by a physical reanimation (as Matthew and Luke were believed to teach).

Holtzmann's role as providing just this credibility for Mark so that his work could be used to reconstruct the liberal portrait of Jesus is clearly described by Albert Schweitzer:

> What attracted these writers to the Marcan hypothesis was not so much the authenticification [*sic*] which it gave to the detail of Mark . . . but the way in which this Gospel lent itself to the a priori view of the course of the life of Jesus which they unconsciously brought with them. They appealed to Holtzmann because he showed such wonderful skill in extracting from the Marcan narrative the view which commended itself to the spirit of the age as manifested in the 'sixties.[11]

The "spirit of the age" was essentially one which probed into the psychological development of Jesus' public career and suggested reasons for his actions and decisions. A Galilean success was followed by a response to political factors, which in turn caused him to escape and to rethink his plan. Only then, frustrated at the impossibility of carrying out his mission in Galilee, did Jesus resolve to go to Jerusalem and make his final bid for the capital.

Basic to this reconstruction is a confidence that the modern interpreter can read between the lines and supply motivations in the mind of Jesus and his reactions to outward events and pressures, which are otherwise lacking in the text. This is what Schweitzer calls the attempt to delineate "the inward and outward course of development in the life of Jesus."[12] At heart, it is a treatment of the Gospel data as a psychological case-study, incomplete in themselves but capable, by a sympathetic weaving together of the visible threads, of forming an imaginative reconstruction and a resultant in-depth analysis.

The Gospel of Mark played a decisive part in this Holtzman-

[11] *Ibid.*, pp. 203f.
[12] *Ibid.*, p. 204.

nian doctrine and in the use he made of it. It had much in its favor. Its portrait of Jesus was sufficiently ambiguous to suggest a purely human Jesus for whom no claims to divinity are made. Its outline could, with slight adaptation, be made to yield a sequential narrative with a plainly visible pattern of development. Its setting in a historical milieu shows that it is no mythical saga. And, above all, the storyline made sense, since it told of an earthly figure, of flesh and blood, who shaped his destiny in response to events as he met them and who concealed his messiahship until the psychologically critical moment when, in the last days of his life, it could be hidden no longer. Yet when it is revealed, it is a spiritual secret appreciated only by the sensitive souls who discover, with Jesus, that the kingdom of God is within them and who are encouraged by Jesus' example of living under the fatherhood of God to live as his children and as brothers together. This is the quintessential doctrine of the liberal theology, classically adumbrated by A. Harnack.[13]

Yet, on the whole, the results were disappointing and ephemeral. "Those who are fond of talking about negative theology can find their account here," wrote Schweitzer at the close of his long recital of the lives of Jesus. Already in the nineteenth century the ground was being prepared for an assault on the Holtzmann doctrine and, more specifically, on the generally accepted notion that a portrait of Jesus as he moved from Galilee to Jerusalem could be etched by a careful and sympathetic drawing together of the Gospel data.

THE MARKAN HYPOTHESIS UNDER ATTACK

In 1906 Schweitzer wrote perceptively about the dominance of the Holtzmannian treatment of Mark, and indicated that the Markan hypothesis had a sort of inevitability which could only be overcome and neutralized by a breaking of the stranglehold which a combination of psychologizing interest in Jesus' life and the liberal portrait of Jesus laid upon the interpretation of Mark.[14] But a decade earlier a slender volume had been released which contained all the potential to attack and disarm the Markan hypothesis, Martin Kähler's *Der sogenannte historische Jesus und der geschichtliche, biblische Christus* (translated into English in 1964 as *The So-Called Historical Jesus and the Historic Biblical Christ*).

[13] No one saw more clearly or expressed more forcibly the main lineaments of theological liberalism than T. W. Manson in his essay "The Failure of Liberalism to Interpret the Bible as the Word of God," in *The Interpretation of the Bible*, ed. C. W. Dugmore (1944), pp. 92-107. His citation of Harnack, *What is Christianity?* (ET 1950 ed.), pp. 68f., is to the point: "The fact that the whole of Jesus' message may be reduced to these two heads—God as the Father and the human soul so ennobled that it can and does unite with him . . . that . . . is therefore religion itself."

[14] Schweitzer, *op. cit.*, p. 204.

1. Kähler engaged in warm polemic against the historicism of his day which produced the vagaries of the life of Jesus portraits. He objected that such attempts at portraiture inevitably led to a false picture, which obscured the transcendental qualities of the biblical Christ. The living Lord, he averred, is essentially the Christ of apostolic proclamation, accessible to us today in a spiritual encounter and not to be dug out of historical documents as though he were "the mere object of historical research, as one can [disinter] other figures belonging to the past."[15]

Many reasons are offered to account for Kähler's opposition to the historiographical methods and theological presuppositions of his day. Central was his conviction that the Gospels do not provide the biographical data which would give us a window of access into the inner life of Jesus. They are—and it is apparent that in context he has his eye set primarily on Mark's Gospel—"passion narratives with extended introductions,"[16] containing the content of early Christian preaching and intended to awaken faith in Christ as Savior.

The Gospels serve an exclusively religious purpose and interest: "Every detail of the apostolic recollection of Jesus can be shown to have been preserved for the sake of its religious significance."[17] The Christ they portray is the Christ of faith, the proclaimed Lord whose encounter with his people is not at the mercy of historical investigation and systematic doubt. Only by insisting on the exact nature of our entrée to the "historic, biblical Christ" can we be delivered from the clutches of historical relativism (for which nothing in the past is absolutely certain) and be given an "invulnerable province" (*sturmfreies Gebiet*), unassailed and unassailable by historical, probing inquiry. The upshot of Kähler's discussion was to place a large question mark against the current doctrine that the Gospels record plain, uninterpreted history, capable of verification by the methods of historical science and revelatory of the secret of Jesus' person to the impartial investigator.

2. Other influences at work in the early part of the twentieth century took up and developed Kähler's historical radicalism. W. Wrede's study of the messianic secret in the Gospels (*Das Messiasgeheimnis in den Evangelien*, 1901) addressed itself particularly to the element of mystery and secrecy in the Gospel of Mark, which reports Jesus as enjoining secrecy about his miracles and messiahship in situations where such commands could hardly be observed. Wrede explained these injunctions to silence as a literary device of the evangelist to account for the absence of faith in Jesus' messiahship during his lifetime. That faith was born at the resurrection and formed

[15] Kähler, *The So-Called Historical Jesus* (ET 1964), p. 92.
[16] *Ibid.*, p. 80n.
[17] *Ibid.*, p. 93.

part of the apostolic preaching, from which it was carried back into the tradition, and superimposed on it. In its pre-Markan form the tradition contained no such messianic awareness; therefore, it must have been Mark himself who devised the theory of a messianic secret and imported it into the tradition as he took it over and edited it.

This particular conclusion of Wrede is not, at this point, the important thing. But what Wrede succeeded in doing was to convince other interpreters that Mark's Gospel is not a record of plain, unvarnished, and straightforward history "as it actually happened," but a dogmatic treatise in which the rationale of the messianic secret is used to account for the Markan story and imposed on it by the evangelist himself.

3. K. L. Schmidt examined, in his 1919 work *Der Rahmen der Geschichte Jesu* ("The Framework of Jesus' Story"), the connecting links or seams which join the separate stories of Mark's Gospel and form them into a continuous narrative. His conclusion was that these notices of time-sequence and place-reference, which appear to carry forward the story and make it into a coherent narrative, do not rest on historical reminiscence or temporal or geographical fact but are editorial additions supplied by the evangelist, who often gathers his material into units on a topical basis of common subject matter, like the collection of "controversy stories" in chapters 2 and 3.

Schmidt reached the verdict that "as a whole there is no life of Jesus in the sense of a developing biography, no chronological sketch of Jesus' history, but only individual stories (*pericopes*) which are put into a framework."[18] By a form-critical method he elaborated Schweitzer's idea that, when Mark's Gospel is examined in sections, not only is there no obvious psychological connection between the sections, but "in almost every case there is a positive break in the connexion."[19] Therefore, attempts to string together the sections and read them as freely flowing narrative, suggesting events of cause and effect, are foredoomed to failure. As Schweitzer put it in a memorable metaphor:

> Formerly it was possible to book through-tickets at the supplementary-psychological-knowledge office which enabled those travelling in the interests of Life-of-Jesus construction to use express trains, thus avoiding the inconvenience of having to stop at every little station, change, and run the risk of missing their connexion. This ticket office is now closed. There is a station at the end of each section of the narrative, and the connexions are not guaranteed.[20]

4. A further factor added its weight to the crushing burden on the Markan hypothesis. The doctrine of *Sitz im Leben* is built on the

[18] Schmidt, *Der Rahmen der Geschichte Jesu* (1919), p. 317.
[19] Schweitzer, *op. cit.*, pp. 333f.
[20] *Ibid.*, p. 333.

principle that each section or *pericope* of the Gospel teaching and narrative may be suggestively placed in the setting of its historical context when we heed its literary form and theological context. The underlying assumption is that Mark's material in particular can be separated out into paragraphs, each of which is a self-contained unit making its point without regard for anything before or after.

This analysis led to a double consequence, both parts damaging to the traditional view of Markan authorship. First, if Mark's role in the process of Gospel-making is confined to the task of collecting and stringing together a set of independent units of narrative and sayings, he can hardly be known as the author of a life of Jesus. He is more accurately described as a compiler, an editor, a hander-on ("*Tradent*" is Dibelius' term)[21] of earlier traditions, which he was content simply to piece together in what has been called "this curious, anecdotal, stop-go manner."[22]

Second, the nineteenth-century understanding of Mark as the scribe of Peter's eyewitness experiences and witness vanishes before the critical assessment of these discrete paragraphs. Form-critically, they give the impression of having been shaped by a number of hands before Mark used them. The uncomplicated picture suggested by Jerome's words, "As Peter spoke, he [Mark] wrote it down," seemed, after this analytic scrutiny, to be almost ludicrous. But even worse (from an orthodox standpoint) was to follow, as the form critic proceeded to pass judgment on the historical worth of the stories. From being regarded as straightforward, historical events of factual, episodic history in the life of Jesus of Nazareth, they came to be seen as idealized reconstructions, worthwhile mainly for the post-Easter church. The entire course of Jesus' career as recorded in the Gospels was considered to be viewed through the refracting prism of the early church.

5. Rudolf Bultmann took up the protests raised by Kähler and extended the pioneering work of the earliest form critics. At the same time he added a new feature, derived from some philosophical indebtedness to a Kierkegaardian type of existentialism and a Lutheran application of the dogmatic principle of justification by faith alone. The result of the weaving together of these divergent strands of influence may be seen in Bultmann's *Jesus* (1926) and in his 1960 lecture "The Primitive Christian Kerygma and the Historical Jesus."[23]

Bultmann's position, both early and later, rests on two considerations. First, on form-critical grounds, he avers that it is impossible to recapture Jesus as he moved in Galilee and Jerusalem and to

[21] Martin Dibelius, *From Tradition to Gospel* (ET 1934), p. 3.
[22] C. F. Evans, *The Beginning of the Gospel* (1968), p. 9.
[23] A translation of this lecture appears in *The Historical Jesus and the Kerygmatic Christ*, ed. C. E. Braaten and R. A. Harrisville (1964), pp. 15-42.

know precisely what took place in the years AD 30-33. He does not deny some historical foundation, and he is willing cautiously to affirm the "having-happened-ness" of Jesus with a modest outline of his Galilean career. But he denies even to this minimum of information any valid theological value, because the Gospels are by definition not concerned with "objective historicity." He stoutly denies any hint that Jesus' personality may be seen in the Gospels. Thus, because there is no estimate of the "inward and outward course of development in the life of Jesus" (Schweitzer's phrase of the original Quest), we can have no sure knowledge of how Jesus anticipated his death. Mark 10:45 is a "prophecy after the event," read back into the lifetime of Jesus. It is conceivable, Bultmann still declares, that he died in utter bewilderment and abject despair, a frustrated and rejected prophet of God.

But as we turn to the second element in Bultmann's reading of the Gospels, we observe that he does not take this skepticism to be too great a loss; indeed, he maintains, it is a necessary loss. For, even if it were possible to learn significant details of the Jesus of history, it would be illegitimate to inquire after them, and the knowledge that might be gained would prove a burden. For faith can never be at the mercy of historical criticism and suspend its activity while the historians debate the problematic issue—"Did it happen?" The person in whom the Christian faith confides is the risen Christ, living in the church and present supremely in the ministry of preaching, in the *kerygma.* The Gospels do not direct faith to a past figure of whom certain historical values may be predicated with more or less certainty, but perform the necessary function of certifying that Jesus of Nazareth once embodied the word of God in his existence in time. About this "Christ-event" (i.e., the appearance of Jesus as an eschatological prophet of God who announced the imminent reign of God) nothing of *theological* significance requires to be known except *that* he once lived, taught, and died. The mere *thatness (das blosse Dass)* is sufficient. All else in terms of his character and recorded words is fraught with problems and vulnerable to doubt. Christian faith can find no resting place in such historical uncertainties, which can never be more than approximations, and must instead seek its point of reference in an existential encounter with the living Christ of the church's proclamation. The only "essential relationship" (*sachliche Verhältnis*) between Jesus and this kerygma on which faith builds is that continuum guaranteed by Jesus' existence. "It is therefore obvious that the kerygma presupposes the historical Jesus, however much it may have mythologized him. Without him there would be no kerygma."[24]

The two roadblocks Bultmann places in the way of any effort at a twentieth-century "life of Jesus" are noted by J. M. Robinson.

[24] Bultmann, *loc. cit.*, p. 18.

Bultmann's "form-critical studies corroborated the view that a Life of Jesus research after the style of the nineteenth century is impossible, and his existential interpretation did not support the thesis that such a Life-of-Jesus research was legitimate."[25] Robinson adds: "Therefore it is not surprising that the critical restudy of [Bultmann's] position by his pupils should begin here."[26] Here the so-called New Quest opens; but it is not our purpose to continue the story in detail beyond this stage.[27]

BULTMANN AND GOSPEL HISTORY

Bultmann's pupils have refused to remain content with their master's position. The chief reason for this was expressed in Ernst Käsemann's October 1953 lecture, which marked the beginning of the so-called "New Quest of the Historical Jesus." While sharing many of Bultmann's presuppositions about Gospel criticism, Käsemann confessed himself unwilling to admit a "disengagement of interest from the earthly Jesus." In a significant statement, he proceeded: "If this were to happen, we should either be failing to grasp the nature of the primitive Christian concern with the identity between the exalted and the humiliated Lord; or else we should be emptying that concern of any real content, as did the docetists."[28]

Käsemann placed his finger on an issue which Bultmann's critics have always regarded as the outstanding weakness, not to say danger, in his attitude to Gospel history. Although his writings are cautiously framed, they still leave the impression that the human Jesus has been lost. To talk about Jesus as an "eschatological phenomenon" is hardly an adequate reply to the criticism that Jesus' human life has been eviscerated. Calling this a twentieth-century version of docetism implies that the overemphasis on the mere thatness, on the factuality of Jesus, as the chief contribution of the Gospel records, evaporates the Jesus of Galilee and Jerusalem and gives his place as a historical person to a cipher, a symbol, an ethereal idea, a mathematical point, which has position but no magnitude. The loss of the Jesus of history seems inevitably to open the road to a gnosticized Christianity which has severed connections with empirical history.[29]

25 J. M. Robinson, *Kerygma und historische Jesus* (1960), pp. 10f.
26 J. M. Robinson, *A New Quest of the Historical Jesus* (1959), p. 12.
27 For an admirable brief statement on the lines pursued in the New Quest, see F. Gogarten, *Christ the Crisis* (1970), ch. 4; and—more simply—Ralph P. Martin, "The New Quest of the Historical Jesus," in *Jesus of Nazareth: Saviour and Lord,* ed. C.F.H. Henry (1966), pp. 31-45. Documentation for what follows will be found in this article, as in several more recent studies. This article now also appears in the symposium, *The Theology of Christ: Commentary* (1971), ed. R.J. Tapia, pp. 394-404.
28 *Essays on New Testament Themes,* p. 46.
29 See A.M. Hunter, *Introducing New Testament Theology* (1957), pp. 152f.

We might press the question of Bultmann's logic here, and query with H. Zahrnt whether there can ever be a historical "fact" without content.[30] But a more effective criticism of Bultmann's implied docetism is to ask why he is embarrassed by a recourse to Jesus' historical person. Part of the answer comes in the way his existentialism takes over from Kierkegaard a peculiar version of religious epistemology—and we may trace this problem back to what Lessing called the "ugly ditch." How can one leap from truths of fact to truths of reason? The leap is made by these men as they are emotionally moved (Lessing), or as they exercise an irrational faith (Kierkegaard), or as they respond in a decision to the church's preaching (Bultmann). But, as John McIntyre has discerned, such a step must remain "non-significant without some contextual historical knowledge. It cannot take place in a vacuum, nor can a decision be made except within a framework of reference."[31]

Similarly, on theological grounds, Bultmann shies away from too close a contact with history, for fear that, if historical knowledge were to turn out to be genuine knowledge (which Kierkegaard had denied), faith would rest on something less than Christ himself. He is driven, therefore, to dissociate faith from history; and to remove theological questions from the realm of history in the interest of securing the invulnerable province of which Kähler spoke. This is clearly brought out by his attitude to the question, "Was Jesus the Messiah?": "Only the historian can answer this question . . . and faith, being personal decision, cannot be dependent upon a historian's labor."[32] Here is a clear instance of Bultmann's disengagement of interest from the earthly Jesus, which shows that he wishes to place the emphasis in his understanding of Christianity on a decision of faith engendered by the preaching of the risen Christ, who, having lived a life whose character is concealed from us today, ascended into the kerygma! Thus, on this view, the kerygma becomes the legitimating instrument by which the figure of Jesus the preacher is turned into the Christ who is preached.

But, as Gogarten rightly asks, what gave the kerygma the right to make this change? If it "claims that in it Christ is present," what is the basis of this claim? With discerning logic he responds,

> What Bultmann ascribes to the work of the kerygma can only be asserted if Jesus who promises salvation is himself the salvation to come, and as such the Christ. . . . But this would mean not only that, as Bultmann holds, the paradox "life dwells in death", which became the reality of salvation in Christ, first became explicit in the kerygma. It would mean even more: that it was already explicitly present "in the words and deeds of the historical Jesus."[33]

[30] H. Zahrnt, *The Historical Jesus* (ET 1963), p. 93.
[31] J. McIntyre, *The Shape of Christology* (1966), pp. 119ff.
[32] Bultmann, *Theology of the New Testament*, I (ET 1952), 26.
[33] Gogarten, *op. cit.*, p. 38.

But on Bultmann's attitude to Gospel history, this offer of present salvation in the historical ministry is the very thing the Gospels do not give; and the Gospels, in his view, do not yet demonstrate the factual unity in the activity and preaching of Jesus with the kerygma.

If Bultmann's reconstruction of Christianity is true, it is a very delicate matter to know what to do with the Gospels. For they are concerned with a human figure, the outlines of whose character and personal presence are to be seen in his assumption of authority (Käsemann), his attitude to sinners (Bornkamm), his faith (Ebeling), his obedience to God (Gogarten), and his conduct (Fuchs). By what he says and does he effectively communicates God's will, for, as he accepts sinners and eats with them, it is implied that so God is graciously disposed to men. And this implies a way back behind the apostolic preaching to the earthly Jesus. That way was first taken by Mark, the author of the earliest gospel writing; and then subsequently developed by the other evangelists.

SOME GUIDELINES CONCERNING GOSPEL HISTORY

The first question to be asked in a sound approach to the Gospels is what these books purport to be. Quite obviously they claim to be reporting historical events which took place in Galilee and Jerusalem in connection with the life and public career of Jesus of Nazareth. Yet as we discussed in the opening chapter, it is clear that they do not offer the reader a biography in the modern sense. They say little about Jesus' antecedents; they are virtually silent about the formative influences on his character or behavior; and they are disappointing as day-to-day chronicles of his doings. Nor do they profess to supply objective history by telling the story of Jesus in an impartial and disinterested way, as though the evangelists were

> court-reporters, [or] . . . newspaper correspondents sending wire dispatches from the scene. They conceive their task to be something quite different. They are concerned to interpret and transmit the traditions in the light of their understanding of Messiah's message and of the needs of their readers.[34]

And the Gospel-writers were certainly not purveyors of myths,[35] professing to extol the mighty deeds of a legendary figure, a cult-hero of a kind of mystery religion, to whom a name could hardly be given.

The real issue is the type of history the Gospels claim to be recording.[36] As a short answer to this question, we may reply that the

34 E. E. Ellis, *The Gospel of Luke. New Century Bible* (1966), p. 9.

35 We are using the term "myth" here in its popular sense as "a purely fictitious narrative involving supernatural persons or natural phenomena."

36 Two very readable accounts of what is involved in this question may be mentioned: F. F. Bruce, "History and the Gospel," in *Jesus of Nazareth: Saviour and Lord*, pp. 89-107; and William Wand, *Christianity: A Historical Religion?* (1971), esp. ch. 10.

Gospels are theological documents which set out the interpreted history of the person Jesus of Nazareth, in whom God visited and redeemed his people (Luke 1:68). In the phrase, "interpreted history," both aspects are to be given equal prominence, and our goal should be to keep them in balance.

"History" is of vital importance because the Gospels record what actually took place in time and space. They are a denial in advance of the false notion, later dubbed docetism, that Jesus was only an appearance and did not assume a truly human nature and possess a fully human body. Indeed, one of the reasons for the writing of the Gospels in the form we have them may well have been the early Christians' concern to put an end to the false teaching that Jesus' body was only a ghostlike apparition and that he never knew human suffering at first hand.

Another factor which contributed to the composition of the Gospels was the desire to give some assurance regarding the authenticity of the events centered in Jesus. Luke's intention as stated in his prologue (1:1-4) is to assure Theophilus that the facts he has assumed to be true as part of his interest in the church's preaching are trustworthy and credible.

If we may hazard a more general impression, much of the Gospels' detail would make no sense if we thought that the evangelists were self-consciously weaving their stories out of thin air and inventing tales about Jesus simply because they had fertile imaginations and wonderful powers of fantasy-making. The impression most readers gain is exactly the opposite (whether or not they accept what the Gospels say as true is beside this point here). Apparently the evangelists thought they were reporting solid history, and that the chief actor in their drama was a flesh-and-blood character, living a human life under Palestinian skies. To be sure, this is not all the Gospel-writers believed, but it is the foundation of their faith. If that foundation is undermined, the essential part of New Testament Christianity is gone and nothing can replace it. As Wand puts it, "We cannot improve our hold upon Christian doctrine and practice while deducting from our belief in its historical evidence. It is inevitable that if we lost our grasp of the historical facts we should soon lose our grip of the Christian life as a whole."[37]

Yet a recovery of bare historical facts is not enough. What we need to know in regard to the sort of history of which the Gospels speak is what those facts mean and how they impinge on our lives. We cannot remain in the posture of a detached, neutral observer, indifferent to Jesus' place in history. We are involved, and have a live interest in what really happened long ago.

Even if we could remain content with a knowledge of "objec-

[37] Wand, *op. cit.*, pp. 63f.

tive historical facts" and could press back in our inquiry to learn "what actually happened" when Jesus walked in Galilee, it would take us no further than an intellectual persuasion that Jesus was a figure of history, perhaps enigmatic, perhaps strangely moving, certainly ambiguous. We would still be outside the kingdom of God, which is entered only by a response and commitment to Jesus. Our faith must rest on the firm foundation of essential fact; it can only become vital and vibrant as it embraces the witness in history to Jesus Christ as Son of God and Lord of life.

To complete the picture, when we look at the data in our Gospels we have no option but to treat them as theological documents which confront us with a challenge and cause us to ask, "What manner of man is this?" For the only history the Gospels are basically interested in is interpreted—or, better, kerygmatic—history. John 20:31 speaks for all the evangelists: "These [signs] are written that you may believe that Jesus is the Christ, the Son of God, and that believing you may have life in his name."

From this perspective, we may infer that the Gospels report history not for its own sake, but as a vehicle of God's redeeming interest and action in his Son. They declare that in this segment of human history God came especially close to men and erected certain "disclosure situations" in which his saving purpose and loving design for the world were revealed to men.[38] To those who were open and sensitive to all that Jesus came to reveal in his life, teaching, death, and triumph, the great disclosure is made. They perceive that in the itinerant preacher-prophet Jesus, God was truly at work, and that he was none other than God's messianic agent sent to establish his kingdom. To the Gospel reader who shares this "secret" through his acceptance of the church's proclamation of the kerygma, the gospel presentation shows that Jesus is now the exalted Lord, still active in history as he was during his earthly ministry, except that what was seen in token and ambiguously in his lifetime is, since Easter, completely and persuasively known.

2. The axiom stated succinctly by T. W. Manson that "a single story or saying may contain the whole Gospel in miniature"[39] fits in with the above proposition. Each Gospel-"section"—whether narrative, parable, miracle-story, or dialogue between Jesus and another person—may be approached with the anticipation that it will disclose

[38] The phrase "disclosure situations" is taken from A. Richardson's discussion in *History, Sacred and Profane* (1964), pp. 223-27. The term derives from I. T. Ramsey, *Religious Language: An Empirical Placing of Theological Phrases* (1957). Richardson's definition is as follows: "In what we are calling disclosure situations there occurs at certain 'historic' moments the discernment of a meaning which provokes a response to what is discerned, an acknowledgement of an obligation, a commitment to an overriding purpose" (p. 224).

[39] T. W. Manson, *The Servant Messiah* (1953), p. 67.

something of God's activity in Jesus. As students of Gospel history, we are responsible first to inquire about the revelation of God in the context of the past event. That exercise in historical inquiry demands a full knowledge of all we can ascertain about the literary, stylistic, cultural, and religious setting of a Gospel passage. Then we shall be prepared adequately and honestly to address ourselves to the theological task—and that is to examine the Gospel stories in a way which anticipates that we may discover there what God was doing.

This is the transition-point from the past event to a present-day encounter with gospel truth. One of the most fruitful suggestions to come out of the current New Quest controversy was made by Käsemann in his celebrated address on "The Problem of the Historical Jesus."[40] He distinguished between what took place *once* (German, *einmal*) and what occurred *once and for all* (German, *ein für alle Male*). Both meanings are traced back to the New Testament phrase, ἐφ' ἅπαξ,[41] but the two senses are distinct in the way Käsemann uses them. We can interpret this distinction as follows. In the life and death and victory of Jesus certain patterns of life were displayed and acted out on the stage of history. This anchors the gospel in the tangible world in which men and women move, with their feet firmly set on the ground. That indispensable "once upon a time" character of Jesus' history is certified by setting his story in a historical and cultural frame. The opening verses of Luke 3 provide the clearest case of this intention, common to all the Gospel authors who adopt the historical framework by their inclusion of contemporary figures such as Herod Antipas and Pontius Pilate.

Out of this historical factuality came the interpretative extension in the light of the post-Easter experience of the living Lord and the awareness that the church's destiny was set in a new age of eschatological fulfilment and promise. It was this consciousness of living on the other side of God's Easter vindication of Jesus that enabled the evangelists to look back on that earthly life of Jesus and interpret it as full of tokens and signs which indicated how the story would end and the ultimate worthiness of the one whom they hailed as Lord and King. It is this understanding of the Gospels as faith-story in which history is pressed into service as a vehicle to contemporize the historical figure of Jesus and reenact his living presence and power in situations confronting the early church which gives them their distinctive literary genre. More specifically, the evangelists read off from the "once upon a time" element in Jesus' life-story those qualities and characteristics which betrayed its "once for all" value. From the human life of Jesus, set in great obscurity yet possessing authority

[40] In *Essays on New Testament Themes*, pp. 15-47.

[41] *Ibid.*, pp. 30f. The reference in the original German is found in *Exegetische Versuche und Besinnungen*, I (1960), 200f.

and power, they extrapolated teaching about the nature of God and his saving designs for the world of men.

The Gospel writers' concern for Jesus' human existence is not to be narrowly conceived as simply a statement of his coming into the world. That would be to agree with Bultmann's virtual concentration on the sheer factuality (the *Dass*). They offer also "certain unmistakable traits of his individuality," as Käsemann calls the evangelists' summary of the nodal points around which the ministry of Jesus gathers. He lists the features which are grouped around "Jesus' message of the gracious God, his critique—conditioned by this message and expressed both in word and work—of the law of Moses and its interpretation, his radical demand for obedience and love, and his death as the logical culmination of his ministry."[42]

These "traits of Jesus' individuality" are precisely the raw materials out of which God's revelation in Jesus came to be formed and interpreted in the apostolic kerygma. To be sure, the message is, as it were, transposed into a new key as a result of the resurrection and the post-Easter situation of the church. Paul, for reasons which are not too clear, can afford to bypass much of the historical detail in the Galilean and Judaean ministry. But he is at one with the authors of the Synoptic Gospels in finding the heart of the gospel in the gracious God, the displacement of Mosaic legalism, the necessity of the cross and its vindication, and the call to obedience. His kerygmatic theology is a transcript of what he believed to be God's saving action in Jesus Christ, just as the Gospels are the dramatization of the same saving action, set in a historical frame. If the apostolic kerygma expresses the essence of the gospel, the Gospels perform the vital service of keeping that essence tied in to a historical setting. "The function of recalling the historical Jesus is thus, within the framework of the Gospel, a permanent necessity." Consequently the New Testament kerygma *does* count the historical Jesus among the criteria of its own validity.[43]

3. The historian's task is thus necessary if the Christian faith is not to lose much of its character and change into a specimen of esoteric theosophy, or be reduced without remainder to an existentialist philosophy, or thrive solely because it appeals to experience. The "historical Jesus," recoverable along the kerygmatic road of inquiry which includes the Gospel literature as well as the apostolic preaching, functions indispensably as a means of recreating those disclosure points at which we glimpse God's divine presence and essence. He is the bulwark against an ever-present docetism, which would turn his name into a cipher or a gnostic password. And further,

[42] Käsemann, "Blind Alleys in the 'Jesus of History' Controversy," in *New Testament Questions of Today* (ET 1969), p. 64.

[43] If we may so turn around Käsemann's question, posed as the problem in a nutshell. "Blind Alleys," *loc. cit.*, p. 48.

the historical bedrock of Jesus of Nazareth delivers us from a subjectivism by reminding us that God acted in Jesus *before* there was any response to the kerygma, and before there was formed a church as a company of believers. Indeed, if there had been no Jesus of Nazareth, there would assuredly have been no congregation claiming allegiance to his name.

But the historian's role, strictly defined, is a limited one. By what is termed "indirect research," the historian can place Jesus in his setting of first-century Palestinian Judaism, with its religious, social and cultural milieu.[44] He can show that the historical evidence suggestively implies that God was present and active in the man Jesus. But only faith can grasp the implication of this history and cry, "Jesus is Lord!" It is the office of the Holy Spirit to awaken that faith and inspire the confession that in this man Jesus God was—and is—mightily at work.

History as a science operates within the categories set by the norm "once upon a time." It has a descriptive and interpretative function, but as a science it must stay within the bounds of its own terms of reference. That entails a commitment to the past, an admission that its raw materials are recurring, not anomalous, and can be explained within the nexus of cause-and-effect. Faith alone perceives a transcendental dimension in history when it views it as the arena of God's activity, the workshop in which his mighty deeds are fashioned, performed, and acknowledged. It is the perception of gospel history with a believing eye that gives to it a "once-for-all" character. Its significance then is grasped as revelational, i.e., unique and salvation-bringing. True, there may be historical parallels and correspondences, but in the last analysis an event which becomes revelatory of God and his purpose will to that extent be in a class by itself and nonrepeatable.

THE PRACTICAL ISSUE

It will be well to say a little about the practical ramifications of the preceding discussion. The upshot of that discussion brings us face-to-face with the question of how Jesus is known today.

First of all, even with the Gospel records open, the moment of revelation cannot be reached simply by an inspection of these documents. If this were the case, all readers who follow the words with intelligence would be believers, and the scholars would be saints. The nineteenth-century "Quest of the historical Jesus" proves the opposite. Reimarus wrote out of an attitude of revulsion to Christianity

[44] E. Stauffer, *Jesus and His Story* (ET 1960), provides possibly the best-known example of this line of inquiry. It draws on the contemporary evidence in Jewish and Graeco-Roman sources "concerning the conditions, events and personalities playing any part in Jesus' story" (p. 8).

which bordered on hatred; of his work Schweitzer wrote, "Seldom has there been a hate so eloquent, so lofty a scorn."[45] Strauss made it his avowed aim, in his study of the Gospels, precisely to discredit the Christian claim based on those documents. Impartial examination of the Gospels *by itself* cannot lead to Christian discipleship, for then the knowledge of Jesus as the Christ and Lord of all would depend on human cleverness and scholarly aptitude in handling ancient texts. Academic expertise is no barrier to personal faith, but, left to itself, it can never be the functional cause of it.

The disclosure of Jesus Christ as Lord is made through the apostolic testimony in the history of the Gospels. Our understanding of the type of historical data the Gospels contain enables us to hold this position, since we have insisted that that history is kerygmatically interpreted from the start. What would be more natural than that the reader today should be introduced to the Christ of the kerygma by an acquaintance with the deposit of living faith which first produced the Gospels? This is the sense of Johannes Weiss's remark that the Gospels are written "from faith to faith," i.e., by men of faith in order to convert and confirm their readers by introducing them to the treasure they themselves have found. Further, this disclosure is made within the context of the church's life and faith and worship and service: the revelation works only in the atmosphere of faith. The media of this saving power may be mentioned as a prelude to Gospel study.

1. What is called the *consensus fidelium* reminds us that we are not the first Christians, and that we stand in a relationship of debt to the past. All Christians who have preceded us and who have led us in the way of Christ by their example, prayer, writing, and influence make it impossible for us to cherish the illusion that we have no heritage shaping us. We bring a great deal of mental furniture, intellectual understanding, and spiritual experience to our study of the Gospels, which reminds us of our past inheritance and of all we owe to the past history of the church, without which there would be no present generation of believers for us to claim our place in. We may be only dimly aware of that factor, yet it guides our search for truth. The existence of the Gospels themselves presupposes a churchly community out of which they first came.

2. The ministry of the preaching office claims a necessary place in the way Jesus Christ is made known to his people. The importance of that ministry is clear from Paul's insistent questions in Romans 10:14, 15. The effect of the proclaimed word, in which the words of Christ are read, expounded, and applied to the concrete situations of modern life is unquestioned: it is to lead men to faith. And "faith comes from what is heard, and what is heard comes by the preaching of Christ" (Rom. 10:17). The Holy Spirit works confluently

[45] Schweitzer, *op. cit.*, p. 15.

with the preaching ministry, and evokes from those who hear the saving response and confession "Jesus is Lord" (1 Cor. 12:3).

3. The Gospel sacraments were instituted by the authority of the Lord and are invested with all the hallowed association of our Christian past from the beginning. Through them we receive pledges of the presence of the living Christ. The operative phrase in the Lord's supper is embedded in the liturgical form: "Do this in remembrance of me." In the Lukan-Pauline tradition, the assurance of Christ's presence is set in the narrative framework of the upper room scene and the interpreting words. Behind the last meal of Jesus with the disciples lay the meals in Galilee and the whole pattern of his ministry, in which meals with sinners played a significant role (Mark 2:15-17; Luke 15:1, 2, etc.). So it is not surprising that the promise of his living power should be given in the context of a meal. The perpetuation of this sacred meal links us inevitably with the past of the Gospel tradition. It recalls our indebtedness to the historical church which gathered first in this upper room and at the post-resurrection meals; and it creates a priceless disclosure scene—what Käsemann calls the *kairos*[46] —for God in Christ to come to his people in every age.

4. We dare not omit a reference to the oblique ministries of Christ, who comes to us on the road of life and meets us in the face of a neighbor and in situations of human extremity and need. Whatever the precise setting of the dramatic parable in Matthew 25:31-46 we cannot today escape its claim on us to serve Christ in a ready response to those in need.[47] "As you did it to one of the least of these my brethren, you did it to me" (25:40) entitles us to think of Christ as present in some way in the poor, the prisoner, the outcast and the socially disadvantaged. And the converse holds out the terrifying warning that our neglect to stretch out the compassionate hand to support and comfort and plead for those whom we can help is tantamount to ignoring Christ's real presence in our world. Nor can we compensate for this blindness and indifference by our religious observances and pious duties. The cup of water offered in his name becomes sacramental of his presence and grace (Matt. 10:42); and the knowledge of Jesus Christ is mediated in the context of doing his will (John 7:17) and serving our fellow men as he did (Luke 22:27).

46 Käsemann, "The Problem of the Historical Jesus," *loc. cit.*, pp. 31ff.

47 The most cogent interpretation of the setting in the Last Judgment drama in those verses is suggested by T. W. Manson, *The Sayings of Jesus* (1949), p. 251. The actions of benevolence (vv. 35-39) refer to the help given the disciples when they were engaged on their apostolic task, when they arrived in a strange town, hungry and thirsty, or when they were worn out and ill through toil and travel, when they were imprisoned for preaching the gospel. "The deeds of the righteous are not just casual acts of benevolence. They are acts by which the Mission of Jesus and His followers was helped, and helped at some cost to the doers, even at some risk."

PART TWO

Backgrounds to the Gospels

The study of any piece of ancient literature is made more meaningful if we can place it in its contemporary setting. That setting would certainly include the historical period of the literature, along with its cultural and social milieu. If the literature in question belongs to the great classics of our human heritage, we shall certainly expect that it will wrestle with profound issues such as life and death, the tragedy and victory of the human spirit, and man's quest for purpose and meaning in his existence. That means that the influences will be not simply sociological and cultural. They will also include the forces of spiritual endeavor and striving.

The New Testament story is the story of God's action in history. Repeatedly the New Testament writers stress that what God has done in Jesus Christ is almost incredible and too marvelous for words. For this action is nothing less than God's initiative in coming to earth in the person of his Son in whom (as Dorothy L. Sayers once remarked) God was writing his autobiography.

But for all this emphasis on the wonderful and supernatural, the Gospels never allow us to forget that this story is part of the stuff of history. It is important, therefore, to learn something of the historical setting in first-century Palestine where this action took place, and of the hopes and ambitions of the Jewish people, both in Palestine and beyond, which were at one and the same time fulfilled and dashed in pieces by the coming of God's messenger and Messiah "in the fulness of time."

CHAPTER THREE

Historical Survey I: Alexander the Great to Herod the Great

The three or four centuries of Jewish history from Malachi to Matthew are a period of special interest and unusual difficulty for the student of the Gospels and the New Testament.

The interest of these years is how they provide a background to the New Testament. Many important developments in Jewish thinking took place within these centuries and prefaced Jesus' coming "in the fulness of time." But most students find difficulty in fitting the period into a clear pattern.

What follows is a brief sketch of the salient features in the period from Alexander's world-shaking conquests to the second Jewish war of AD 132-135. The present chapter will follow the story in outline up to the death of Herod the Great in 4 BC. The next chapter covers the remainder of this period, from the birth of Jesus to the middle of the second century of our era.[1]

THE COMING OF HELLENISM

When the Old Testament closes, the Jews are under their Persian masters. Alexander defeated the Persians at the battle of Issus (334 BC) and then turned southward to Egypt. In 332 BC all Palestine fell before him, and the Jews were exposed to Greek culture. Evidently viewing himself as divinely chosen to unify mankind,[2] Alexander

[1] Many excellent guides are available to fill in the details of this period. To list a few: E. R. Bevan, *Jerusalem Under the High Priests* (1904); W. O. E. Oesterley, *The Jews and Judaism during the Greek Period* (1941); C. F. Pfeiffer, *Between the Testaments* (1959); D. S. Russell, *Between the Testaments* (1960); and *The Jews from Alexander to Herod* (1967); B. Reicke, *The New Testament Era* (1968); and F. F. Bruce, *New Testament History* (1969).

[2] The evidence of Alexander's sense of destiny is debated. W. W. Tarn, *Alexander the Great* (1948), calls attention to passages in the literature where Alexander is said to receive an oracle to inform him that he was God's son, charged with the task of bringing all nations together; and to

dreamed of one world mastered by the essentially civic Greek culture. Hellenization, especially in the mid-second century, posed acute problems for the Jews. Alexander's vision was a challenge to Jewish particularism and more importantly to the Jewish conviction that God had revealed himself to his people and that no mortal man dare set himself up as a rival to God.

The unifying force in Alexander's effort to bring together into a political entity the civilizations of east and west was to be Greek culture. The conquered peoples were to adopt "the Greek way of life," a policy later described as "hellenization."

These terms "Greek way of life," "hellenization," with which the RSV renders the Greek of 2 Maccabees 4:10, 13, are expanded on to indicate in a concrete situation what happened when a ruler decided to import essentially Greek practices and impose them on his subjects. The passage in 2 Maccabees 4:10-17 gives a list of features, five in number.

1. The gymnasium served both as a training-ground for athletic fitness and a social center, catering to the need for comradeship and sportsmanlike competition. The gymnasium played a vital part in expressing the Greek outlook on life. It included a frank, uninhibited acceptance of the naked human body, in contrast to the Hebrew association of nakedness with shame and guilt—an idea that is attested throughout the Bible from Genesis 3:7 to Revelation 3:18. Moreover, Jews in the gymnasium could not disguise their circumcision, the mark of their ancestral faith, unless they chose to do so by a reverse surgical operation to make themselves appear uncircumcised, thus "repudiating the holy covenant" (1 Macc. 1:15), as many did.

2. As meeting points for social contact the gymnasiums functioned as headquarters for guilds of young men called *ἔφηβοι*, youths who had arrived at manhood, 18 years of age in Athens. During the year in which young men were so ranked, they wore a distinctive uniform—a broad-brimmed hat (2 Macc. 4:12), a cloak, and high-laced boots. These garments became marks of social distinction and formed part of the ostentation and civic pride of the young men, especially in state processions. Civic virtue was wedded to physical prowess and social snobbery.

3. Another feature of "the Greek way of life" was the stadium, where sports—wrestling, discus throwing, horse racing—took place. The author of 2 Maccabees 4:14 laments that Jewish priests were deserting their sacred offices at the altar to be spectators and

the passages where his policies are described as calculated to break down all national and racial boundaries. On the other hand, E. Badian, "Alexander the Great and the Unity of Mankind," *Historia*, 7 (1958), 425ff., has raised some telling points against these interpretations of the data. See the recent discussion by J. Ferguson, *The Heritage of Hellenism* (1973), pp. 8ff.; and J. R. Hamilton, *Alexander the Great* (1973).

participants in the arena games, "putting the highest value upon Greek forms of prestige."

4. Entertainment of a different kind from that which appealed to the Jews was integral to the Greek ethos. This was the practice of the dramatic art in the Greek theater, which had been developed to a finesse by the Athenians in the fifth century. Every city in the Greek world had its theater. That civic necessity did not come easily to the Jewish way of life, for Judaism had no interest in theatrical representations and no actors.

5. The most powerful and abiding influence of Hellenism was the use of the Greek language. Greek culture spread through the medium of the language, which was a grief to orthodox Palestinian Jews, who believed that Hebrew was uniquely sacred and who came to associate the learning of Greek with an invitation to apostasy from the ancestral faith.

The importance of Alexander is seen in this intermingling of cultures, which went far to destroy the parochialism and exclusivism which had marked the Jewish way of life from the beginning. Also, for the first time with Alexander's universal conquest, a single language, Greek, became widely understood and accepted. This was to have an obvious bearing on the later dissemination of the Christian gospel in Greek.

When Alexander died in 323 BC, his kingdom was divided into three parts, Macedon, Asia, and Egypt, and each segment ruled by one of his generals or their successors. In 311 BC Palestine came under the rule of the Egyptian kings, the Ptolemies. In 30 BC the latter fell to the Romans. The other part of Alexander's domain to prove influential was the Seleucid Kingdom in Babylon, which later annexed much of Asia Minor and part of Palestine. Its capital was Antioch in Syria. But constant dynastic strife during the second century led to the gradual dissolution of the Seleucid realm, and in 63 BC it became part of the Roman world.

THE MACCABEAN STRUGGLE

By the battle of Panium in 198 BC Antiochus of Syria gained the Jewish kingdom from the Ptolemies. With the accession of Antiochus IV in 175 BC, the stage was set for the conflict which pitted the Jews against the Syrians, sparked by the Maccabean revolt.

During the suzerainty of the Ptolemies in the third century BC, the Jews in Palestine were given considerable freedom to retain their institutions and language and practice their customs. This had the effect of building up the prestige and power of the high priesthood in Jerusalem. Outside of Palestine the Jews of the Dispersion were more pervasively exposed to Greek influences, which had the effect of liberalizing their religion and encouraging them to speak Greek. About

250 BC there were so many Jews living in Egypt who spoke only Greek that a translation of the Old Testament was begun. From the story that it was the work of seventy Jewish translators, it derives its title of Septuagint (LXX).

In Palestine no such inroad of Greek culture was allowed. This insularity of Palestinian Judaism explains the hostility to innovations brought by the Syrians and in turn the fervor with which the Syrians tried forcibly to impose hellenistic culture on what they thought was a backwater religious group. But the real issue was religious, more than cultural. The fierce opposition to Syrian influence came about because the Jews felt convinced that to adopt hellenic ways would be an act of idolatry and apostasy from their faith.

The test came in 168 BC. Antiochus IV claimed the title "Epiphanes" ("God-manifest") and decided to set in motion a policy of hellenization. So ferocious was his determination that Polybius suggested he might better be nicknamed "Epimanes" (madman). The rites of the Jerusalem temple were abolished to make it an altar to Zeus. The worship of pagan gods became compulsory in Palestine; following the precepts of the Mosaic law was forbidden; circumcision, Sabbath observance, and the keeping of the festivals were all prohibited.

The people on whom this was being imposed were not fully hostile to Antiochus. Already there had appeared an infiltration into Jewish life as hellenistic Jews in Jerusalem were hospitable to these measures of the Syrian king. The Jews were divided among themselves. The nucleus of a strong hellenizing party was the priestly aristocracy, led by the brother of Onias the high priest, Jason (a Greek name for Joshua), who favored the introduction of Greek customs. Various signs of hellenistic culture had been embraced, particularly the use of Greek as a spoken language.

But the greatest offense Antiochus' policy caused came to expression in the time of the high priest Menelaus, who permitted Antiochus to plunder the temple. Jewish sensibilities were shocked (1 Macc. 1:21f.; 2 Macc. 4:32). Faithful Jews wondered why a pagan like Antiochus had been permitted by God to act so arrogantly. "It was the sense of abandonment by its God, which made the bitterness of the anguish to the heart of Israel."[3] Consequently, a group of Jewish loyalists banded together to preserve Judaism. They were called "pious ones" (or *ḥasîdîm*).

Up to this point the opposition to hellenization had been political. But, encouraged by hellenistic Jews, Antiochus, who was furious that strict Jews would not recognize Menelaus and would set the Jewish law above the divine right of kings, determined to stamp out Judaism and set in motion a chain of events which made armed

[3] Bevan, *op. cit.*, p. 82.

resistance inevitable. The stage was set at the village of Modein, where a priest named Mattathias refused to obey the king's agent and sacrifice to Zeus. A renegade Jew then came forward and prepared to make his offering. In the sight of the assembled villagers, Mattathias killed him and the king's officer and pulled down the altar. His act was a sign for widespread rebellion. The Maccabean revolt had begun.

Mattathias fled with his five sons to the mountains where the Hasidim joined him. They were willing to join in this crusade because of the religious issues involved and because they were stunned by the mass slaughter of their fellow Jews who had refused to defend themselves on the Sabbath. This led to a change of tactics; and the Jewish loyalists became guerrilla freedom-fighters waging an offensive war on the Syrians.

Before his death, Mattathias chose his son Simon to succeed him as leader. Another son Judas became commander of the freedom army, and took the name Maccabee (most likely from the Hebrew *maqqābāh*, meaning "hammerer"). The war went in the Maccabees' favor, with victories over the Syrians at Beth-Horon and Maspha (within sight of Jerusalem). The latter victory opened the way for the return of the Jews to the holy city. This rehallowing in the month Kislev, 164 BC, was thereafter commemorated as Hanukkah (see 1 Macc. 4:36-59; it is the feast mentioned also in John 10:22).

For eighteen months there was peace while the Syrians made an expedition to Persia. But although the situation that was the immediate cause of the war had been resolved and religious freedom won back, there was a military stalemate which required the war to continue. The Syrians still held the Acra, the military fortress in the temple area. Judas had been given the taste of victory in the field; and he wanted to capitalize on his success by a total conquest, but he found the Syrians too great a match, and had to endure defeats. Increasing militarism under his successor Jonathan alienated the Hasidim, who were satisfied with what had been achieved (religious liberty) and had no desire to gain political independence.

Simon, who followed Jonathan, carried the war to victory when in 143-142 BC he gained independence, declared himself high priest and drove the Syrians from the Acra. A new chapter opened here, since Simon received, at the instigation of the Jewish council, the office of high priest to be invested in himself and his descendants. In 140 BC he accepted this appointment and became high priest, military leader, and official representative to the people—three offices concentrated in one person. A token of this new takeover of power is seen in the titles given to Simon.[4]

[4] 1 Macc. 13:42 speaks of this new situation: "People began to write in their documents and contracts, 'In the first year of Simon the great high priest and commander and leader of the Jews.' " Cf. Josephus, *Antiquities* 13.6.7.

THE HASMONEANS

This introduced the era of the Hasmoneans, as they are called, the family of Mattathias who aspired to political lordship in Palestine.[5] John Hyrcanus began to reign in 134 BC. Under him Judaea became completely free from Syria, even to the point of minting coins in John's own name. No previous Jewish ruler had done this, and it was a sure sign of his claim to political independence, a freedom that lasted 66 years. The Jewish state, now thoroughly politicized, began to develop some territorial ambitions and conquered Moab, Samaria, and Edom, on whom the Jews forcibly imposed their religion.

During the reign of John Hyrcanus, the strife between the Pharisees and Sadducees over the attitude to the law of God began. Both agreed that the rules laid down in the books of Moses were binding, but in the Maccabean age religious customs not sanctioned by the law had come to be accepted. The Sadducees, a priestly aristocracy, proposed to make these new customs lawful by priestly decrees; the Pharisees, who were laymen intensely jealous for the law, refused to grant this additional authority to the priesthood and gave an important place to an oral tradition which they believed God had entrusted to Moses for transmission down the years and of which they were custodians. The Pharisees supported John at first, but later withdrew their backing. Perhaps this was because he aspired to the kingship, or (as D. S. Russell suggests)[6] perhaps they saw John's assumption of the high priestly office as a profanation of the priesthood by a man with political ambition and lust for secular power and military importance.

The reins of power, on Hyrcanus' death in 104, were seized by his eldest son Aristobulus, whose reign lasted only one year, long enough, however, for him to aspire to the kingship, though it is uncertain whether he actually claimed the title in his domestic relations or not. The historian Strabo says that it was his brother and successor Alexander Jannaeus who made a bid for the title "king"; at all events the latter's long reign (103-76 BC) well deserved the kingly inscription he placed on coins minted during his time in office.

Jannaeus increased his dominion by military expansion which gave him territories as extensive as the old kingdom of David and Solomon.[7] The Pharisees opposed him on the ground of his secularist interest and his coarse habits. Jannaeus retaliated by showing his fierce treatment of the Pharisees. On one occasion he had eight hundred of them put to death by crucifixion; and it is likely that the enormity of this event is recorded in the Nahum commentary from the Dead Sea

[5] See the genealogical tree of the Hasmonean family, p. 63.
[6] D. S. Russell, *The Jews from Alexander to Herod*, p. 67.
[7] Josephus, *Antiquities* 13.15.4.

scrolls: "He used to hang men alive on trees, as was never done before in Israel, for he that is hanged alive on a tree . . . [Deut. 21:23]."[8]

After a stormy period during which Alexander had to suffer the consequences of his opposition to the Pharisees (who at one point called on Syrian troops to help them in their struggle), he apparently came to a different frame of mind. He counseled his wife Alexandra to make peace with the Pharisees, hoping in this way to win over the people's allegiance. This is what she did, according to Josephus, after her accession in 76 BC: "She permitted the Pharisees to do as they liked in all matters, and also commanded the people to obey them."[9]

The aristocratic Sadducees, now in disfavor, found a champion in Alexandra's son Aristobulus II. When it became clear that, on the queen's imminent death in 67 BC, the kingship would pass to the elder son Hyrcanus II, Aristobulus took the initiative and gathered an army with a threat of civil war.

THE COMING OF THE ROMANS

Internecine strife between the brothers was inevitable. But after a skirmish at Jericho, the prospect for peace appeared in a concordat between them, by which Hyrcanus consented to retire from the position of king, leaving the way clear for the more energetic and popular Aristobulus II to be acclaimed. That might have solved things, but for an enigmatic figure waiting in the wings, the half-Jew Antipater. Though a descendant of the Edomites, the age-old enemies of the Jews, Antipater had gained considerable wealth and popular influence; now he saw his chance to test his strength against Aristobulus. He persuaded Hyrcanus to enlist foreign mercenaries to regain the position he had forfeited to his brother.

This stalemate brought the Romans to the scene and into Palestinian politics. The Roman general Pompey had come east to subdue King Mithridates of Pontus. Aristobulus was able to secure the services of Pompey's lieutenant Scaurus, but Pompey decided to support Hyrcanus, since he regarded Aristobulus as the more dangerous threat to Roman power in the eastern provinces. After an engagement, Aristobulus was forced to surrender. The temple garrison held out, and was besieged, falling in 63 BC. Pompey did something which left an indelible mark on Jewish mentality: he entered the holy place, where no Gentile had previously dared to penetrate. Though Pompey

8 Text published by J. M. Allegro, *JBL*, 75 (1956), 89-95. For a commentary on the words "hanged alive," see N. Wieder, "Notes on the New Documents from the Fourth Cave of Qumran," *Journal of Jewish Studies*, 7 (1956), 71f. Josephus' account of the incident is given in *Antiquities* 13.14.1f.; and *Jewish War* 1.4.5f.

9 Josephus, *Antiquities* 13.16.2.

refrained from looting the temple treasure, his act of trespass and sacrilege was never forgotten.

Grief over Pompey's invasion and the Sadducees' corruption of the court are reflected in the Pharisaic document, *The Psalms of Solomon*, written around 50 BC. These noble pieces of literature bemoan the sad condition of Jerusalem; they accuse the Sadducees as princes who have betrayed their trust; yet they express the hope that a new king will arise as a second David to rule over a purified and free people. He will expel occupying Roman troops and Sadducean usurpers and bring in God's kingdom of Israel's prosperity and dominance over her enemies. Not surprisingly this king holds a special relationship to God; he is the Lord's anointed or Messiah (17:32; 18:5).

Following Pompey's triumph, Aristobulus was sent as a captive to Rome. Hyrcanus was deposed from kingship and granted the titles of high priest and ethnarch (ruler of the people). The real power was vested in the Idumean Antipater. This détente marked the decline and eclipse of the Hasmonean house, and all future policy was to be shaped by the occupying Romans.

Antipater was clearly a man under pressure. He knew that his control rested on his continuing favor with the Romans, which in turn depended on throwing in his lot with whatever faction in Roman politics seemed most likely to be successful. He also had troubles on the domestic front with the defeated Hasmoneans, who were not willing to take a reversal without countermeasures. Moreover, Antipater was at a disadvantage as an Idumean rather than a full Jew, especially since he owed his post to the Romans.

On the international scene Antipater first supported Pompey, but when Julius Caesar achieved power after the defeat of Pompey's party in 48 BC and Pompey's murder in Egypt, Antipater deftly transferred his support. Caesar rewarded him with the office of procurator of Judaea and granted concessions to Jews both in their holy land and in the Jewish dispersion outside Palestine. In March 44 BC, the republican party in Rome, led by Brutus and Cassius, killed Caesar. Once more Antipater found it politic to redirect his allegiance to the new masters of the Roman world. But in the changeover of power, he was assassinated in 43 BC, leaving his energetic son Herod in control.

HEROD THE GREAT

The active life of this man spans the years 37-4 BC, years of great importance for the Jewish people. In Herod, history recognizes the character of an ambitious man, yet his ambition was not selfish in spite of the contradictions of his nature. On the one hand, he attempted to rule in a civilized, rational, and constructive manner; on the other he was plagued with a violent disposition, and at the end of his career he lost command of events and fell victim to the matrimonial intrigues he brought on himself by his polygamous relationships. To sum up in a sentence this kaleidoscopic character, we can hardly do better than to use the words of his recent biographer Michael Grant: Herod's "ambition was to keep the Jews intact and prosperous, in their own country, without losing the cooperation and protection of the Roman empire."[10]

Before Herod could establish his rule he had to secure his position. After Antipater's death, Brutus and Cassius were defeated at Philippi (42 BC). Following his father's policy, Herod made peace with the victor, Mark Antony. He was recognized as joint tetrarch along with his brother Phasael and was given control of Judaea. This was soon to be challenged. The Parthian tribes in the east launched a campaign against Rome. Antigonus, the sole surviving son of Aristobulus, joined in alliance with them. This put pressure on Antipater's sons. Phasael was captured and committed suicide; Herod escaped to Rome; and Antigonus ruled as high priest and king in Jerusalem.

But Herod was in favor at Rome. In 39 he secured the title of "confederate king" from the Roman senate and proceeded to Palestine to claim his possession. He was thwarted at first because of insufficient Roman military backing, but eventually, with his hold on Galilee secured, he laid siege to Jerusalem and put Antigonus to the sword, in a great slaughter. The rule of the Hasmoneans had finally come to extinction.

In 31 BC the civil war which had broken out between Antony and Octavian was resolved in Octavian's victory at Actium. Herod was quick to transfer his allegiance to the victor, who in turn transferred Cleopatra's lands and possessions held in Palestine to him. This gave Herod a vast territory comparable with the kingdom Alexander Jannaeus had ruled. Octavian's favors indicate the success of Herod's policy of casting his lot with Rome. For his part, Octavian was sufficiently alive to the menace of the Parthians in the east to want a bulwark of defense in Herod's kingdom. It also was a matter of Octavian's expediency to give Herod a commanding status, for he wished to water down "the Hebrew nationalism of the central homeland by infusing non-Jewish elements, in the hope that a more or less Hellenised type of client state would emerge . . . governed by an administration of the normal Greek type."[11]

Herod, too, was eager to repress the nationalist spirit and to cultivate relations with the Romans on an international scale. This policy reflected Herod's realization that politics is the art of the

[10] Michael Grant, *Herod the Great* (1971), p. 13.
[11] *Ibid.*, p. 97.

possible. He was willing to accept the inevitable restrictions on Jewish independence, to seek peace within his borders, and to collaborate with the Roman authority. In the eyes of the more turbulent nationalists, he must have appeared as a traitor to the Jewish cause. It is likely he chose to do what he did because of his ethnic background as an Idumean, which left him less than wholeheartedly in sympathy with the Jewish revolutionaries. He was prudent enough to concede that national survival would come by working with, not rebelling against, the Roman overlords who bestrode not merely Palestine but the Mediterranean world like a colossus.

Herod's government at home was typically hellenistic. An important part of that ethos was centered in city life. He busied himself with fine building programs, establishing palaces in Jerusalem and Jericho and residences and public works in the provinces, especially in Samaria which was renamed Sebaste after the Greek word for the Latin "Augustus." He also erected a new harbor-town, named Caesarea after the emperor. Evidence can still be seen there of Herod's theater, and doubtless there were originally the other elements of Greek city life to be seen—gymnasiums, baths, and marketplaces to cater to a population estimated at 50,000. At Masada, on the southwest side of the Jordan river, Herod built a fortress, now a place of sacred pilgrimage to the Jews because it was there that a last stand was made by Jewish freedom fighters at the close of the first Jewish war in AD 72-73. In securing the place as a national shrine the Israeli government has uncovered precious relics of Herod's palace built there.[12]

Perhaps the most noteworthy building project associated with Herod is the Jerusalem temple. Begun in 20 BC on the site of the second temple of Zerubbabel, this rebuilt edifice was to be the climax of Herod's life's work, for which he hoped to be remembered with everlasting gratitude by the Jewish people. After 18 months' work the sanctuary was completed, though remaining parts on the precinct had to be finished, and the final touches were not put to the completed whole until AD 63, seven years before its destruction by the Romans. But the scheme of reconstruction and beautification was Herod's brainchild, for which he claimed the honor with deep pride.

These magnificent projects needed budgetary support. In addition Herod's client relationship with Rome was underwritten by taxes he was required to pay. Poll taxes and land revenues were levied, with a system of sales tax imposed on purchases and sales. The collection of these taxes was farmed out to private concerns, and the network of "tax collectors" (later called *publicani* in Latin) was responsible. But there was no oppression at this stage.

[12] See Y. Yadin, *Masada: Herod's Fortress and the Zealots' Last Stand* (1966).

GENEALOGICAL TREE OF THE HASMONEAN FAMILY

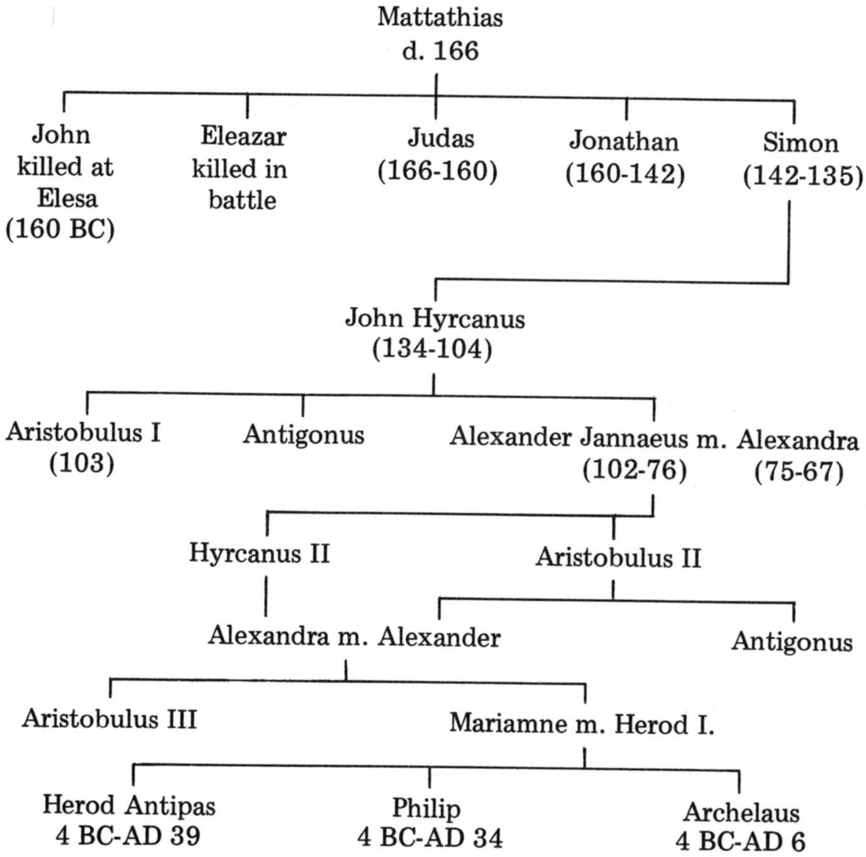

In spite of all these attractive aspects of Herod's rule, he was not popular. His public image is sadly defaced by his reputation as an individual who, in a position of autocratic eminence within his family and court, was obsessed with suspicion and fear, and showed that obsession by his cruel and hasty removal of all he suspected of being enemies. Herod's polygamy committed his family to deep suspicion and fearsome revenge. Especially in the closing years of his reign his life was saddened by the plots of his sons and the hatred of his people. Three of his sons were murdered. To check the disaffection of the people, Jerusalem was honeycombed with informers and spies, and those who lay under suspicion were dispatched without mercy.

One matter particularly irked the sick and aging king. The expectation of a messianic figure rose high in popular imagination.

Herod naturally saw in this prospect a threat to his own safety and control. He repressed the supporters of this hope with stern measures. In this context his eventual response to the visit of the Magi—the massacre of the Bethlehem babies—is explained (Matt. 2:1-21).

Herod angered the Pharisees, chiefly by requiring an oath of allegiance to himself and his policies. About 17 BC he had issued an order for the act of fealty, and the Pharisees and Essenes asked to be excused on the grounds that they disliked using God's name in oath-taking and that the Essenes objected to oaths as such. Ten years later Herod insisted on complete obedience, and included a pledge of loyalty to the emperor. This was evidently calculated to demonstrate his unwavering pro-Roman commitment. The Pharisees objected and were lightly punished, but the incident is indicative of a general mood of malaise and uneasiness throughout Herod's realm. It is a further illustration of the underlying hatred he felt for all that represented the Hasmonean spirit; and popular opinion, which Herod was never able to overcome, still considered the Hasmoneans the rightful rulers of the Jews.

Herod's illness, which caused him some mental disturbance at the end, led to his death in 4 BC. His kingdom was divided among his surviving sons.

CHAPTER FOUR

Historical Survey II: The Rule of the Romans

THE DIVIDED KINGDOM AT HEROD'S DEATH

The three sons of Herod—Archelaus, Antipas, and Philip—each in turn applied to Rome for the terms of their father's will to be ratified. Augustus agreed, and the disposition of power was as follows.

1. By far the most energetic of the sons, Herod Antipas (4 BC to AD 39) suffered from several of his father's unfortunate moral propensities. Also, like his father, he was a great builder; and he erected a great city on the banks of the Sea of Galilee, which he named Tiberias after the reigning emperior (*c.* AD 22).

After many years of marriage to the daughter of a Nabatean king, Antipas contracted an illicit union with his niece and sister-in-law Herodias. He had met her in Rome when she was the wife of his brother Herod Philip; and he persuaded her to marry him after she had induced him to abandon his Nabatean queen. The offensiveness of this act caused some stir, and it formed the occasion on which John the Baptist was imprisoned and later martyred (Mark 6:14-29).

Not only the Jews were affronted by this marriage union. Herodias' father, the Nabatean king Aretas IV, was later to gain his revenge on Antipas; and her brother Agrippa became an effective agent in securing Antipas' downfall. First, the Nabatean king invaded Peraea in AD 36 and dealt a crushing blow to Antipas' forces. Agrippa, too, had designs on Antipas' kingdom; and he informed against him, accusing him of plotting with the Parthians in the east. Having failed to answer those charges, Antipas was banished to Lyons in Gaul. Herodias decided to accompany him into exile and oblivion, leaving the way clear for Agrippa to assume rulership in Galilee.[1]

[1] For fuller detail see F.F. Bruce, *Herod Antipas, Tetrarch of Galilee and Peraea* (1966), and (at greater length) H. Hoehner, *Herod Antipas* (1972).

2. Philip (4 BC to AD 34) was a stay-at-home ruler, confining his attention to his tetrarchy of Ituraea and Trachonitis (Luke 3:1) in the upper Jordan region on both west and east banks. He refounded the city of Paneion, which he renamed in honor of the Roman emperor Philip's Caesarea or, in Latin, Caesarea Philippi, to distinguish it from the larger city of that name on the Mediterranean seaboard. He also established the city of Bethsaida and made it into a winter residence. There he died in AD 34, and as his estate had no heir the region he ruled over passed under the control of the legate of Syria.

3. Archelaus (4 BC to AD 6) inherited all the character deficiencies of his father. His office as ethnarch in Judaea, Samaria, and Idumaea was short-lived because of his oppressions. The occasion of Archelaus' outbursts was a rising fervor of hope that God's kingdom would be established in Judaea and the Jews would be able to throw off all Roman domination. Archelaus' ferocious manner of quelling these uprisings led both Jews and Samaritans to protest to the emperor. Augustus, fearing that Archelaus' callousness and obvious disfavor with the people would lead to widespread revolt, banished him to Vienne in AD 6. Judaea became a Jewish province administered by a procurator (*praefectus*), chosen from the lower order of *equites* but answerable to the emperor himself.

THE PROCURATORS

At the time of Archelaus' removal, the Roman legate in Syria was Publius Sulpicius Quirinius. He proceeded to take steps to determine the taxable responsibility of the Judaean province now that Judaea was to pass directly under Roman rule. These measures included a census. This event raised a storm of opposition, which provoked the armed rebellion of Judas of Galilee and brought the Zealots onto the stage of history. Though the uprising failed, it was an ominous sign that many Jews were convinced that one day they would succeed by force of arms in driving the Romans from their land. However, Rome took steps to confirm its control over Judaea by appointing Coponius as first procurator (in some English translations of the Gospels, the word is rendered governor).

1. During the reign of Tiberius Caesar, so Luke 3:1 records, Pontius Pilate was the fifth prefect, coming to his appointment in AD 26 and holding it until AD 37. Several incidents prior to Jesus' trial give proof of Pilate's inflexibility and self-will (to use descriptions of him by Herod Agrippa to the emperor Gaius in AD 40). On three occasions he is recorded to have showed his contempt for the Jewish people, though on two of those he was forced to relent and change his mind.

Out of their fear of idolatry, the Jews in Jerusalem refused to tolerate any graven image in the city. Incoming Roman soldiers were thus required to remove the image of the emperor from their standards. Pilate tried to avoid this loss of prestige by ordering the soldiers to enter by night and leave the standards untouched. The Jews protested; and when a showdown became inevitable at Caesarea, they refused to be cowered by the soldiers' threats, offering to die rather than surrender their principles. Pilate realized he was defeated, and backed down by consenting to remove the standards from Jerusalem.

Pilate faced a similar situation when he set up votive tablets in the palace of Herod on Mount Zion. The Jews regarded this act as tantamount to a violation of Jerusalem's sanctity as God's city and successfully appealed to the emperor for their removal. Pilate acquiesced.[2]

A third attack on Jewish sensibilities was more effective. Pilate seized a portion of the temple treasure to finance construction of a new aqueduct to increase the water supply in Jerusalem. The protest was made that it was sacrilegious for the sacred money of the temple to be devoted to secular purposes. Pilate insisted; and when the Jews (including, perhaps, if Luke 13:1 refers to this episode, a number of Galilean pilgrims in the temple courts) raised a violent remonstrance, Pilate put them down with great violence and some slaughter.

Some have found the reason for Pilate's detestation of the Jews in his close association with Sejanus, prefect of the praetorian guard in Rome. Before his fall from favor in October, AD 31, Sejanus exercised a powerful influence on Tiberius and led him to adopt an anti-Semitic policy. After Sejanus' death, his protégé Pilate may have felt bereft of support and obligated to pacify the Jews in Jerusalem if he was to remain in favor with the emperor, whose policy changed to a pro-Jewish one. John 19:12 may report the chief priests' innuendo aimed at Pilate's most vulnerable spot: "If you release this man, you are not Caesar's friend."[3] The phrase "Caesar's friend" may be an allusion to the special privilege (*amicus Caesaris*) Pilate enjoyed. At Jesus' trial he was under pressure and afraid of losing that favorable place in Roman society.

Some years thereafter Pilate was again put in an awkward position when a Samaritan prophet appeared who promised to unearth the vessels used by Moses in the tabernacle. He was probably bidding to be hailed as a Samaritan "restorer" in fulfilment of the expectation of Deuteronomy 18:15. In Pilate's eye this would have been equivalent to a messianic claim. His method of dispelling the gathering around the prophet was to resort to considerable violence. His brutal methods were reported to the emperor, and he was recalled to Rome

[2] On this incident, see P.L. Maier, "The Episode of the Golden Roman Shields at Jerusalem," *HTR*, 62 (1969), 109-21.

[3] So P.L. Maier, "Sejanus, Pilate, and the Date of the Crucifixion," *Church History*, 37,1 (1968), 3-13; cf. A.D. Doyle, "Pilate's Career and the Date of the Crucifixion," *JTS*, 42 (1941), 190-93.

to justify his conduct in AD 37. We know no more of him; for before he could reach Rome, Tiberius had died. Tradition represents Pilate's later years as given up to remorse, though this is perhaps only pious reflection due to the inclusion of his name in the Apostles' Creed.

2. Pilate's successor Marullus was later replaced not by a Roman governor but by a Jewish king, Herod Agrippa I, who ruled from 41 to 44. The Roman procurator Fadus was then appointed in 44. He managed to keep a firm hand on Judaean political pressure points. The Pharisees adopted a quietist posture, believing that the Romans were the divine agents of chastisement to whom the Jews must submit as a penalty for their sins. At the opposite end of the spectrum the Zealots preached a holy war against Rome and stirred up an undercurrent of unrest and opposition. Under Fadus' successors, lawlessness and resentment against foreign rule simmered, until it reached a boiling point during the procuratorship of Florus (AD 64-66).

3. Of particular interest for reading the New Testament are four of the seven procurators who held office between 44 and 66. Felix was appointed in 52 and ruled until 60. During his procuratorship Paul was arrested and detained for trial. Felix had to deal with disturbances caused by a number of revolutionaries who persuaded people to follow them into the wilderness promising that their freedom from Rome would be gained there. A reference to this type of bogus leader is found in Matthew 24:23-26, which concludes with Jesus' warning: "If they say to you, 'Lo, he is in the wilderness,' do not go out. . . ." Similarly, such anti-Roman activity is alluded to in Acts 21:38, which mentions an Egyptian wonder-worker, put down by Felix, who led his devotees in the desert and promised them victory over the Roman garrison in Jerusalem.

4. If Felix's character contained unattractive features—the Roman historian Tacitus wrote a verdict for posterity in the remark that Felix "exercised the power of a king with the spirit of a slave"[4]—the man appointed to succeed him in 59 was of a different caliber. This was Festus. However, he was unable to reverse the deteriorating situation of suspicion and animosity between Jews and Romans. Nor did he take action to favor Paul's case, as we learn from Acts 25 and 26. Festus died in AD 62, to be followed by Albinus after a brief interruption. This short interim is noteworthy because it provided the opportunity for the Jews to indict James, the Lord's brother, and bring about his death.

5. Albinus (62-64) inherited an unpromising situation from his predecessors. Jewish revolutionaries called *sicarii* ("men of the dagger") caused terrorism throughout the province. Albinus endeavored to suppress them but with little success. He gave in to their

[4] Tacitus, *Annals* 12.54; *History* 5.9.

demands for blackmail and lost ground in his campaign against them. The stage was obviously being prepared for a final confrontation between Jewish resistance and Roman authority. With Florus the combustible material exploded.

6. Florus had acquired a reputation for avarice and corruption. He exceeded all previous limits set on his lust for wealth and power when he raided the temple treasure on the pretext that money was required for the imperial service. This action infuriated the Jews, and when they demonstrated against Florus' sacrilege, he retaliated by brutal reprisals. Leading citizens were crucified and the Roman troops were given a free hand to plunder and pillage part of Jerusalem.

As a further means of protest Eleazar, the captain of the temple, incited the priests to discontinue the daily sacrifice on behalf of the emperor's well-being. This was interpreted by the Romans as an act of treason. Attempts to repair the breach of Jewish-Roman relations failed, and the enmity was made irrevocable in September 66 by an insurgent attack on the garrison in the Antonia fort in which all the Romans there were killed.

An earlier attack had been made on a Roman fort at Masada, west of the Dead Sea. This encampment was held by a left-wing guerrillas of the Jewish resistance, the Zealots. Hearing of the attack on the Romans in Jerusalem and inspired by a leader Menahem who claimed a messianic role, they marched on Jerusalem and occupied a portion of the city. Rivalry between the Jewish factions led to blows, and Menahem was caught and killed. The Zealots managed to get back to Masada, where they held out until the final phase of the Jewish war in 73 or more probably 74.[4a]

THE JEWISH REVOLUTIONARY WAR

At the outset of the revolt in 66, the Jews were encouraged by the victory of their forces over Cestius Gallus, governor of Syria. The news of his defeat gave fresh courage, and the revolt spread throughout Palestine. The emperor Nero dispatched his able general Vespasian to subdue the outbreak. First he attacked Galilee where he mopped up Jewish insurgents and captured a young Jewish military commander named Josephus, who had just returned from Rome, and the noted Zealot John, who had held out for a time in Gischala. While Josephus remained a prisoner, placing himself on the side of the Romans by his prophecy that Vespasian would be the next emperor, John escaped to Jerusalem.

During the winter of AD 67-68 a civil war raged in Jerusalem

[4a] For the date of the fall of Masada in April, AD 74, see E. Schürer, *The History of the Jewish People*, i, ed. G. Vermes and F. Millar (1973), pp. 512, 515.

between the forces of John and the priest Ananus, who led a more moderate faction. Vespasian swept through Peraea, Samaria, and Idumaea and was poised for an attack on Jerusalem. Then news came that Nero had died (June 68) and there was disturbance in Rome. Vespasian returned to Caesarea where he was subsequently proclaimed emperor.

He took up the task of besieging Jerusalem in June 69 but was recalled to Rome to take charge of imperial affairs. He entrusted the Roman interest in Judaea to his son Titus, who laid siege to Jerusalem in April 70. After five months of resistance, the temple area held by John of Gischala fell and the sanctuary was burned down. Three weeks later the upper city, where John and his fellow Zealot leader Simon Bargiora had fled, was taken. The Romans surged into Jerusalem and killed all whom they could find.

Simon, John, and others took refuge in underground caverns, but were forced to surrender. The most inaccessible pocket of resistance was the encampment at the fortress of Masada, west of the Dead Sea, which held out for another three or more years. In order to take it the Romans had to erect a huge causeway from the nearest mountain to the top of the fortress; and it stands today as a memorial to Jewish patriotism which refused to surrender. When the Romans eventually gained this summit, only one old woman was left alive; in April or May 74 the garrison of Jewish patriots had committed mass suicide by consent rather than fall into enemy hands.

The Zealot leaders in Jerusalem were punished and the city was leveled, with only the western wall remaining to give some protection to a resident Roman garrison. Josephus' life was spared. After his capture earlier in the war, he had been imprisoned, and subsequently released to attend Titus at the siege of Jerusalem as a negotiator between the Romans and Jews. Though these efforts failed, Titus at his request spared the lives of a number of Jews and allowed them to keep certain sacred books. Josephus' sympathies, however, lay with policies of cooperation and appeasement; and his writings show no concern to be identified with the Jewish freedom-fighters of Jerusalem and Masada who chose to die rather than surrender their ancestral faith.

Josephus returned to Rome, was made a Roman citizen, and received rewards from the Romans for his services. The Jewish religion, however, survived even in Palestine, thanks largely to the enterprise of a leading rabbi, Johanan ben Zakkai, who accepted Roman domination and sought to live with it. He petitioned Vespasian to be allowed to set up a rabbinical school at Jamnia in western Judaea. A new Sanhedrin was convened, and much attention was given to rebuilding the Jewish way of life. Especially in the legislature these Jewish schools set about classifying and codifying the oral law, a task carried on by succeeding generations, notably by the rabbi Aqiba.

In one respect the Jamnia school has an important bearing on the understanding of the New Testament. The Jewish Christians were not in great favor in the eyes of the Jewish people. At the beginning of the war in 66, the Jerusalem community had acted on an oracle and had fled to Pella, in Transjordan,[5] thus preserving its identity. In the period of Jamnia reconstruction it was not averse to seeking a liaison with the synagogue. The need for national solidarity within a renewed Judaism required that unity be achieved at the level of the local synagogues. To protect themselves from weakening due to the presence of Jewish Christians, the synagogues inserted a test clause into their daily congregational prayers, known as the Eighteen Benedictions. The prayer cursing the heretics was inserted around the year 90 to detect the presence of Jewish Christians who would reveal themselves by their silence during the imprecation sought on "Nazoreans and heretics" (*mînîm*).[6]

How great the breach became between orthodox Judaism and the Jewish Christian section within the synagogue is not certain. What is indisputable is the definite break that came at the time of the Second Jewish War, AD 132-135, as Eusebius observes in Book IV of his *Church History*.

THE END OF THE JEWISH STATE

Between AD 73 and 132 there were occasional rebellions against Rome by Jews in the lands to which they had earlier been dispersed. For instance, in 114 Trajan's campaign against the Parthians in the east suffered defeat; and this incited Jews in North Africa to rise up, only to be crushed in 115-117.

The Jews in Jerusalem were left in peace, and a measure of resettlement and rebuilding was allowed. But there was no substantial revival of Jewish religious life centered in the holy city. The old temple tax paid by Jews throughout the area in the period before 70 was diverted, on Vespasian's insistence, to the temple treasury of Jupiter Capitolinus at Rome, and a later extension of the scope of this taxation policy caused resentment.

Even more violently opposed was Hadrian's edict forbidding the practice of circumcision in 132. This came soon after Hadrian's order in 130 that a new city, to be called Aelia Capitolina, should be built on the ruins of Jerusalem. It was to have a temple dedicated to the god Jupiter and to be a shrine for emperor-worship. The implica-

[5] Eusebius, *Church History* 3.5.3. There is a careful discussion of this text by S. Sowers, "The Circumstances and Recollection of the Pella Flight," *ThZ*, 26.5 (1970), 305-20. L. Goppelt, *Jesus, Paul and Judaism* (1964), p. 131, points out that these Jewish Christian "Nazarenes" were branded as traitors and deserters by the bulk of Jewry.

[6] See C.W. Dugmore, *The Influence of the Synagogue upon the Divine Office* (1944), p. 4.

tion of this building plan was clear for the nationalist Jews to see: there would be no Jewish temple rebuilt.

These actions stirred the spirit of a Jew named Simon, to whom a leading rabbi of the day, Rabbi Aqiba, gave the title *Bar-Kokhba* ("son of a star"), a name taken from the Old Testament: "A star shall come forth out of Jacob, and a sceptre shall rise out of Israel" (Num. 24:17). The messianic pretensions of the name are apparent, and the significance of the claim made by and for Simon was not lost on the Romans. The revolt was put down at great cost to both sides and not before 135. Simon's surname appears in recently discovered fragments from the Dead Sea area of Wadi Murabba'at, in which he is called Simon ben-Kosebah.[7]

After the war, Aelia Capitolina was built as a Roman colony, and a temple in which Hadrian's statue was contained erected. The Jews were forbidden to enter the city. As far as the fourth century, the ban was in force, except for one day a year when the Jews were allowed to weep at the temple site. This restriction remained until the end of the Six Day War in 1967.

[7] The results of these findings have been published by Y. Yadin, *Bar Kokhba* (1971).

CHAPTER FIVE

Foundations of Judaism

The period following the Council of Jamnia (*c.* AD 90) was marked by a growing concern on the part of a reconstituted Judaism to define more precisely the nature and authority of its religious faith. Much of what is loosely called rabbinic Judaism was not formulated until this period, though rabbinic beliefs and practices no doubt also belonged to New Testament times before they became formally standardized later. We must first consider the chief elements in the literature which was to form the corpus of rabbinic Judaism and then note other literary sources important for understanding first-century Jewry.

LITERARY SOURCES

1. *Rabbinic literature.* The foundation of orthodox Judaism was the biblical law, known by its Hebrew title "Torah," which in fact is more properly translated "direction" than "law." Essentially, "Torah" meant the five books of Moses, to which supreme authority was given, but this was supplemented by oral teaching handed down from Moses' time as an expansion and explanation of the written law of the Old Testament. Those responsible for this chain of teaching—referred to in Mark 7:5 as "the tradition of the elders"—were called the Tannaim or scholars. The description of the Jewish leaders as "the elders" is drawn from Joshua 24:31, and was referred to in the composite document which later reduced the oral law to written form. This written compilation is known as the Mishnah (meaning "repetition").

Rabbinic literary activity falls into two parts. The descriptive term for the oral tradition, later codified in the Mishnah, is halakah (a Hebrew term for walking, which suggests the practical application of the Mosaic law in everyday situations). Halakah may be defined as an exposition of legal precepts, offering direct and authoritative direction and guidance for a life of obedience. For all practical purposes, the rabbinic corpus became embodied in the sixty-three sections or tractates of the Mishnah. The remaining rabbinic writings, which found no place in the Mishnah, became incorporated into the Tosephta, which was similar to the Mishnah but lacked its special authority.

It is almost inevitable that a definition of a legal precedent will later prove inadequate and require refinement. So, too, with the Mishnah. Its precepts in turn became the subject of commentary and amplification, and this comment, along with some sayings (baraita) of the rabbis of the premishnaic period, forms what is called Gemara.

The final stage of growth and development of Jewish law came in the Talmud, the collected wisdom of the rabbis, achieved by the addition of the Mishnah and the Gemara. The Talmud exists in two forms, corresponding to the two main centers of rabbinic study. The "Jerusalem Talmud" was first issued in Tiberias *c.* AD 250; the Babylonian edition came much later, *c.* AD 500.

The other sphere of rabbinic literary enterprise is the world of haggadah, sermonic, practical illustrations of the narrative portions of the Torah. This expository and interpretative work is found mainly in Midrash, which is a comprehensive description of this kind of literature including such examples as a commentary on Exodus (known as Mekilta), on Leviticus (Siphra), and on the Pentateuch as a whole (Midrash rabbah).[1]

Other specimens of literature which open the door to Jewish faith and practice in New Testament times are the Targums—Aramaic paraphrases of the Bible designed to meet the needs of the worshipers in the synagogue who did not understand the biblical Hebrew of the lessons[2]—and liturgical texts for worship services both in the synagogue (e.g., the Eighteen Benedictions) and home (e.g., the Passover haggadah, used for the domestic celebration of Passover).

2. *The Septuagint.* The Jewish people in the New Testament era were distributed over a wide geographical region. More than 150 cities in the Roman empire are known to have had synagogues at this period. For several centuries an important segment of Jewish population had lived in Egypt, where they had come to speak the language of the area—Greek.

The Jews who lived in Alexandria during the third and second centuries BC had lost much of their understanding of Hebrew. Yet they wanted to comprehend the message of their ancient sacred writings. The problem was faced by the production of the Septuagint, whose origin is told (with legendary details added) in the *Letter of Aristeas*, the work of an unknown Jew living about 170 BC. The letter, allegedly from an official, Aristeas, in the court of Ptolemy in Egypt, to his brother Philocrates, tells how the Egyptian king wanted a translation of the Jewish law and sent Aristeas to Jerusalem to bring

[1] Examples of the rabbinic writings referred to in these paragraphs may be found in C.K. Barrett, *New Testament Background: Selected Documents* (1956), pp. 139ff.

[2] See M. McNamara, *Targum and Testament* (1972).

back skilled and scholarly interpreters. He returned with seventy-two scholars, who labored for seventy-two days on the island of Pharos, and eventually produced the Greek translation they were commissioned to make. From their number the name *Septuaginta* (Latin for "seventy") or LXX (in Roman abbreviation) was given.[3] The legend's only substance is perhaps that the books of the law were translated into Greek for the benefit of Greek-speaking Jews in Egypt during the time of Ptolemy II in the middle of the third century BC.

The law was probably the first part of the Hebrew Bible to be translated, then the prophets, and finally the writings. More books were translated into Greek than were later recognized as canonical or authoritative; the balance of the books form what we know today as the Old Testament Apocrypha. These additional books are important for the data they supply to assist our understanding of Jewish thinking in the period between the Testaments. C. K. Barrett draws attention to three major aspects of Jewish thought that surface in these apocryphal books: the concept of wisdom as an intermediary between God and man; ethical teaching which emphasizes God's providence shown to the Israelite righteous; and the hope of the after-life, which is bright even if martyrdom is the destined lot of the Maccabean faithful.[4]

In sum, the Septuagint provides an important source of knowledge for understanding the Jewish faith prior to and during the New Testament period. It was, furthermore, the Bible of the early church and the prime instrument in Christian missionary preaching to the Jewish and hellenistic world to show how God's salvation had been accomplished "in accordance with the scriptures" (1 Cor. 15:3).

3. *The Qumran scrolls.* Since 1947, when the first discoveries of scrolls hidden in caves near Qumran by the banks of the Dead Sea were made, our knowledge of life among a group of Jewish emigrants to a monastery in that area has increased greatly. The work of classifying the Dead Sea scrolls according to their contents and intent is still proceeding. The earlier discoveries have yielded the following items of literature important for New Testament study: *The Rule of the Community* (1QS), *The Rule of the Congregation* (1QSa), *Hymns of Thanksgiving* (1QH), *The War Scroll* (1QM), and the commentary (*pesher*) on the Book of Habakkuk (1QpHab)—all from cave 1; and the *pesher* on the book of Nahum (4QpNah) from cave 4.[5]

4. *Josephus.* Despite his Roman name, Flavius Josephus was a

[3] For this legend, see Barrett, *op. cit.*, pp. 213-16; with the alternate version from Philo printed on pp. 210-13. Both versions agree in crediting the Alexandrian king Ptolemy Philadelphus, 283-245 BC, with sponsoring this translation.

[4] *Ibid.*, pp. 216ff.

[5] Among the numerous available sources on the scrolls is a useful student's guide, M. Mansoor, *The Dead Sea Scrolls* (1964). See also W. S. LaSor, *The Dead Sea Scrolls and the New Testament* (1972), with a bibliography of introductory works on the scrolls.

Jew, born of noble and priestly ancestry in Palestine *c.* AD 37-38. His personal history is recounted in his *Life*, which includes the information that he became a Pharisee as the result of a deliberate effort to select the best Jewish group with which to identify himself.

Josephus' voluminous writings record Jewish history from the standpoint of a historian who himself shared in the public life of his times. As we saw above, in the Jewish War of AD 66-70 he led Jewish resistance in Galilee after his return from Rome, where he had gone to secure the release of some priests who had been arrested. He was involved in the struggle as a military commander in Galilee, then captured by the Romans and brought before Vespasian, only to be released after he offered his services to the Romans.[6] As a mark of gratitude he took Vespasian's family name Flavius. Josephus was an eyewitness of the final tragic stages of the war. Later, in Rome, he saw the triumphal procession of the Romans and the captive trophies borne from Judaea, an event commemorated in Titus' arch. He received Roman citizenship, and devoted his final years to his literary tasks.

The writings of Josephus included *The Jewish War*, a propaganda piece intended to urge on the inhabitants of Syria the need to collaborate with Rome by showing how disastrous the war of AD 66-70 had been for the Jews. In the twenty books entitled *The Antiquities of the Jewish People*, published *c.* AD 93, he sought to extol the virtues of the Jewish people from the creation to his own day and to commend them to a non-Jewish readership. His *Life* was an apology for his own part in the Jewish War and a defense against charges brought against him. An apology on a larger scale against allegations brought against the Jewish people formed the substance and theme of his treatise *Against Apion.*

In evaluating Josephus as a historical source we should observe certain factors that colored his accounts. First of all is the apologetic, propagandistic motive in his writing, which often led him to exaggerate and distort the evidence. Furthermore, he virtually eliminated messianic expectation from his description of the Jewish faith. The reason for this was its potential damage to his presentation of the Jews as loyal to Rome. The title "King of the Jews" would be as abhorrent to Roman ears as to his own, for he had learned and practiced the art of compromise by his collaboration with the Romans in AD 66-70. Finally, it must be recalled that Josephus was an apologist on behalf of his race, anxious to conserve what he considered the best elements in the national character and to dismiss all

[6] A modern parallel to this dramatic change of allegiance is General Reinhard Gehlen, Hitler's chief of intelligence on the Russian front until the closing of World War II, when he went over to the Americans and became the head of an intelligence organization directly supported by the CIA. The last phase of his career was as a leader in West German intelligence. See E. H. Cookridge, *Gehlen: Spy of the Century* (1972).

revolutionary tendencies in recent history as the misguided efforts of nationalistic zealots and unprincipled gangsters who plunged the nation into bloody conflict. Josephus' own life and career were, of course, involved in this characterization, and his history-writing is not objective. Yet his sources are invaluable and as a Jewish historian of this period he has no rival.[7]

5. *Philo.* No precision can be attached to the dates suggested for Philo's birth and death. His life evidently spanned the period of Jesus' life, and during most of it he seems to have lived in Alexandria in Egypt—an important key to his outlook and writing. Philo was a wealthy Jew chosen at one time to represent his fellow-Jews in Alexandria on an embassy to Rome (AD 39). His account of this mission is recorded in his book *The Embassy to Gaius.*

Philo's interest to the student of the New Testament lies in his writings. Among these are his expositions of the Greek version of Genesis, in which he extracts the maximum allegorical and homiletical value from the text—or, rather, imports his own philosophical and religious notions into the verses and then reads them out in a verse-by-verse exegesis. These allegorical interpretations were intended to serve the practical purpose of convincing his contemporaries that the wisdom of the Greeks was already anticipated in the Hebrew Scriptures and, indeed, was indebted to the Hebrew revelation given through Moses. In one tract *Who is the Heir?* Philo claimed that Moses anticipated the doctrine of opposites taught by the Ionian philosopher Heraclitus.

A second class of Philo's writing was biographical. He used Old Testament heroes and heroines to symbolize moral qualities: Noah was regarded as a type of righteousness; Sarah and Hagar were played off against each other (as in Gal. 4, where Paul, though not quite in the manner of Philo, discusses who are the heirs of Abraham). This allegorical treatment of the Old Testament was one way in which Jews of the Dispersion managed to reconcile their belief in the authority of the sacred text with a looseness in observing the Jewish law. From Philo the mystical sense of Scripture became a concern taken over in Christendom by the Alexandrian school, led by Clement and Origen, whose work decisively influenced the medieval church.[8]

BELIEFS AND PRACTICES OF PALESTINIAN JEWS

A saying attributed to the high priest Simeon the Just (third century BC) epitomizes the genius of Jewish religion before and during Jesus' ministry: "By three things is the world sustained: by the Law, by the

[7] For a modern assessment see H.W. Montefiore, *Josephus and the New Testament* (1962); R.J.H. Schutt, *Studies in Josephus* (1961).

[8] See J.D. Wood, *The Interpretation of the Bible* (1958), pp. 50ff., 71ff.

[temple-] service, and by deeds of loving-kindness."[9] God has made himself known supremely in his law, with its commandments and promises, written in the Pentateuch and unwritten in the rabbinic tradition. Man is called on to study, obey, and safeguard this for posterity. This is Israel's heritage and the sign of the nation's election. "Beloved are Israel, for to them was given the precious instrument; still greater was the love, in that it was made known to them that to them was given the precious instrument by which the world was created" (i.e. the Law).[10] The service (*'abôdāh*) is the cultic worship of God, centered in and conducted at the Jerusalem temple. "Deeds of lovingkindness" (*g^e^millûṯ ḥasādîm*; lit. handing-out of kindnesses) are acts of human compassion, generosity, and concern by which the Jew shows his fellow-feeling and the practical application of his religion.[11] Matthew 5:16 may be an adaptation of this principle to a Christian context.

Within the institutional framework of Judaism, the temple held pride of place. But it was not alone, as we shall observe: the Sanhedrin and the synagogue also played an important role.

1. As the center of Jewish worship and focal point of national pride, the Jerusalem shrine claimed an unrivaled place in the Jewish religion. The sense of reverence evoked by a sight of this building (which Herod the Great began to reconstruct in 20 BC) is remarked by Josephus. Visitors to the holy city were impressed by the architecture of the temple and its precincts.[12] The rabbis exclaim with a pardonable exaggeration: "He who has not seen the Holy Place in its detailed construction has never seen a splendid building in his life!"[13] And there is the evidence of this pride in the disciples' outburst, "Look, Teacher, what wonderful stones and what wonderful buildings!" (Mark 13:1).

For two reasons the temple and its worship was a symbol of all the Jews held dear. It gave proof of Israel's election as the special people of God, for God had promised to make his name known at the holy place in Jerusalem ever since the Deuteronomic Code (Deut. 12). Moreover, it stood as a monumental reminder and pledge of God's accessibility to his people through the cultus.

The sacrificial system was maintained by a hereditary priesthood,[14] divided into twenty-four "courses" or family groups who

[9] *Aboth* (="Sayings of the Fathers") in the Mishnah, 1:2. Translation in H. Danby, *The Mishnah Translated from the Hebrew With Introduction and Brief Explanatory Notes* (1933), p. 446.

[10] *Aboth* 3:15 (Danby, *op. cit.*, p. 452).

[11] On "deeds of lovingkindness" as an important part of Jewish piety, both private and public, see J. Jeremias, *Jerusalem in the Time of Jesus* (ET 1969), pp. 126-34.

[12] Josephus, *Jewish War* 5.5.6.

[13] *b. Sukkah* 51b.

[14] On the hereditary character of the Jerusalem priesthood, see Jeremias, *op. cit.*, pp. 213-21.

served in rotation (see Luke 1:5). These priestly families were responsible for the daily public sacrifices, at dawn and mid-afternoon, and many private sacrifices. On the chief festival occasions and on the Day of Atonement, all twenty-four courses served together. These festivals were Passover, Weeks (Israel's harvest thanksgiving), Booths (a reminder of Israel's wilderness experience), and Dedication (recalling the rededication of the temple after its defilement by Antiochus Epiphanes in the days of the Maccabees).

The annual Day of Atonement ritual was performed by the high priest, who alone could enter the innermost sanctuary of the holy place as the nation's representative and confessor. This was his most important privilege and awesome duty, for which his personal life of sanctity and his authorization were intended to fit him. He also had the right to offer the main sacrifices when he chose, especially on the Sabbath and other "high days." The office of high priest was thus one of considerable stature, jealously guarded by an elaborate custom of investiture. The candidate for high priest had to be certain of the absolute purity of his descent, and presumably able to trace back his "line" to Aaron and his sons.

Other temple functionaries included the captain of the temple (*sāgān*), who was responsible for the conduct of the worship, and the chief priests (*οἱ ἀρχιερεῖς*; Acts 4:1) who belonged to the priestly aristocracy, an upper stratum of Jerusalem society to which the ordinary priests had no access. This was bitterly resented by the latter, as the Talmud and Josephus make plain; and it came to a head in internecine strife within Jerusalem society just prior to the fall of the city in 70. But the chief priests held the reins of power through the Sanhedrin.

2. The supreme court of Judaism, known as the Council or Sanhedrin, was made up of seventy-one members. The chief priests were in control; and the high priest acted as president. The other members of the Council were scribes and elders. The "elders" were nonpriestly members of the body, whose representation grew out of the desire of the people to be heard in national affairs. The reference in Luke 19:47 to the "principal men of the people" is apparently to the elders. Joseph of Arimathea (Mark 15:43; John 19:38-42) belonged to this lay nobility, who were represented by the heads of the principal families resident in Jerusalem.

The main function of the Sanhedrin was as a judicial body in hearing and settling all cases not determined by the lower courts. Its civil jurisdiction was limited to Judaea proper, but it commanded wide respect, and many Jewish communities submitted voluntarily to its religious authority. It heard accusations of transgressions against the law of Moses, and of blasphemy; and it assessed the claims of would-be prophets. Accused men were given every opportunity to have their name cleared. The rules of procedure were weighted on the side of exoneration and acquittal, though it is not certain how closely the later codification of early tradition resembled the procedures in operation at the time of Jesus' trial and condemnation. The issue raised by the statement in John 18:31—"It is not lawful for us to kill anyone"—has been keenly debated as to whether or not the Jews had the right to carry out capital punishment. Probably this limitation was in force at the time of the trial of Jesus, but John's Gospel may be consciously ambiguous here to indicate the deeper spiritual meaning of Jesus' death (18:32).[15]

3. The origins of the synagogue are lost in antiquity. The term refers both to the building in which a company of Jewish men meet for prayer and study of the Law and to the assembly of Jews in such a place. The idea, if not the actual institution, probably dates back to the Babylonian exile. When Solomon's temple was destroyed and sacrificial worship ceased, the study of the law became central in the Jewish cultus. On the return from exile, the rebuilt temple did not replace the important prominence given to Scripture study and congregational prayer. It was at these points that the synagogue came into its own and fulfilled a persistent need.

Two factors made the synagogue important during the decades of Jesus' ministry and the apostolic church. One was its availability. A synagogue was independent of buildings specially consecrated for worship. This fact gave the local synagogue an appeal which the central sanctuary at Jerusalem could never have. Any ten male Jews could associate as a synagogue, as they formed a quorum (*minyān*); the synagogue was free from the necessary encumbrance of a priestly cultus, as the temple required.

Second, the network of country synagogues became a powerful factor in the conservation of Jewish religious life because they were in the hands of laymen. The majority of the influential class of scribes, i.e., professional students and exponents of the Torah and its tradition, were laymen identified with the Pharisees. (The term "scribe," it should be noted, refers to a person's profession; "Pharisee" refers to his allegiance to the Pharisee party, a much larger group than the scribes.) During the Seleucid era the priesthood, exposed to foreign influence, became easily hellenized. After the Roman conquest the priesthood was, in the eyes of the nationalists, further contaminated. So it is not surprising that spiritual authority passed over from priest to scribe, especially in Galilee where nationalist feelings had run high since Judas' abortive uprising. Perhaps there was another reason to hold the scribes in great respect: Jeremias argues that they possessed and guarded a secret teaching which could not be divulged to

[15] See R.P. Martin, "Trial of Jesus," in *New Bible Dictionary* (1962), pp. 1295f. On the question of Jewish illegalities, see D.R. Catchpole, *The Trial of Jesus* (1971), ch. 4.

unauthorized people, and this knowledge gave to their profession a mystique and an authority.[16]

The place of the synagogue in Jewish village life provided the scribes a platform. The synagogue combined a center of worship with a center of instruction; indeed, worship was understood within an educational framework. The chief officers of the synagogue are referred to in the New Testament literature: the 23 elders; the ruler, who superintended the worship services, presided over the affairs, and regulated the business in hand (for the synagogue was also a law court for minor offenses); the collector of alms and messenger of the assembly;[17] and the attendant (Luke 4:20), who was janitor and teacher in the school which was held in the synagogue building throughout the week.

Among these officials the real power lay with the scribes and especially with the leading teachers, who attracted young pupils from all parts of the Jewish world. These principal men established schools in Jerusalem, where they trained their students and sent them into the synagogues to be teachers and guides of the people. The most famous of the rabbis were Shammai, whose school represented the strict interpretation of the Law and its rigorous application to everyday life, and Hillel, who adopted a more lenient approach. Many anecdotes are told of these two teachers. One well-known story tells of a Gentile who came to Shammai and asked to be taught the whole law while he stood on one foot. Shammai was enraged at his impertinence and drove him away with a stick. Then the man went to Hillel with the same request. Hillel replied: "Never do to your neighbor what you would hate to have done to yourself. This is the whole law; all the rest is commentary." This advice was welcome, and Hillel's reputation enhanced as the counsel he gave was put into practice. He said: "Be of the disciples of Aaron, loving peace and pursuing peace, loving mankind and bringing them nigh to the Law."[18]

The synagogue became an important vehicle for Jesus' proclamation (Mark 1:21-28; 3:1-6; 6:2f.; Matt. 4:23; Luke 4:15, 16-30, 31ff., 44; 6:6; 13:10ff.; John 6:55; 18:20), and Paul and his missionary colleagues later made use of the synagogues of the Jewish dispersion (Acts 13:5; 14:1; 17:1, 10, 17; 18:4, 19). The use of the synagogue as a springboard from which to send forth the gospel message of Israel's hope and salvation to those who gathered as committed Jews or loosely attached "God-fearers" was also adopted by Apollos at Ephesus (Acts 18:26). The Jewish synagogue was an

16 Jeremias, *op. cit.*, pp. 240ff.

17 This title (*šᵉlîaḥ ṣibbûr*) plays an important part in the background to the New Testament word "apostle"; see T.W. Manson, *The Church's Ministry* (1948), pp. 40ff.

18 *Aboth* 1:12 (Danby, *op. cit.*, p. 447).

important link in dissemination of the good news. More than likely, its pattern of worship had a formative influence on the early Christians.[19]

Jewish scholars have helped us to form a picture of the essential pattern of synagogue worship, though some facets remain debatable.[20] For the period before the destruction of the temple in 70 the New Testament (esp. Luke 4:15-21) is a most valuable source of information but very few precise details are given in any contemporary document. The three main elements of synagogue worship were praise, prayer, and instruction. The note of corporate praise opened the service, in accord with the Talmudic principle "Man should always first utter praises, and then pray."[21] This procedure may underlie the order of the elements of Christian worship in 1 Corinthians 14:26, which begins with a "hymn." In the synagogue, the "ruler" summoned the "minister" (see Luke 4:20) to invite someone from the congregation to commence the service with this "call to worship." To the words "Bless ye the Lord, the one who is to be blessed," the people responded: "Blessed be the Lord . . . for ever," in the spirit of Nehemiah 9:5. At the outset worshipers were thus invited to think of God and to acknowledge his greatness and blessing.

Prayers in Jewish worship fall into two parts. The first group comprises two lovely utterances: the *Yôṣēr*, which means "he who forms" and takes up the theme of God as Creator of all things; and the *'Ahābāh*, which means "love" and is concerned both to recall God's love for his people and to pledge their obligation to love him in return. This ends with the words, "Blessed art thou, O Lord, who hast chosen thy people Israel in love." Immediately thereafter comes the *Shema'*, which is a confession of faith and benediction. Its name derives from its first word, "hear." The congregation recites the formula of Deuteronomy 6:4, "Hear, O Israel: the Lord our God is one Lord." As soon as they come to the word "one," the leader adds, "Blessed be the name of the glory of his kingdom for ever and ever." The emphasis on the unity of God has always been the central Jewish confession, and the word "one" is given special prominence in the liturgy. Rabbi Aqiba is reported to have died with this Hebrew word (*'ehad*) on his lips. The full form of the *Shema'* consists of Deuteronomy 6:4-9; 11:13-21; and Numbers 15:37-41.

The second division of united prayer comes next. It is introduced by reciting the prayer known as "true and firm" (is this

[19] The standard work on this indebtedness is C.W. Dugmore, *The Influence of the Synagogue upon the Divine Office.* See also W.O.E. Oesterley, *The Jewish Background of the Christian Liturgy* (1925).

[20] Two straightforward accounts may be mentioned, apart from the more technical works: G. Dalman, *Jesus-Jeshua* (1929); and P.P. Levertoff's essay, "Synagogue Worship in the First Century," in *Liturgy and Worship*, ed. W.K.L. Clarke (1932).

[21] See *b. Berak.* 32a.

word—the *Shema'*—to us for ever). The "minister" then summons a member of the assembly to lead in the "prayer proper," i.e., the Eighteen Benedictions. The man appointed steps forward in front of the ark and, with his face turned towards it, leads the united intercessions of the company, who reply with "Amen." The blessings cover a wide range of themes, partly expressing praise, partly petitioning for spiritual and material benefits, partly supplicating for those in need (exiles, judges and counselors, and the chosen people). The tone of these prayers is captured in the last one: "Grant peace upon Israel thy people and upon thy city, and upon thy inheritance, and bless us all together. Blessed art thou, O Lord, the Maker of peace." Perhaps these precise words were on the lips of Jesus as he entered, according to his custom, the synagogue for worship in his day.

Once the prayers were said, the service assumed the form which has given to the synagogue its distinctive ethos—the emphasis on Scripture reading and exposition. The Jews themselves called the synagogue the house of instruction. Instruction was given by two means. First, the law and the prophets were read by members of the congregation. Since the original biblical Hebrew was not understood by all present, a translator would turn the Scripture lessons into the vernacular, usually Aramaic. Next came the homily or address based on the passages read. Any person in the assembly who was considered suitable was invited to deliver this "sermon"—as proved the case both at Nazareth (Luke 4:21ff.) and at Antioch (Acts 13:14ff.). The service concluded with a blessing and the congregational Amen.

Modifications of this basic pattern were sometimes made, depending on the season of the year and the day of the week (market days, Monday and Thursday, had shorter Scripture lections). But the ingredients which provide the staple diet of synagogue worship—praise, prayer and instruction—are found in every case.

The evidence we have given shows how well founded is the thesis that "Christian worship, as a distinctive, indigenous thing, arose from the fusion, in the crucible of Christian experience, of the Synagogue and the Upper Room. . . . The typical worship of the Church is to be found to this day in the union of the worship of the Synagogue and the sacramental experience of the Upper Room; and that union dates from New Testament times."[22]

[22] W.D. Maxwell, *An Outline of Christian Worship* (1945), p. 5.

CHAPTER SIX

Jewish Parties in Jesus' Day

In a naive piece of his autobiography Josephus tells something of the choices open to him as an inquiring youth:

> While still a mere boy, about fourteen years old, I won universal applause for my love of letters; insomuch that the chief priests and learned men of the city used constantly to come to me for precise information on some particular of our ordinances. At about the age of sixteen I determined to gain personal experience of the several sects into which our nation is divided. These, as I have frequently mentioned, are three in number—the first that of the Pharisees, the second that of the Sadducees, and the third that of the Essenes. I thought that, after a thorough investigation, I should be in a position to select the best.[1]

At nineteen Josephus finally settled on the Pharisees as "the best"—a phrase which unconsciously captures the ethos of Pharisaism with its superior claim and lofty self-characterization.

THE PHARISEES

The Books of the Maccabees speak of a group of nationalists called the "pious ones" (*ḥasîdîm*), who rallied to the support of Mattathias at the outbreak of the revolt in 167 BC. They had earlier opposed the hellenizers who formed a priestly aristocracy and deliberately courted foreign influences and customs. The Hasidim found a champion in Onias, one of the few priestly members of their protest group; and they took a firm stand against the corruption of the traditional faith by alien importations. If they were distressed at the ease with which the priestly line became won over to worldly ways, disillusionment was in store for them when, at the close of the revolt in 164 BC, the

[1] Josephus, *Life* 9f. Josephus' term for "sect" is *αἵρεσις* (derived from the verb "to choose"), a word used in the New Testament to indicate the Jewish estimate of the party of Nazarenes (Acts 24:5,14) and the official Jewish groups (Acts 5:17; 15:5; 26:5). Josephus deliberately omits the fourth *αἵρεσις*, the Zealots, whom he describes elsewhere (*Antiquities* 18.1) as the "fourth philosophy." His detestation of this movement as made up of anarchist revolutionaries accounts for his omission.

victors became themselves oppressors and strove after territorial gain and political ambition. The rise of the Hasmoneans as important figures on the world stage must have brought grief to the pacifist, otherworldly, quietist Hasidim, who were interested only in securing spiritual freedom from Syria.

It is usual to trace the origins of the Pharisees (as successors to the Hasidim) and the Sadducees, who promoted a hellenizing policy and formed a continuing priestly nobility, to this period of Jewish history. Indeed, the term Pharisees derives from the Hebrew word *pārāš*, meaning "separated"; but separated from *what* or *whom* is an unresolved question. The traditional view is that they strove ardently for complete obedience to the law, and in so doing kept themselves aloof from the rest of their compatriots—the "people of the land," as they were called, who professed no such zeal. The Pharisees' tendency to exclusiveness was certainly well-attested, and accords with Josephus' classic description of the Pharisees in the time of Queen Alexandra (78-69 BC): "a body of Jews with a reputation of excelling the rest of their nation in the observance of religion, and as exact exponents of the laws."[2]

Josephus remarks on the rise of the Pharisee party during the reign of Jonathan (*c.* 145 BC), and he states that the first rift between the Hasmonean dynasty and the Pharisees came in the time of John Hyrcanus (134-104 BC).[3] Thus their name may have arisen from their withdrawal from the Maccabean house when the successors of the first freedom-fighters turned their ambition to gaining political power.

Other derivations of the name Pharisee are much more speculative, e.g., T.W. Manson's theory that the term was coined as a nickname by their opponents who charged them with being theological innovators and borrowers of ideas (e.g., the resurrection of the dead) from Persian sources.[4] A later idea is that they were protesting against "the priestly fanatics of the law at Qumran, in view of the sect's acute messianic speculations";[5] and this, it is held, led to the name they were given.

In any case, there is no doubt about the Pharisees' way of life and main tenets. High on the list was belief in divine providence, by which both human history and individual lives are shaped and governed. Yet man has freedom of choice, which ensures his responsibility. A rabbinic dictum crisply defines the relationship: "All is foreseen, but freedom of choice is given."[6] A reflection of this belief in a combination of God's control and man's accountability to do the right thing is the advice of Gamaliel in Acts 5:34-39. The supreme authority

[2] *Jewish War* 1.5.2.
[3] *Antiquities* 13.10.5f.
[4] See T.W. Manson, *The Servant Messiah*, pp. 18f.
[5] So K. Schubert, *The Dead Sea Scrolls* (1960), pp. 38ff.
[6] *Aboth* 3:16 (Danby, p. 452).

of the Torah and its scribal interpretation played a decisive role in Pharisaic teaching. More than once Josephus speaks about the Pharisees as "accurate interpreters of the law."[7]

The Pharisees entertained firm messianic hopes, which centered in a coming kingdom of God and a resurrection of the dead. The righteous dead would share in that victory for God's cause as they were raised. The messianic beliefs of the Pharisees are set forth in the *Psalms of Solomon* 17 and 18,[8] which look for the appearing of a princely Messiah of David's family to restore Israel's fortunes on earth. The hope of a victorious kingdom was extended to include those who had died in expectation. This hope arose from the need to "justify the ways of God to men" when the Maccabean martyrs perished before the triumph was assured. It is at this point also that foreign influences are suspected of entering the Pharisees' world-view, notably from Persia, with the rise of belief in spiritual powers, both angelic and demonic, in the form of an elaborate angelology.

Above all, the Pharisees had organization as well as ideas. A definite society was created, with rules of membership and a much-respected ethos. Pharisaic groups formed "fellowships" or "communities" (*ḥăbûrôṯ*), which met for association, study, and meals on Friday afternoons prior to the Sabbath. Their communities were closed, clearly conscious of their identity.[9] Yet, in spite of this exclusivism and tightly knit structure, the Pharisees exerted a powerful influence, partly because of their earnestness and devotion, partly (if Jeremias' view is recalled; see above, pp. 80f.) because they were guardians of a secret discipline and esoteric teaching. But they were popular mainly because they were the people's party and represented a serious effort to keep the Jewish faith and practice alive in the towns, villages, and hamlets of first-century Palestine.

THE SADDUCEES

Like the Pharisees the Sadducees first came into prominence during the reign of John Hyrcanus, whose cause they championed after his quarrel with the Pharisees.[10] Their name is usually taken to derive from Zadok, a priestly figure in Solomon's time (1 Kings 1:32ff.), a view supported by the later priestly composition of the Sadducees. Not all were priests, however; and the Sadducees are more accurately characterized as a party of wealthy, property-owning laymen residing in Jerusalem. This lends some plausibility to T. W. Manson's theory

7 Cf. n. 2 above; *Antiquities* 17.2.4. The word *pārāš* may also refer to interpreters or exponents of the law, thus suggesting another possible etymology for the name Pharisees.

8 See ch. 8 below, pp. 107-114, for further discussion.

9 See J. Jeremias, *Jerusalem in the Time of Jesus*, p. 247.

10 Josephus, *Antiquities* 13.10.5f.

that there is a linguistic connection between the name Sadducee and a term in Aramaic meaning "civic official." The Greek equivalent of the latter would be *σύνδικοι* (English, "syndics"), referring to the civil servants charged by the Romans with financial duties in Palestine.[11]

Whatever the derivation of their name, the Sadducees represented a power bloc in Jerusalem, centered on the temple and its prestige, which supported the status quo. Their political outlook was conservative, and they were anxious not to disturb the structure of a society in which they enjoyed both wealth and power. Messianic expectation held no attraction for them; they were quite content with the services and security of the traditional temple worship. They collided with the Pharisees in matters of belief as well as general attitude. They rejected the addition of the oral tradition to the law, and insisted that final authority rested alone on the five books of Moses. Beliefs not found in the Torah they refused (e.g., resurrection and the extensive angelology), though they did not deny the remaining parts of the Hebrew Bible.

Even before the collapse of the status quo in AD 70 Sadducee power had begun to wane. When the temple fell and the Jewish privilege came to an end, its power was lost completely, never to be regained.

THE ESSENES

Even more deserving than the Pharisees of the title "separated people" were the Essenes. Ordinarily, their name is taken to be derived from the Aramaic *ḥasyā* ("pious" or "holy"). If this is the case, it links the Essenes with the *ḥasîdîm* of the Maccabean period, from whom the Pharisees emerged; but there is some doubt about this derivation. A safer theory bases the emergence of the Essenes in the second century BC on historical grounds. F.F. Bruce links the particular *ḥasîdîm* out of whom the Essenes came with the people referred to in the Book of Daniel as those who impart wisdom (cf. 11:33ff.; 12:3). They were persecuted when Antiochus Epiphanes was on the rampage; although they received "a little help" from the Maccabean warriors, they knew intuitively that suffering and affliction was their destiny until a time of final victory. When a Maccabean victory did come, it led to a time of disillusionment, as we have seen; and part of the *ḥasîdîm*, despairing of a new order to be set up in Jerusalem in this time of apostasy, migrated to the desert.[12] Scriptural authority for this withdrawal was discovered in Isaiah 40:3: "In the wilderness prepare Yahweh's way; make straight in the desert a highway for our God." So it came about

[11] See Manson, *The Servant Messiah*, pp. 12f.; and *The Sayings of Jesus*, pp. 295f.

[12] F.F. Bruce, *New Testament History*, pp. 101f.

that encampments of Jews—referred to by Josephus, Philo, and Pliny the Elder—were found in the Judaean desert.

Josephus speaks of the Essenes as a monastic community, practicing celibacy and holding their possessions in communal ownership.[13] Philo agrees with this description and extols the virtues of their plain, unencumbered life, in which intellectual pursuits were a group study of the Scriptures and devotion to ceremonial laws. He finds these practices attractive as part of his advocacy of the argument that only good men are really free.[14] Pliny's description of the settlement north of Engedi, near the Dead Sea, matches the information in the other two writers. If allowance is made for certain rhetorical flourishes in Pliny's idyllic description, its greatest relevance is that it allows us to see a geographical connection between these Essenes and the community whose headquarters have been unearthed at Khirbet Qumran—the people of the Dead Sea scrolls.

If the identification of the community of the Dead Sea scrolls as a type of Essene brotherhood is accepted, it is possible to introduce the literature of the scrolls into the discussion of the practices and beliefs of the Essene movement. Four items are particularly important as background to the New Testament.

1. Some light is shed on John the Baptist, who chose the Jordan valley and the Judaean wilderness as his habitat, in the light of Isaiah 40:3. Luke's reference to John's being "in the wilderness till the day of his manifestation to Israel" (1:80) is tantalizing, and has been used to suggest that John grew up in the Qumran community before he began his public ministry. Certainly his ascetic way of life and stern message are similar to what we know of the Qumran recluses.

2. The special place accorded in this community to the interpretation of Scripture (the Old Testament), aided by the example of their leader, who was called the Teacher of Righteousness, is significant for understanding how these same books were read by the early Christians. Several interpretative principles are common to both groups, notably the awareness of living in days when the fulfilment of Old Testament prophecies was taking place and a heavy sense of destiny, of standing at the dawn of a new age of God's dealings with his people.

A clear distinction should be made at this point. The Qumran community saw in their teacher a herald of the new age, to which they still looked forward. Christians were convinced that the kingdom of God had already arrived, at least in its first stage, in Jesus' ministry; and they looked back on it as the focus of the kingdom's power, and ahead to the climax of his saving work. The Qumran expectation was, of course, not fulfilled: during the Jewish War in AD 66-74 their monastery was attacked and destroyed.

[13] *Antiquities* 18.1.5.
[14] *Every Good Man is Free* 75ff.

3. The ascetic practices of the Essenes; the use they made of a solar calendar of 364 days; their developed theology of the Holy Spirit, which made a great deal of the "spirit of truth" and the "spirit of wickedness" (suggesting a clear ethical distinction between the two paths of truth and error); their obvious self-conscious identity as a special people, "the children of light"—all these elements are informative parallels to, or at least analogies with, the New Testament message and its interpretation.

4. Probably the greatest importance of these manuscript discoveries and the light they cast on the Essenes at Qumran, is purely historical. Through this body of information, we have been introduced to the literature of a detached monastic, celibate sect with rigorous discipline and a world-denying spirit that contrasted sharply with the other Jewish parties, who stayed in the arena of public life and made their presence felt in Palestinian affairs during the first half of the first century of the Christian era.

THE ZEALOTS

The Zealots inspired a degree of hostility among the other parties in Judaism. Josephus, for example, accused them of causing the great rebellion of AD 66.[15] Occasionally the term is used in the sense of "brigand" or "bandit."[16] The origin of the Zealots is usually traced to Judas of Galilee, who in AD 6 raised the standard of revolt in the name of Israel's refusal to pay tribute to a heathen emperor. Josephus calls him a "sophist" and the founder of a sect of his own with no common allegiance to the other groups within Judaism.[17]

The actual term Zealot dates back only to AD 66, though the concept of zeal for God has a long history in Israel, stretching back to Phinehas (Num. 25:7-13; cf. Ps. 106:28-31), who, consumed with indignation at the lax morality of the Israelites at Baal-Peor, took a decisive step to stem the tide. Thereafter he became an idealized character and an example of a commendable virtue (Sir. 45:23). At the time of the Maccabees this zeal burst out in armed resistance, as Mattathias rallied the villagers of Modein with the cry, "Let every one who is zealous for the law and supports the covenant come out with me!" (1 Macc. 2:24ff.).

Strangely, Josephus fails to make the connection between the spirit which motivated the Maccabeans and that which led the opponents of Rome to take up arms. We can only account for this by Josephus' own prejudice.[18] Certainly the principles which inspired both groups run in parallel lines. What underlay both movements is

[15] Josephus, *Antiquities* 18.1.6.
[16] Mishnah *Sanhedrin* 9:6 (Danby, p. 396).
[17] Josephus, *War* 2.8.1.
[18] See W.R. Farmer, *Maccabees, Zealots and Josephus* (1956), pp. 18-22.

aptly described by S.G.F. Brandon as a return to the theology of the holy land, which was part of Israel's heritage.[19] Since the Exodus and settlement in Canaan God's providence had been seen in his consolidating the people of Israel in his land. By national faithfulness within the covenant relationship Israel would be assured of Yahweh's deliverance and protection and perpetual possession of the land. For a foreigner to invade or exact tribute was thus an affront to Israel's theocratic destiny which had to be resisted.

F. F. Bruce points to another factor to explain Josephus' hostility to the Zealots. The Zealots were hostile to the Jewish establishment, particularly the priestly hierarchy and the wealthy nobles. They formed a proletarian backlash, and at least part of the reason for the war against Rome in 66-74 was a protest raised by the common people within Israel against aristocratic privilege and priestly status, such as Josephus himself enjoyed.[20]

POPULAR RELIGION IN PALESTINE

The population of Palestine in Jesus' day has been estimated at five or six hundred thousand.[21] It would be a mistake to assume, however, that the total membership of the four religious groups described above was at the half-million level. Those who belonged to these "parties" constituted only a fraction of the whole people. Josephus gives the total number of Pharisees, Sadducees, and Essenes living in Palestine as thirty thousand—or about one in twenty. Even this may be generous, since he may have overestimated the members of his own party, the Pharisees.[22] Moreover, there were 3½ million Jews living outside of Palestine. It is estimated that they constituted about seven percent of the population of the Roman Empire. This Dispersion, as it was called, had a distinctive hellenistic ethos and culture.

The general population in Palestine—the 95% not affiliated with a religious party—was frowned on and contemptuously dismissed by the Pharisees as "people of the land" (*'am hā-āreṣ*), on the ground that they did not observe the rules of tithing and ritual purification (see John 7:49; Luke 18:9-14). Basically the Pharisees dismissed all whose interest in religion was only casual and sporadic. Rabbi Eliezer (about AD 90) is recorded as answering the question "Who is an *'am hā-āreṣ*?" with the dictum, "He who does not recite the *Shᵉma'* morning and evening." Yet the issue went deeper than belief. On a practical level the Pharisees called the mass of the people "Jews who made themselves as Gentiles" because of their apparent lack of concern to take their national distinctiveness seriously.

19 S.G.F.Brandon, *Jesus and the Zealots* (1967), pp. 62f.
20 F.F. Bruce, *New Testament History*, p. 100.
21 So J. Jeremias, *Jerusalem in the Time of Jesus*, p. 205.
22 *Ibid.*, p. 252.

The common people were alienated from official religion. No matter how much they admired the zeal of the Pharisees and were impressed by the grandeur of the temple ritual, accepting the religious regimen was, for the mass of them, an invitation to assume a heavy yoke (cf. Acts 15:10). Jesus distinguished his call to discipleship (Matt. 11:28-30) from the impositions made on people by the legalistic and merit-conscious religion of the Pharisees (cf. Matt. 23:4). The eager response, especially in Galilee, to messianic and revolutionary men is not surprising in view of the pressures of economic need from heavy taxation and the spiritual frustration caused by Pharisaic idealism. This was proved by the ready followings commanded, for example, by Judas in AD 6 and Simon bar-Kokhba in AD 132.

One additional feature in the total picture of life in first-century Palestine should not be overlooked. In Hebrew thought the connection between poverty and piety is very close. Especially in the period of hellenization, when alien ideas were brought in to challenge the Israelite notion of national theocracy, those who compromised their faith gained material affluence as a reward for their services. On the other hand, poverty and deprivation were the lot of the godly who chose to remain aloof from Syrian and Greek influences.

This has led to a supposition that in Jesus' day certain circles of people—called "the poor" (*anāwim*)—awaited the arrival of God's kingdom in a nonviolent, passivist way. Distinct from Pharisees and Zealots, these "quiet in the land" practiced their religion in obscurity, waiting contentedly for the fulfilment of their hopes. They cherished the Psalmists' aspirations to live on, through the stress of their present times, to see the coming of God's kingdom, when the Messiah would save the poor and the afflicted (Ps. 72:2, 4, 12, 13) who cry to God for deliverance from the ungodly rulers (Ps. 13:2, 4).

Some scholars argue that Jesus came from this stratum of Palestinian society, but of this there is no certainty.[23] It is more probable that the songs in Luke 1 and 2 can be credited to this group of messianic pietists who "looked for the consolation of Israel" (Luke 2:25) and prayed for the redemption of Jerusalem (Luke 2:38). The families of Simeon and Anna may have preserved the best of the religious aspirations of this enclave within Judaism. At any rate, the literature of this period reflects this trend no less than the "official" line of religious belief and practice.

JESUS AND HIS CONTEMPORARIES

How far was Jesus influenced by the movements of thought around him? Was he indebted to his contemporaries for ideas in his preaching?

[23] H. Lietzmann, *The Beginnings of the Christian Church* (ET 1949), p. 38. Cf. G. Bornkamm, *Jesus of Nazareth* (ET 1960), pp. 202f.

Did he share aspirations in common with them? Did he identify himself with prevailing teachings? Was the cause of any who stood in the same historical and cultural milieu espoused by him? Some have argued that he could not have stood aloof and unaffected by the currents of nationalism and politics which swirled around him. No loyal son of Israel who claimed to stand within the succession of Israel's holy men and prophets could have remained uninvolved. But if so, is there any reason to believe he became involved with one of the four parties in the Judaism of the first century?

Jesus chose not to join the migration to the desert and become an Essene recluse. His very presence in the midst of Galilean life and his special attachment to Jerusalem as the city of the great king (Matt. 5:35; Luke 13:31-35) necessarily implicated him in the political fortunes of his people and in the issues of freedom and loyalty to Rome. Jesus' presence in Palestinian life, dramatized by the criticism that he was *too* involved with people and shared their social habits and kept company with the riff-raff of the day (Luke 15:1, 2; 7:34, 35, 39), precludes the idea that he accepted the Essene way of life.

Nor is there any real meeting point between Jesus and the Sadducees. They represented the landed gentry, the wealthy aristocrats of society, and with them Jesus apparently had little in common. It is a plausible suggestion that Jesus took up a negative attitude to these privileged members of the upper class, not only on the ground of their beliefs (Mark 12:18-27) but more pointedly because of their inhumanity and indifference to the crying social needs at their doorstep (Luke 16:19-31; cf. Matt. 25:31-46).[24]

The attempt has also been made to point to certain resemblances between Jesus' teaching and that of the Pharisaic theology. There are, indeed, undeniable links between them.[25] But at three points, at least, Jesus broke decisively with Pharisaic orthodoxy and its practical outworking. He refused to acknowledge the authority of their scribal tradition (Mark 7:9-13); he discounted their rules for ritual purification (Mark 7:1-8, 14-23); and he consorted with the very people, "publicans and prostitutes," whom the Pharisees treated contemptuously and dismissed as outside the pale of salvation (Luke 7:34). Both his words of forgiveness and his actions of welcoming and seeking out the company of these "Jews who made themselves as Gentiles" and accepting their hospitality at a meal are significant, as recent studies have shown.[26]

[24] T.W. Manson, *The Sayings of Jesus*, pp. 295ff. comments as follows on Luke 16:19—"Now there was a rich man, who was clothed in purple and fine linen and who feasted sumptuously every day . . ."—"Anyone, in the days of Jesus, hearing this description would think at once of the priestly aristocrats of Jerusalem"; and he goes on to supply additional reasons for believing that this parable was directed at the Sadducees (in spite of Luke 16:14).

[25] See C.G. Montefiore, *Rabbinic Literature and Gospel Teachings* (1930).

[26] N. Perrin, *Rediscovering the Teaching of Jesus* (1967), pp. 102ff.; J. Jeremias, *New Testament Theology*, I (ET 1971), 113ff.

That leaves the Zealots as a possible party identification for Jesus. As far back as the eighteenth century it was proposed that Jesus' message must have been addressed to the political situation of his contemporaries. H.S. Reimarus wrote: "Jesus must have been well aware that by such a plain announcement of the kingdom of heaven, he would only awaken the Jews to the hope of a worldly Messiah; consequently, this must have been his object in so awakening them."[27] Regardless of the logical incoherence of Reimarus's argument, it clearly overlooks Jesus' repeated rebukes to his hearers for their false notions of the kingdom of God and his strenuous efforts to train the disciples to see the reality of his understanding of the term. Further developments of the thesis of Jesus' political involvement have come from Robert Eisler, and in our day the proposition that Jesus could not, and did not, stand outside the political arena of his time has been taken up and elaborated by S.G.F. Brandon.[28] This hypothesis merits a close look, coming into vogue as it does at a time when the political climate is ready for it. The notion of revolution is gaining great acceptance in certain Christian groups, especially in the emerging nations of Latin America and Central Africa. If it can be shown that Jesus was aligned with a revolutionary movement such as the Zealots, the ramifications will go far beyond the academic.

First of all, it is worth mentioning that the Zealots were not all that Josephus would have us to believe. They were not a first-century version of the Mafia, nor a band of lawless gangsters who profited from a life of crime. They were basically fervent, nationalistic patriots who carried their ancestral beliefs in the sanctity of their country into explosive action. Zeal for God and his law stood high on the list in their manifesto, and their rallying call was "For Yahweh, for his land, and for freedom."

How could Jesus have resisted the appeal of this slogan? Brandon's reply is that he did not stand apart but he accepted the Zealot portfolio *with modification.*[29] Brandon's thesis makes an inferential appeal to Jesus' patriotism: that a loyal Jew could not have ignored the political tensions and turmoils of his day and refused to take sides in his nation's struggle against Rome, the occupying power.

But what of the concrete evidence? Is there ground for believing that Jesus' sympathies lay with the current nationalist and anti-Roman mood of his times?

1. There is the documentary evidence that Jesus had at least one disciple who was—or had been—a Zealot. Luke 6:15 preserves the true meaning, "the Zealot," of the description given to Simon, which Mark, possibly with some embarrassment, has veiled in his phrase "the

27 See *Reimarus Fragments* (ed. C.H. Talbert) (1970), p. 137.

28 R. Eisler, *The Messiah Jesus and John the Baptist* (ET 1931); S.G.F. Brandon, *Jesus and the Zealots.*

29 The qualification is important, as Brandon remarks in response to critics. See his final rejoinder, "Jesus and the Zealots: Aftermath," *BJRL*, 54 (1971), 47-66.

Cananaean" (3:18). "Sons of thunder" (Mark 3:17), moreover, may suggest not simply a violent temper, but a sympathy with violent methods. Finally, some scholars have maintained that the name Judas Iscariot betrays his allegiance to the *sicarii* or dagger-men, whose aims resembled those of the Zealots.[30]

2. Jesus is reported to have followed a policy of noncollaboration with the Romans. By various tokens he is thought to have registered his opposition. In the debate on the imperial tax (Mark 12:13-17), his ruling *could* be interpreted as condoning refusal to pay. The Zealots objected to the tax on the ground that Yahweh's people were governed directly by him and all taxes were a religious due. Brandon suggests that the original form of words in this story—revised by Mark to clear Jesus of Zealot sympathies—contained a clear declaration by Jesus that the tax was wrongly imposed and should be refused. Even after Mark's alleged revision of the debate, the text could be interpreted to mean: When you have paid all that you rightfully owe to God, there will be nothing left to be rendered to Caesar!

Jesus' opposition to Rome was raked up at his trial (Luke 23:2 , 35-38) and led to his condemnation as a pretender king whose claim rivaled that of Caesar. If a man is known by the company he keeps, it is not unnatural that Jesus should be bracketed with Barabbas, whose political involvement is clear from Mark 15:7, which refers to his role in "the uprising" against Rome. The companions of Jesus at Calvary were Zealots, dying on their own admission for their complicity with deeds of violence (Mark 15:27).[31]

3. Finally, Jesus' preaching, activity, and positive counsel all furnish examples of a revolutionary policy. He announced an imminent end of the old order and a new rule of God (Mark 1:15). The people caught his message (John 6:15) and hastened to proclaim him their king, even by force. The Jewish authorities sensed the danger that if Jesus were allowed to continue and to draw a following, the Romans would clamp down on the Jews as a whole, branding them a rebellious nation (John 11:48). Jesus faced his final ordeal with no blinkered piety. He made certain that his disciples were armed, ready to resist and to fight their way through at a moment's notice (Luke 22:35-38). How else do we make sense of the words, " 'Let him who has no sword sell his mantle and buy one. . . .' And they said, 'Look, Lord, here are two swords.' And he said to them, 'It is enough' "?

This is an impressive case for identifying Jesus with Zealotism, a case with sufficient diversity to give it a cumulative force that cannot

[30] See R.P. Martin, "Judas Iscariot," in *New Bible Dictionary*, pp. 673ff.; also B. Gärtner, *Iscariot* (1971).

[31] "Robbers," the RSV rendering of the Greek λῃσταί, does not quite fit the meaning. Josephus uses the word for guerrilla-like bandits. Cf. Luke 23:39-43.

be ignored. But there are important flaws that come to light on closer examination.

1. The place of Simon within the apostolic circle cannot prove that Jesus consciously approved of the Zealot movement. For the Twelve also included the tax-collector Matthew, who would have been regarded from the Zealot standpoint as a quisling, one who had sold his country out to the Romans. Clearly Matthew abandoned his occupation (Matt. 9:9); may not Simon have renounced his past association and yet have retained his name (as Matthew did) as an identity title (Acts 1:13)? It says much for the breadth of Jesus' appeal that he called men from the opposite ends of the political spectrum, and suggests that he thereby transcended political affiliations in binding men together in a higher loyalty to himself and God's kingdom.

2. Mark 12:13-17 can hardly be stretched to assert categorically a pro-Zealot position. Any argument on the basis of what the original version of Mark's story might have been is doubtful. It seems clear, at any rate, that Jesus deliberately left the issue in a certain state of ambiguity. Evidently he saw no necessary opposition between the claims of Rome and those of the Jewish faith. Such an interpretation is consonant with Jesus' attested practice of leaving his hearers to interpret his message in the way they chose (e.g., Mark 11:27-33).

Jesus refused to be impaled on the horns of a false dilemma; for the issue was not "giving" voluntarily to Caesar, but "paying" what was due. Neither a direct affirmation nor denial of Caesar's claim would convey the exact impression he wished to give. To say "Yes, pay the tax to Caesar," to accept the legitimacy of Roman authority, would be to align himself with the Herodian party and place an imprimatur on the existing social order.[32] To reply "No, refuse to pay the tax," would have the effect of countenancing violent revolt. What Jesus did was to return an evasive answer, probably with an ironical twist, insisting thereby that there was no incompatibility between political obligation and religious allegiance in the matter under debate. This, at least, is how Paul understood it (Rom. 13:1ff.): God's control extends over everything, including what Caesar claims as his. The Jews acknowledge the divine sovereignty in that Caesar is permitted to rule over God's people and to mint coins with his image imprinted on them (vs. 16). If they admit to a possession of Caesar's coinage, they must pay the tax in that coin.

To that extent Jesus refused to embroil himself in contemporary politics, and veered to the Pharisaic line of waiting for God to bring in his kingdom without human support and in his own time and

[32] The Herodians (Mark 3:6) were not, strictly speaking, a separate party within Judaism, but a group who promoted the interests of Herod Antipas, tetrarch of Galilee, who held his position at Rome's pleasure. See H.H. Rowley's study of the Herodians in *JTS*, 41, o.s. (1940), 14-27.

way. This conviction accords with his teaching as reported elsewhere (Luke 17:20f.). He proclaimed the kingdom as a present reality, and he awaited its coming at some future time. Whether present or future, however, it was wholly God's work; and while man could prepare himself to enter that kingdom, he could not bring it in or thwart its arrival. In fact, Jesus' words in Matthew 11:12 are best understood as a rebuke to the Zealots, who claimed to take the kingdom by force (cf. Luke 16:16).

Jesus therefore ran the risk of misunderstanding. It was always possible that his message would be distorted and misapplied. This is precisely how it turned out at the time of his arraignment, on a political charge (Luke 23:2).[33] His crime was that he claimed to be a king. This was both true and false—true in that he proclaimed the kingdom of God and regarded himself as the one through whom that rule would be established; false if the term were given political overtones. But the latter association was made by the Jews in Pilate's hearing, and Pilate could not afford to ignore the possible ramifications of a messianic claimant who had something to do with a kingdom and was thus an overt threat to Roman rule (and, incidentally, to his own tenure as prefect).

3. The abortive attempt to crown Jesus (John 6:15) says more about the crowd's aspirations than about Jesus' intentions. For that reason, he fled and disowned any attempt to mount a throne as a social provider or on the wave of a popular uprising. This brings to our attention the importance of the temptation narrative (Matt. 4:1-11 = Luke 4:1-13). At the outset of his ministry Jesus faced the question of the nature of God's kingdom and the way it would be brought in. Then, as he was to do throughout his ministry, he rejected the false trails set before him. He would not minister simply to the bodily and social needs of men; nor would he stun them into allegiance by resorting to the spectacular; nor would he bow down to Satan's war-chariot and try to do God's will by Satan's methods.

Chiefly for that reason, his saying about selling one's coat to buy a sword (Luke 22:35-38) must be reexamined. Elsewhere in Luke's Gospel (12:51) extreme language had borne a metaphorical meaning. Jesus had come to issue a call which will brook no rivals. He claimed a total allegiance, even at the expense of alienation, division, and hostility within close-knit family units (12:52, 53). Matthew's version of this teaching (Matt. 10:34ff.) uses the metaphor of a sword as an alternative to domestic peace and family harmony. In the words quoted in Luke 22 Jesus looks ahead to the same situation after the stress and trial awaiting him and his disciples. They must be prepared for new experiences of hostility and rejection.

The disciples construe his saying literally, and proffer two

[33] So O. Cullmann, *Jesus and the Revolutionaries* (1970), pp. 45-47.

swords. Jesus does not correct them or chide them for their gross misunderstanding: the hour is too late for a lesson. He swiftly replies, "It is enough," meaning "No more of this talk," a biblical idiom (cf. Deut. 3:26) intended to bring a conversation to an abrupt conclusion. There is no word here about armed resistance. Quite the contrary. Jesus' mind is moving on to the destiny which awaits him, and for which he has prepared himself in his Gethsemane prayers. This interpretation accords with the recorded teaching of Jesus (Matt. 5:38-41, where a nonresistance of personal evil is to be understood).[34]

4. Finally, the argument that Jesus must have been stirred by patriotic sentiment and thus drawn to the cause of the Zealots is not persuasive. His love for his people and nation and their sacred traditions may be readily conceded, but there are other ways of expressing a true patriotic spirit than by a response to the nationalist call to arms. In the Old Testament no man felt more keenly the sorrows of his people in captivity than did Jeremiah, yet he spoke out *against* resistance and counseled collaboration with the invading army (Jer. 29, 30, 40)—hardly the obvious position for a patriot! At first glance, we would choose the fierce denunciations of Nahum, in a different decade, exulting over the fall of Nineveh. But which of them was the more courageous and loyal lover of his people?

We conclude that Jesus cannot be numbered among the Zealots or their sympathizers. His program was not political, though it had political implications. It was centered in God and his kingdom, which claimed first loyalty and called for a total surrender. Jesus announced that rule as imminent and soon to be established; and he called for allegiance to himself as a response to God's call through him. That is why he stood outside the welter of movements in his day. He was "the Man who fits no formula,"[35] solitary in his distinctiveness and unique in his relation to God and the people he came to call. But he was under no illusion that they would flock to his side (Matt. 11:6), for the enigmatic Jesus was bound to offend.[36]

[34] Cf. T.W. Manson, *The Sayings of Jesus*, p. 341.
[35] E. Schweizer's phrase, in *Jesus* (ET 1971), ch. 2.
[36] See G. R. Edwards, *Jesus and the Politics of Violence* (1972).

CHAPTER SEVEN

Jewish Literature as New Testament Background

It is customary to make a fourfold classification of the literature which formed the background of the New Testament writers and may conceivably have influenced them. First of all, there are books of historical narration; second, teaching books, both narratives written to convey instruction and straight didactic works; third, apocalyptic literature (to which we shall return in the next chapter); fourth, additions to canonical works serving the function of giving theological content and placing extra emphasis on the points made in the books. Additions to Esther give it a strengthened "theological" character, and compensate for the absence of the name of God from the canonical portions of the book. Additional and extensive prayers are put into the mouths of Azariah and the Three Martyrs as an interlude set between Daniel 3:23 and 24, forming a polemical tract against idol worship.

The term used to describe these Jewish writings is "apocrypha," which derives from a Greek word meaning "hidden." The precise application of this term to the books is not clear. Perhaps the books were thought of as "hidden" because they were worn out and consigned to a *genizah* or storeroom; or perhaps it was because they contained mysteries thought too deep for the uninitiated; or perhaps because they contained—or were believed to contain—heretical teaching. In support of the second explanation is the evidence of *4 Ezra* 14:44ff., which mentions 94 books—24 of the canonical Old Testament, and another 70 to be delivered only to the wise among the people, which formed the apocrypha.[1]

It is clear that the term apocrypha gradually took on a pejorative sense; and the teaching of this literature came to be regarded as

[1] See W.O.E. Oesterley and T.H. Robinson, *An Introduction to the Books of the Old Testament* (1934), p. 9. The common reckoning of the number of Old Testament books at 24 considers the twelve minor prophets as one book, the "two-volume" books (Samuel, Kings, Chronicles) as one book each, and Ezra-Nehemiah as one book.

questionable from an orthodox standpoint. The Palestinian rabbis called these books "outside books" (*ḥiṣônîm*), to indicate their being outside the sacred collection of the Hebrew canon and used by heretics. The Jews of the Diaspora took a more liberal attitude, and included a number of additional books in the Septuagint. These extra books, found in the Greek canon but not in the Hebrew list, form, for all practical purposes, the apocryphal literature.

In the category of history books, the two books of Maccabees hold first place. First Maccabees tells the story of the Jews from the time of Antiochus IV to John Hyrcanus. It was written by an ardently patriotic Jew, an enthusiastic supporter of the Hasmoneans (5:61f.), "that family to whom it was granted to bring deliverance to Israel." Evidently a contemporary of the characters whom he brings onto the stage at the time of the Maccabean struggle, the author shows a first-hand knowledge of Palestinian topography. His praise for the Romans (ch. 8) would seem to indicate a date of composition much earlier than Pompey's desecration of the temple in 63 BC; and the most likely date is around the turn of the first century BC.

First Maccabees, though a historical work, is written with the didactic purpose of showing the reality of God's providence in time of conflict and struggle for national survival. Faithfulness to the Torah is the hallmark of Maccabean piety (2:61-64), and this example is held up for emulation before the readers. However, the lessons of God's presence with his people are not explicitly drawn, since God's name never appears as such but is referred to under such appellations as "Heaven" (3:18, 50; 4:10). A good case can be made that 1 Maccabees is written from a Sadducean standpoint. The author has reverence for the Torah and temple, and he makes no reference to evil high priests. The virtual absence of references to miracles and the fact that no resurrection hope is mentioned as a prospect for the loyal martyrs of Israel conform to the thesis of Sadducean origin.

Second Maccabees is a more religiously oriented document. Like its companion, it was written in Hebrew and later rendered into Greek. Despite its name, 2 Maccabees is earlier in date. Its first author was Jason of Cyrene (2:23), who wrote extensively in five volumes. A later abbreviator reduced this to one book, evidently by 124 BC according to the date supplied in 1:9, 10.

Second Maccabees is more patently an instructional and edifying work, intent on stressing the religious faith of the martyrs as an example to later times. Representative of this is the remark in 6:31 (NEB) about the martyrdom of Eleazar: "by his death he left a heroic example and a glorious memory, not only for the young but also for the great body of the nation." Pharisaic teaching is prominent in this work, and attention is repeatedly drawn to the hope of the resurrection of the just (7:9; 14:46; cf. Heb. 11:33-38). Angelic helpers are part of the story (3:23-30; 10:29-31; 11:6-10); and intercessory prayer, not only of angels but also of the saints of long ago, plays an effective part in securing divine victory (15:12-16).

TEACHING MANUALS

Two valuable documents belonging to the classification of teaching manuals must be mentioned. They are Ecclesiasticus and the Wisdom of Solomon.

Ecclesiasticus is the popular name of a book more strictly called The Wisdom of Jesus son of Sirach (Sirach was actually the author's *grandfather*). Sirach was a scribe and teacher in Jerusalem with special interest in training young people in a deep knowledge of the Scriptures and the acquisition of practical wisdom. The Hebrew original of this book was composed about 180 BC, and translated into Greek by the author's grandson Jesus soon after his arrival in Egypt in the 38th year of Ptolemy VII Euergetus, 132 BC. The preface, however, was written when Euergetus died—in 116 BC—or later.

The name of Wisdom in the title is important. The emphasis on wisdom has antecedents in many Near Eastern lands, especially Egypt. Similarly, the Jews had, from earliest times, summed up and preserved their experience of life in the form of proverbs and gnomic sayings. "Wise Men" were a class prominent in court circles, especially since Solomon's time.[2] Solomon was looked on as the traditional depository of wisdom, in view of the stories which gathered around his name (1 Kings 4:29-34). The Book of Proverbs reflects something of the Israelite traditions for training court officials, mentioned in connection with Solomon's entourage (1 Kings 4:1-6).[3] Later, after the Dispersion, collections of logia, or oracles, praising wisdom or showing its practical application to daily life, were to be made by exiled Jews.

The Hebrew pursuit of wisdom was not like the Greek *philosophia*, or "love of wisdom," for the Hebrew idea centers in the Torah. This is clearly brought out in Sir. 1:1: "All wisdom is from the Lord; [wisdom] is with him for ever." When Hellenism made a bid for Jewish loyalty, wisdom literature came into its own, for through it the sages attempted to draw men from the false wisdom of Greek thought and pagan religion. They personified wisdom (as a woman),[4] and set her forth as the embodiment of God's law.

[2] Cf. D.A. Hubbard, "The Wisdom Movement and Israel's Covenant Faith," *TB*, 17 (1966), 3-33.

[3] See W. McKane, *Prophets and Wise Men* (1965).

[4] The Hebrew word for wisdom (*ḥôkmā*) is feminine, as is the Greek σοφία. The growth of the idea is traced by H. Ringgren, *Word and Wisdom: Studies in the Hypostatization of Divine Qualities and Functions in the Ancient Near East* (1947), pp. 95ff.

Two directions taken by this personification (or, better, personalization) are important for New Testament study. Both lines of development have their starting-point in Proverbs 8:22-31, "the most obvious evidence in Prov. for the hypostatization of Wisdom."[5] Here wisdom takes on the form of a personal being, especially created by God before the world and serving as a sort of ground-plan of creation.

This twin characterization of wisdom as possessing premundane existence and assuming an importance as God's agent in creation is carried forward into Sirach's thought. In Ecclesiasticus wisdom possesses a real existence before the world (1:4); she was made by God (1:9), and from the beginning of time (24:9). God in turn created the world by her, though this thought is conveyed only obliquely (1:9). More important for Jesus ben Sirach is the necessity that wisdom regulate the affairs of men and guide the conduct of human life. It is especially the mark of Israel's privilege that God has imparted the gift of wisdom to the nation and that wisdom has condescended to make her abode with Israel: "Among all these [the nations] I sought a resting place; I sought in whose territory I might lodge. Then the Creator of all things gave me a commandment. . . . And he said, 'Make your dwelling in Jacob, and in Israel receive your inheritance' " (24:7f.).

The author of Ecclesiasticus goes on to equate wisdom with the Torah by suggesting that wisdom becomes embodied in God's law. This is a practical application, intended to make a bid for Judaism's place as the center of divine revelation. His contention is simply that the divine wisdom resides in Israel and in Israel's precious heritage, the law. "If a man masters the law, wisdom will be his" (15:1; cf. 21:11; 24:12; 34:8). Israel's possession is meant to be shared by the Gentiles, to whom, in part, ben Sirach directs his appeal (24:19-22). But his main stress is to encourage his fellow-Jews, in both Palestine and the Dispersion, to stand firm in their ancestral faith and abide by their inheritance in the possession of wisdom incarnated in the Torah.[6]

The Wisdom of Solomon comes out of a time of persecution, or at least of severe testing. The author's overt purpose was to strengthen the faith of his fellow Jews living in Alexandria in Egypt, who were apparently in danger of forsaking their religion. The author has four purposes in view—encouragement to stand firm in the hope of immortality (1:6-8; 2:1-20); a warning against those who had abandoned the faith (2:21-24) and assurance for those facing acute trial and suffering (2:10ff.); a demonstration of the folly of idol-worship (14); and a proof of the superiority of the Jewish faith. He shows Jews inclined to forsake their faith in favor of hellenized philosophy that

[5] *Ibid.*, p. 99. There are also some important clues in Job 28.
[6] See G.F. Moore, *Judaism*, I (1927), 263-80. For a recent study, see G. von Rad, *Wisdom in Israel* (1972), ch. 13.

they have no reason to be envious of the wisdom of the pagans, since they possess the true wisdom.

The author's attitude is pluralistic, combining elements from Platonic and Stoic cosmology with his ancestral faith. What he produces, in effect, is an attempt to rewrite Proverbs 8 in the light of Stoic doctrine.[7] The concept of wisdom is transformed by comparison with the teaching in Proverbs 8 and Sirach 24. Wisdom's pre-mundane existence as a creation of God is replaced by the eternity of wisdom, who is described in some lofty terms on which Paul (Col. 1:15-20) and the author of Hebrews (1:3) will later draw: "Like a fine mist she rises from the power of God, a pure effluence from the glory of the Almighty; she is the brightness that streams from everlasting light, the flawless mirror of the active power of God and the image of his goodness" (7:25f. NEB). This text points in one direction: wisdom is coeval with God, and shares his eternity.

There is also development in the other direction we mentioned. The master-workman idea, found in Proverbs 8:30 and in Sirach 1:9, gives way to the concept of wisdom as a spirit (1:6) or an ethereal substance. She is an immanent spirit which informs the mind of man rather than a force in creation (8:1). Wisdom becomes linked with God's holy spirit (9:17; 1:7). This leads on naturally to the idea of wisdom as entering into human life as a spiritual power, imparting knowledge and guiding men in the path of duty (8:7-9).

Wisdom teaching in this book is matched by the author's concern for man's immortality, and he bases this on man's relationship to God. No explicit mention is made of the resurrection of the body (cf. Dan. 12:2; 2 Macc. 7); rather the hope beyond death is set in the soul's survival and protection by God's care (3:1-9). But this is a hope extended only to the faithful in Israel. The "godless" (3:10) are promised no such reward.

[7] T.W. Manson, *On Paul and John* (1963), p. 143.

CHAPTER EIGHT

Apocalyptic Literature and Its Hope

In traditional theology the term "eschatology" refers to the study of the four "Last Things" (death, judgment, heaven, and hell). In modern biblical theology the term is used more specifically, carrying the meaning of a decisive disclosure of God's presence and power in some historical event which manifests a token of the divine rule to be established at the end of the age.

We shall begin our study of this aspect of the New Testament background with a look at the development of Israel's understanding of God's rule in the world. The biblical writers whose work we see in the Old Testament historical and prophetic books took their stand on Israel's faith that history is the arena of God's activity. They were convinced that his purposes are accomplished in and through the processes of the historical order, that is, in events of political, economic, and social significance occurring on the stage of world and national history. God is the Lord of history, and he shows his sovereignty in the way he arranges and disposes the destinies of men and nations. This faith is reflected, for example, in Amos 9:7:

> "Are you not like the Ethiopians to me, O people of Israel?"
> says the Lord. "Did I not bring up Israel
> from the land of Egypt,
> and the Philistines from Caphtor
> and the Syrians from Kir?"

Implicit in this conviction of the divine control of history was the belief that God had a special providence for Israel and that he reserved a unique destiny for "his people." This is made explicit in Amos 3:1, 2: "Hear this word that the Lord has spoken against you, O people of Israel, against the whole family which I brought up out of the land of Egypt: 'You only have I known of all the families of the earth.' " Israel is called to serve God in a special way, but there were elements in her history which acted as barriers to the fulfilment of that goal. In part, Israel's own perversity and unfaithfulness frustrated the divine purpose, but evil empires also opposed the establishment and success of the Jewish theocracy which was to mirror and exemplify God's reign in Jerusalem. Thwarting circumstances entered into the picture, and turned the Israelite ideal of "one nation under God" into a broken dream.

The Hebrew prophets of the eighth and seventh centuries BC still cherished the hope that Israel's repentance and renewal would lead to recovery of this lost ideal. To be sure, it would not be an easy recovery, in spite of the facile use in popular religion of the phrase "Day of Yahweh" (Amos 5:18f.) to denote the desire for God to intervene and promote Israel to a superior place. The exile shattered all such easy-going hopes. Yet even the exilic messengers of divine wrath and mercy (Jeremiah and Ezekiel) still clung to the prospect that Israel would be restored and revived in her land. Then, as a purified nation, Israel would fulfil her God-appointed destiny in the world, and at her head would be a new king from David's revived family.

Prophetic hopes were nourished through the Babylonian exile (586-536 BC). But new factors entered on the scene. Israel's leaders in exile were brought into direct contact with world empires and compelled to take into their understanding of God's control of history the unwelcome if undeniable reality that God was permitting these pagan rulers to chastise Israel for her sins. Indeed, so heavy was the burden of national disgrace and humiliation that many teachers of Israel despaired that historical events could ever again serve to vindicate their cause.

Added to this onset of pessimism and dejection was the contact Israel in exile had with some ideas of Iranian religion. This ancient form of Persian Zoroastrianism taught a continuous cosmic struggle between forces of good and evil; the hope of a sudden interposition of God on earth; the resurrection and judgment of all men; the destruction of the world by fire; and the final victory of God and a new beginning of world history.

Some have argued that this teaching exercised a deep influence on Jewish thought and led to the creation of new hope, which expressed itself in unheard-of ways. In particular, it is maintained, the cosmic dimensions of world history and the prospect of the victory of God's kingdom over all the earth, even to the angelic and demonic regions, can be traced to this influence. Of this clear connection we cannot be sure, but what is more apparent is the rise of a new outlook on life and the future after the exilic experience. Various explanations have been supplied for the onset of this new, decisive role for transcendence and cosmic metaphors. The setting of the Jewish hope is now shifted from the hope of a revived earthly rule with a new Davidic king reigning in Jerusalem, and the seer's vision is enlarged to include the triumph of God in heaven and earth.

Dissatisfaction with the Hasmonean theocracy has been suggested as the chief cause of the rise of apocalyptic (as it is called).[1] Disillusioned with the Maccabean priest-kings, religious Jews averted their hopes to a sudden inbreaking of God's rule as a supernatural power unaffected by human effort or resistance. Another view proposes that it was the temple cult which alienated sections of post-exilic Judaism and drove them away from the priestly tradition into the arms of apocalyptic expectation.[2] A simpler idea is that the exile did away with all consciousness that Israel was a special people. Some post-exilic writers do reflect this sense of abandonment of divine calling. At this time of national crisis, Israel's legitimate tradition and prophetic destiny came to an end, and the new writers had to choose a new vehicle of expression, both theological and literary, for conveying their message. This they found in apocalyptic.[3]

THE RISE OF APOCALYPTIC ESCHATOLOGY

Several features historically mark most examples of apocalyptic literature, and the list that follows covers some of these more important aspects.[4]

1. The visionary experience of the seer announces the content of his message, which is usually conveyed in an extended dialogue between himself and a heavenly counterpart (e.g., Zech. 1:18f.; 4:1). The apocalyptist is visibly overcome by the situation which meets him, whether as a problem posed to faith or an encounter with heavenly realities. He may fall into a trance, or lie prostrate on the ground, or manifest great agitation in his spirit.

2. The use of ancient names—Enoch, Abraham, Moses, Ezra—to conceal the identity of the seer is a common device, which leads to the description of apocalyptic literature as pseudonymous, though this word is misleading if meant strictly, since there was apparently no intention to deceive the readers. It was not imagined that these ancient worthies of Jewish history were the actual authors; rather, the seers used these names either because they were unable to claim personal authority for themselves (since the stream of prophetic inspiration had dried up; Ps. 74:9; Zech. 13:3), or because they felt a

[1] See O. Plöger, *Theocracy and Eschatology* (1968).

[2] So R.G. Hamerton-Kelly, "The Temple and the Origins of Jewish Apocalyptic," *VT*, 20,1 (1970), 1-15.

[3] This is G. von Rad's explanation, *Old Testament Theology* (ET 1962), pp. 91, 352ff.

[4] Klaus Koch, *The Rediscovery of Apocalyptic* (ET 1972), pp. 23ff., is the source of several of the examples that follow. For a popular statement of the issues involved, see L. Morris, *Apocalyptic* (1973), and for some differing emphases, G. E. Ladd, "Apocalyptic and New Testament Theology," in *Reconciliation and Hope. Festschrift for L. Morris*, ed. R.J. Banks (1974).

kinship with the men of old and believed themselves to be at one with them, since they shared the same divine inspiration and were conscious of belonging to the same group of God's messengers.[5]

3. The message of the apocalyptic writers is a strange blend of despair and hope. As far as human nature and its prospect of recovery from the ravages of evil is concerned, the seers are pessimistic. No hope of restoration seems possible unless God graciously and mightily intervenes. Yet this confidence in God strikes a hopeful note, since they believed that the last word in history would be uttered by God, whose sovereign purpose would be seen in his final act. Then his lordship would be demonstrated by "the unique divine initiative at the end of history, when God would not use human freedom to achieve His purpose in an act which could be regarded from the human side as man's, but when He would Himself act in a way as solely His own as His act in creation had been."[6] This anticipation is the ground of their hope.

4. The present struggle between God's people on earth and their enemies is unequal because of the cosmic setting of the real conflict. The imbalance is most obvious to the seers, because they can see the spiritual powers of evil arrayed against God's saints on earth. Thus, their thought is dualistic. They see the earthly struggle of the Jewish people in the light of the great rivalry between God and his enemy, the Satan—or Beliar, or Mastema, or Azazel—whatever name is given to the personification of evil. But there is no doubt as to the issue of this engagement, and the ultimate victory of God is assuredly predetermined.

5. Because the setting of the apocalyptic literature is otherworldly, it is natural that the language used is symbolic and dramatic. Angels and demons are the contestants; they engage one another through the medium of mythological and zoological figures, such as dragons, monsters, members of the animal kingdom, and species of reptiles.

6. Above all, the apocalyptists address a message of hope and encouragement to their readers, and call for patience in the interim between the dark present and the glorious future. The future was sure, since God's purposes cannot fail and the end is foreordained; meanwhile the saints must endure.

The center of the seers' hope was the establishment of the kingdom of God, which would replace all earthly empires. Sometimes this rule of God is set on earth (Dan. 7:14; *Enoch* 41; Rev. 11:15); later apocalyptic literature (e.g., *4 Ezra; 2 Baruch*) more often thinks of it as a new beginning in world history and as a new eon supervening on the old order which passes away.

[5] This is D.S. Russell's thesis, stated in *The Method and Message of Jewish Apocalyptic* (1964), pp. 127-39.

[6] H.H. Rowley, *The Relevance of Apocalyptic*[2] (1947), pp. 154f.

The mediator of this new age is variously described as the Messiah, the Son of Man, or the elect one. There is a certain fluidity in the relationship this figure bears to God. Sometimes he is a human person; sometimes angelic; sometimes celestial and divine. Because this figure is so important as a background of the New Testament message of Jesus and his first interpreters, we shall devote a separate section to this subject. In particular, we shall look at two specimens of the pre-Christian literature which portray a deliverer in antithetical terms, first as an earthly king of David's family, then as a celestial figure ruling a transcendent kingdom. Both aspects are represented in the New Testament, so it is important to fix the background with some precision.

THE DAVIDIC MESSIAH

There is ample evidence in Jewish literature and the Gospel narratives that the expectation of a Messiah as a second David ran high. Part of the evidence may possibly be found in the *Testament of the Twelve Patriarchs* (second century BC), which also contains the presentation of Messiah from the priestly tradition associated with Levi.[7] But the chief source of our knowledge of a messianic figure who was expected to be a descendant of David's family and exercise an authority as military leader and liberator of the Jewish people is the *Psalms of Solomon.* Fortunately we can date these documents with some accuracy.

From allusions made in chapters 1, 2, 8, and 17, we gather that Palestine at the author's time was suffering from the alarms and threats of war. A hostile army was approaching, led by a foreign commander, "a man alien to our people" (17:7). He came from the ends of the earth (8:16)—i.e., Rome—and laid waste the armies and the territories in his path. It seems clear that only one character fits this description, especially since the record goes on to relate that this man whose heart was alienated from God committed the infamy of desecrating the holy place in the temple at Jerusalem (17:13ff.). It is of course the Roman general Pompey who is in view; and his invasion of Palestine in 63 BC suggests the earliest possible date for the *Psalms of Solomon.* Pompey was murdered in Egypt in 48 BC; and this event seems to be referred to in 2:30, 31. This date would set the other terminal point for the book.

The decades between 70 and 40 BC were times of conflict between the Pharisees and the Sadducees in Palestine. The descriptions given in these psalms of the Sadducees as "sinners" who had usurped and defiled the priesthood and laid claim to rulership of the Jewish people show clearly that the author is a Pharisee. His theological

[7] See Russell, *op. cit.*, pp. 55ff., 316ff., for pertinent information.

beliefs shine through his writings, notably where he asserts the divine sovereignty over Israel and his belief in the Torah as God's witness on earth. This confirms his Pharisaic connections, which are further illustrated by his understanding of the Messiah.

Chapters 17 and 18 contain full descriptions of this Pharisaic picture of the Messiah (esp. 17:23-51; 18:6-10). Twice (17:36; superscription to 18) the agent of God's rule (hailed in 17:23 as such—"Behold, O Lord, and raise up for them their king, the Son of David") is called God's anointed. This shows his office as Messiah, and is probably the first time in Jewish literature that the title is used in an official way in reference to the ideal king of the future.[8]

The Messiah, then, is called to his task by God as one who belongs to David's line. He is a human prince, yet equipped for his task with spiritual graces. The Holy Spirit endows him (17:42; 18:8) and qualifies him as a leader free from sin and dedicated thoroughly to God's service (17:41f.). So his trust is in God and not in his military prowess (17:37f., 44). He enjoys the divine blessing (17:43) and can inspire his people to seek the same qualities of spirit he so illustriously possesses (17:28ff.).

The two-part mission of the Messiah is clearly defined. On the negative side he is to overthrow the Gentiles who have dared to set foot on God's land and enter his holy place (17:24, 27). Having overthrown these overlords, he will expel the sinners from God's inheritance, i.e., drive out the Sadducean princes who have gained unlawful possession of the priesthood. The words of chapter 17, "They to whom thou madest no promise took away our place," bemoan this act of usurpation and the false assumption of authority on the part of the Sadducees.

Messiah's constructive task will be to set up God's kingdom, making Jerusalem his capital and reviving the glory of the ancient cultus of the temple. The dispersed tribes of Israel will be regathered (17:26f.), and he will protect and nourish them as a shepherd cares for his flock (17:45). In this capacity he acts as God's vicegerent, since in the theocratic kingdom God's lordship is acknowledged (17:42) and the ruler is the Lord's anointed (the text in 17:32 should read: *βασιλεὺς αὐτῶν χριστὸς κυρίου*). Yahweh is his God (17:28, 41; 18:8) and his king (17:38).

The days of Messiah's rule under God are days of indescribable blessedness (17:44; 18:6) and unparalleled prosperity for Israel. The nation is elevated to a rank of supremacy, with Jerusalem the acknowledged chief city of the world, "a place to be seen in all the earth" (17:30). Part of this picture of Israel's dominance is the submission of the Gentile nations, who will be either broken in pieces (17:23) or brought in subjugation under Israel's rule (17:30).

Hopes of a Davidic Messiah are also given in the *Assumption of*

[8] So Russell, *ibid.*, p. 318.

Moses, an apocalypse written in the first half of the first century of the Christian era. It is Pharisaic in outlook, and contains the pious hopes of a patriotic Jew who counseled his fellow-countrymen to be patient and to await deliverance from the Romans in God's own time and way.

PSALMS OF SOLOMON: TEXT AND TRANSLATION WITH NOTES

Some of the material in the *Psalms of Solomon* is quite indispensable as a background to New Testament Christology. In this section, the text of parts of chapters 17 and 18 is given in Greek, with an English translation, and some notes on the issues raised by these verses. To relate these verses to the New Testament data is to be impressed at how far the *Psalms of Solomon* prepare both negatively and positively for the revelation of messiahship in Jesus.

TEXT

17:21 Ἰδέ, κύριε, καὶ ἀνάστησον αὐτοῖς τὸν βασιλέα αὐτῶν υἱὸν Δαυιδ
εἰς τὸν καιρόν, ὃν εἵλου σύ, ὁ θεός, τοῦ βασιλεῦσαι ἐπὶ Ισραηλ παῖδά σου
22 καὶ ὑπόζωσον αὐτὸν ἰσχὺν τοῦ θραῦσαι ἄρχοντας ἀδίκους,
καθαρίσαι Ιερουσαλημ ἀπὸ ἐθνῶν καταπατούντων ἐν ἀπωλείᾳ,
23 ἐν σοφίᾳ δικαιοσύνης ἐξῶσαι ἁμαρτωλοὺς ἀπὸ κληρονομίας,
ἐκτρῖψαι ὑπερηφανίαν ἁμαρτωλοῦ ὡς σκεύη κεραμέως,
24 ἐν ῥάβδῳ σιδηρᾷ συντρῖψαι πᾶσαν ὑπόστασιν αὐτῶν,
ὀλεθρεῦσαι ἔθνη παράνομα ἐν λόγῳ στόματος αὐτοῦ,
25 ἐν ἀπειλῇ αὐτοῦ φυγεῖν ἔθνη ἀπὸ προσώπου αὐτοῦ
καὶ ἐλέγξαι ἁμαρτωλοὺς ἐν λόγῳ καρδίας αὐτῶν·
26 Καὶ συνάξει λαὸν ἅγιον, οὗ ἀφηγήσεται ἐν δικαιοσύνῃ,
καὶ κρινεῖ φυλὰς λαοῦ ἡγιασμένου ὑπὸ κυρίου θεοῦ αὐτοῦ.
27 καὶ οὐκ ἀφήσει ἀδικίαν ἐν μέσῳ αὐτῶν αὐλισθῆναι ἔτι,
καὶ οὐ κατοικήσει πᾶς ἄνθρωπος μετ' αὐτῶν εἰδὼς κακίαν·
γνώσεται γὰρ αὐτοὺς ὅτι πάντες υἱοὶ θεοῦ εἰσιν αὐτῶν.

. . . .

32 καὶ αὐτὸς βασιλεὺς δίκαιος διδακτὸς ὑπὸ θεοῦ ἐπ' αὐτούς,
καὶ οὐκ ἔστιν ἀδικία ἐν ταῖς ἡμέραις αὐτοῦ ἐν μέσῳ αὐτῶν,
ὅτι πάντες ἅγιοι, καὶ βασιλεὺς αὐτῶν χριστὸς κυρίου.
33 οὐ γὰρ ἐλπιεῖ ἐπὶ ἵππον καὶ ἀναβάτην καὶ τόξον
οὐδὲ πληθυνεῖ αὐτῷ χρυσίον οὐδὲ ἀργύριον εἰς πόλεμον
καὶ πολλοῖς (λαοῖς) οὐ συνάξει ἐλπίδας εἰς ἡμέραν πολέμου.
34 Κύριος αὐτὸς βασιλεὺς αὐτοῦ ἐλπὶς τοῦ δυνατοῦ ἐλπίδι θεοῦ,
καὶ ἐλεήσει πάντα τὰ ἔθνη ἐνώπιον αὐτοῦ ἐν φόβῳ.
35 πατάξει γὰρ γῆν τῷ λόγῳ τοῦ στόματος αὐτοῦ εἰς αἰῶνα,
εὐλογήσει λαὸν κυρίου ἐν σοφίᾳ μετ' εὐφροσύνης·
36 καὶ αὐτὸς καθαρὸς ἀπὸ ἁμαρτίας τοῦ ἄρχειν λαοῦ μεγάλου,
ἐλέγξαι ἄρχοντας καὶ ἐξᾶραι ἁμαρτωλοὺς ἐν ἰσχύι λόγου.
37 καὶ οὐκ ἀσθενήσει ἐν ταῖς ἡμέραις αὐτοῦ ἐπὶ θεῷ αὐτοῦ·
ὅτι ὁ θεὸς κατειργάσατο αὐτὸν δυνατὸν ἐν πνεύματι ἁγίῳ
καὶ σοφὸν ἐν βουλῇ συνέσεως μετὰ ἰσχύος καὶ δικαιοσύνης.

. . . .

18:4 ἡ παιδεία σου ἐφ' ἡμᾶς ὡς υἱὸν πρωτότοκον μονογενῆ
ἀποστρέψαι ψυχὴν εὐήκοον ἀπὸ ἀμαθίας ἐν ἀγνοίᾳ.
5 καθαρίσαι ὁ θεὸς Ισραηλ εἰς ἡμέραν ἐλέους ἐν εὐλογίᾳ,
εἰς ἡμέραν ἐκλογῆς ἐν ἀνάξει χριστοῦ αὐτοῦ.
6 Μακάριοι οἱ γενόμενοι ἐν ταῖς ἡμέραις ἐκείναις
ἰδεῖν τὰ ἀγαθὰ κυρίου ἃ ποιήσει γενεᾷ τῇ ἐρχομένῃ
7 ὑπὸ ῥάβδον παιδείας χριστοῦ κυρίου ἐν φόβῳ θεοῦ αὐτοῦ
ἐν σοφίᾳ πνεύματος καὶ δικαιοσύνης καὶ ἰσχύος

TRANSLATION

17:21 Behold, O Lord, and raise up for them their king, the son of David,[a]
At the appointed time which, O God, you did choose,[b]
That he may reign over Israel, your servant.[c]

And gird him with strength, that he may shatter unrighteous rulers,[d] 22
And may cleanse Jerusalem from the Gentiles[e] that trample her down in destruction.

Wisely and righteously let him expel sinners from the inheritance, 23
And destroy the sinner's pride as a potter's vessel,

With a rod of iron may he break in pieces all their resources. 24
Let him destroy the lawless Gentiles by the word of his mouth.

At his rebuke the nations[f] shall flee from his presence, 25
And he shall convict sinners in the thoughts of their hearts,

And he shall gather a holy people,[g] whom he shall lead in righteousness, 26
And he shall judge the tribes of a people that has been sanctified by the Lord, his God.

And he shall not permit unrighteousness to lodge any more in their midst, 27
Nor shall any person who approves of evil[h] dwell with them.
For he shall recognize them, that they are all God's sons.[j]

. . . .

And he, as one taught of God, shall be a righteous king over them.[k] 32
And there will be no unrighteousness in their midst in his days.
Because they are all holy people, and their king is the Lord's anointed.[l]

For he shall not place his hope in horse or rider or bow, 33
Nor shall he multiply for his advantage gold or silver for war,[m]
Nor shall he gather confidence from many (people)[n] against the day of battle,

The Lord himself is his king, the hope of him who is mighty through his hope in God, 34
And he will have mercy[o] upon all the nations that come in fear into his presence,

For he will smite the earth with the word of his mouth for ever.[p] 35
He will bless the Lord's people with wisdom and gladness.

And he himself will be pure from sin so that he may rule a mighty people. 36
He will rebuke princes and expel sinners by the might of his word.

And he will not grow weary all his days because he relies on his God; 37
For God will cause him to be powerful by the holy spirit;[q]
And to be wise by the counsel of understanding with strength and righteousness.

. . . .

18:4 Your disciplining[r] is ours [O God], as upon a son who is firstborn and special,[s]
To convert our obedient souls from the unteachableness due to ignorance.

5 May God cleanse Israel against the day when he shows mercy in blessedness,
Against the day he chooses to lead in his anointed one.[t]

6 Happy are they who will be born in those days,[u]
To see the Lord's goodness which he shall bring upon a generation to come,[v]

7 Under the chastening rod of the Lord's anointed, who lives in the fear of his God,
With the wisdom that comes from the spirit and righteousness and might.

NOTES

17:21-25: These verses describe what is largely the destructive work of God's messianic king. Specifically, he is the agent, under God, for the purging of Jerusalem, which is defiled by the presence of alien armies (the Romans) and a corrupt, illegitimate priesthood (the Hasmonean priest-kings and their collaborators). He will deal summarily with both groups, and clear the ground for a renewed Jewish theocracy in which he will rule as God's vicegerent.

[a] The promise to David's family that a future ruler will establish God's house goes back to 2 Sam. 7:8-16. It was later reinterpreted and reapplied to developing needs within the Jewish community (Pss. 89:20-38; 132:11-18; 1 Chron. 22:8-10); see G. von Rad, *Old Testament Theology*, I, 310ff. The prophecy assumed an importance in the eschatological and messianic expectation at Qumran and among the early Christians. See O. Betz, *What Do We Know About Jesus?* (1968), pp. 88f., 96f., 101-103.

[b] God's choice of an appropriate time (καιρός) for the messianic reign to begin recalls Mark 1:15.

[c] Israel is God's servant (παῖς). The word can also mean "son" (cf. Ex. 4:22).

[d] The "unrighteous rulers" are the Sadducean princes, whose right to rule the author disputes.

[e] The oppressing Gentiles are the Romans, with special reference to Pompey's invasion in 63 BC and his trespass into the temple sanctuary. According to the next verse, they are "lawless" (or, possibly, "law-breaking") by their defiance of God's holy ordinances concerning the "holy place" of the sanctuary.

[f] "Nations" (ἔθνη) are especially the Roman Gentiles, whose expulsion from Israel's covenant land (God's "inheritance," vs. 23) is confidently awaited when Messiah comes to reign.

17:26-32: The scene changes to display Messiah's office as ruler, shepherd, and teacher of God's people. The verb tenses are future, as the Psalmist looks forward to the fulfilment of God's appointed hour (vs. 21).

[g] "Holy people" (λαὸς ἅγιος) identifies the Pharisaic ideal of Israel as a purified remnant separated from others by a resolute determination to practice God's laws with utter seriousness. They are a people "sanctified by the Lord, his God."

[h] A possible side-glance at those who saw no harm in cooperating with the Romans.

[j] This is the recognition given to the pious endeavorers who are left after Messiah's purifying task is completed. The Greek verb γινώσκειν probably reflects the Hebrew verb "to know" (*yāda'*) in the special sense of "call and acknowledge" (Amos 3:1-2). Messiah owns this people as truly members of God's family, "a holy people" (vs. 32).

[k] Messiah's rule is always "under God," who is Israel's true king as well as Messiah's (vs. 34).

[l] This is a passage of some textual uncertainty. The underlying Hebrew apparently read *m^e šîaḥ Yahweh*, the Lord's anointed, which is the Greek text as printed. A Christian scribe has probably altered this expression of Jewish hope (seen in Luke 2:26) to bring it into line with the Christian confession (e.g., Luke 2:11; Phil. 2:11). The change needed would be slight, from Χριστὸς Κυρίου to Χριστὸς Κύριος, and even more understandable if the early manuscripts had abbreviated both κυρίου and κύριος as $\overline{\text{KY}}$.

17:33-37: The personal character of Messiah is exemplary. In particular, he is seen as a warrior figure (vs. 35) who leads Israel to freedom and then is installed as Israel's captain, possessed with superhuman power and spiritual gifts which qualify him to exercise a benevolent rule over God's people. The destiny of his (and Israel's) enemies is less happy. They are either destroyed or subjugated to Israel's control.

[m] The contrast with Solomon is intentional. He extended the nation's empire by an expansionist economic policy, but the price was a heavy one and involved him in compromise, as his reign was reduced to that of any Near Eastern potentate of his day. Cf. Deut. 17:16f.

[n] The text has a possible lacuna after πολλοῖς, "many." If πολλοῖς by itself is the correct reading, it would be translated: "Nor shall he gather confidence from (?) a multitude (?) for the day of battle"; following R. H. Charles, *The Apocrypha and Pseudepigrapha of the Old Testament in English*, II (1913), 650; cf. C.K. Barrett, *The New Testament Background: Selected Documents*, p. 249. The suggestion has also been made that πολλοῖς is not the correct reading. Several conjectures have been made: ἄλλοῖς (others), παλτοῖς (javelins), ὅπλοῖς (weapons), or, most plausibly, πλοίοις (ships; cf. Solomon's foreign commerce and navy, 1 Kings 9:26ff.).

[o] The text reads ἐλεήσει ("he will have mercy"); but this seems not to accord with the context. Messiah's attitude to the Gentiles is one of

hostility, not mercy. Emendations have been proposed, suggesting ἀλοήσει ("he will thresh").

[p]Cf. Isa. 11:4 (LXX): *πατάξει γῆν τῷ λόγῳ τοῦ στόματος αὐτοῦ*. RSV: "he shall smite the earth with the *rod* of his mouth."

[q]This link between the spirit (of God) and power (*δυνάμις*) paves the way for the New Testament picture of Messiah as endued with the Holy Spirit's gift of strength (Acts 10:38; Rom. 1:4).

18:4-7: The Psalmist voices the confession and hope of his people in the expectation of the new age about to dawn. The installation of Messiah will be a sure sign of God's favor and Israel's joy. This is the sequel to a prayer in 17:45: "May God hasten his mercy to Israel."

[r]"Disciplining" (*παιδεία*) is Israel's experience of adversity, shortly to be relieved by Messiah's coming and rule.

[s]There are two important terms here: *πρωτότοκος* ("first-born") and *μονογενής* (lit. "only-born"). The New Testament links are Col. 1:15 where Jesus Christ is *πρωτότοκος πάσης κτίσεως*, first-born with rights over all creation; and John 1:18, *μονογενὴς θεός* (which is to be preferred to the reading *μονογενὴς υἱός*, even though the context may support the latter), the only God. In both cases, Israel's relationship to God is carried over and applied—in a richer sense, to be sure—to Israel's Messiah and the church's Lord.

[t]The text has *ἐν ἀνάξει χριστοῦ αὐτοῦ*, which would strictly mean "when he (God) brings up his anointed." This may suggest a doctrine of a pre-existent Messiah (*Enoch* 48:3; *2 Esdras* 7, but the context argues against this). T.W. Manson, *The Servant Messiah*, p. 28, n. 1, makes the plausible suggestion that one syllable has been omitted in the transmission of *ἀνάξει*, and that the original was *ἀναδείξει*, which yields the translation, "For the day of destiny when his Messiah is installed" or manifested. For the noun *ἀναδείξις*, see Luke 1:80.

[u]The blessedness of living in Messiah's time recalls Luke 10:23f., and prepares for the gospel teaching. See T.W. Manson, *The Sayings of Jesus*, pp. 80f.

[v]The description "a generation to come" is in line with the Jewish demarcation of time between "this age" and "the age to come," and sets the stage for New Testament eschatology. Cf. *2 Esdras* 7:50: "The Most High has made not one age but two."

THE "CELESTIAL" MESSIAH

Quite distinct from the figure which emerges from the literature we have been discussing is the type of messianic personage who appears in the more "apocalyptic" literature known by the name of Enoch. This corpus builds on the tradition represented in Daniel, especially chapter 7. There the seer is presented with a vision of four beasts symbolizing four world empires. The fourth beast has ten horns but these are attacked by a little horn. The latter represents the persecuting ruler, Antiochus Epiphanes, and his appearance is followed by the great judgment held by the Ancient of Days (God). The fourth beast is then killed, and power over all the earth is given to a human figure, "one like a son of man" (7:13), who represents God's saints.

Daniel's "son of man" is the starting-point for a development which blossoms fully in *Enoch*, a composite work which has been preserved in Ethiopic. Our interest centers in the central portion of chapters 37-71, known as the Similitudes or Parables of Enoch.

To date, no part of this section has been found among the scrolls from Qumran. Some scholars contend that this is no accident. In their view, these chapters of *Enoch* are post-Christian, whether written by a Jew or Jewish Christian.[9] This conclusion is by no means compelling, and a more likely dating for the document is during the reign of Herod the Great,[10] even if some of the references can be suspected of later Christian tampering.

The importance of this section is that it contains an entirely spiritualized conception of the Messiah and his kingdom. Four titles applied in the New Testament to Jesus are found in the ascription to the Enochian figure: Messiah, the righteous one, the elect one, and the Son of Man. Indeed, he is hailed as a divine being: "And his glory is for ever and ever, and his might unto all generations" (49:2). The kingdom over which he rules transcends all national bounds: "And he shall be the light of the Gentiles" (48:4). He stands in a special relationship to God, and is brought out onto the stage of a cosmic drama to be acknowledged and revered by all, both human and spiritual powers. This revelation of a hidden, pre-existent Son of Man is a sign of the world's judgment and betokens the establishment of a heavenly kingdom.

> They see that Son of Man sitting on the throne of his glory: And the kings and the mighty and all who possess the earth shall bless and glorify and extol him who rules over all, who was hidden; for from the beginning the Son of Man was hidden and the Most High preserved him in the presence of his might and revealed him to the elect (62:5-7).

In the same sequence of thought, a later apocalypse known as *2 Esdras* (or *4 Ezra*) contains several apocalyptic visions of a savior figure. The most famous is the vision of the man from the sea (ch. 13), which may be dated at the outbreak of the Jewish War of AD 66. Both in this section as in the earlier eagle vision (ch. 11 and 12), the Messiah is a supernatural being, pre-existent, heavenly, revealed by God.

> This is the anointed and whom the Most High has kept unto the end of days (12:32).

[9] So J.T. Milik, *Ten Years of Discovery in the Wilderness of Judaea* (ET 1959), p. 33.

[10] E. Sjöberg and M. Black; cited by Russell, *op. cit.*, p. 52.

> The same is he whom the Most High has kept a great season, who by his own self shall deliver his creatures: and he shall order them that are left behind (13:26).

Clearly in this literature we are dealing with a conception of Messiah quite different from the nationalistic, earthly figure found in other parts of the pre-Christian writings. Both strands are well-attested, and both are found in the background of New Testament Christology.

PART THREE

How the Gospels Came to Be Written

Talking about the study of the Four Gospels might suggest that we are to inspect these four books as separate, published works. But we must bear in mind that these books did not mysteriously fall down from heaven as completed wholes. They had to be written. That process—on its human side (as Christians, we want also to recognize that these little books form part of the total library of holy Scripture, inspired by God)—requires that the authors had to give attention to assembling their materials and arranging them in some order. We know that this was their method of operation, for Luke tells us as much in the preface to his Gospel (1:1-4). The question is, How much of the Gospel material was already in existence before the evangelists set about their task? With that question goes another: Can we today know anything about the processes which were at work shaping the materials before they came into the hands of a Matthew, a Mark, or a John?

These two questions are the concern of this section. There are other issues as well. One has to do with the purpose of the Gospel writers. This matter can only be settled once we have asked about their literary interdependence. To investigate how far the first three Gospels agree in their reporting and how far they are individually distinctive is the province of the Synoptic problem, which we shall discuss in chapter 11.

Behind all questions about the Gospels is that of the authenticity of the text. How far can we be sure that what we have today in our Greek and English Testaments represents what the first writers intended to record? In chapter 12 we shall have a brief introduction to the science and method of textual criticism.

CHAPTER NINE

Early Traditions About Jesus

The inquiry into how the Gospels were composed is largely a speculative one, since the Gospel records of Jesus' career and achievement have come down as completed wholes and self-contained books. They do not offer much indication that they were put together in stages and as compilations by different authors. Each of the Gospels as a literary unit appears on the face of it to be the work of its author, not a symposium.

But first impressions can be misleading. While we do not expect to find the literary devices modern writers use to denote their dependence on other writings (footnotes, for example), there are some clear signs that the evangelists have incorporated earlier material. To separate out the layers of tradition and to assign them to a suitable life-setting in the activity of the early Christian groups who assembled and used them are the tasks of literary criticism.

Literary criticism includes form criticism and editorial criticism as well as the more strictly defined task of source criticism. We shall be looking in turn at each part of this total enterprise. To begin, however, we may look to the Gospel of Luke for encouragement in the task of trying to discover what materials the evangelists had already in hand as they began their work of Gospel writing.

THE THREE STAGES

Referring to Luke 1:1-4, W. Michaelis comments, "This self-witness [to the growth of the Gospel tradition] is of inestimable value to us."[1] The force of this observation invites us to look at the grounds for it. The great value of this Lukan text is simply that it provides concrete evidence of the three stages in which the tradition prior to and including the evangelist's own work was built up.

1. There is, first of all, the deposit of testimony Luke refers to

[1] W. Michaelis, *Einleitung in das Neue Testament*[2] (1954), p. 14.

in recalling those "who from the beginning were eyewitnesses and ministers of the word." The exact nature and extent of his indebtedness to eyewitness material is a matter of considerable debate in recent study.[2] But it seems reasonably safe to conclude that there was at the foundation of the Gospel tradition a basis of historical reminiscence and reporting on which the later evangelists drew.

2. The second stage comprises the work of "many," to whom Luke pays tribute, who attempted to fashion a narrative out of the material which was shaped by what was known as "the ministry of the word." These early writers used whatever traditions lay to hand, which came into their possession through their contact with the early preachers and catechists (instructors of new converts). Little is positively known of these ventures at Gospel writing, with this exception: we are able to identify at least one of Luke's predecessors in this field, namely Mark. If there is any writer in early Christianity whose task is suitably described by Luke 1:1, it is John Mark, the evangelist known to us from the Gospel record which the church fathers associated with him.

3. The third stage is Luke's own contribution as one who "followed all things accurately [RSV margin] for some time past," and who sought to write "an orderly account" with a distinct purpose in view (vs. 4).

Three key terms in this section shed special light on Luke's own self-witness and his intention to meet his readers' needs.[3] First is παρηκολουθηκότι (vs. 3), best translated (as in Arndt-Gingrich's version of Bauer's *Lexicon*) "having investigated" (everything carefully from the beginning). The verb indicates Luke's care and thoroughness in seeking out the necessary information; and it is a witness, on his own account at least, that he went about his task in a methodical and diligent way.

Second, the verb form of κατηχέω (vs. 4) speaks of the way in which Theophilus had been initiated into a knowledge of Christian truth. He had come to an understanding of "the things which he had been taught as a catechumen." This knowledge was already his possession; now Luke will help him to a fuller apprehension of it and a firmer grasp of its significance and value.

Perhaps the single most important key to Luke's purpose as a Gospel writer is his term ἀσφάλεια (vs. 4). By his efforts as a composer of an "orderly account" of Jesus' activity and achievement, which the

[2] See, for example, D. E. Nineham's comprehensive survey of the problem, "Eye-witness Testimony and the Gospel Tradition," *JTS*, 9,1 (1958), 13-25; 9,2 (1958), 243-52; 11,2 (1960), 253-64. There is a critique of Nineham's assessment by A. T. Hanson, "The Quandary of Historical Scepticism," in *Vindications*, ed. A. Hanson (1966), esp. pp. 90ff.

[3] For a recent statement on these issues, see A. J. B. Higgins, "The Preface to Luke and the Kerygma in Acts," in *Apostolic History and the Gospel*, ed. W. W. Gasque and R. P. Martin (1970), pp. 78-91.

subsequent chapters will contain, Luke intends that Theophilus will be assured that the truth he has embraced rests on a *firm foundation.* This is the most adequate meaning of Luke's term ἀσφάλεια. His record aims at providing an objective reliability (as in Acts 25:26) rather than a subjective certainty (which is the sense of Acts 2:36); and he is concerned to establish the solidity of the facts of the gospel (which Theophilus has already learned as a new convert), probably in the face of false teaching already on the horizon (Acts 20:29ff.).[4]

Luke's purpose, then, seems clear. He is laying claim to an authority, partly derived from his predecessors and partly personal, to write his Gospel (and his second volume, the Acts of the Apostles). His intention is to give Theophilus a solid basis in reliable narrative and witness for his newly found faith as a Christian and to fortify him to resist the encroachment of false teaching.

We can now broaden our inquiry to examine the various ways the tradition was preserved.

THE EARLY CHRISTIAN ENVIRONMENT

Three Greek terms are used in a technical sense to denote aspects of how the gospel story was handed on in early Christianity.

1. κήρυγμα. This is the common word for the public proclamation of the good news of Jesus Christ to the non-Christian world (1 Cor. 1:21).[5] It is the announcement of all that God in Christ has done for men. It was no bare statement of facts, nor even a combination of historical events with a statement of their significance. As can be seen from the specimens of the kerygma in Acts (2:14-39; 3:13-26; 4:10-12; 5:30-32; 10:36-43; 13:17-41), the preaching "always closes with an appeal for repentance, the offer of forgiveness and of the Holy Spirit, and the promise of 'salvation,' that is, of 'the life of the Age to Come,' to those who enter the elect community."[6] Two other elements are found in early Christian preaching—a preparatory apologetic and rationale for God's having sent the Messiah, and a rebuttal of false notions, both Jewish and pagan (e.g., Acts 3:18, 24; 13:27; 17:29-31).

2. διδαχή. The ministry of teaching (Acts 2:42; 4:31; 5:42; 6:2), by which new believers were instructed in the duties, discipline, and ethos of the Christian communities, was important in the primitive church. The task of those endowed with the gifts of "exhortation" (παράκλησις—Acts 4:36: Rom. 12:8) and of "prophecy"[7] (Acts

[4] So H. Schürmann, *Traditionsgeschichtliche Untersuchungen zu den synoptischen Evangelien* (1968), pp. 253f.

[5] See C. H. Dodd, *The Apostolic Preaching and its Developments* (1936), pp. 7ff., for a classic presentation of this theme.

[6] *Ibid.*, p. 23.

[7] See E. E. Ellis, "The Role of the Christian Prophet in Acts," in *Apostolic History and the Gospel*, pp. 55-67.

13:1; 1 Cor. 14:3) served the practical purpose of encouraging believers to endure suffering and to maintain hope. Much of this instruction would be given in a liturgical context as Christians assembled in services of worship, especially in connection with the breaking of bread.[8]

3. κατηχέω. This verb, meaning "to instruct," suggests a catechetical responsibility accepted by the leaders of the early Christian groups.[9] The clearest allusion to such teachers is in Galatians 6:6, where the person who is "taught the word" is counseled to "share all good things" with the one who teaches him (the latter to be equated, according to Beyer, with the teachers of 1 Cor. 12:28; Eph. 4:11). Although the actual class of catechumens does not appear in church history until early in the third century, there is some evidence of its early place in the church.[10] Interested inquirers and seekers were given instruction in Christian belief and practice in anticipation of the day when they would be ready to accept full privileges and responsibilities as church members. There is Jewish precedent for this procedure, as interested Gentile seekers were trained in preparation for proselyte baptism. And it would seem that several verses in the New Testament indirectly attest to a rudimentary catechumenate (Acts 8:32-37; 18:25; 20:20; Col. 1:6; Eph. 4:20f.; 1 Pet. 2:2; 5:1; 1 John 2:12-24). Pre-baptismal instruction later played an important role in educating new Christians in preparation for their initiation in the body of Christ.

These are the three main types of activity in which Christians would draw on the deposit of traditions handed down. They had to have the basic facts of Jesus' ministry in order to spell out the meaning of the gospel in their public preaching. They drew on the oral traditions, later written down for their ministry of instruction and teaching. They needed the materials of these traditions to train recent converts in apostolic belief and practice. It is not difficult to believe that in such a situation the sections of tradition which later became assembled to form the four Gospels would be preserved and transmitted. We may venture to state this more specifically: our completed Gospels are the result of the evangelists' assembling materials of the life and activity of Jesus which first played a functional role in the early church. To put it in another way, the units of tradition of which our Gospels are composed are the literary deposits of the oral preaching, teaching, instruction, and worship of the early communities, whose purpose was to awaken faith and to confirm Christian certainty.[11]

[8] O. Cullmann, *Early Christian Worship* (ET 1953), pp. 20ff.

[9] See H. W. Beyer, in *TDNT*, III, 638ff.

[10] See W. Robinson, "Historical Survey of the Church's Treatment of New Converts, With Reference to Pre- and Post-baptismal Instruction," *JTS*, 42 o.s. (1941), 42-53.

[11] So Michaelis, *op. cit.*, p. 18; see also C. F. D. Moule, *The Birth of the New Testament* (1962), ch. 5, esp. p. 93.

Can we identify any group of traditions later employed by the evangelists and say what impulses moved the first Christians to assemble these small units of the material or *pericopae* (sing. *pericope*) into a connected sequence? Let us look more closely at several of these proposed groupings.

THE PASSION STORY

The proclamation and defense of the kerygma called for repeated reference to the closing events in Jesus' life. It is one of the most assured results of modern study that, even if the first believers had apparently little interest in preserving a chronicle of Jesus' day-to-day activity, they made an exception with respect to the events from the Last Supper to the somber details of Good Friday and its sequel.[12]

There are compelling reasons for our confidence in being able to isolate these events in the account of Mark (14—16), for from the character of these chapters it is evident that Mark found them already in a block of narrative and took the material over into his Gospel. The conclusion stands that "the incidents in the Passion appear to have been the first to be collected together in anything like a historical narrative."[13]

Several strands of evidence support the thesis of the formation of the passion story before Mark. For one thing, Mark 14 and 15 have a stylistic character different from the rest of the gospel. Further, Matthew and Luke, in their parallel accounts of the last meal, the arrest, the trial, and the crucifixion did not feel able to modify Mark's account to the extent they did earlier in their Gospels. To be sure, the two later evangelists add significant details not present in Mark, but they supplement and enrich Mark's account *within his framework.* Even Luke, who utilizes a passion narrative which may justifiably be claimed to be independent of the Markan model, still operates within the general sequence of events set by Mark. The fourth evangelist, too, follows the Markan order closely,[14] especially from the arrest of Jesus onwards (John 18:2-11; par. Mark 14:45-50), where there is, as Jeremias remarks, "a continuous narrative style in the synoptic manner."

On the assumption that there existed a narrative framework of the story of Jesus' passion, we have still to ask why Christians were interested in these events. The first claim made in the early preaching was that the Messiah has come and that his name is Jesus of Nazareth (Acts 2:22ff.). But at the heart of this assertion lay the implication

[12] For the nine episodes which make up the material from the last meal to the resurrection appearances, see C. H. Dodd, *History and the Gospel* (1938), pp. 80ff.

[13] D. E. Nineham, *Saint Mark* (Pelican Gospel Commentaries, 1963), p. 23.

[14] J. Jeremias, *The Eucharistic Words of Jesus*^{2} (ET 1966), pp. 94ff.

that God has revealed himself in this person who suffered death on a Roman cross. This bold statement would immediately be challenged from two sides.

A Jewish objection would be registered that a crucified Messiah is a contradiction in terms. Messiah is a term meaning God's anointed; it was an honorific title describing God's agent in redeeming his people. As such, Messiah was seen as standing in a relation of special favor and blessedness. Death on a cross meant precisely the opposite, according to Deuteronomy 21:23: the criminal sentenced to death by impaling was *ḥērem*, under a ban and outside the covenant relationship with God and his chosen people.[15] The absurdity, then, of the Christian claim that Jesus was truly God's Messiah would be patent; and a fuller account was needed to demonstrate that, in spite of the seeming contradiction, God was at work in the human condemnation of Jesus, who died because of a false charge and who made no confession of personal guilt. Paul's preaching of the cross proved a stumblingblock (*σκανδάλον*) to the Jews (1 Cor. 1:23; Gal. 5:11). The passion narrative would help to overcome this objection by relating the circumstances of his death, which showed him innocent of the charge brought against him. The resurrection then set the seal of God on his life of obedience to God's will (Rom. 1:4; 4:25; Phil. 2:9-11).

Additionally, a Gentile demur was likely. From that side the suspicion was probable that Jesus was merely a common criminal, who deserved to die. In any case, his weakness and submission in death would be thought to prove that he could not be divine, since according to Greek thought the divine cannot suffer. We may refer to a scene in Aristophanes' play *The Frogs* (ll. 632ff.). In a dialogue between two travelers, set in the underworld, the dispute is over their identity—which is a god and which is his slave? It is decided to settle the matter by finding out which of the two can feel bodily pain:

> You should flog him well,
> For if he is god he won't feel it.
> Whichever of us two you first behold
> Flinching or crying out—he's not the god.

Moreover, the contemporary religious world in which the gospel was first preached was familiar with itinerant "holy men," impressive personalities having a reputation for marvelous deeds or powers. The message of Jesus spoke of suffering and submission to hostile forces, which led to an ignominious death on a Roman gibbet. Some rationale for this tragic ending would be required, which both showed how Jesus consistently refused to summon supernatural aid to deliver himself from death and demonstrated that God's wisdom and

[15] Cf. W. D. Davies, *Paul and Rabbinic Judaism*² (1955), pp. 227f.

saving purpose were displayed in this suffering figure (2 Cor. 13:3, 4; cf. 1 Cor. 1:24; 2:7).

On two counts, then, a connected sequence of stories offering some insight into how and why Jesus consented to suffer was required. For the Jews, the apologetic had to stress how God was fulfilling his promised word in Messiah's death and to show that certain events long ago predicted were part of God's age-old plan of redemption. There is heavy emphasis on these themes in early Christian preaching in the Acts-kerygma (2:23-31; 3:18; 10:43; 13:27, 29, 32ff.) as well as in a credal statement which has been justifiably traced back to the Jerusalem church (1 Cor. 15:3ff.).[16]

The line pursued by these kerygmatic statements was intended to convince open-minded Jews that Jesus was no apostate suffering the fate of a heretic or a revolutionary. Jesus was indeed condemned to death and died on a cross. Technically he died "under a ban" (Deut. 21:23)—and so outside of a covenant relationship with God. But this judgment came on him for no personal demerit. Rather, he was voluntarily and vicariously enduring divine displeasure as a Savior of others. Paul explicates this in a way which suggests that it was a common understanding of Jesus' death in the mission churches (Gal. 3:13); its relevance for a mission preaching to the Jews under Judaizing pressure would be even more apparent. C. H. Dodd comments on the need which the assembling of the passion story was designed to meet:

> The Church was committed, by the very terms of its *kerygma*, to a formidable task of biblical research, primarily for the purpose of clarifying its own understanding of the momentous events out of which it had emerged, and also for the purpose of making its Gospel intelligible to the outside public.[17]

The second need which the passion narrative met is found in the Gentile question. As it is framed by K. L. Schmidt, the argument is that part of the interest in the passion story was in answer to the natural question in the mind of inquirers.[18] "How could Jesus have been brought to the cross by the people who were blessed by his signs and wonders?" The answer is given in the set of historical panels which together formed the passion narrative. They tell the story of Judas' betrayal, the disciples' fear, the Jewish authorities' malice. They show how fickle the Jewish populace were when pressure was put on them, and yet how Jesus foresaw his destiny in terms of rejection and humiliation, so that the end did not take him by surprise. All of this would further vindicate Jesus' claim to be an innocent sufferer and set the blame at the door of the Jewish leaders.

[16] See Jeremias, *The Eucharistic Words of Jesus*, pp. 101ff.
[17] *According to the Scriptures* (1965), p. 14.
[18] *Der Rahmen der Geschichte Jesu*, p. 305.

Yet, at a deeper level, it would indicate Jesus' own command of the situation and his obedience to the divine will.

We should take brief note of some other possibilities suggested to account for the rise of the passion story. S. G. F. Brandon and P. Winter argue that the story of the cross was told tendentiously, in order to shift the blame for Jesus' death from the Romans to the Jews.[19] The purpose would be to make life tolerable for Christians in Rome at the time immediately after the Jewish revolt in AD 70, when the Jews were in disfavor and Christians had no desire to be closely linked with them. Mark, it is contended, adapted the tradition to concentrate all blame on the Jews and to make them appear as chief instigators of the death of Jesus.

Two critical comments may be made. On Brandon's showing, Mark is still left with the greatest obstacle—to explain away the *Roman* crucifixion of Jesus. If he freely invented a narrative to make the Jews appear in a bad light, why did he not delete altogether the story of the cross and have Jesus die by stoning at the hands of the Jews as a heretic (Lev. 24:14; Deut. 17:2-7)? At the time when the church needed, in Winter's view, to dissociate itself from the Jews and seek favor with the Romans, the Romans themselves had already taken a hostile attitude to the Christians (Nero's persecution was in AD 64). No mere retelling of the crucifixion story would avail to deflect that animosity.

A novel view, stated by H. Conzelmann and accepted by J. M. Robinson, maintains that the traditions about Jesus arose from a need to clothe the "bare facticity" (Bultmann's *das blosse Dass*) of Jesus and the declaration of the cross as the instrument of salvation with enough personal detail to prevent the message from falling into an assertion of an unreal incarnation, which virtually denied the Lord's humanity.[20] Thus, "Christ died" (1 Cor. 15:3) may have become little more than a cipher in the hand of early Christian gnostics, whose cry may be heard in 1 Corinthians 12:3, "Jesus be cursed." In other words, they rejected all interest in the earthly Jesus and concentrated their attention on the heavenly, pneumatic Christ, seen as an ethereal spirit.

A variation of this view is given by E. Schweizer, who suggests that Mark had to impose on an already existing tradition of Jesus as a "divine man" (θεῖος ἀνήρ) the paradox of a victory-through-humiliation pattern, and give the historical circumstance in which the life of Jesus arose by making corrective use of the Jesus-tradition and replac-

[19] S. G. F. Brandon, *The Trial of Jesus* (1969); P. Winter, *On the Trial of Jesus* (1961). For an acute critique, see A.N. Sherwin-White, "The Trial of Christ," in *Historicity and Chronology in the New Testament* (1965), pp. 97-116.

[20] J. M. Robinson, *Journal of Bible and Religion*, 30 (1962), 198-208.

ing the un-Christian understanding of existence (bound up with Jesus as an impressive wonder-worker) which had permeated the tradition with a Christian understanding of existence.[21]

We shall come back to this general approach in our section on Mark's Gospel, here simply noting its suggestiveness as a possible reason why Christians were initially interested in assembling the data of the passion story.

John Knox offers a psychologizing rationale of the passion story.

> Paul tells us that in his preaching to the Galatians, Jesus Christ was "publicly portrayed" as crucified before their very eyes (Gal. 3:1). The Crucifixion had to be *pictured.* Men must see and feel it, imaginatively entering into the sufferings of Christ and sensing the awful significance of what happened on Calvary. The story of the Passion must be told in such a fashion that the stark reality of it be felt and the full redemptive meaning of it be realised. The early preachers would have dealt with the Crucifixion . . . in the manner of dramatists.[22]

Knox's theory is not capable of proof. It would seem to be too modern a view, and its weakness is apparent when he argues for it thus: "We can be sure of this, if for no other reason, because preachers still deal so with the Gospel materials."

J. Jeremias appeals to the use of significant passion sayings in the conceptual and liturgical life of the early church. The passion narrative formed the milieu in which these sayings were preserved and used. These *verba Christi* ("words of Christ") would be treasured and recalled in the context of the passion scenes because of their importance for the church's life in the world.[23] They are:

Mark 14:24, which shows how the church found the *raison d'être* for the practice of the eucharist in Jesus' words in the upper room.

Mark 10:45 and *Luke 22:27* both point back to Jesus as servant of God who both atones for his people's sins and is the pattern of the church's ethical life—a truth taught in catechesis and particularly applicable to new converts.

Luke 23:34 is connected with the life of prayer, both Jesus' and his followers' (e.g., Acts 7:60). We can well imagine the value of this prayer for one's enemies in time of persecution.

Luke 22:35-38 and *Mark 14:27f.* have to do with persecution. The Markan text further offers assurance that the Shepherd's presence will be with his sheep, and that he will regather (at the final time) the scattered flock (Zech. 13:7-9; 14).

21 E. Schweizer, *The Good News According to Mark* (ET 1970), pp. 380-86.
22 John Knox, *The Death of Christ* (1959), p. 19.
23 J. Jeremias, *The Central Message of the New Testament* (1965), pp. 45ff.

THE RESURRECTION NARRATIVES

The case of the resurrection narratives is not exactly the same as the passion story. The evidence allows us to say that the first Christians felt it sufficient to report that certain persons had visited the tomb and found it open and/or empty, and that Jesus appeared to certain individuals and groups. There was no attempt to produce a single standardized account. It is possible, however, to suggest a couple motives for the preservation of these stories.

1. C. H. Dodd has written suggestively on the apologetic purpose of the lists of appearances to specified individuals and groups.[24] Dodd argues that they were assembled "to provide interested enquirers with a guaranteed statement of the sources of evidence upon which the affirmations of the *kerygma* were grounded."[25] Two facets of this apologetic value are to be seen. First is an emphasis on recognition (ἀναγνώρισις: this is a term taken from Greek drama, in which the crucial point was often a recognition scene, when the god or hero revealed himself, not unlike Gen. 45:1-4 in the Hebrew saga). The recognition of the Lord by the disciples (John 21) would have evidential value as showing that they were not predisposed to believe in a resurrection, which burst on them suddenly and without warning. In the second place, the word of command addressed to the disciples would later validate the church's claim to be a missionary agent and to be the community of the risen one.

2. A second purpose for preserving the resurrection stories is a eucharistic one. One of the interesting links in the post-resurrection narratives is the connection between Jesus' appearances and the celebration of a meal (Luke 24:13-35; John 21:1-14; cf. Acts 1:4; 10:41; and the spurious Markan appendix, 16:14). This suggests that the resurrection sections were used to give a rationale for the church's celebration of the Lord's Supper and that they expected his risen presence to greet them there just as he came to his first disciples at a post-resurrection meal.[26]

This view ties in with the observation made above that traditions about the risen Lord were preserved in the church's liturgy. This can be justified exegetically on the basis of 1 Corinthians 11:26, where the verb "proclaim" (καταγγέλλειν) reflects the Hebrew verb *higgîth* ("tell a story"), thus linking it with the narration of the drama of the exodus from Egypt in the Passover Haggadah. In Jewish custom it was a duty to tell the story of Yahweh's deliverance of Israel from bondage at the Passover meal table.[27] Paul takes over this notion in a

24 In *Studies in the Gospels*, ed. D. E. Nineham (1955), pp. 9ff.
25 *Ibid.*, p. 33.
26 See O. Cullmann, *Early Christian Worship;* W. Rordorf, *Sunday* (ET 1968), pp. 215ff., 243ff.
27 See S. R. Driver, *Literature of the Old Testament*[9] (1913), p. 487.

Christian context, once he has Christianized the Passover feast (1 Cor. 5:6, 7); and he may well envision a telling of the drama of the new redemption in the historical events of Messiah's death and deliverance.[28]

OTHER NARRATIVE UNITS

Early preachers (we learn from Acts 2:22) were accustomed to call attention to the "mighty deeds" (δυνάμεις) which accompanied and accredited Jesus' ministry. At least one purpose of Jesus' miracles was that of certifying that God was at work in the ministry of the Messiah. The background to this lies in the Jewish apocalyptic notion that when the new age of deliverance dawned, the regime of Satan or Beliar would be overthrown by the power of God. As *The Assumption of Moses* has it:

> And then his [God's] kingdom will be manifest in all his creation;
> And the devil will have an end,
> And with him all sorrow will be removed.
> Then the messenger will be commissioned,
> Who has been established in the highest place;
> And he will immediately liberate them from their enemies.

The Gospels explain many of Jesus' mighty works in terms of the imagery of the defeat of demons, the cessation of Satan's power, and the inbreaking of divine rule into human lives in the person of Jesus (Mark 1:15; Luke 10:9-11; Matt. 10:7; 12:28 = Luke 11:20; Matt. 11:12; Luke 17:20f.).

The language in which the stories are told is a further witness to the role the miracle stories played. E. C. Hoskyns has drawn attention to the strange vocabulary of Mark 7:32. The word μογιλάλος there has its sole parallel in biblical (and non-biblical) literature in the LXX of Isaiah 35:6, where it renders the Hebrew *'illēm*, "speaking with difficulty." Hoskyns concludes that Jesus' miracles, in the early church's estimate, looked beyond physical healing to the presence of the Messiah in the midst of his people, to the spiritual benefits of forgiveness and new life which that presence brings, and above all to the awakening of faith in the eschatological fulfilment of God's saving power, revealed for the redemption of Israel.[29]

M. Albertz first identified and isolated what he termed controversy stories, i.e., stories which told of a conflict between Jesus and his Jewish opponents (notable in Mark 2-3).[30] These records of

28 For discussion see R. P. Martin, *Worship in the Early Church* (rev. ed. 1974), pp. 115, 126f.

29 E. C. Hoskyns and N. Davey, *The Riddle of the New Testament*, pp. 119f. Alan Richardson has elaborated this thesis in the monograph *The Miracle Stories of the Gospels* (1941).

30 M. Albertz, *Die synoptischen Streitgespräche* (1921).

statement and counterstatement were preserved because they provided case material which could be used as ammunition for Christians in their post-resurrection controversies with Jewish debaters. There is no proof of this view, but the theory has plausibility. We can easily imagine the relevance in such contexts of Jesus' teachings on the law, the Sabbath, and ceremonial defilement, which would be crucial debating issues between the followers of Jesus and their first Palestinian audiences.

CONNECTED STORY OR LOOSE SECTIONS?

Were the first Christians content simply to use separate tracts (passion story, resurrection traditions, apologetic materials) as independent and isolated units? Or were they concerned to know what a sequential story of Jesus looked like?

We have seen that the early preaching did not give a connected account of Jesus' ministry on a day-to-day basis, as though the evangelists were working with a chronicle set in careful time-sequence. The plain evidence is that in the unlikely event Mark does contain such a chronological scheme, the later evangelists felt at liberty to alter it, depart from it, and to return to it at will. The outline of Jesus' movements in the Fourth Gospel only compounds the problem of trying to weave all the events into a connected whole, which was the undertaking of Tatian in his *Diatessaron*, made in AD 170. For the evangelists, biographical considerations seem to have counted for little. There are just not sufficient data to reconstruct Jesus' "personality" as a first-century Jewish teacher.

Nor can we say that Jesus left his disciples with a compendium of teaching, either written down (a non-Jewish trait) or committed to memory. This theory that part of the Gospel tradition was regarded as "holy word" and passed on to the disciples as a verbally correct deposit was first suggested by H. Riesenfeld in 1957.[31] The appeal in this argument is to the rabbinic practice of memorization and transmission of oral tradition which (it is maintained) had attained the fixed process of sequence in the first century. But the trial balloon sent up by these Scandinavian scholars has met with heavy weather.

In the first place, we cannot be certain that the method of transmission of teaching had attained this degree of fixity in the Judaism of the first century. The New Testament, furthermore, virtually denies this rigid pattern of transmission, for Jesus was distinguished from the rabbinic teachers (Mark 1:22, 27) as one who taught informally and spontaneously, not in dependence on others or by

[31] For his development of this thesis, see Riesenfeld's 1957 essay, now rep[rinted] in *The Gospel Tradition* (1970). It is elaborated by Birger Gerhardsso[n,] *Memory and Manuscript* (1961).

citation of precedent. His disciples were not rabbinic students, "plastered cisterns, losing not a drop," but apprentices engaged in practical work rather than learning arguments and debating points.[32] Nor is there any appeal to a holy tradition (ἱερὸς λόγος) in Paul. On the contrary, it is Paul who rebukes Peter, who of all persons would have been the guarantor, if there was one, of a "sacred deposit" (Gal. 2:6f., 11).

Most damaging to the Scandinavian hypothesis is that it does not allow us to explain the differences in the tradition in which events and sayings are given different settings and different formulations. The saying "The Son of man came to [seek and to] save the lost," for example, appears in different contexts in Matthew 18:11 and Luke 19:10; and Jesus' teaching about the shepherd means in Matthew 18 his concern for weak church members, whereas in Luke 15 he uses the same imagery in defense of his outreach to the despised strata of Palestinian society.

The most that can be affirmed is that the skeletal framework available to the pre-Markan evangelists set the story of Jesus in some elementary order. It is tempting to see an outline of this order in Acts 10:37-41, as C. H. Dodd argued in a classic presentation.[33] But no fixed sequential outline of the ministry seems to have been settled in the pre-Markan era. Even after Mark the later Gospel writers modified and re-arranged his material for their own purposes. Yet the existence of floating *pericopae*, each designed to meet a religious and practical need, may well have awakened a desire to know the reason for these events. Why did Jesus provoke hostility? Why did he enter Jerusalem, there to be betrayed and condemned? Did he anticipate his fate, and forewarn the disciples? Did he glimpse his triumph and look beyond defeat and death to victory and his continuing presence with his own?

In any case there was evidently no compelling interest to write a *vita Jesu* at this early stage. As Vincent Taylor puts it memorably, Christian hands were full of jewels, but there was no desire to weave a crown.[34]

32 See T. W. Manson, *The Teaching of Jesus*² (1935), pp. 237-40.
33 "The Framework of the Gospel Narrative," *ExpT*, 43,9 (1932), 396ff.; repr. in *New Testament Studies* (1952), pp. 1-11. Opposing this view is D.E. Nineham, *Saint Mark*, p. 28n.
34 Vincent Taylor, *The Formation of the Gospel Tradition* (1933), p. 175.

CHAPTER TEN

Form Criticism and Redaction Criticism

FORM CRITICISM

The discipline of form criticism aims at inquiring into the "form"—the literary structure or genre—of the Gospel sections (*pericopae*) at a time when traditions concerning Jesus were circulating by word of mouth. Admittedly we know the "form" of the stories only by their later written evidence, but a strong case can be made that the present written form contains signs which point to the earlier, pre-literary stage of the Gospel tradition. A critical and comparative method for locating, analyzing, and studying this pre-written stage of the tradition originated in Germany (where it is called *Formgeschichte*, literally "form history") and was first applied by German philologists to folklore, community legends, and fairy tales. It set out to identify and classify the forms in which folk traditions are contained and transmitted, and to discover the laws or principles which govern their persistence and history from one generation to another.[1]

To the study of the Bible this method was first applied by H. Gunkel, who studied the creation stories of Genesis in this light.[2] In the period directly following World War I, the same methods were applied to the study of the Gospels. The pioneers in this field were M. Dibelius, who published *Die Formgeschichte des Evangeliums* in 1919, and R. Bultmann, who wrote *Die Geschichte der synoptischen Tradition* in 1921.[3]

We may enumerate four axioms which regulate this approach to the pre-literary stage of the Gospel tradition.

1. The stories and sayings of Jesus were first circulated in

[1] See K. Koch, *The Growth of the Biblical Tradition* (1969).

[2] H. Gunkel, *Schöpfung und Chaos* (1895).

[3] Both works were later translated into English: Dibelius in 1934, *From Tradition to Gospel;* and Bultmann in 1964, *The History of the Synoptic Tradition.*

small independent units, though an exception to this, as we have seen, was the passion narrative.

2. These self-contained stories can be classified according to literary form or type. Various labels and subdivisions are suggested. Dibelius began with the clearly attested preaching of the early church, and isolated certain sections of the life story of Jesus as "paradigms," which he thought were used as sermon texts or illustrations. Bultmann called them "apophthegms" and broadened the scope of the milieu in which the stories were valued. He classified them according to catechetical and controversial situations in the life of the early church as well as pointing to their more obvious usefulness found in public preaching.

Various other classifications have been made. The simplest one is perhaps that of Vincent Taylor, who made a twofold division:[4] pronouncement stories, in turn made up of two examples, controversy stories (Mark 2:1-12; 3:1-6) and conversations with Jesus on the part of inquirers (Mark 10:17-22; 12:28-34) ending with a memorable dictum of Jesus; and miracle stories (Mark 5:22-43). This latter group was labeled "tales" by Dibelius. Both he and Bultmann think that their purpose was to extol the merits of Jesus as a hellenistic wonder-worker.[5]

3. The relative age and historical value of the Gospel units can be determined by using certain criteria for considering their antiquity and consequent veracity. Among these criteria are length (expansion denoting a later development and embellishment); names (addition indicating a later development and embellishment); and the presence of Semitisms (pointing to an earlier stage).[6]

4. Underlying the approach of form criticism is the doctrine of *Sitz im Leben*, the persuasion that each unit may be placed in an appropriate life-setting in the early church, and that this *Sitz* determined not only the form but shaped the content of the *pericope*.[7]

In spite of some adverse attitudes to form criticism, especially in its early years,[8] a number of its positive contributions to our understanding of primitive Christianity and its documents have come to be recognized.

4 V. Taylor, *The Formation of the Gospel Tradition.*

5 See, for a recent treatment, H. D. Betz, "Jesus as Divine Man," in *Jesus and the Historian*, ed. F. T. Trotter (1968), pp. 114-33. But see later, p. 220.

6 These criteria have recently been challenged by E. P. Sanders, *The Tendencies of the Synoptic Tradition* (1969), who shows that no cast-iron set of laws can be adhered to.

7 Here, too, there is a measure of truth and error. See T. W. Manson, *Studies in the Gospels and Epistles*, ed. M. Black (1962), pp. 5-8.

8 These reservations are voiced in F. J. Badcock, *ExpT*, 53 (Oct. 1941), 16ff.; and A. H. McNeile and C. S. C. Williams, *Introduction to the Study of the New Testament*[2] (1953), pp. 52-58.

1. Form criticism demonstrates that each unit links Jesus' words and deeds with the life and faith of his followers. It shows that early Christian witness was not oriented to the past, as though the church were continually harking back to some golden age when Jesus lived on earth. Quite the contrary: they were conscious of his living *presence*. The first believers did not understand Jesus as a "museum piece."[9] Form criticism is a timely recall of the living link between what Jesus had said and done long ago and what he was doing and saying in the ongoing life of the church.

2. The fact that the *pericopae* were preserved in the corporate life of the church is a check on a possible obsession with individual experience. The form critics emphasized that the Gospels were regarded as social possessions, embodying not the individual recollections of isolated pockets of believers but the corporate testimony of a witnessing and worshiping community. Here was a safeguard against the human possibility of turning a private, esoteric experience into a universal truth.[10]

3. Form criticism entered a protest against the tyranny of source criticism, and it corrected the mistaken notion that the evangelists were mere "scissors-and-paste" editors, handling texts and documents in an academic way. Rather, we are introduced to a living community pulsating with vitality, whose transcripts of united experience the Gospel writers record by their assembling of the current traditions.

4. Form criticism provides a hermeneutical key for our interpretation: namely, that the Gospels are religious documents, most appreciated when we bring to them a faith like that of their original writers and the community in which they worked.[11]

Still, some cautionary observations about the limits of the form-critical method are in order. E. Fascher has observed that form criticism offers a new and fine instrument in the Gospel historian' hand, but it is only one among many.[12]

1. The form critic's questionable denial of interest in th course of Jesus' ministry eventuates in historical skepticism, as repre sented by Norman Perrin, who confesses: "The most that the presen writer believes can ever be claimed for a gospel narrative is that it ma represent a typical scene from the ministry of Jesus."[13] This concl

[9] To use G. Bornkamm's vivid expression, *Tradition and Interpretation i Matthew* (ET 1963), p. 52.
[10] See F. C. Grant, *The Gospels* (1957), p. 1.
[11] C. H. Dodd, *About the Gospels* (1950), p. 22, referred to by J. L. Pric *Interpreting the New Testament* (1961), p. 159. Dodd writes: "Th Church not only remembered and reported facts. It lived them. If we hav understood this, we are near to the secret of the Gospels."
[12] *Die formgeschichtliche Methode* (1924), p. 228.
[13] *Rediscovering the Teaching of Jesus*, p. 29.

sion is reached by the use of criteria for authenticity which are too restricted[13a]; and it completely overlooks the controls provided by eyewitnesses. Dibelius was not guilty of such an omission, since he believed that the "paradigms" were assembled by those who had witnessed the events in Palestine.[14]

2. This leads directly to our second criticism: form criticism ignores the presence and influence of eyewitnesses (αὐτόπται; cf. Luke 1:2).[15] This omission can lead to the fallacy that communities, not individuals, write books,[16] and needs the challenge of Riesenfeld and Gerhardsson and the Scandinavian school of oral transmission.[17] We earlier (see above, p. 130) offered a critique of this approach, yet some value remains in the admission that there was direct continuity between the disciples of Jesus and the leaders of apostolic Christianity.

3. In its attempt to move from literary analysis to historical appraisal (*Sachkritik*) form criticism assumes a willingness on the part of early Christians to invent sayings of Jesus and retroject them into his public ministry. This facility is an unproven assumption of Norman Perrin, for example, who writes: "The early Church absolutely identified the risen Lord of her experience with the historical Jesus and *vice versa*."[18] T. W. Manson counters this with a call for historical examples. He points out that the Holy Spirit is much in evidence in Paul, but references to him in the Synoptic Gospels are few and far between.[19]

4. We may raise, finally, a question which strikes at the roots of form criticism's literary procedures. Is there any literature really comparable with the Gospels as far as literary genre is concerned? If not—and we may appeal to Amos N. Wilder for this view[20] —much of

13a For a recent discussion, see D. G. A. Calvert, "An Examination of the Criteria for Distinguishing the Authentic Words of Jesus," *NTS*, 18 (1972), 209-19.

14 See Kümmel's review, *The Journal of Religion*, 49 (Jan. 1969), pp. 59-66.

15 See T. F. Glasson, "Kerygma or Martyria?" *SJT*, 22 (Mar. 1969), pp. 90-95.

16 See R.M. Grant, *A Historical Introduction to the New Testament* (1963), p. 302.

17 Cf. B. Gerhardsson, *Memory and Manuscript;* and his *Tradition and Transmission* (1964).

18 *Op. cit.*, p. 26.

19 *Studies in the Gospels and Epistles*, p. 7.

20 Wilder maintains that the earlier form critics compared the Gospel literature to pagan Greek writings. "This proved on the whole a blind alley. The existing Greek literary forms were almost all sophisticated and artistic. They belonged to a different world. Even much Jewish literature in Greek—Josephus, the Letter of Aristeas, etc.—was determined by a professional literary tradition, and was consciously artistic and written for a wide public . . . [whereas] the primitive Christian writings from AD 50 to as late as 160 . . . fall outside the history of literature properly so called. They were sub-literary products and naïve in the best sense"; *The Language of the Gospel* (1964), p. 44.

the analytical work is called in question, though formal similarities remain.

REDACTION CRITICISM

Markan scholarship moved decisively beyond form critical evaluation with the ground-breaking proposals of Willi Marxsen.[21] The form critics had been concerned mainly with the literary structure and "type" of the individual units which made up the Gospels; thus their task was one of classification and analysis. But an indirect result of this was to cast the evangelists in a new role. If the several *pericopae* were only loosely strung together and existed as independent units or blocks, the work of the evangelist could be seen as more like that of a compiler than a creative writer. His task was thought of more as that of a collector of traditions, who put the units together into sections of teaching material, rather than as that of a Gospel-writer who designed a work from start to finish.

Since Mark is seen on this view[22] as an arranger of "essentially disconnected stories," which he strung loosely together and which in no sense formed an "outline" of the ministry of Jesus, it is not unnatural that his identity should be virtually lost in a welter of separate traditions of which he is the purveyor. Redaction criticism now protests against this understanding of the evangelist's role, and calls for a more constructive appreciation of what the Gospel writers were seeking to do in arranging the traditions they took over.

A programmatic statement by G. Bornkamm was given in his 1956 essay "End-Expectation and Church in Matthew."[23] Commenting on the "new direction" in which form critical research must be continued, Bornkamm expounded the meaning of "editorial criticism":

> The Synoptic writers show—all three and each in his own special way—by their editing and construction, by their selection, inclusion and omission, and not least by what at first sight appears an insignificant, but on closer examination is seen to be a characteristic treatment of the traditional material, that they are by no means mere collectors and handers-on of the tradition, but are also interpreters of it.

The last few words give the clue to the new understanding of the Gospel writers' role. The aim and intention of a *redaktionsgeschichtlich* treatment of the Gospels is to overturn the dictum of Hoskyns and Davey that "the evangelists write as historians and not as theolo-

21 *Der Evangelist Markus* (1956; ³1959); ET *Mark the Evangelist* (1969).

22 Represented most recently by D. E. Nineham's 1963 Pelican commentary *Saint Mark*.

23 The essay originally appeared in German in *The Background of the New Testament and its Eschatology. Festschrift C. H. Dodd* (1956), pp. 222-69; now it appears in translation in *Tradition and Interpretation in Matthew*, pp. 15-51.

gians."[24] The evidence for this reversal lies in what is called the *Tendenz* of the Gospel material. Why are certain incidents included in the way they are? Why are they couched in the particular language used? Evidence is also found in the telltale clues of editorial redaction seen in the "seams" or connecting links between the *pericopae* and in the alterations, adaptations, and emphases the evangelists have made to the *pericopae* they have received and used.

On a broader front, the discipline and method of redaction criticism has addressed itself to the following issues.[25]

1. Attention is shifted from the small, independent units into which form criticism had separated the Gospel materials to the Gospels as literary wholes.

2. As a result of this change of perspective, the evangelists emerge from the role of simple collectors and handers-on (*Tradents*) of the material they assemble and are reinstated in their own right as authors, who by their selecting and editing of the material impose on that material a distinctive theological stamp. In a phrase used by J. Rohde, they do not simply hand on the story, but by placing it in a particular context and editing its details they become the earliest exegetes of it.[26]

3. We are invited to penetrate beneath the layers of those Gospel data which can be identified as traditional and to seek the elements of the evangelists' editorializing work. We are encouraged to enter and explore the world of the evangelist himself—or more plausibly the community of which he was a member—and seek to understand what the Gospel sections *and the completed whole of the Gospels* would have meant in those situations.

4. So we are bidden to inspect the "third life-setting" of the Gospels,[27] the setting which provides explanatory contexts for the evangelist's own work. For Marxsen this entailed a study of the historical and theological background which provoked the evangelist to publish his literary work under the novel caption "Gospel." Marxsen needed to find the "occasion," which he called a catalyst, required to cause the author to assemble, edit, and then make public in written form what we know as a Gospel. Assuming that Mark had before him a collection of loosely connected sections of narrative and teaching, what impulse moved him to set them into a coherent pattern which conveyed a unified message? It cannot have been by accident that his

24 *The Riddle of the New Testament*, p. 147.

25 For fuller details see J. Rohde, *Rediscovering the Teaching of the Evangelists* (ET 1968); R. H. Stein, "What is Redaktionsgeschichte?" *JBL*, 88 (1969), 45-56; and N. Perrin, *What is Redaction Criticism?* (1969).

26 *Op. cit.*, p. 12; cf. p. 20.

27 For this analysis, see Marxsen, *op. cit.*, p. 23. The first and second *Sitze im Leben* are Jesus' own earthly life and that of the primitive church which transmitted the tradition.

Gospel was born, for "it is not at all obvious that this totally disparate material should finally find its way into the unity of a Gospel."[28]

The precise historical event and its attendant theological ramifications to which Marxsen looked in defense of his view that Mark published his Gospel at the outbreak of the Jewish War in AD 66 will be considered in a later section. But redaction criticism does not stand or fall by the correctness of this part of Marxsen's thesis. His innovation was to rescue Mark's Gospel from a piecemeal form critical dissection. By reinstating it as the work of a theological author, he has enabled us to stand back from the Gospel and see its architecture and message as a whole rather than being concerned with the minutiae of the structure, size, and shape of each pre-Markan brick and with the constituency of the cement and mortar.

In addition to Marxsen's study of the Second Gospel, we may note in passing two other studies in redaction criticism of the Gospels. G. Bornkamm has applied the insights of this method to the Gospel of Matthew.[29] He believes that the author of the First Gospel was a hellenistic Jewish Christian whose work has a twofold situation in focus—Pharisaic Judaism in the period after the fall of Jerusalem in 70; and hellenistic Christianity, for which the law had lost its validity and whose attention was focused on the heavenly *kyrios*.

The Third Gospel has also been the subject of examination from a redaction critical point of view. H. Conzelmann's study of Luke shows him to be a theologian reflecting on Mark, yet modifying the earlier Gospel in a number of significant ways.[30] Conzelmann sees Luke as having set out to write a "Life of Jesus," adopting the conscious role of a historian (though not in the modern sense). He notes Luke's interest in geography and travel, which he uses to produce a coherent narrative which is still theologically oriented to a salvation-history scheme. According to Conzelmann, the key to Luke's thought is the recession of the hope for the imminent appearance of Christ. In its place Luke has put a salvation-history program, which proceeds by stages. The key verse he sees as Luke 16:16, which suggests a threefold schema: (1) the time of Israel (the law and the prophets); (2) the time of Jesus, of dawning salvation;[31] (3) the time of the church, between the ascension and the parousia, which is open-ended, yet not short.[32]

28 *Ibid.*, p. 17.
29 Bornkamm, *Tradition and Interpretation in Matthew.*
30 Conzelmann, *The Theology of St. Luke.* For a critique, see H. Flender, *St. Luke: Theologian of Redemptive History* (ET 1967); and I. Howard Marshall, *Luke: Historian and Theologian* (1970).
31 Hence the title of Conzelmann's book in German, *Die Mitte der Zeit* (the middle of time).
32 See pp. 246f. for a more extended consideration and critique of Conzelmann's thesis.

CHAPTER ELEVEN

The Synoptic Problem

Luke 1:1-4 witnesses to the work of "many" who were Luke's predecessors in the field of Gospel composition. Just how many such accounts were in existence when Luke wrote we do not know. Of one Gospel account we have sure knowledge—Mark. Two centuries of source criticism have inspected the first three Gospels and reached the fairly unanimous conclusion that the measure of agreement between Matthew, Mark, and Luke can be explained only as the result of literary interdependence.

Comparative study of the three Gospels reveals both differences and similarities among them. The "synoptic problem," then, is basically the question of how these similarities and differences can be explained most satisfactorily. The story of the synoptic problem may be divided into three stages.[1]

1. *Pre-critical explanations*, which were offered early in church history in the interest of harmonization (Tatian) or simplicity (e.g., Augustine, who said that Mark came after Matthew and shortened his work).

2. Later *appeals to the unknown*, whether in the form of an oral gospel (Herder, 1796; Gieseler, 1818) adapted by the evangelists to their particular needs or early collections of apostolic fragments (Schleiermacher, 1817) or an original gospel (*Urevangelium*) now unhappily lost but surviving in our canonical records (Michaelis, 1777; Lessing, 1778). The common assumption of these hypotheses—that there was a foundation document on which the evangelists drew as they rendered this basic source into Greek or into a Gospel suited to their constituents' needs—faces a large objection: that numerous strict correspondences between the three Gospels *in Greek* presuppose an interdependence rather than an independent drawing on a basic docu-

[1] More detail is supplied in W. G. Kümmel, *Introduction to the New Testament*[14] (ET 1966), pp. 37ff.; and D. Guthrie, *New Testament Introduction*[3] (1970), pp. 123ff.

ment. The common order of events in Jesus' life—even extending to trivial details—is a point against all forms of tradition-theory, as Hoskyns and Davey note.[2]

3. *Notions of interdependence.* These began in 1789 with J. J. Griesbach, who sought to show that one Gospel used others. Griesbach arrived at the order Matthew—Luke—Mark. On this foundation of a comparative method Lachmann (1835) reached a better solution: Mark—Matthew—Luke, by announcing the priority of Mark and the dependence of the other two Gospels on it. Lachmann's work was given classic shape by Holtzmann (1863), who asserted the priority of Mark (or an original version of Mark called *Urmarkus*); the use of Mark as a source by Matthew and Luke; and the existence of a common source used (later) by Matthew and Luke.[3]

MARKAN PRIORITY

The case for regarding Mark's Gospel as the first of the three synoptics to be written is cumulative and progressive. It rests on the following data and their interpretation.

1. *Common subject matter.* Mark has 661 verses, of which 601 are found in Matthew and Luke. Matthew reproduces 90% of Mark's material; Luke over 50%. Only three or four of Mark's 88 *pericopae* are missing from the other two synoptics.[4]

2. *Common outline and order.* The sequence of Mark's narrative is supported by one or both of the synoptics. Wherever Matthew or Luke departs from Mark, the other is usually found supporting him; and there is no case in which Matthew and Luke agree in point of arrangement against Mark. The parallelism in the order of Matthew and Luke begins where Mark begins and ends where Mark ends.[5]

3. *Common usage of language.* Matthew usually abbreviates Mark's literary style, yet he employs 51% of the actual words of Mark. Luke similarly shows a literary dependence on Mark's vocabulary, reproducing 50% of his words.

4. *Rare constructions and unusual words.* Some of these unusual Markan usages are retained by Matthew and Luke. When there is "improvement," it is always by Matthew of Mark, or by Luke of

[2] *The Riddle of the New Testament,*[3] p. 76. Comparing Mark 10:13-34, Matt. 19:13—20:19, and Luke 18:15-34, they comment: "Such identity of order cries out for some explanation other than that three evangelists wrote three independent narratives."

[3] There were further modifications of this thesis in B. H. Streeter, *The Four Gospels* (1924); and F. C. Grant, *The Gospels.* Both argue for a "four document" or "multiple source" hypothesis. We will treat this variation later, pp. 151ff.

[4] Cf. H. B. Swete, *The Gospel According to St. Mark*[3] (1927), p. lxix.

[5] As the tables in Kümmel, *op. cit.,* pp. 46f., show.

Matthew and Mark.[6] This is a decisive point against the oral theory.

5. *The meager agreement between Matthew and Luke* in the triple tradition. Luke's agreement with Matthew against Mark is especially small—a mere 6%.

6. *The Markan style.* Styler argues that "of all the arguments for the priority of Mark, the strongest is that based on the freshness and circumstantial character of his narrative."[7] There are cases in which Mark's ruggedness (2:7) or embarrassing statements (6:5) or use of material open to ambiguity (8:31-37) is either modified (Matt. 13:58) or omitted altogether.

7. In at least one place Matthew shows that he is following Mark. In Matthew 14:3-12 the author slips in the appellation king to describe Herod. This seems clearly to be drawn from Mark 6:17-29.

Still, a few obstacles remain to a full acceptance of Markan priority.[8] In the first place, why would Luke apparently omit all reference to the contents of Mark 6:45—8:26 if he had our canonical Mark in front of him?[9] A number of suggestions have to do with the contents of Luke's copy of Mark's Gospel. A later hand, it is argued, may have added this section to Mark after Luke had used an earlier draft. However, there is no textual dislocation and the style is uniform. Another argument is that Luke perhaps used a mutilated copy of Mark.[10] Or, it has been suggested that Luke's version of Mark followed a particular textual tradition, such as a Caesarean[11] or a Western text.[12] Another hypothesis is that Luke used an otherwise unattested version of Mark, which omitted this passage.[13] This, however, is an argument from ignorance.

Some other suggestions are that the section was deliberately omitted by Luke because he had an aversion to adding "doublets" (*two* feedings, *two* walkings on water). So argues H. Schürmann.[14] Yet there are doublets in Acts (e.g., 10—11), though not quite the same

6 For instance, κράββατος in Mark 2:4ff. is improved by κλίνη (Matt. 9:2ff.). κράββατος, meaning a poor man's pallet, is a Macedonian loanword (Moulton-Milligan, *Vocabulary of the Greek New Testament*, p. 357). Similarly, in point of grammar, ἐφυλαξάμην ("I kept") in Mark 10:20 is corrected to ἐφύλαξα (with the same meaning but the more usual form of the past tense) in Matt. 19:20.

7 G. M. Styler, in C. F. D. Moule, *The Birth of the New Testament*, p. 230.

8 For an extended critique of the priority of Mark, see D. Wenham, "The Synoptic Problem Revisited: Some New Suggestions about the Composition of Mark 4:1-34," *TB*, 23 (1972), 3-17. But see n. 21.

9 Cf. Kümmel, *op. cit.*, p. 49: "The omission . . . is . . . puzzling." See also H. Conzelmann, *The Theology of St. Luke*, pp. 52-55.

10 Streeter, *op. cit.*, pp. 76ff.

11 J. P. Brown, "An Early Revision of the Gospel of Mark," *JBL*, 78 (1959), 215ff.

12 T. F. Glasson, *ExpT*, 55 (1944), 180-84.

13 So B. Reicke, *The Gospel of Luke* (1965), p. 35.

14 "Die Dublettenvermeidungen im Lk," *ZKTh*, 76 (1954), 83ff.

kind as in Mark 6—8. Perhaps the section was accidentally omitted by Luke by what textual critics call haplography, in which the reader's eye wanders from one incident to a similar one in a later part of the book. The suggestion is that Luke's eye jumped from Mark 6:42-44 to 8:19-21. Or, because Mark's narrative takes Jesus on a long journey to the north and west (Tyre and Sidon), Luke may have omitted the section in order not to break his journey motif en route to Jerusalem (9:51).[15]

A second question posed to the advocates of Markan priority is how one explains the agreements of Matthew and Luke against Mark in the triple tradition? This teasing question was first posed by F. C. Burkitt.[16] He explained many of the agreements as due to grammatical and stylistic variants (e.g. Matt. 7:16 = Luke 6:44); or else scribal and editorial corrections may account for them.[17] In any case, the number of such passages is very small and insignificant.[18]

Since some doubts about Mark's priority do linger, we may look briefly at the viable alternatives that have been proposed.

1. B. C. Butler accepts the link between Peter and John Mark, and explains the freshness of Mark's style in this way, but argues that Peter had access to Matthew's Gospel while speaking, and that this access has led to Mark's freshness.[19]

2. L. Vaganay postulates two main sources of our Gospels—Q in Greek, and an Aramaic source which later became our Matthew.[20] Once this is granted, neither Matthew nor Luke need have used Mark as a source, though Vaganay supposes that Luke did in fact do so.

3. W. R. Farmer offers the most thoroughgoing critique of Mark's priority. In fact, he wishes to revert to Griesbach's order by placing Mark last.[21] This is a prime example of *reductio ad absurdum*, and puts his whole method in doubt. Farmer appeals to three arguments: verbal agreements of Matthew and Luke against Mark; the reflection of Mark's order in Matthew and Luke and the consideration that both of them never diverge from it at the same time; and features in Mark which he says betray lateness and align it with second-century apocryphal Gospels.

[15] G. H. P. Thompson, *The Gospel according to Luke* (1972), p. 20.

[16] *The Gospel History and its Transmission* (1906), pp. 42-58.

[17] K. and S. Lake, An *Introduction to the New Testament* (1938), pp. 6f.

[18] See N. B. Stonehouse, *Origins of the Synoptic Gospels* (1963), pp. 61-63.

[19] Butler, *The Originality of St. Matthew* (1957). He follows a line pursued earlier by J. Chapman, *Matthew, Mark, Luke: A Study in the Order and Interrelation of the Synoptic Gospel* (1937).

[20] Vaganay, *Le problème synoptique* (1954). L. Cerfaux, *The Four Gospels* (ET 1960), argues similarly, though placing the Greek Matthew later than Mark.

[21] Farmer, *The Synoptic Problem.* For a devastating review of Farmer's work, see F. W. Beare in *JBL*, 64 (1965), 292-97; cf. the editorial review in *ExpT*, 77 (1965), 1-3. For a recent treatment of Markan priority, see C. H. Talbert and E. V. McKnight, "Can the Griesbach Hypothesis Be Falsified?" *JBL*, 91 (1972), 338-68. Their answer is Yes.

Farmer's first two considerations can be explained as well on the basis of Markan priority. His third argument strains credulity to the limit. It is by no means cogent to insist with Farmer that lifelike details, the use of people's names, and Aramaisms are signs of lateness. A final—and fatal—objection to Farmer's arrangement of Gospel sequence is that the scheme makes it too difficult to account for Mark's appearance at all. Vividness and freshness are not to be secured by copying extant materials.

THE PROBABILITY OF Q

The presence of an underlying source, mainly composed of sayings of Jesus, behind the Gospels of Matthew and Luke is the hypothesis of Q (so named because it is the first letter of the German word *Quelle*, "source" or "spring"). The existence of this common body of teaching, from which the two evangelists have drawn, is inferred from an inspection of those passages where the Matthew and Luke columns of a Gospel synopsis run in close parallel. The supposition of Q has, however, come under close and critical scrutiny in the last few decades. Some opponents of the theory have in recent years become so emotionally stirred as to register their disavowal of the hypothesis in terms like "unnecessary and vicious"[22] and with the comment that " 'Q' stands for 'quirk' and should be wholly forgotten and promptly dispatched to the limbo of forlorn hypotheses."[23]

The arguments for the postulate of Q's existence may be set down as follows:

1. There is in the synoptic tradition a quantity of common matter found in the Gospels of Matthew and Luke. Out of more than two hundred verses where a measure of correspondence has been found, there are several cases in which the agreement is verbally exact. We may cite Matthew 3:7-10 = Luke 3:7-9, which has a precise agreement of 63 words, with only minor variations within the text. Other instances of such parallel reporting—and, in some cases, verbatim correspondences of the words used—are Matthew 7:7-11; 11:4-6; 12:43-45; 24:45-51; and parallels.

On the other hand, there are cases where the two Gospels diverge when reporting what are ostensibly the same accounts of Jesus' teaching. Vincent Taylor has examined these passages and suggested four reasons for the divergence. First, there may be editorial modifications. Each evangelist had the liberty of making minor editorial alterations in transmitting the text. A second source of differences may be different recensions. One may cite here Matthew 5:3f. and Luke 6:20f., and the two versions of the Lord's Prayer (Matt.

[22] B. C. Butler, *op. cit.*, p. 170.
[23] C. S. Petrie, " 'Q' Is Only What You Make It," *NovT*, 3 (1959), 28-33.

6:9-15 and Luke 11:2-4).[24] G. Bornkamm uses this flexibility to argue that "Q is still relatively close to the oral tradition, and remained exposed to its continuing influence."[25] A third explanation for the cases where there are parallel versions of the same report yet no exact correspondence in the wording is that these may be places where Q and Matthew's special source (sometimes called M) have overlapped. Then, Luke has followed Q and Matthew has preferred M. Finally, the idea of a composite Q document has been proposed to account for the discrepancies between Matthew and Luke. The theory is that there were two editions of Q, an Aramaic source R (showing variations between Matthew and Luke) and T (where there is close agreement). This view has been criticized severely;[26] but in a modified form it has been refurbished in the more recent idea that Matthew's Q is a Greek production, whereas Luke's Q is a primitive translation from Aramaic.[27]

2. Between the two Gospels the order is in the main the same where they record common teaching, but there are divergences. This has raised the question of which order is to be preferred. The main evidence shows that Luke's sequence is the more compact and unified, while Matthew's teaching is scattered throughout his Gospel. Some have tried to show that Matthew's version of Q is contained in the blocks of his teaching, and that each Q section ended with the same formula ("When Jesus had completed all these sayings").[28] But the Lukan insertions of Q seem to have kept the order in a better state of preservation, because his editorial procedure is less open to obvious influence (e.g., ecclesiastical and liturgical) than Matthew's.[29]

3. What W. G. Kümmel regards as "the decisive proof" for Q's existence lies in the presence of the double tradition—the sayings that occur twice in the synoptics, of which one example comes from Mark and the other apparently not. Hence, it is concluded that the second must come from a source that contains an independent tradition, which is Q.[30] The data can be best appreciated in a table. The left-hand column shows the texts in the triple tradition (Mark, Matthew and Luke); the right-hand side indicates the same saying found elsewhere in the double tradition.

24 See for the different tendencies of the prayer J. Jeremias, *The Lord's Prayer* (ET 1964).

25 *Jesus of Nazareth*, p. 218.

26 See T. W. Manson, *The Sayings of Jesus*, pp. 20f.

27 M. Black, *An Aramaic Approach to the Gospels and Acts*[3] (1968), pp. 270ff.

28 See A.H. McNeile and C.S.C. Williams, *Introduction to the Study of the New Testament*,[3] p. 81.

29 V. Taylor, "The Original Order of Q," *New Testament Essays in Memory of T. W. Manson*, ed. A. J. B. Higgins (1959), pp. 246-69.

30 W. G. Kümmel, *op. cit.*, p. 52. For an earlier announcement of this conclusion cf. J. C. Hawkins, *Horae Synopticae*[2] (1909), pp. 80ff.

Triple Tradition	Double Tradition
Matt. 13:12; Mark 4:25; Luke 8:18	Matt. 25:29; Luke 19:26
Matt. 16:24f.; Mark 8:34f.; Luke 9:23f.	Matt. 10:38f.; Luke 14:27; 17:33
Matt. 16:27; Mark 8:38; Luke 9:26	Matt. 10:32f.; Luke 12:8f.
Matt. 24:9, 13; Mark 13:9, 13; Luke 21:12, 17, 19	Matt. 10:19f., 22; Luke 12:11f.

As a result of this investigation, reconstructions of Q (see pp. 150f. below) consist entirely of teaching, with a negligible amount of narrative. Most scholars agree that there was no passion story.[31] This raises a large question: What purpose did Q serve?

T. W. Manson has confidently suggested four answers.[32] Q was written as a manual of pastoral care; to show the personal interest of the disciples in the Master; for its apologetic value in the Gentile mission; and to demonstrate the need for the Palestinian community to defend itself. Of these the first is believed to be the most powerful.

Tödt has criticized Manson, reasoning from the absence of a passion story in Q to the conclusion that Q's theology is "kerygma-less," belonging to a different theological world from Mark, and offering a rival Christology and a different doctrine of salvation.[33] Specifically, Tödt argues that Q has an interest in Jesus as the Son of Man who fulfils Psalm 118:21ff. But this Christology is based on an understanding of salvation that sees Jesus as the exalted Son rather than the one who atoned by his death for his people's sins. Furthermore, Tödt contends, Q emphasizes the words of Jesus (against Mark and Paul who offer a theologoumenon of redemption). And, according to Q's teaching on the future, the vindication of Son of Man is awaited in the future parousia (as in Acts 3:20ff.). But this postulate of a rival kerygma is doubtful, for the only early Palestinian church we know of is already confessing Christ crucified (1 Cor. 15:3-5).[34]

Since the case for Q's existence is uncertain, we should pause to consider some counter-arguments.

1. There have been doubts over the contents of Q. There are no agreed limits to the Q material, and it is difficult to see any inner coherent structure to the material proposed as belonging to it. It looks like a ragbag of "odds and ends"; and this feature is offered as an argument against it.

2. There is no certainty as to the order of its sections. Luke's order is usually accepted as more reliable (i.e., better preserved) than

[31] For a contrary opinion, see F. C. Burkitt, *The Earliest Sources for the Life of Jesus*[2] (1922), pp. 103-106.

[32] *The Sayings of Jesus*, pp. 15ff.

[33] H.E. Tödt, *The Son of Man in the Synoptic Tradition* (ET 1965), pp. 241ff.

[34] So Kümmel, *op. cit.*, p. 56. But this is criticized by D. Lührmann, *Die Redaktion der Logienquelle* (1965), pp. 94f., since in his view Q is the product of the hellenistic church. See later, p. 149.

Matthew's, but there is a case for Matthean superiority.[35] If this latter is correct, it would stultify the case for Q, for it would mean that Luke drew on Matthew.[36]

3. The conclusion has been drawn that Luke did in fact use Matthew's Gospel. This is Austin Farrer's contention in his well-known essay "On Dispensing with Q,"[37] and some Roman Catholic scholars argue that Luke used a "proto Matthew" in Aramaic.[38]

4. Farrer argues that there are no precise contemporary parallels to the type of document Q is supposed to be. The nearest extant one is the *Gospel of Thomas* in the Jung Codex, yet there are still differences, not least in the matter of the respective *Gattung* or literary form and usage of the two "documents."[39]

5. If Q did exist, why was it allowed to disappear? T. W. Manson replies that the early Christians had no interest in archives.[40] Yet so indispensable a collection of *logia* of Jesus as Q is depicted to have been may well have had antiquarian interest, and it would hardly be so lightly valued as to be allowed to perish as a separate document.

6. An argument partly from evidence and partly from logic is elaborated by T. R. Rosché, who points to the unusual methods employed in Matthew and Luke's preservation of Jesus' sayings in Q as over against the other methods used in handling sayings in Mark.[41]

We may conclude that many scholars today speak less confidently of Q as a document, preferring to call it a "layer of tradition" or "stratum,"[42] or even a cipher for oral material found in Matthew and Luke.[43] Perhaps the best summary is that of W. L. Knox:

> It is necessary to insist that Q is simply a hypothetical document; its claim to have existed rests on its being the best hypothesis to explain the fact that there is much material to be found in these two Gospels [Matthew, Luke] which shows so close a resemblance of wording (sometimes amounting to complete identity) that it must have been derived by both of them from a common written source, or at least an oral source which was regarded as authoritative and memorized by Christian teachers.[44]

35 Stated by McNeile and Williams, *op. cit.*, p. 81.
36 D. Guthrie, *op. cit.*, p. 150.
37 *Studies in the Gospels*, ed. D. E. Nineham, pp. 55-86.
38 So, e.g., L. Vaganay, *op. cit.*
39 On this question see the full discussion by J. M. Robinson, "LOGOI SOPHŌN: On the *Gattung* of Q," in *The Future of our Religious Past* (Bultmann *Festschrift*) (1971), pp. 84-130. See also R. McL. Wilson, " 'Thomas' and the Growth of the Gospels," *HTR*, 53 (1960), 231ff.
40 *The Sayings of Jesus*, pp. 19f.
41 "The Words of Jesus and the Future of the 'Q' Hypothesis," *JBL*, 79 (1960), 210-20. See also H. Palmer, *The Logic of Gospel Criticism* (1968), pp. 167ff. Rosché's article has been carefully and critically scrutinized by C. E. Carlston and D. Norlin, "Once More—Statistics and Q," *HTR*, 64 (1971), 59-78.
42 Cf. E. Fascher, *Textgeschichte als hermeneutisches Problem* (1953), p 76; M. Dibelius, *From Tradition to Gospel*, p. 235.
43 G. Bornkamm, *Jesus of Nazareth*, p. 218; see also R. H. Fuller, *The New Testament in Current Study* (1962), p. 88.
44 *The Sources of the Synoptic Gospels*, II (1957), 3.

There is considerable value in the existence of this layer of tradition, whatever its precise form.

1. Its early provenance, in a Palestinian setting, takes us back to the earliest type of Christianity.[45] Support for this assertion is found in Q's picture of Jesus' ministry, according to which the Jewish people, with their organized life in Palestine, seem very much "alive and well." Furthermore, the Q version of the mission charge (Luke 10:2-12) still restricts this mission to Israel (as in Matthew's archaic source, 10:5, 6; 15:21-28), though there are hints of an expansion (esp. in Luke 13:28-30). Also, Q's kerygma has links with the preaching immediately following Pentecost (Acts 2, 3), in which Isaiah 53 is not yet used as a passion text and, on the basis of Psalm 118:22ff., the resurrection is seen as a vindication of Jesus' claim. But this does *not* necessarily imply a rival kerygma, as Tödt's reconstruction would suggest.

2. The early Christians' desire to preserve the Lord's words is evidenced by Q, though there was no intention to codify his teaching or produce a verbally correct and rigid compendium.[45a]

3. Some attempt has been made to find a route back through Q to the historical Jesus. H. Schürmann argues that some of Q was collected during Jesus' ministry and used by the disciples in their preaching mission (Mark 6:7-13; Luke 10:1-12).[46]

4. An unsolved question is that of the extent of Q's knowledge of Jesus' mission. Some scholars are content to describe Q as a digest of the sayings of Jesus, much like the prophetic books of the Old Testament, which present the prophets' oracles with a minimum of narrative framework. These oracles are often introduced with an account of the prophet's call but they do not include any account of his death. So Q might be designated as "The Book of the Prophet Jesus."[47] E. Bammel, however, argues on the basis of Luke 22:29f. that Q is parallel with the testamentary literature of later Judaism (e.g., *Testament of the Twelve Patriarchs*) and that it contained a

[45] See R. N. Longenecker, *The Christology of Early Jewish Christianity* (1971).

[45a] The description of Q as catechesis needs modifying in the light of W. D. Davies' discussion, *The Setting of the Sermon on the Mount* (1964), pp. 366-86. He insists that the key to Q's chief emphases is the note of crisis that sounds throughout the material. This crisis is precipitated by Jesus' announcement of the New Age of grace, and centers in his person and claim. His position is well argued, though some doubts may be entertained over his method of comparing Q's so-called catechesis with the exhortation material in the epistles. It could be that the former belonged to the Palestinian church life, whereas the hortatory data in the Pauline and Petrine literature represent Christian ethical patterns adapted to life in Graeco-Roman society. The absence of points of contact, therefore, is more to be expected than wondered at.

[46] Set forth in his essay in *Der historische Jesus und der kerygmatische Christus* (1961), pp. 342-70; later reprinted in his *Traditionsgeschichtliche Untersuchungen zu den synoptischen Evangelien*.

[47] F. F. Bruce, *St. Matthew* (1970), p. 3.

passion story told in terms of a rejected son of man and a martyred teacher of wisdom, with the message of the cross spelled out in terms of an "example to be imitated."[48]

5. The issues of tradition and redaction have been raised in reference to Q. Recent studies have sought to locate the Q source in a suitable *Sitz im Leben* in the light of its theological motifs.[49]

P. Meyer sees Q's theology as that of a persecuted community undergoing vigorous opposition at the hands of Jews. The self-identity of the Q community is governed by the prototype of the prophets in the Old Testament, who also were rejected. The motifs of the document are consolation for the faithful and judgment on the enemies.

A. P. Polag distinguishes three phases in Q's Christology. The earliest step in the evolution of the tradition is the setting of the Q material in Jesus' own lifetime (specifically Luke 7:18-23 and parallels, and 11:14-23 and parallels); this is similar to Meyer's view. Here the emphasis falls on Jesus' activity and authority as heralding God's saving action. Jesus' ministry shows signs of God's saving power in the present; and he overcomes Satan by announcing a kingdom at hand. The call is to follow Jesus, and the judgment on Israel as a disobedient people is sounded. But no christological titles are found at this stage, and there is no interest in Jesus' person or his teaching about the future. The message is ethical in the sense that it enshrines Jesus' call to discipleship, which in turn is based on his authority.

At the resurrection, according to Polag, a new era opened. Here he corrects Tödt, for whom the resurrection meant simply a resumption in relations between Jesus and his followers. Polag argues that a new situation was created in the resurrection, marked by a more profound call to decision which was based on a renewed interest of the community in scriptural exegesis. This led to a renewal of the preaching to Israel and produced more interest in Jesus' enigmatic person and his relationship to God. Scriptural proofs were added, and to this second redaction the introductory *pericopae* (the Baptist's preaching and Jesus' temptations) were added, as were the final christological elements, such as the titles of sonship and the work of the Holy Spirit. The later redaction indicates a change of *Sitz im Leben* from a post-Easter setting to one which enlarges the circle of the Christian

48 E. Bammel, "Das Ende von Q," in *Verborum Veritatis: Festschrift G. Stählin* (1970), pp. 39-50.

49 See M. Devisch, "Le document Q, source de Matthieu. Problematique actuelle," in *L'évangile selon Matthieu. Redaction et Théologie*, ed. M. Didier (1972), pp. 71-97. The chief works discussed by Devisch are P. D. Meyer, *The Community of Q* (doctoral dissertation, Univ. of Iowa, 1967); A. P. Polag, "Zu den Stufen der Christologie in Q," *Studia Evangelica*, 6 (1968), 72-74; and D. Lührmann, *Die Redaktion der Logienquelle;* cf. P. Hoffmann, *Studien zur Theologie der Logienquelle* (doctoral dissertation Münster, 1968); and "Die Versuchsgeschichte und der Logienquelle," *Biblische Zeitschrift,* 13 (1969), 207-23.

mission (though it is still within Palestine) and takes in elements derived from the church's liturgy.

D. Lührmann sees eschatology as a deciding factor in Q's redaction. Prominent features are the teaching of Israel's opposition and of the impending salvation of the church as Jesus comes as son of man to save his people and to execute judgment on Israel. This eschatological perspective Lührmann dates after the Palestinian period of the church's life, and he maintains that Q picks up hellenistic traditions, which are evident in the "hellenized" theology of the christological confession (Luke 10:21f. = Matt. 11:25-27) and in the opposition to Israel from the Gentiles, a theme often referred to in Q. Interestingly, this interpretation is exactly the opposite of T. W. Manson's. The latter thought that Q had "a friendly attitude towards Gentiles"[50] and that its teaching contained a tacit invitation to them. The hellenistic origin of the final formulation of Q (AD 50-60) is opposed by P. Hoffmann, who argues that Q comes out of a nonviolent, nonrevolutionary Christian group, motivated by love for one's enemies and showing an aversion to the messianic struggle against Rome.

One of the most recent treatments of Q and its setting in early Christianity is that of Graham N. Stanton.[51] His chief contribution is an attack on Tödt's supposition that Q was composed with *one* specific purpose in mind. While it is shown that Q has a firm conviction regarding Jesus' role as "the coming one" and "the herald of good news to the poor" (Matt. 3:11f. = Luke 3:16f.; Matt. 11:2-6 = Luke 7:18-23) and announces Jesus, in the temptation story (Matt. 4:1-11 = Luke 4:1-13), as entering on his mission as God's son and servant, anointed with the Spirit, this picture is not incongruous with the possibility that the community behind Q may well have cherished materials which explained his rejection and passion. Stanton thus opposes the idea that Q's Christology was a passionless kerygma and argues that we must not conclude from the absence of a specific passion narrative in Q that the community was uninterested in the significance of Jesus' death and vindication. On the contrary, Q's interest in his resurrection and continuing presence as Son of Man requires that Q's community must have asked itself why Jesus had died.

The upshot of recent discussion is to postulate a much wider purpose for Q than Tödt, Lührmann and others have been willing to grant and to submit that Q may well have played a part in instructing members of the community as well as functioning as an evangelistic tool. Stanton wants to synthesize the earlier insight of T. W. Manson (whom he does not mention by name, however) with the kerygmatic purpose of Q suggested by Tödt and later writers.

50 *The Sayings of Jesus*, p. 20.

51 "On the Christology of Q," in *Christ and Spirit in the New Testament: Festschrift for C.F.D. Moule*, ed. B. Lindars and S.S. Smalley, pp. 27-42.

From the variety of these current proposals it is clear that the last word on Q has yet to be spoken. The Q source, in Devisch's words, has not yet yielded its final secrets.

THE CONTENTS OF Q

The following chart lists the sayings which may be thought of as constituting the Q source.

I. *The Preparation*
  A. John's preaching of repentance (Luke 3:7-9; Matt. 3:7-10)
  B. The temptation of Jesus (Luke 4:1-13; Matt. 4:1-11)

II. *Sayings*
  A. Beatitudes (Luke 6:20-23; Matt. 5:3, 4, 6, 11, 12)
  B. Love to one's enemies (Luke 6:27-36; Matt. 5:39-42, 44-48; 7:12)
  C. Judging (Luke 6:37-42; Matt. 7:1-5; 10:24; 15:14)
  D. Hearers and doers of the Word (Luke 6:47-49; Matt. 7:24-27)

III. *Narrative*
  A. The centurion's servant (Luke 7:1-10; Matt. 7:28a; 8:5-10, 13)
  B. The Baptist's question (Luke 7:18-20; Matt. 11:2, 3)
  C. Christ's answer (Luke 7:22-35; Matt. 11:4-19)

IV. *Discipleship*
  A. On the cost of discipleship (Luke 9:57-60; Matt. 8:19-22)
  B. The mission charge (Luke 10:2-16; Matt. 9:37, 38; 10:9-15; 11:21-23)
  C. Christ's thanksgiving to the Father (Luke 10:21-24; Matt. 11:25-27; 13:16, 17)

V. *Various Sayings*
  A. The pattern prayer (Luke 11:2-4; Matt. 6:9-13)
  B. An answer to prayer (Luke 11:9-13; Matt. 7:7-11)
  C. The Beelzebub discussion and its sequel (Luke 11:14-23; Matt 12:22-30)
  D. Sign of the prophet Jonah (Luke 11:29-32; Matt. 12:38-42)
  E. About light (Luke 11:33-36; Matt. 5:15; 6:22, 23)

VI. *Discourse Against the Pharisees* (Luke 11:37—12:1; Matt. 23)

VII. *Sayings*
  A. About fearless confession (Luke 12:2-12; Matt. 10:19, 26-33; 12:32)
  B. On cares about earthly things (Luke 12:22-34; Matt. 6:19-21 25-33)
  C. On faithfulness (Luke 12:39-46; Matt. 24:43-51)
  D. On signs for this age (Luke 12:51-56; Matt. 10:34-36; 16:2, 3)
  E. On agreeing with one's adversaries (Luke 12:57-59; Matt. 5:25, 26)

VIII. *Parables of the Mustard Seed and Leaven* (Luke 13:18-21; Matt 13:31-33)

IX. *Other Sayings*

A. Condemnation of Israel (Luke 13:23-30; Matt. 7:13, 14, 22, 23; 8:11, 12)
B. Lament over Jerusalem (Luke 13:34, 35; Matt. 23:37-39)
C. Cost of discipleship (Luke 14:26-35; Matt. 10:37, 38; 5:13)
D. On serving two masters (Luke 16:13; Matt. 6:24)
E. On law and divorce (Luke 16:16-18; Matt. 11:12, 13; 5:18, 32)
F. On offenses, forgiveness and faith (Luke 17:1-6; Matt. 18:6, 7, 15, 20-22)
G. The day of the Son of Man (Luke 17:23-27, 33-37; Matt. 24:17, 18, 26-28, 37-41)

FURTHER SYNOPTIC STUDIES

Let us look at some tentative conclusions so far reached in synoptic studies. With a large measure of consensus, the priority of Mark as the first of the Synoptics is accepted, as is the existence of a "sayings source" (whether written or oral) on which Matthew and Luke drew.

These relatively simple solutions were taken two steps further by B. H. Streeter in his Four Document Hypothesis and Proto-Luke theory, the latter defended and amplified by Vincent Taylor.[52] According to Streeter's version of the Proto-Luke theory, Luke first combined Q and his special source about AD 60, and some twenty years later expanded Q and L in compiling his Gospel. The Lukan passion narrative, he said, was composed by Luke, and is found to contain extracts from Mark.[53] Diagrammatically the advance from the two- to four-document theory may be seen thus:

Two Documents

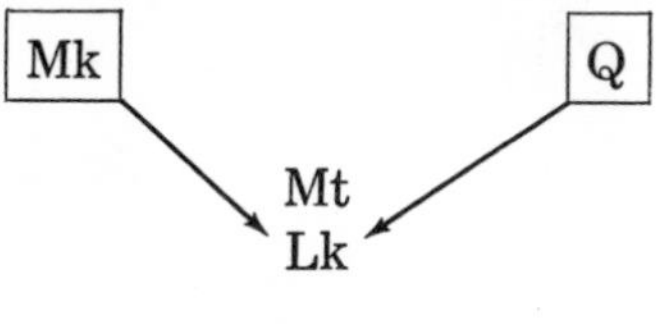

Four Documents

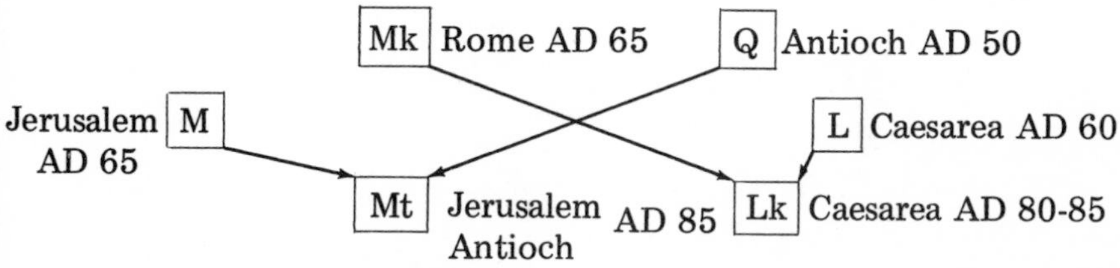

The three departures in synoptic studies associated with Streeter are: separation of material peculiar to Matthew (M) and Luke

52 Streeter, *The Four Gospels;* Taylor, *Behind the Third Gospel* (1926).
53 Streeter, *op. cit.*, p. 222.

(L); assignment of a place of origin for these sources in church centers;[54] and the postulate of an earlier draft of Luke's Gospel consisting of a joining of Q material plus Luke's special source at a time prior to Luke's use of Mark.[55]

About the Four Document Theory, we may remark that M cannot be demonstrated. It is best regarded as a body of tradition—oral or written—seen in distinction from Q. This view does justice to the data provided by this material (such as non-Lukan parallels to the Sermon on the Mount, ch. 5-7; the mission charge, ch. 10; the woes on the Pharisees, ch. 23; and Matthean parables and isolated sayings, 12:11, 12; 13:52; 15:22b-24; 18:15-22; 19:28), to the Judaic character of many texts, and to Matthew's literary methods. But L looks like a distinct stratum, composed of fourteen parables, various sayings (12:13-15; 13:1-5, 31-33; 14:7-14; 16:14f.; 22:24-30), and certain narratives (the widow of Nain's son, the mission of the seventy, Martha and Mary, the ten lepers, Zacchaeus, and parts of the passion narrative).

The Proto-Luke hypothesis seeks an explanation of the construction of the Third Gospel. Consider this simplified diagram of Luke, based on Vincent Taylor's analysis of the components of the Gospel:

BIRTH STORIES	Q + L	6:12—8:3	Q + L	9:51—18:14	Q + L	PASSION NARRATIVE

Almost all of the Markan material is set in four blocks, and is drawn from Mark 1:21—3:6; 4:1—9:40; 10:13-52 and 11:1—14:16. This is clear from Jeremias' revised diagram.[56]

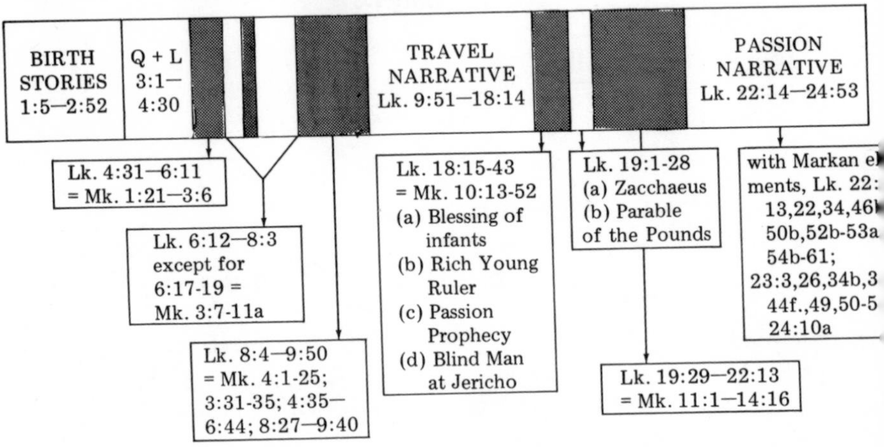

[54] *Ibid.*, p. 230. This notion was taken even further by F. C. Grant, *op. cit* p. 51.

[55] For a recent review of the birth of Proto-Luke theory and attitudes to i see V. Taylor, *The Passion Narrative of St. Luke*, ed. O. E. Evans (1972 ch. 1, 2.

[56] See J. Jeremias, *The Eucharistic Words of Jesus*, pp. 97f.

Prior to Streeter, the building of Luke had been schematized thus:

Lk = Mk (foundation) + Q (6:12—8:3) + L (9:51—18:14)
+ Birth Stories

Streeter reversed this, to read:

Lk = (Q + L) + (20 years later?) Mk + Birth Stories
Proto-Luke = 3:1—4:30; 5:1-11; 6:12—8:3; 9:51—18:14; 19:1-28, 37-44, 47, 48; 22:14—24:53

The conclusion is that, if Proto-Luke is proved, it is a document slightly earlier than Mark and completely independent of it. This is an important contribution to New Testament studies, for reasons we shall enumerate later.

We may now consider some of the arguments advanced for the Proto-Luke reconstruction of the growth of Luke's Gospel:[57]

1. The proportion of Markan material in Luke's Gospel is small, relative to the whole Gospel (the ratio is about 1:3).

2. The peculiar distribution of Markan and non-Markan material in alternate blocks contrasts with the situation in Matthew's Gospel, where the sources are woven together. Q material is found only in the passages represented by white spaces on our diagram, where it is combined with L. The inference may be drawn that Markan sections are "insertions" into an already existing whole.

3. From the content of the sections, Streeter and Taylor argue that Luke appears in the passion narrative to have added only short extracts from Mark to a non-Markan source,[58] while observing Mark's order.[59] This happens as well in Luke 21:12-38.[60]

4. Markan blocks in no sense form a continuous whole; they are rather "topical panels." Non-Markan sections, on the other hand, do present a continuous story (= white portions).[61]

5. The Proto-Luke hypothesis explains "Markan omissions" in Luke either because Luke preferred a parallel or similar version in (Q + L) or because he did not need the Markan matter omitted to expand his first draft.

[57] For a popular statement, see V. Taylor, *The Gospels*[5] (1945), pp. 38ff.

[58] In a final statement of his position, Taylor cites the following Markan elements in Luke—22:1-13, 22, 34, 46b, 50b, 52b-53a, 54b-61; 23:3, 26, 34b, 38, 44f., 49, 50-54; 24:10a; *The Passion Narrative of St. Luke*, p. 119. Cf. Streeter, *op. cit.*, p. 222.

[59] V. Taylor, The *Passion Narrative of St. Luke*, pp. 33, 124. Contrast W. G. Kümmel, *Introduction to the New Testament*, p. 94.

[60] See Taylor, *The Passion Narrative of St. Luke*, p. 32, drawing on *Behind the Third Gospel*, pp. 102-109. Statistical analysis, Taylor avows, proves "that on occasion Luke does insert extracts from Mark into non-Markan sources."

[61] Especially this may be demonstrated in the passion narrative; Taylor, *The Passion Narrative of St. Luke*, pp. 120f.

6. This hypothesis explains Luke's "new beginning" in 3:1ff., the genealogy after the first reference to Jesus *in that document* (Q + L) in 3:23-38, and does justice to the prologue (1:1-4) of Luke's Gospel and to his method of construction in the Book of Acts, where the "we-sections" are additions.

Recent study of the composition of Luke's Gospel[62] has focused on the themes of the passion narrative (Luke 22:14—24:53) as a test-case for the general hypothesis embracing the whole Gospel. J. Jeremias has concluded about the distinctive Lukan material of 22:14ff. that it "is no longer built upon a Markan basis but comes from *Urlukas*."[63] He maintains that "Luke incorporated the Markan material into his own and not *vice versa*."[64]

Source analysis has been undertaken by Schürmann and Rehkopf.[65] Schürmann concludes that the greater part of 22:14-38 derives from a special source; and he reduces the Markan element to a minimum of vv. 20b, 22, and 34. This conclusion does not materially prove the Proto-Luke theory, but it is consonant with it.[66]

Rehkopf casts a wider net and restates the Proto-Luke hypothesis, omitting only 6:17-19 from Streeter's allocation to (Q + L) and adding 21:34-38 to the composition. The passion narrative regarded as pre-Lukan is augmented by the inclusion of 22:21-23, and Rehkopf rejects the view that 22:14 and 33f. are based on Mark.[67] His concessions of Markan insertions in the Lukan passion narrative are limited to 22:20b, 26, and 52b-53a.

G. B. Caird refurbishes the hypothesis of Streeter and Taylor, and sets down seven considerations which seem to him to support the case for Proto-Luke, even if they lack the force of probative evidence.[68] He rightly focuses his interest on 3:1—4:30 and 22:14—24:53, and shows that the evidence is lacking to demonstrate that Luke has used Mark as a primary source in these sections. Rather, Luke's policy of editorial composition is better described as one of not having deliberately altered Mark's account in those places where there is an overlap. Instead, he has omitted Mark's version because of a preference for Q or his own special source (L). Thus, to give an example, the visit of Jesus to Nazareth is not a free rewriting of Mark

62 For a useful conspectus of this discussion see V. Taylor, *ibid.*, ch. 3.

63 Jeremias, *The Eucharistic Words of Jesus*, p. 99.

64 *Ibid.*, p. 99n.

65 H. Schürmann, *Quellenkritische Untersuchungen der lukanischen Abendmahlsberichtes Lk. XXII. 7-38* (1953-57); F. Rehkopf, *Die lukanische Sonderquelle* (1959).

66 See O. E. Evans's editorial note in Taylor, The *Passion Narrative of St. Luke*, p. 29, referring to H. Schürmann's review of Rehkopf's book, now reprinted as "Protolukanische Spracheigentümlichkeiten?" in *Traditionsgeschichtliche Untersuchungen zu den synoptischen Evangelien*, pp. 209-27.

67 *Op. cit.*, p. 30.

68 G. B. Caird, *Saint Luke* (Pelican Gospel Commentaries) (1963), pp. 23-27.

6:1-6 but an independent tradition derived from L. The same editorial policy is seen in 22:14—24:53, which shows a reliance on a non-Markan source, to which Luke has added occasional supplements from Mark.

Caird further bolsters these arguments from editorial procedure with some details. For example, whereas Matthew and Mark never use the title "Lord" (κύριος) of Jesus in their narratives, Luke does so fourteen times. This is Luke's handiwork, since it occurs in both Q and L, but it does not appear in the parts of the final edition of the Gospel where Luke's use of Mark has been suspected. Also, there is a variation in the use of other terms within the two strata of (Q + L) and Mark. Jewish lawyers are called νομικοί in the former, and γραμματεῖς in the Markan passages.

This leads Caird to the tentative conclusion that when he came into possession of the Gospel of Mark, Luke did not feel he should recast his existing framework (Q + L). Rather he inserted Markan panels into the existing sequence of the first draft of his Gospel. If the Proto-Luke hypothesis is rejected, Caird argues, we are left with the anomaly that Luke has "used wide editorial freedom in rewriting his sources,"[69] which is a feature not borne out by the evidence of other parts of Luke's compositional work.

Critical handling of the Proto-Luke hypothesis has centered on several diverse items:

1. Proto-Luke passages, often described as "a miniature Gospel," fail to live up to that title. They form only an amorphous collection of narrative and discourse. But Streeter never claimed that (Q + L) formed a complete Gospel, and his caution about this is confirmed by the absence of the noun εὐαγγέλιον in Proto-Luke.

2. Luke's use of Mark in the passion narrative is believed by some to be a fatal objection, since then it is more likely that Luke has enriched Mark with his own special material. But Taylor has shown that a concession that Luke knew and used Mark's framework is not damaging, and that the Markan verses are found in a series of short sections of the Lukan passion story, not spread evenly throughout it, as would be expected if Luke were embellishing an existing Markan document with his own insertions.

3. A denial of Luke's use of sources lies at the base of W. G. Kümmel's argument that the evangelist has drawn on a number of orally transmitted features or accounts and has transformed Mark's passion narrative on the basis of such tradition. This accords with the recent understanding of Luke as a creative writer, less bound to written tradition, who dealt flexibly with oral material, on which he imposed his own peculiar theological stamp. For example, the so-called "travel narrative" (9:51—18:14 or 19:27) is artificially con-

[69] *Ibid.*, p. 23.

structed. Also, on this view, Luke edited both Q and Mark to bring out his own *Tendenz.*[70] E. E. Ellis follows suit, contending that the work of Luke is a unity, conceived as such in the evangelist's mind.[71]

There are assessable values in the Proto-Luke hypothesis (or something like it), which we may briefly tabulate.

1. It picks up links with the Fourth Gospel, especially having to do with the passion, and to that extent witnesses to the existence of reliable traditions of the life of Jesus that are not found in Mark.[72]

2. It ties in with Pauline theology, especially in the Last Supper accounts. If the so-called Longer Text (Luke 22:19b-20) is accepted, this contains the command to repeat the celebration of the Lord's supper in remembrance of Jesus, as in 1 Corinthians 11:24, 25.

3. It suggests the existence of an authority comparable with Mark yet presenting more of a "life of Jesus," as evidencing early Christian interest in Jesus as a person, not simply a kerygmatic cipher.

4. It perpetuates a species of "primitive" Christology which proclaimed Jesus as son and servant (cf. Acts 2 and 3) and a soteriology (mainly based on Q) which echoes early Palestinian beliefs.

CONCLUSIONS ON THE SYNOPTIC PROBLEM

We shall now bring together several loose threads in the form of some tentative conclusions. First of all, in terms of literary analysis of the three synoptic Gospels, the *most* that can be affirmed is displayed schematically as follows:

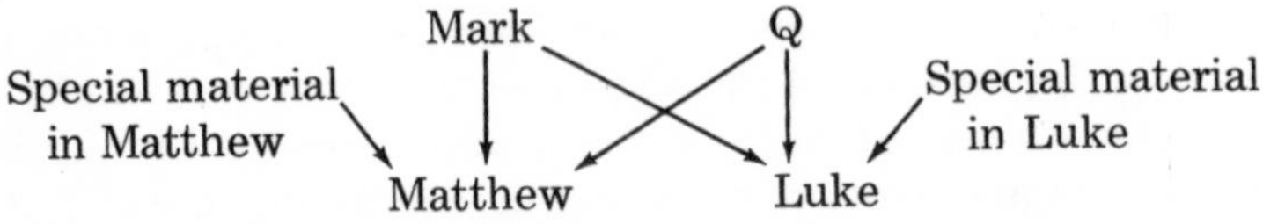

This chart would be misleading if it were seen to suggest that all the factors and sources in Gospel criticism are equally demonstrable. Obviously this is not the case. For example, the arguments for the priority of Mark are more defensible than those for the existence of documents (e.g., Q) or sources which *ex hypothesi* are unprovable. Before we begin talking about documents whose presence we can know only by inference, we must ask, What standard of proof should be required for reconstructed books?[73] It is usually assumed that if Q is acceptable to the documentary critic as the best explanation of the similarities and differences between Matthew and Luke, the historian

[70] W. G. Kümmel, *op. cit.*, pp. 93-95.
[71] E. E. Ellis, *The Gospel of Luke*, p. 27.
[72] See S. I. Buse, "St John and the Passion Narratives of St Matthew and St Luke," *NTS*, 7 (1960), 65-76.
[73] H. Palmer, *The Logic of Gospel Criticism*, p. 167.

should also accept that Q once existed as a book and should regrade his evidence accordingly. But by definition Q exists only as a material common to Matthew and Luke and is known inferentially. We can hardly ask the critic to produce it, for then it would not be "lost."[74] On the other hand, it is clearly insufficient merely to suppose that there must have been *somewhere* for the evangelists to get their stories. Other explanations of Matthew's and Luke's common material are possible. But are they as likely as the Q hypothesis? If we want to argue from Q, we must first show that this material belonged together in a document (but only if we are determined to insist that Q was a homogeneous corpus with definable limits). Finding literary unity is one thing; imposing a mechanical unity by our method of analysis is something different.[75]

Palmer's scrutiny of the logic needed to determine Q is a welcome clarification of the reasons many critics now avoid the logical impasse by admitting that Q is a convenient cipher for common material without maintaining that it once existed in tangible form. The most we can know about Q, L, and M is that they stand for traditions on which the evangelists drew, though they are *a priori* likely if we accept the main principles of redaction criticism, including the view that each Gospel is the deposit of church teaching in a given area or situation. Form criticism, too, adds its witness to a period in which oral tradition went through stages of modification, accretion, and collation.

A second point worth noting is that none of this represents testimony that is directly at first hand, with the possible exception of that which reached Mark through Peter (if we are to believe Papias) and the traditions of the apostle Matthew which the evangelist has incorporated into his Gospel. We may ask ourselves whether it is a loss that we have no stenographic typescript of Jesus' ministry and teaching; or, as Nineham argues, are we better placed to appreciate the ministry of Jesus when we read it through the later reporting of those who stood back from the events and therefore saw it in greater perspective?[76]

In the third place, the Gospel of Mark had not yet attained canonical status in this period, for the later evangelists felt free to adapt and alter his order and wording. Mark, itself a Gospel written to meet a specific situation in the church (at Rome?), is now subject to editorializing treatments by Matthew and Luke, though they do follow his main outline and direction.

74 A printing error in a recent book on the subject illustrates the point. In a diagram displaying the hypothetical sources of the synoptics, Luke's special source appears as "Photo-Luke." The question would not be so problematic if such photographic evidence were available!

75 Palmer, *op. cit.*, p. 171.

76 D. E. Nineham, "Eye-witness Testimony and the Gospel Tradition," *JTS*, 9.1 (1958), 13-25, 9.2 (1958), 243-52, 11.2 (1960), 253-64.

Students will need to ask whether Guthrie's treatment[77] really faces this fact of editorial adaptation and alteration. The conviction that the Spirit guided the evangelists cannot override the observable facts that there are many instances when the details of the same incident as recorded by the Gospel writers are given differently in the triple tradition, and Jesus' words are recorded in new situations and for different purposes. We should therefore inquire why this is so before seeking to frame a doctrine of a verbally correct Gospel record or attempting a forced harmonization.

Fourth, faced with the problems associated with divergent transmission of what appear to be details of the same story (e.g., the centurion's servant, the rich young ruler, and various healing accounts), we may most safely (if unexcitingly) admit that we simply do not know exactly what happened, that the data do not enable us to decide one way or the other.[78] Attempts at harmonization break down, and there is no easy way of fitting all the facts into a coherent and intelligible whole. Therefore we should conclude that the evangelists did not think it vitally necessary to record these stories in a verbally exact way and to follow their sources word-for-word. Let us look at this point in more detail.

1. We may speculate that the Gospel writers were theologically motivated and wished, by the form in which they tell the stories and by the way they angle the historical detail, to enforce a didactic point or a theological truth for the benefit of their audiences in the churches. But these are at best only conjectures, though in some cases (e.g., Matthew's interest in the law, Luke's universalistic teaching) theological *Tendenz* may be taken as highly probable.

2. Perhaps we should begin with the facts as we have them, namely, that the evangelists did not record the incidents and sayings of the men and women around Jesus in the same way because their supreme interest and concern lay in another direction. Those who appear on the stage of the gospel drama appear not for their own sakes but for the sake of Jesus, who is the chief *dramatis persona*. The evangelists can afford to differ over minor issues (how many blind men were there? were they met by Jesus before or after he entered Jericho? Matt. 20:29-34; Mark 10:46-52; Luke 18:35-43) because they wish to concentrate attention on the main event, Jesus himself.

Similarly, they can be loose in reporting the actual words spoken (what precisely did the young ruler say?) because they want to

[77] The discussion in D. Guthrie, *op. cit.*, pp. 230-36, is singled out for convenience since it is accessible to most students.

[78] D. E. Nineham recalls that "R. H. Lightfoot was often to be heard lamenting: 'If only they would say "we do not know".' New Testament scholars, he suspected, tend to have a false sense of obligation to decide definitely one way or the other even when the evidence does not really permit of such a decision." "... *Et hoc genus omne,*" in *Christian History and Its Interpretation: J. Knox Festschrift* (1967), p. 209.

focus on the punchline of the story, which is the saying of Jesus. This helps us see that the important thing for the first Christians was not that a Gentile came directly to Jesus or sent a delegation of Jews (though the variant tradition has a secondary importance for each evangelist's *Tendenz*) but Jesus' remark that he had not found faith like this man's in Israel. That was the saying which the evangelists cherished, irrespective of what they did editorially with the historical framework of the story.

3. A larger issue looms in the question whether the Gospel writers ever felt free to read back from the post-resurrection ministry of the Lord and the experience of the congregations any sayings of Jesus that we now find embedded in the context of the earthly ministry. A case in point is Matthew 18:15-20, which clearly has a later church situation in view. Is Jesus giving instruction in advance, or does this entire passage reflect the mind of the Lord communicated to the congregation through the prophets of the New Testament church in a way similar to the *verba Christi* recorded in Revelation 2-3? The former alternative, though possible, seems strange, for why should Jesus give a promise (Matt. 18:20) that can only be understood in the light of the later Christian experience of public assembly? So the question is left wide open. If we knew more about the authority of early Christian prophets (cf. the *Didache*), we would be better able to answer it. Perhaps, however, it is more academic than vital, since the words of Jesus are now embedded in canonical Scripture and for that reason gain their authority regardless of their origin, just as we read Revelation 3:20 as a true word of Christ today.

Our fifth conclusion from this look at the synoptic problem is that Mark is valued as the first written Gospel. The value of the theories of Q and Proto-Luke is that we are thereby introduced to an independent tradition, which is of comparable weight though coming out of a different milieu.

Sixth, the final product in the three completed Synoptics determines each of the *pericopae* that makes up that whole. In a sense this is arguing in a circle:[79] we know the meaning of each pericope from the larger whole and the whole is made up of the several parts. This is what form criticism has taught us; and it needs to be complemented by a redaction criticism which sees the evangelists as proceeding by selective emphasis,[80] adaptation, inclusion, and omission to place a theological stamp on the tradition they have received.

Finally, the aim of the evangelists is theological. That theological purpose is seen in the use to which they put the historical

[79] "There is no way of escape from the so-called 'hermeneutical circle'—the understanding of the whole from its parts, and of the parts in the light of the whole"; R. S. Barbour, *Traditio-Historical Criticism of the Gospels* (1972), p. 19.

[80] See B. Reicke, *The Gospel of Luke*, esp. pp. 72ff.

materials at their disposal. They interpret the material[81] in the light of their pastoral (Matthew), polemical (Mark), and apologetic (Luke) concerns. Christology, ethics, and theodicy are in the background of their evangelical task; and there is value in discovering a catalyst[82] or in investigating "adversary theology," i.e., the controversial situation the evangelists are addressing by way of exposure and corrective.

[81] Once more, the question comes down to the kind of history the Gospels contain. An earlier section used the phrase "interpreted" or "kerygmatic" history. That description can now be reinforced on the basis of our overview of synoptic study. A contemporary illustration may be helpful. In the reported dialogue between Judge Julius Hoffman and Norman Mailer at the "Chicago Seven" trial, Hoffman urged Mailer to stick to the facts.

Mailer: The facts, sir, are nothing without their nuances.

Hoffman: But you're too high priced a writer to give us all this detail for free. Just answer the questions. (Quoted in *The Guardian Weekly*, Feb. 7, 1970.)

The gospels offer us facts and their nuances; and there is no way of having the facts shorn of those interpretative meanings.

[82] See W. Marxsen, *Mark the Evangelist.*

CHAPTER TWELVE

An Introduction to Textual Criticism

The aim of the textual criticism of ancient literature may be stated succinctly: to deduce from all the extant material which is available what the original author wrote. Applied to the New Testament documents, textual criticism seeks to recover, as far as is possible, the original text of the New Testament writings. This purpose is given striking expression by one of the most distinguished names in modern textual studies. In a letter to his fiancée, Tischendorf declared this as his objective: "I am confronted with a sacred task, the struggle to regain the original form of the New Testament."

A couple of presuppositions underlie this goal, which has beckoned New Testament textual scholars for two hundred years. The first is that none of the original manuscripts of the New Testament has survived. Second is that before 1450—the date of the invention of printing by movable type—New Testament manuscripts were copies of copies, and this method of transmitting the text included the inevitable risk of error, especially when words were not separated. In these centuries there was no punctuation and no accentuation on the Greek letters. Moreover, scribes and copyists, in their endeavor to use all the available space on the papyrus and parchment, left no unfinished lines. The joining together of the letters in a cursive form of handwriting often made for ambiguity when a later scribe wished to know how the letters were to be divided to make a word.

On account of this, it is only to be expected that mistakes would creep in. The two obvious categories of such errors are accidental and deliberate, and we shall look at some examples of each. First, textual critics recognize five types of accidental errors:

TEXTUAL ERRORS

1. The technical terms used to describe mistakes in transmission accurately denote whether the scribe erred from defective hearing or defective eyesight. Mistakes of this kind are called itacism. Similar

vowel sounds could lead to confusion when the text was read aloud and the scribes relied on their hearing to record it. In Colossians 1:7 the texts divide between the readings of *ημεις* ("us") and *υμεις* ("you"). Romans 5:1 contains another example of this confusion between vowel sounds: the slight distinction between the long and short vowel sounds produces a difference in meaning: *εχομεν* ("We have") or *εχωμεν* ("Let us have"). Poor eyesight may account for other instances of confusion. Consider the Greek OC ("who") and $\overline{\Theta C}$ (a contraction of *θεός*, "God"). We can see from the apparatus attached to a critical edition of 1 Timothy 3:16 how these two conflicting readings could arise by the omission of the ligature (which is better attested) and the inclusion of a short stroke across the letter omicron to make it a theta.

2. When the scribe's eye inadvertently passed over from one word or phrase to another of similar form or sound (parablepsis), an omission would result known as haplography. A good example is found in Codex Vaticanus (B) at John 17:15, where the phrase *εκ του* before *κοσμου* has led to the omission of all that follows in view of a corresponding *εκ του* before *πονηρου*.

3. Another scribal quirk is caused by the reverse process. This is a doubling of words (dittography) as the writer's eye returns to the place he has just written down and he repeats himself. An example of this occurs at Romans 7:25 where one group of textual witnesses reads "Thanks to God" (*χαρις τω θεω*) and another group has *ευχαριστω τω θεω*. In all likelihood, the eye of the scribe whose work formed the basis for the later tradition deceived him into writing *τω* twice, and so he has manufactured a verb (*ευ*)*χαριστω* by the repetition of *τω*.

4. Homoioteleuton is an omission caused by the similar sound at the end of two phrases or lines. The example of haplography at John 17:15 in Codex Vaticanus given earlier contains the error of homoioteleuton as the scribe's eye passed from the first *εκ του* to the second *εκ του*, which stood like the first at the end of the line.

5. We should also include in the general category of mistakes due to accidental causes the possibility of total or partial destruction of the writing materials, which were made of perishable substances liable to rot when wet or damp and to become brittle and frayed when exposed to hot climatic conditions. Some papyrus leaves became frayed at the edges. The ink used by the scribes was a mixture of water and carbon (in the form of soot or lamp-black), and in time this would fade and the writing would naturally become illegible. These circumstances would produce a defective text. The most obvious instance is Mark 16:8, if it is the case that the authentic Markan ending has perished, leaving only a truncated form at verse 8a.

Under the heading of deliberate alterations we should include the following, recalling that the scribes also acted as editors and sought to add intelligibility to the task of reproducing faithfully what lay before them.

1. The most easily understandable method of securing an intelligible text was that of producing harmonization. In the accounts of Paul's conversion in Acts, the warning about "kicking against the goads" given in Acts 26:14 is carried backwards and inserted in the text of Acts 9:4 in order to secure a harmonious agreement. Similarly, Jesus' words at the Last Supper are brought into liturgical symmetry by some manuscripts; and Second Peter shows influences borrowed from Jude's epistle, where there is common matter.

2. More problematic is the presence of dogmatic tendencies, that is, alterations made for theological reasons. There are not many such tamperings with the New Testament text. The best-known example is the text of Matthew 1:16, where the Sinaitic Syriac text has the reading "Joseph to whom was betrothed Mary the virgin begot Jesus who is called the Christ." This text seems to reflect an Ebionite (i.e., Jewish Christian) tendency to regard Jesus as the natural son of Joseph.[1]

Other clear cases where the theological influence of the scribes may be suspected are in the area of moral teaching. At Hebrews 6:4 the bulk of the textual witnesses read *αδυνατον* (=impossible), indicating that there is no second chance for those who apostatize after baptism. The second-century *Shepherd of Hermas* discusses this issue, and promises one "second chance." This kind of pastoral problem seems to underlie the reading in Codex Claromontanus, which substitutes the Latin *difficile* to tone down the apparent rigorism of the best recoverable text.

Occasionally there are explanatory or qualifying additions inserted by a scribe who wished to leave the teaching in no doubt. An example of this is Galatians 3:1, where the phrase "that you should not obey the truth" is added; another is Romans 8:1 where certain traditions amplify what it means to be "in Christ" by expanding the text, "who do not walk after the flesh, but after the Spirit."[2]

These scribal additions probably began as marginal notes or comments. Later they were incorporated into the text. There are examples of another type of addition in Codex Bezae (see later p. 166), which adds after Luke 6:4: "on the same day, seeing one working on the sabbath day, he [Jesus] said to him, 'Man, if you know what you are doing, you are blessed; but if you do not know, you are accursed and a transgressor of the law.' "

[1] See J. N. Birdsall, in *The Cambridge History of the Bible*, I, *From the Beginnings to Jerome* (1970), 334. For a more recent discussion, see Bruce M. Metzger, "The Text of Matthew 1:16," in *Studies in New Testament and Early Christian Literature: Essays in honor of Allen P. Wikgren*, ed. D. E. Aune (1972), pp. 16-24.

[2] See M. A. King, "Should Conservatives Abandon Textual Criticism?", *Bibliotheca Sacra*, 130 (1973), 35-40.

In all, the variations supplied by these additions are not numerous, and the New Testament text is remarkably free from drastic interpolation and editorial overworking.

THE TASK OF TEXTUAL CRITICISM

To the question of how the text critic goes about his task, the answer may be found in Karl Lachmann's principles of textual criticism, enunciated by three Latin terms.[3]

1. *Recensio*. This is the process of setting the evidence in groups and working back from recent to most ancient forms by observation of common errors. This leads to the discovery of "text-types." B. F. Westcott and F. J. A. Hort pioneered here, producing the following scheme:

WESTCOTT-HORT'S RECONSTRUCTION (1881)
of Text-Types *(Stemma)*

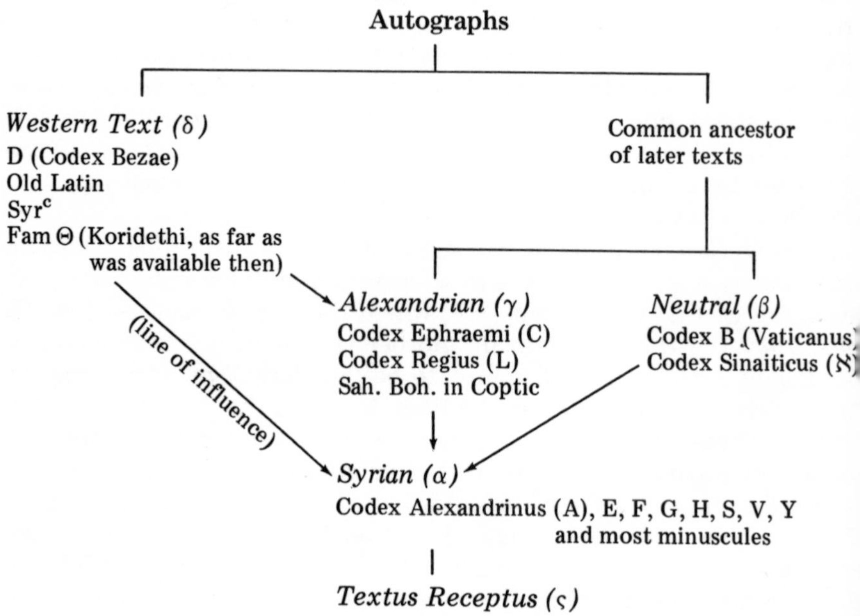

The α-text is a Greek text from the fourth century onward. Westcott and Hort called it the Syrian or Antiochian text. This is a "mixed" text, produced by an editor or a group of editors who wished

[3] For a more recent statement of these principles see P. Maas, *Textual Criticism* (1958); and G. Zuntz, *The Text of the Epistles* (1953), pp. 8ff.

to secure a smooth and complete text.[4] It is represented by Codex Alexandrinus (A) in the Gospels only, the later uncial manuscripts, and the great bulk of minuscule manuscripts. The Textus Receptus is its latest form.

The β-text is a Greek text in Codex Vaticanus (B) and its allies. Westcott and Hort called it Neutral, and made it their chief authority, believing it to be most free from later corruption and contamination. The paragraph in which Westcott and Hort set down their judgment on B and Codex Sinaiticus (א) is worth quoting.

> It is our belief (1) that the readings of א B should be accepted as the true readings until strong internal evidence is found to the contrary, and (2) that no readings of א B can safely be rejected absolutely, though it is sometimes right to place them only on an alternative footing, especially where they receive no support from Versions or Fathers.[5]

The γ-text was regarded by Westcott and Hort as a revised form of the β text made in Alexandria. It is preserved more or less in Codex Ephraemi (C), Codex Regius (L), Codex 33, and the Coptic versions.

The δ-text is a Greek text of Codex Bezae (D) and its allies, the Old Latin and Old Syriac versions. Westcott and Hort called this text Western; and Hort characterized it as harmonistic with a predilection for paraphrase.

2. The second part of the critic's task is *examinatio:* assessing the quality of the most ancient readings which have been generated by the process of *recensio.* The reading which satisfies all requirements is considered to be original.

3. Where the tradition fails to yield such a satisfactory reading, the critic strives, by *emendatio*, to recover by means of conjecture the original wording, which failed to reach the archetype of the extant evidence. Probably the most celebrated example is 1 Peter 3:19, where it has been suggested that εν ω και ("in which also"—viz. the spirit—Christ preached to the souls in prison) should in fact read Ενωχ ("Enoch" preached to the souls in prison).[6]

SOURCES

There are three sources of information for the textual critic: manuscripts—uncials, minuscules, and lectionary readings; versions; and citations in the early church fathers. Into this final class fall Tatian's *Diatessaron*, a second-century harmony of the Gospels,[7] the quota-

4 See Hort's description of the Syrian text, *The New Testament in the Original Greek* (1881), pp. 134f.
5 *Ibid.*, p. 225.
6 On this conjecture see B. M. Metzger in *Journal of Religion*, 32 (1952), 256f.
7 See B. M. Metzger, *Chapters in the History of New Testament Textual Criticism* (1963), pp. 97-120.

tions made by Origen both before and after his settlement at Caesarea in AD 231, and those by Cyprian, Bishop of Carthage in North Africa (died AD 258), who witnesses to Codex Bobbiensis (*k*). Our attention however, will be directed to the first two sources.

Manuscripts are subdivided into the following types:

1. Papyrus manuscripts are denoted by the letter P plus a number raised to a superior place; e.g., P^{45} (Chester Beatty papyrus: Gospels-Acts, third-century Caesarean, in codex form), P^{46} (Pauline epistles, third century), P^{66} (Bodmer papyrus; fragments of John, *c.* AD 200, codex). The most famous is probably P^{52} (Rylands papyrus John 18:31-34, 37f.). Dated in the first half of the second century this discovery proves that John's Gospel was in circulation in Egypt at this early time. The latest papyrus discovery is P^{75}, a codex of Luke and John. The editors date it between AD 175 and 225, and it is the earliest extant copy of Luke and one of the earliest of John. An interesting reading in John 10:7 gives "I am the shepherd [rather than "door"] of the sheep"; and in Luke 16:19 the name of the rich man in Jesus' parable is given as Neve.

2. Uncial manuscripts were written from the fourth to the tenth century. The following are the most important uncials, along with their standard designations.

Codex Sinaiticus (ℵ or S) was discovered by Count Tischendorf in 1844. The first hand (ℵ*) dates from the fourth century readings from later scribal correctors of the manuscript are indicated by raised letters ($\aleph^a$, $\aleph^b$).

Codex Vaticanus (B) has been in Rome since before 1475. It is a fourth-century manuscript placed in Egypt, perhaps at the command of the emperor Constantine. It is the chief authority for the β text.

Codex Alexandrinus (A) came from Alexandria to the British Museum in London. It is fifth-century and of mixed text-type—α in the Gospels, β elsewhere in the New Testament.

Codex Ephraemi (C) is a palimpsest, i.e., a vellum manuscript written on and then reused after the surface had been scraped to remove the original writing. Its name comes from the fact that it also contains the sermons of Ephraem of Syria. It is fifth-century and of mixed type.

Codex Bezae (D) is named for the continental reformer Theodore Beza, who brought it to Cambridge in 1581. It is a fifth-century authority for the δ text in Old Latin. As noted above, it adds a long interpolation after Luke 6:4. Also, there is an interesting additional reading at Acts 19:9, where D supplies the notice that Paul's preaching in the lecture room of Tyrannus was from 11 a.m. to 4 p.m., i.e., at a time when the Ephesians were enjoying a siesta and Tyrannus had no use for the hall.

There are two main manuscripts in this family. The Freer manuscript (W), in Washington, DC, has a mixed type, is fifth-century and in Mark 16 has a special reading (the Long Ending). The second i

Codex Regius (L), an eighth-century codex of the Gospels. It is important for its witness to two endings of Mark, both the traditional 16:9-20 and the shorter ending.

Codex Koridethi (Θ) is eighth-century and of a mixed type (cf. Matt. 27:16f.), with a Byzantine text in Matthew, Luke, and John, but a text in Mark similar to that used at Caesarea in Origen's day.

3. Minuscules are smaller editions, written on vellum and in codex form from the ninth century onwards, to meet current needs. Twenty-four hundred minuscules exist (mainly α text), and are divided into families, two of the nine famous being fam. 1, identified by Lake (hence sometimes referred to as λ); and fam. 13, the Ferrar group (hence ϕ). Both these families have textual affinities with the Caesarean type of text in the third and fourth centuries.

There are three principal groups of versions used by the textual critic. These are translations of the New Testament into the main languages of the Christian mission—Latin, Syriac, and Coptic.

1. Latin versions include the Old Latin, which had its home in North Africa. The most important witness to it in North Africa is Codex Bobbiensis (*k*). The Vulgate was a revision of the Old Latin made by Jerome in 386.

2. Several Syriac versions exist. The Old Syriac is preserved in two manuscripts which, however, are incomplete. One is an edition made by William Cureton in 1858, and is referred to as Syr^{c}. The other is a palimpsest manuscript discovered in 1892; it is denoted Syr^{s}. The two were copied in the fifth and fourth centuries respectively, though they witness to a text three centuries earlier. The influence of Tatian's *Diatessaron* (*c.* AD 170) on them is debated. They represent a Western type of text. The Philoxenian (Syr^{ph}) and Harklean (Syr^{h}) Syriac versions may in fact not be two versions at all but a single version in two editions. The Palestinian Syriac version represents a translation in Aramaic, dated in the fifth century. It seems to be based on a Greek text of the Caesarean type, independent of the other Syriac versions. Syr^{h} is an important witness (next to D) to the Western text of Acts.

3. Coptic is the most recent form of the Egyptian language. During the early period of church history, several Coptic dialects were spoken. In Upper Egypt the dialect was Sahidic; around the northern delta the Bohairic dialect prevailed. These are the two most commonly used in New Testament translations. In the Fayyumic dialect there appeared the sub-Akhmimic version, which contains a papyrus codex of John's Gospel. This has been dated *c.* AD 350-75. Like the Sahidic version it witnesses to the Alexandrian type of text.

4. Other versions of the New Testament were made for use in the Eastern churches, including Armenian, Georgian, Ethiopic, Gothic, and Arabic translations.[8]

[8] See J. N. Birdsall, *loc. cit.*, pp. 364ff.

TEXTUAL CRITICISM: HISTORY AND METHODS

Once the classification of different manuscripts and versions of the New Testament has been accomplished, the harder task comes of forming a judgment on which reading or readings is or are to be preferred in any given case. To see how this is done, a short, skeletal history of textual criticism is useful.

1. The starting-point for our purposes is provided by Erasmus who prepared a printed edition of the New Testament in Greek, which he published in 1516. He used some good minuscules which represented the Byzantine text. This edition was followed by Stephanus from 1546 onwards. The preface to the edition in 1633 contained the Latin words, "*Textum* ergo habes, nunc ab omnibus receptum"—"[The reader] thus has the text which is now accepted by everyone." From this statement arose the designation Textus Receptus, i.e., the standard text (TR or ς). This is the text underlying the King James Version of 1611, and was the main Greek text until 1881.

2. Building on the work of their predecessors, especially Griesbach and Lachmann, B. F. Westcott and F. J. A. Hort began a new phase of textual criticism in 1881 with the publication of the *New Testament in the Original Greek*. Their work set forth certain principles of textual criticism. First, of individual readings, the most probable is that which best explains its rivals. Second, "knowledge of documents should precede final judgement upon readings."[9] Third, authorities are to be grouped in families of manuscripts descended from a common ancestor. This approach derived from Lachmann, who established the genealogical method of determining the *stemma* or family tree of manuscripts, and of demonstrating their descent from an archetype.[10] Fourth, the character of the groups thus determined must be estimated.

For Westcott and Hort, the third principle was the most important, and in their hands it produced four groups of text-types, as we saw above—α, the Syrian or Antiochian text (third to fourth century); β, the Neutral text, including ℵ B; γ, the Alexandrian text found in ℵCL; and δ, the Western text, including D, Old Latin, and Old Syriac. Of these, Westcott and Hort championed the Neutral text,[11] and evaluated the other text-types in the light of this preference. The Western text they regarded as a corruption; the Syrian as a mixture of texts worked over by Lucian of Antioch (AD 300-350) with a view to producing a simplified text, and they ignored it. The Alexandrian text they took to be the result of modifications taking place in Alexandria.

9 *Op. cit.*, II, 31.
10 See J. N. Birdsall, *loc. cit.*, pp. 309ff., for a critical assessment and reevaluation of this method.
11 *Op. cit.*, II, 225.

Westcott and Hort analyzed conflate readings in eight cases which, they averred, indicate the later origin of the Syrian text. The "mixed" reading in α is the result of a combination of β and δ readings. Luke 24:53 may be given as an example. The α reading *αινουντες και ευλογουντες τον θεον* (read by A and the mass of manuscripts) is, they argue, a conflation of the β reading *ευλογουντες τον θεον* (read by ℵBCL bo) with the δ reading *αινουντες τον θεον* (read by D a b Vulg Augustine). Further evidence for the lateness of the α text they found in the ante-Nicene criterion: no reading strictly belonging to α is found in any church father before Chrysostom, whereas β, γ, and δ types are found.[12] Distinctive α readings are doubtful in their claim to be original.[13] This observation led Westcott and Hort to dismiss the Syrian text as worthy of indifference in the eyes of the modern critic.

Investigations and new discoveries since the time of Westcott and Hort have modified their understanding of the situation somewhat. The theory is sound, but the nomenclature is dubious. For example, "Syrian" (?) is taken as "Neutral," which is too optimistic since γ is only a revision of β. Also, Westcott and Hort were too quick to dismiss the δ text.

3. B. H. Streeter marked a new chapter in the history of textual criticism. His book *The Four Gospels*, published in 1924, led to a reevaluation of the Westcott and Hort theory. Streeter made several contributions of special note. He changed Westcott and Hort's

STREETER'S REVISION (1924). *The Four Gospels*, p. 26

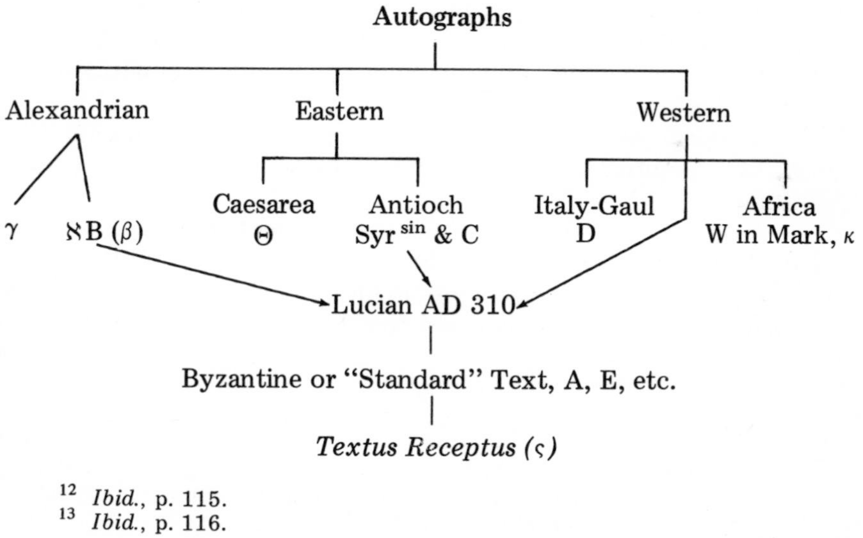

[12] *Ibid.*, p. 115.
[13] *Ibid.*, p. 116.

nomenclature α to "Byzantine," because it was the standard text from the fourth century to the Middle Ages. Under Westcott and Hort's nomenclature β he included the manuscripts they had grouped as γ. This he called Alexandrian, to show that he rejected γ as a separate family. He broke up δ into four families, corresponding to geographical regions. This may be shown diagrammatically:

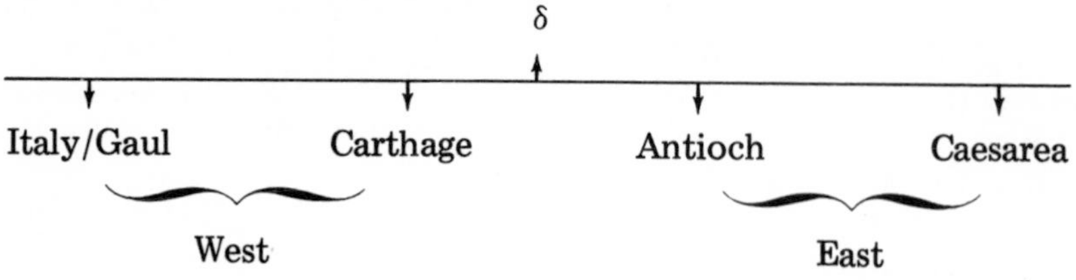

Streeter emphasized the immense importance of early local texts.[14] The textual critic's aim was to recover local texts of the great churches and then to work back to a common original that explained them all.[15]

This guiding principle led Streeter to assess the value of the manuscripts and so to group them in three general ways. First, all manuscripts later than the fifth century should be ignored, except when they differ from the prevailing Byzantine text.[16] Second, prominence should be given to pedigree, not age,[17] and pedigree research should begin with Mark.[18] Third, emphasis should be given to the importance of the great centers of Christianity. Streeter identified these as Rome, Alexandria, and Antioch. Lesser value was given to lesser places like Caesarea. On Streeter's hypothesis, those great metropolitan areas, which contained the episcopal sees, were repositories of the text traditions. The geographical distribution is as follows:

Alexandria was the home of Westcott and Hort's β as well as Streeter's γ. This is primarily represented by B, and secondarily by ℵ, L, and the Coptic version.

Antioch was the home of the Greek text underlying the Old Syriac, i.e., Sinaitic, Curetonian, and Peshitta, when it differs from Byzantine.

Caesarea was the home of the manuscript tradition of Θ (Codex Koridethi, published in 1913), with secondary authorities in family 1 and family 13, certain minuscules, and W.[19] The argument is important because Streeter believed that Θ represented a text already

14 *The Four Gospels*, p. 38.
15 *Ibid.*, p. 39.
16 *Ibid.*, p. 44.
17 *Ibid.*, p. 50.
18 *Ibid.*, p. 64.
19 See R. P. Blake and K. Lake, "The Text of the Gospels and the Koridethi Codex," *HTR*, 16 (1923), 267-86.

MAP TO SHOW NEXT-DOOR NEIGHBOR AFFINITIES
(Streeter, *op. cit.*, p. 106)

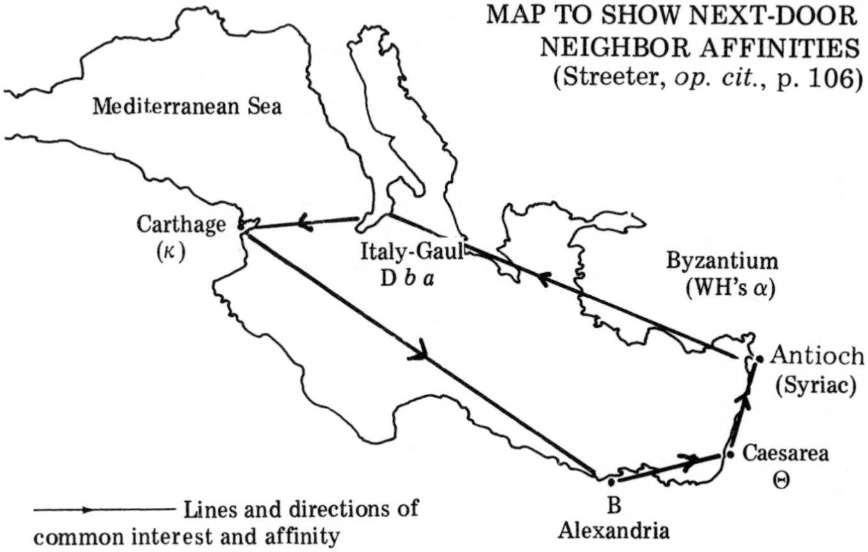

at Caesarea when Origen moved there in AD 231, and not one made by him.[20]

Italy (Gaul) is represented in D, Tatian (*c.* AD 170), and Irenaeus (*c.* AD 185).

Carthage in North Africa witnesses to *k* (Codex Bobbiensis, a fourth- or fifth-century Roman text used by Cyprian).

Byzantium is the home of Westcott and Hort's α (TR), found in A E S and later manuscripts. Streeter joins Westcott and Hort in regarding this part of the family as comparatively worthless.

We may review, in capsule form, some conclusions which Streeter drew. First, he held that while groups are identifiable, each member is related to its next-door neighbor far more closely than to remoter members of the series.[21] Secondly, the practice of presenting manuscripts in alphabetical order is misleading. One should simply quote in groups, e.g., ℵB and its allies, D and its allies, Θ, Old Syriac, and TR. Third, the reliance of Westcott and Hort on β was unfortunate, because all local texts have suffered from assimilation. But Streeter supports ℵB, while insisting that manuscripts should be weighed, not counted.

4. Developments since Streeter have been occasioned partly by new discoveries (P^{45}, Bodmer II P^{66}) and partly by a more rigorous scrutiny of his principles. This has led to the following conclusions:

First, Streeter's "local texts" theory is sound, but it is not too exact, as may be seen in the example of Origen, who witnesses to several textual traditions in one locale.

[20] *Op. cit.*, pp. 101f.
[21] *Ibid.*, p. 106.

Second, doubt has been cast on Streeter's view that Origen used the Alexandrian or β text until AD 230, and thereafter a Caesarean text at Caesarea. He used a Caesarean text at Alexandria. This was the critique of Streeter made by T. Ayuso, who argued that the so-called Caesarean text belonged to an Egyptian provenance, not however based in Alexandria.[22] This "family" has cohesion, but is represented by two subtypes: (a), formed by P^{45} W, the minuscule families 1 and 13, and Cursive 28; and (b), formed by Θ, 565 and 700, Origen, and Eusebius. On this view subtype (a) came into Origen's hands later, which explains the phenomenon of the pre-Caesarean evidence, such as P^{45}, which indicates that Origen knew and used at least two different textual traditions—and perhaps three.[23]

Third, the rest of the New Testament falls into three groups: Alexandrian, Western, and Byzantine.

Fourth, recent work on the Byzantine text (α), which was poorly regarded by Westcott and Hort and Streeter alike, shows that this is not a worthless text consisting only of late and conflated readings. Citations in the church fathers (especially Photius in the ninth century) show how varied were the streams that flowed into this river. G. Zuntz in particular has sought to show that the Byzantine readings may be ancient, and insists that the Byzantine readings which recur in Western texts must be ancient, since the two streams of tradition (with P^{46} as a witness to the Western reading) never met after the fall of the Empire.[24] G. D. Kilpatrick has endeavored to show that Byzantine readings may contain original texts by arguing that forms customary in hellenistic Greek but later condemned by the Atticists appear in the Byzantine text, which suggests that α does preserve a measure of original readings.[25]

Fifth, a fresh evaluation of the Western text (δ) has enhanced the general appreciation of its value. Indeed, since Streeter's time, it has been shown not to be a homogeneous family but one represented by a wide diversity of authorities. In particular, two types of pre-Vulgate Latin text belong to the Western tradition. Irenaeus witnesses to the D text in Gaul; and this tallies with the Latin *a* and *b*, while at Carthage the primary authority is *k* for Matthew and Mark, and secondarily the Greek W for Mark 1-5 and the Latin *e*.

Finally, discoveries since 1881 have enriched our knowledge of the extant materials. Especially noteworthy are the Sinaitic Syriac, the Koridethi manuscripts, the Freer manuscript (W), the Chester Beatty papyrus P^{52}, and the Bodmer papyri. In addition some twenty-eight

[22] T. Ayuso, "¿Texto cesariense o precesariense?" *Biblica*, 16 (1935), 369-415.

[23] See J. N. Birdsall, *loc. cit.*, p. 353.

[24] G. Zuntz, *The Text of the Epistles*, pp. 49-57.

[25] G. D. Kilpatrick, "Atticism and the Text of the New Testament," *Neutestamentliche Aufsätze: Festschrift J. Schmid* (1963), pp. 125-37.

papyrus fragments came to light in the 1940s, the majority of them belonging to the Byzantine text-type.[26]

5. We may conclude our account of the history of the textual criticism of the New Testament with a brief mention of some principles useful for deciding which reading is to be accepted.

Bengel's rules are *difficilior lectio potior*—the more difficult reading is to be preferred; *brevior lectio potior*—the shorter reading is to be preferred (this is less obviously demonstrable); and "a reading which explains other rivals" is on that account superior. Griesbach stressed that, in determining a correct reading, the manuscripts must be weighed as well as counted. Streeter introduced the emphasis of giving preference to local texts, with certain modifications suggested by the interrelations between the ecclesiastical centers where these texts flourished.

The method of eclecticism in textual criticism—the stance of reasoned "choice" in the light of all the available data, is safer than a more mechanical following of genealogical succession. There is far less optimism today about the utility of the genealogical method in selecting readings. The metaphor of manuscript families has been replaced by the imagery of a river, which receives many tributaries and confluences, and by an alternative approach, called "rational criticism."

> Since no one manuscript or text-type is any longer acknowledged as "the best," the ideal should be that all manuscripts be thoroughly examined and their place in the history of transmission known. The judgement of readings will treat the variants revealed by this process—with full cognisance of the documents in which they are preserved—and will assess their claim to originality or the reason for their creation. This latter process and the establishment of a text by its means is known as "rational criticism," that is, it is "reasoned out," and not somewhat blindly and automatically pursued, as stemmatics has sometimes been in a degenerate form.[27]

[26] B. M. Metzger, "Recently Published Fragments of the Greek New Testament," *ExpT*, 63 (1951-52), 309-11.

[27] J. N. Birdsall, *loc. cit.*, p. 311. For "rational criticism," see H. K. Moulton, "The Present State of New Testament Textual Criticism," *The Bible Translator*, 16 (1965), 193-98.

PART FOUR

The Four Gospels

We are now in a position to take a look at the individual books known as Gospels. In a sense all the study of the preceding twelve chapters has been preparatory to and in anticipation of this exercise. We need to come to these deceptively simple books with some background information; and this information the preceding chapters have tried to provide.

It will be clear as we proceed that each of the following chapters is written in a different way. It would have been possible to describe the Gospels, each in turn, under common headings, such as authorship, date, readers, purpose, and the leading features. This method has much to commend it if the student is concerned to take a survey of the Gospels and their content. But if we want to ask questions about the theological intent of the evangelists and the setting of these books in early Christianity, no such uniform method is adequate.

Our study of Mark does follow more traditional lines. The present author has written fully in another book about the real issues raised in Markan studies today. Matthew's Gospel needs special attention, since the big issue is one of the composition of this Gospel. Our chapter on Luke is similarly descriptive of the chief emphases in that first volume of a two-part work, and our conclusions about it will be provisional until we look at the Acts of the Apostles in the second volume. Modern study of John is centered on the issues of tradition and redaction, and the structure of this enigmatic yet captivating work.

In each case we need to set our study in the context of what contemporary students and scholars are saying, so no apology is required for the selected footnote references.

CHAPTER THIRTEEN

The Gospel of Mark

MARK IN THE EARLY CHURCH

The Gospel according to Mark has had a checkered history since the time of its publication. The first Christian reaction to it was one of enthusiastic acceptance and acknowledgment of its authoritative witness to the life of the Lord. This is borne out by a number of attested facts. The Gospel was used by the other synoptic evangelists; it was possibly known to the Johannine evangelist;[1] and it was familiar to the author of the *Gospel of Peter*, a second-century "Passion Gospel."[2]

Later attestation in early Christian literature comes from Hermas (*c.* AD 130), who refers to Mark 6:52 and 8:17 (*Mand.* 4.2.1); Tatian, whose harmony of the Gospels (the *Diatessaron*, *c.* AD 170) used Mark as one of the sources; and Irenaeus (AD 180), who regarded it as one of the canonical documents, adding the testimony: "After their [Peter and Paul's] departure, Mark the disciple and interpreter of Peter did also hand down to us in writing what had been preached by Peter." In the next decade Clement of Alexandria endorsed this statement: "Mark wrote his Gospel from matter preached by Peter."

But as far as direct citation of the text of the Gospel is concerned, little evidence is forthcoming from the early centuries. That it was known and highly regarded is clear; but it is singular that the apostolic fathers and apologists (in the second century) are reticent.[3]

Moreover, Mark's position in the order of the Gospels is unsettled. It was never placed first; and in some of the lists (e.g., the Old Latin, and the Greek manuscripts D and W) it is placed last. Irenaeus' celebrated likening of the Gospel writers to the four cherubim of Ezekiel 1 and the four living creatures of Revelation 4 reflects the

[1] B. H. Streeter, *The Four Gospels*, pp. 397ff. See below, p. 273.

[2] Cf. L. Vaganay, *L'évangile de Pierre* (1930).

[3] Cf. P.N. Harrison, *Polycarp's Two Epistles to the Philippians* (1926), pp. 285-88 on Polycarp's knowledge of the Gospel.

prevalent embarrassment concerning the place and office of the Second Gospel, for unlike the other three Gospel writers, Mark is depicted as an eagle, lion, man, and an ox in successive parts of patristic writing. Apparently the fathers could not make up their mind which characterization best fitted him.

No commentary on Mark was written before that of Victor of Antioch (in the fifth century). There is evidence that the Gospel was mainly neglected on the ground that its contents were embodied in the larger Gospels of Matthew and Luke, which not only incorporated much of the Markan material but in the process smoothed out the rugged and unstylistic character of Mark's writing. Added to this is the commonly held (until the rise of modern criticism) theory of the literary relations of the first three Gospels that Matthew was the first Gospel to be written and that Mark was "one who followed Matthew's footsteps and shortened his gospel" (*pedisequus et breviator Matthaei*), as Augustine put it.

Thus, the facts of the early dissemination and recognition of Mark point to two conclusions. First, the book was immediately received on its publication as a fundamental witness to the life of Jesus; and it began its career in the church with a prestige which was at its maximum just after it was written.[4] This feature has led to the belief that the Gospel was circulated with the backing of some important church—traditionally supposed to be the church at Rome where Peter's authority assured it a ready acceptance in the churches throughout the Christian world.

Second, with the incorporation of Mark into the later evangelical records, its popularity waned. Its text is seldom quoted in the following centuries. As a consequence of the modern assessment of Mark as the earliest of the Gospels to be written and the claim that it records an objective statement of Jesus' historical life—two suppositions which derive from the work of H. J. Holtzmann[5]—Mark's Gospel has come into its own once again; and the last century of biblical scholarship has witnessed a resurgence of interest in this book and its writer, in L. Housman's words—

> The saint who first found grace to pen
> the life which was the Life of men.

JESUS' PUBLIC MINISTRY ACCORDING TO MARK

Mark's Gospel opens with a summary of the mission of John the Baptist (1:1-13) as a frontispiece to the narratives of the baptism and temptation of Jesus. The latter events are the gateway to the public ministry of Jesus, which is depicted in two large sections: the Galilean

[4] A.E.J. Rawlinson, *The Gospel According to St. Mark* (Westminster Commentary) (1925), p. xxv.
[5] Holtzmann, *Die synoptischen Evangelien* (1863).

ministry (1:14—9:50) and the Judaean ministry (ch. 10—13). The former is further divided into a summary of the Lord's work in eastern Galilee (1:14—7:23), with his headquarters at Capernaum; and his later ministry in northern Galilee (7:24—9:50). Returning to Capernaum, he thence journeys further south into Judaea (10—13). This section concludes with his triumphant entry into Jerusalem (11:1-27), his controversies with the Jerusalem religious authorities (11:27—12:44) and his apocalyptic discourse (13:1-37). The remainder of the book is taken up with a full, graphic depiction of the circumstances of his arrest, trial, crucifixion, and burial (14:1—15:47), coming to a victorious but abrupt end with the account of how three women, arriving at Jesus' tomb, found it empty and heard an angel bidding them to return with the disciples to Galilee (16:1-8).

1. *Introduction*

The appearance of John the Baptist marks the historical setting of Jesus' public ministry. It is possible that the exordium of the entire Gospel in this paragraph should read: "The beginning of the good news of Jesus . . . was John the Baptist's preaching of a baptism of repentance." This view, adopted by some Greek church fathers and in modern times by C. H. Turner,[6] would find confirmation in Acts 1:22; 10:37; and 13:24, 25, all of which place the baptizing ministry of the forerunner as the frontispiece of the public appearance of him in whom the gospel was actualized. Alternatively, verse 1 may be the title of the first section and stand as a verbless caption. More plausibly still, it is the title of the entire Gospel.[7]

The verses of the frontispiece (1:1-8) focus on John's distinctive practice. Of the many features of this messianic herald's work,[8] none is more important than his baptizing his fellow Jews in preparation for the coming of God's rule; and of his baptisms no single one is more significant than his receiving and baptizing his cousin Jesus of Nazareth (1:9-11; cf. Matt. 3:13-17; Luke 3:21-23; John 1:24-34). This event provided a fixed starting point for the public ministry.

At his baptism Jesus received an anointing of the Holy Spirit (cf. Acts 10:38) and a summons to messianic service. The pattern of that service is clearly shown in the Father's announcement, "Thou art my Son, the Beloved; with thee I am greatly pleased" (1:11). This verse is a striking linkage of two Old Testament passages (Ps. 2:7 and Isa. 42:1)—a coronation formula for the messianic Son and a portrayal of the Suffering Servant of God. There is also a possible underlying

6 "The Gospel According to St. Mark," in *A New Commentary on Holy Scripture*, ed. C. Gore *et al.* (1928), *ad loc.*

7 For a further discussion of these alternatives, see above, pp. 25-27.

8 See T. W. Manson, *The Servant Messiah*, pp. 36-49; and W. Wink, *John the Baptist in the Gospel Tradition* (1968), ch. 1.

motif in the wording, which recalls Genesis 22, where Isaac is depicted as Abraham's beloved child. That chapter received a Targumic interpretation in the light of Isaiah 53, so the various backgrounds may very well merge together.[9] Thus the messianic servant-son begins a ministry of service and obedience which will culminate in his atonement for his people's sins.[10]

Jesus' baptism and temptation are tied together (1:12, 13). In the Jordan the call came which marked the commencement of his public work. What that call involved was made clear in the weeks of solitude in the wilderness. Mark simply notes the fact; the other Synoptics give a dramatic and revealing account in which the lines of temptation are clearly drawn, and their significance for Jesus and his future ministry carefully spelled out. William Manson rightly observes: "In the background of the experience there undoubtedly lie the Messianic ideas of Jesus' race and time."[11] To Jesus "these traditional Messianic ideas of his people appear not as divine inspirations, but as Satanic perversions of the truth." The importance of this background cannot be overrated. Jesus—the temptations tell us—will not use any of the possible methods by which success could be achieved or accept any contemporary role open to him. To use the apt descriptions of H. E. W. Turner, he will not be an economic Messiah, ministering solely to the bodily and social needs of men, nor a sign-giving Messiah, compelling belief by a theatrical display of supernatural ability, nor a political leader, ambitious to captivate the kingdoms of the world by Caesar's methods.[12]

Instead, Jesus began his ministry with the clear intention of being God's servant *in God's way*. His first announcement of the inbreaking of God's rule into human life (1:14f.) picks up an earlier promise (*Psalms of Solomon* 17:21): "Behold, O Lord, and raise up for them their king at the decisive hour which thou didst choose." His subsequent activity, however, will show how he was to purify the current notions of the kingdom from all misconceptions and political associations and give it a content in terms of service and suffering unto death (Mark 10:45).

2. *The Ministry in Galilee*

Jesus' activity following the initial declaration (1:14f.) began with a call to the masses in Galilee, accompanied by a call to individuals (1:16-20). This latter act is important because it shows that

9 So G. Vermes, *Scripture and Tradition in Judaism* (1961), pp. 202ff.
10 Cf. O. Cullmann, *The Christology of the New Testament* (ET 1959), pp. 66f.
11 *The Gospel of Luke* (1930), p. 36. Cf. J. A. Kirk, "The Messianic Role of Jesus and the Temptation Narrative," *EQ*, 44 (1972), 11-29, 91-102.
12 *Jesus, Master and Lord* (1953), pp. 98ff.

Jesus purposed from the beginning to create a new society. He was not simply teaching people in a vague, amorphous group; he intended to collect disciples,[13] who should later be his messengers (3:14).[14] These disciples were learners of a practical craft, and in the company of their Master they were to catch his spirit.

A Sabbath day's teaching in the synagogue (1:21-34) made a significant impression not only on the human bystanders but also on the spirit-world, now stirred to violent resistance. A summary paragraph (1:32-34) speaks of his healing ministry, directed to both physically sick and mentally disordered people. Both afflictions were thought to be caused by demonic influence; and he must first "expel the demon." In consequence of these acts, Jesus' fame was spreading (1:28); and he sought retirement and renewal, responding to an insistent request to meet the crowds with a quiet determination not to get too caught up in a growing popular movement (1:35-39).

At some unspecified place (1:40) Jesus is confronted by a leper who seems more to doubt his willingness than his ability to help (cf. 9:14-27). Jesus was moved with anger (so vs. 41 in a good manuscript tradition, to be preferred as the "harder" reading), for reasons at which we can only guess; and he cleansed the leprous man, bidding him comply with the law (which had proved powerless to aid him in his extremity) and cautioning him to keep a secrecy which would conceal the identity of the healer. D. E. Nineham comments on the placement of the story here in Mark: the account and its sequel are so placed to depict Jesus as fully obedient to the law of ritual cleansing (based on Lev. 14), just as an earlier verse had shown his respect for the Sabbath (vs. 32).[15] This illustration of Jesus' loyalty is set as a frontispiece to what follows, to show that Jesus is no ruthless iconoclastic reformer, but breaks with rabbinic Judaism only when it comes into fundamental collision with the will of God expressed in his ministry.

In the healing of the paralytic (2:1-12) his controversy with official Judaism begins to be felt. The question of the debate in this story turns on vs. 9: "Which is easier?" Both declarations of healing and forgiveness are easy to *say*—and equally difficult to accomplish. Jesus then proceeds to criticize his adversaries: "You have nothing to say to either his moral or physical condition; I have both the solving word *and* the effective help." But the really criminal offense in the eyes of the rabbis was that Jesus pronounced forgiveness himself, thus usurping a prerogative which belonged exclusively to God (see John 5:18 in the context of John 5:1-16).

The call to Levi the tax official is intercalated into a group of

[13] As the fine study by R. N. Flew, *Jesus and His Church*[2] (1943), shows convincingly.

[14] Cf. E. Schweizer, *Lordship and Discipleship* (ET 1960).

[15] *Saint Mark, ad loc.*

stories which show the developing controversy between Jesus and his opponents. These narratives[16] indicate the nature of the disagreement between Jesus and scribal orthodoxy and orthopraxis in his day. The way the conflict will be resolved is not in doubt (3:6). There were several things about Jesus' ministry which shocked his rabbinic audience.

First, he claimed to forgive sins, which drew out the murmured comment: Why does this man talk like this? Who can forgive sins except God himself?

Second, he chose to consort with the *'am hā-āreṣ*, the "people of the land"—tax collectors and other bad company, who were treated by the Pharisees as beyond the pale of true religion, for whom no hope of salvation is possible (Luke 15:1; John 7:49). Further, he even called one of them to be his disciple. The position of *publicanus* in Roman-occupied Palestine was particularly obnoxious to the loyal Jews, smacking of compromise with the hated invaders and affording an opportunity for extortion and fraud.

Third, the fact that Jesus' disciples did not fast occasioned serious questioning (2:18-22). The immediate background to this is the Jewish picture of the messianic "good time coming," which is likened to a wedding feast. By refusing to fast and commit his followers to fasting, Jesus was tacitly announcing that the messianic age had begun. The feast is now to be enjoyed and everyone is to be happy. But he is under no illusion that everyone shares that joy and darkly hints that an ominous future will await him and his own (2:20), because God's kingdom in him and official Judaism are scarcely compatible and must affect each other either by way of Jesus' revitalizing Judaism or (more probably) a distinct break and a new beginning. "New wine calls for fresh wine skins" (vs. 22).

Fourth, Jesus' Sabbath violations offended the Jews, who treated his disciples' plucking the ears of corn as falling within the category of "reaping and threshing," one of the thirty-nine schedules of work forbidden on the holy day. The Master counters this objection with the assertion that the claims of the ministry override the Sabbath rules; and even the venerable Sabbath day (believed by the Rabbis to antedate creation) is to give place to the Son of Man, i.e., Jesus and his followers, in the exercise of the work of the kingdom.[17] Later he would turn this claim to priority into a prayer: "Give us today bread for the coming day" (of service in the interests of the kingdom). A further case of Sabbath breaking—the man with the withered hand restored (3:1-6)—brings this series of conflict-stories to

[16] First isolated and examined by M. Albertz, *Die synoptischen Streitgespräche.*

[17] See T. W. Manson, "Mark 2:27f.," *Coniectanea Neotestamentica,* 11 (1947), 138-46 on this meaning of Son of Man.

a close; yet the notice of vs. 6 points unmistakably to the way in which the future will be shaped.

A generalizing summary (3:7-12) epitomizes the first phase of the ministry. The Lord's immense popularity is attested, calling forth reactions of gratitude and, more importantly, hope that here may be the new leader of God's people, the heaven-sent Messiah. Yet official Judaism is shocked by his unconventional ways and annoyed by the carefree attitude he shows to the law whenever the claims of the ministry cut across its authority. As he fulfils the messianic program enunciated in Luke 4:16-39, the Jewish leaders are growing alarmed and suspicious at his mounting success and influence.

The appointment of the Twelve (3:13-19) serves a double purpose. They are to learn the secrets of the kingdom by personal acquaintance as learner-apprentices,[18] and they are then to become missionary-apostles to the world. In both ways they form the nucleus of the church.

The reader is next introduced to Jesus' immediate family and relatives. They appear in a strange light, reminding us that Jesus encountered misunderstanding and opposition from his own kinsfolk and friends as well as official animosity. Both groups are seen to be ranged against him in this section. Judaism failed to perceive that his power was a sign of his divine credentials. His wonders they attributed to an alliance with Satan. The family, on the other hand, credits him with madness because of the strange behavior he shows and his obstinacy *vis-à-vis* the authorities. Both charges are frankly rebutted as blasphemy against the Spirit, a deliberate "debunking" of what is God-given, and are invested with solemn warnings.

Up to this point Jesus' public ministry has been conducted either in the network of Galilean synagogues or in private conversation. With the mounting hostility of the synagogue leaders he turns to the open-air preaching (4:1) and to a new type of teaching: instruction by parables. Parables are vivid observations (says T. W. Manson) of nature and human nature. They speak of everyday, commonplace things, events, and situations. Having gained our interest and sympathy, they bid us take a further step: to consider the best in life as a hint of, or a stepping stone towards, what God is like. Thus they set out a standard by which we can measure what we ought to be. In Manson's words, "The parables show us what kind of God we must believe in and what kind of persons we must be." Jesus teaches by parables to make clear the nature and genius of God's kingdom in direct contrast to misconceptions and perversions of the nature of God and his offer current in popular and official teaching. This designation of the parabolic method is one of the chief contributions

[18] For the underlying Aramaic of "disciple" in direct contrast to the rabbinic idea, see T. W. Manson, *The Teaching of Jesus*^{2}, pp. 237ff.

of J. Jeremias, who describes them as his "weapons of warfare."[19] By these powerful words Satan's realm is invaded and his "house robbed" (3:27).

The story of the sower and his seeds speaks of the effectiveness of Jesus' own teaching; indeed, it is a parable about parables. In the explanation appended to the simple tale (4:14-20) we learn that despite waste, failure due to human unresponsiveness, and Satanic counter-measures, there is a crop which crowns the preacher's task (likened to the farmer's work) with success and gives him encouragement to go on. Jesus' own ministry is illumined by this piece of self-revelation; and its application in this parable to early Christian preaching in Mark's day is obvious.

Further parabolic warnings and encouragements indicate more about the nature and outward growth of the kingdom. This may be summed up simply: speed or tardiness of growth are human standards not always applicable to farming. The farmer is known for his patience (James 5:7), and is not overanxious concerning the seed he buries in the ground. Preachers may similarly leave the issue with God, whose word they sow. God will take care of his own kingdom—and fervid nationalist calls to arms are misplaced. In the mustard seed simile (4:30-32) the accent falls on the inclusiveness of the rule of God, embracing the Gentiles, who are pictured as "birds of the air" (as in Ezek. 17:23; 31:6; Dan. 4:11, 12, 21 and in rabbinic usage).[20]

Three examples of Jesus' acts of power follow in 4:35—5:43. First is the storm on the lake (4:35-41), which recalls parallel Old Testament passages teaching that ability to control the sea and subdue tempests is characteristic of divine power (Ps. 89:8-9; 93:3-4; 106:8-9; 107:23-30; Isa. 51:9-10). In the Near Eastern background of these Old Testament texts lies the imagery of the monster "chaos" (Hebrew *teₑhôm*) subdued by the powerful god.[21] Of more significant interest to Mark's first readers would be the Old Testament picture of sleep in the midst of upheaval as a token of perfect trust in the sustaining and protective power of God (Ps. 4:8; Prov. 3:23-24; Job 11:18-19; Lev. 26:6). When Yahweh seemed to be "asleep," i.e., inactive, in the face of his people's danger, he would be invoked to "awake" (Ps. 44:23-24; 35:23; 59:4; Isa. 51:9). To the church in Mark's day, threatened by persecution and fearful of the outcome, the reassuring and commanding word of its unseen Lord, "Peace! Be still!" would come home with special relevance.

The second act of divine power—the cure of the Gerasene madman—is notable for its wealth of personal detail, including a reported conversation between Jesus and the demoniac (vv. 6-10, 18-20). The incident is set on Gentile territory, although the exact

[19] *The Parables of Jesus* (ET 1954), p. 19.
[20] Cf. the evidence in J. Jeremias, *Jesus' Promise to the Nations*, pp. 68f.
[21] Cf. G. von Rad, *Old Testament Theology*, I, 150ff.

location is hard to determine. The "Gerasenes" were Gentiles who lived in Decapolis, the ten-town federation east of the Sea of Galilee (see vs. 20); and there is some plausibility to Hoskyns and Davey's suggestion that this incident follows on directly from the preceding one to parallel the activity of God in Psalm 65. God stills the roaring of the sea . . . and the tumult of the peoples (Ps. 65:7).[22]

The Lord's power over disease and death (5:21-43) is shown in the third narrative. In fact, two stories are here merged into a unit of Gospel tradition. The raising of Jairus' daughter is obviously the chief event, and the finale receives an extra dramatic effect by the intercalation of the other account of the woman with the hemorrhage (vv. 25-34), which interrupts Jesus' movement to the scene of need and hopelessness. Early Christian confidence in the face of man's last enemy (1 Cor. 15:26) is well illustrated by the report of Jesus' explanation, "The child has not died, she is only asleep."[23] The skeptical reaction which greeted this sentence ("They only laughed him to scorn") may portray the pagan derision of the claim of eternal life made by Mark's church.[24]

After these impressive accounts of the Lord's wonder-working power and human response in faith and devotion, the next *pericope*, by way of stark contrast, returns to the unsympathetic attitude of his family. Not surprisingly in such a hostile atmosphere in Nazareth, Mark appends a realistic comment: "He could not perform any miracle there, except that he put his hands on a few sick people and healed them. And he was astonished at their unbelief" (a statement modified by Matthew and Luke). This is a quiet reminder that the Markan Jesus was not a hellenistic thaumaturge, a θεῖος ἀνήρ ("divine man") bestowing his favors to build up his reputation. Rather, he worked in a congenial atmosphere where hope, expectancy, faith, and spiritual sensitivity were present, at least in germ.[25] The plain declaration that he could not perform miracles as though they were akin to conjuring tricks may be a sign of Mark's anti-docetic strain, as well as a sad commentary on the rejection of the apostolic message by Messiah's own people in the later decades. In addition, there is a possible Markan polemic against Paul's charismatic opponents (2 Cor. 10-13). Nor is it by chance that the success of the Twelve, whose mission is placed in the next section (6:7-13), also points in the direction of the subsequent Gentile mission in the apostolic church, as R. H. Lightfoot notes.[26]

22 *The Riddle of the New Testament*, p. 123.
23 Cf. Alan Richardson, "Death," in *A Theological Wordbook of the Bible*, ed. Richardson (1950), pp. 60f., for a discussion of New Testament passages which use "sleep" of death.
24 See A. Richardson, *The Miracle Stories in the Gospels*, p. 74.
25 See R.P. Martin, *Mark: Evangelist and Theologian*, ch. 6.
26 *History and Interpretation in the Gospels* (1935), p. 113.

Such a "sending forth" (vs. 7 uses the important Greek verb ἀποστέλλειν) completes the purpose hinted at in ch. 3. "Their task is an extension of the ministry of Jesus,"[27] coupling a call to repentance with a ministry of healing. From all indications (e.g., Luke 10:1-20) this mission met with some success. As an indirect proof of such a response from the people, Herod's reaction of alarm is noted (vv. 14-16).

The interesting comparison of Jesus with John *redivivus* leads to the narration of the Baptist's death, also reported in Josephus, who attributes Herod's hostility to political motives, as though John were a menace to the security of the state.[28] Mark mentions motives which are more personal, though not inconsistent. A. E. J. Rawlinson adds:

> Both [accounts] are no doubt *bona fide* and independent: it is a mistake to try to harmonize the two. Josephus' version will give the facts as they presented themselves to a historian who wrote sixty years later, and who was concerned to trace the political causes of a war. The story in Mk will be an account, written with a certain amount of literary freedom, of what was being darkly whispered in the bazaars or market-places of Palestine at the time.[29]

There are clear indications to betray the Palestinian origin of this *passio Johannis*, possibly preserved as an independent fragment by his disciples (Matt. 14:12) and later incorporated into this Gospel.

The popularity of Jesus, augmented by the measure of success granted to the apostles' mission, provoked a crisis. The climax is reached at the conclusion of the following two *pericopae* (6:30-56). Various motives seem to have entered into Mark's placing of these stories side-by-side. Both accounts illustrate the disciples' dullness (vv. 51, 52) in the face of the plain evidence of Jesus' manifest power—first, to provide a messianic banquet;[30] second, to assert his control of natural forces (as earlier at 4:35-41). But the historical context of vs. 44 has been perceptively noted by T. W. Manson: that Jesus was confronted with an ugly situation with dangerous forebodings of a messianic uprising.[31] The crowd comprised five thousand men.[32] They are described as "sheep without a shepherd." Matthew 14:13, 14 tends to moralize this incident by observing the compassion of Jesus to a hapless crowd, but Mark's use of the sheep-shepherd metaphor points in a different direction. They are likened to a leaderless mob, an army without a general (1 Kings 22:17), dangerous to all if stirred to a violent anti-Roman demonstration. John 6:15 states this possibil-

[27] So T. W. Manson, whose book *The Church's Ministry* is written to elaborate this theme.
[28] *Antiquities* 18.5.1-2.
[29] *Op. cit.*, p. 82.
[30] See A. Schweitzer, *The Mystery of the Kingdom of God* (ET 1950), pp. 103ff.
[31] *The Servant Messiah*, p. 71.
[32] The Greek ἄνδρες may be significant. Matt. 14:21 adds "not counting women and children," as though to stress that these were strong men, or "he-men."

ity expressly. So Jesus' problem was not simply to feed the crowd, but to quiet them and persuade them to go home in peace.

Shortly after this incident, on which the Fourth Gospel's commentary is most revealing (6:66-71), Jesus retired from Galilee. It is possible that the dangerous enthusiasm of his professed followers urged him to this course of action (7:24-30). F. C. Burkitt's suggestion that the northern journey was virtually a flight from the long arm of the police of Herod Antipas is not incompatible with this reconstruction. H. E. W. Turner adds a further note with the reminder that he withdrew partly to prepare his disciples more thoroughly for the true understanding of his messianic vocation.[33] Recent events had shown how little they had imbibed this teaching and how greatly they needed fresh insight into the meaning of his ministry, if they were to be his "apostles" (6:30), i.e., his accredited representatives or *šᵉlûḥim* in the rabbinic term underlying *apostoloi.*

Opposition to the ministry was felt not simply from Herod and the Romans. The Jewish leaders were mounting an attack. The discussion of ritual washings (7:1-23) focuses attention on the gravamen of the charge the scribes brought against him: he was disregarding "the tradition of the elders" (7:5, 8, 9) with a sovereign freedom and a tacit assumption (Mark does not draw out the implications of this) that he as Messiah brings in the new age, in which the authority of the Torah is rendered invalid. On the surface, the conflict is over the scribal interpretation of the Mosaic law, particularly in the matter of solemn vows, which—if taken deliberately, as distinct from rash vows undertaken in error—were treated as irrevocable, and had the effect of making property "offered to God" (*qôrbān*) sacrosanct even though the plainest human obligations were neglected. Jesus calls the discussion of the legitimacy of such vows out of the realm of the academic to that of the practical and the immediate, emphasizing simple human rights and duties in the light of the will of God for the family. Similarly, ritual lustrations cannot displace the prime importance of a clean inner life (vv. 15, 20-23). A more calculated blow to the authority of scribal tradition could hardly be imagined; and by upturning the regime of the tradition of the elders, invested by the Pharisees with great dignity, Jesus declared the irreconcilable opposition of God's kingdom to their religious code.

3. *An Extension of the Ministry in Scope and Depth*

The journey beyond the northern bounds of the Galilean territory brought Jesus into quasi-Gentile country for an indefinite period of time; but certainly the withdrawal cannot have been long after the springtime of the feeding of the multitude, dated by Mark

[33] *Op. cit.*, p. 110.

6:39 (cf. John 6:4). Encounter with the Gentile people and their varying needs occupies the next section of the Gospel (7:24—8:26), though Jeremias observes that the territory of Tyre and the region lying between Galilee and Caesarea Philippi was then still inhabited by descendants of the northern Israelite tribes. "It would have been to these outposts of Israelite population and Jewish religion that the mind of Jesus first turned when he extended his activity so far to the north,"[34] although the precise geographical data are uncertain (in vs. 31 Sidon may be a misreading of Saidan, a variant form of Bethsaida).

Incidents recorded in this section include the blessing of a Syrophoenician woman, explicitly named as a Gentile (vs. 26), and the cure of a deaf-mute (7:31-37). The technique of performing the latter miracle is unusual, and has points of contact, at least in form, with hellenistic magical cures.[35] The rarity of this kind of narrative argues strongly for the essentially Jewish setting of the rest of the miracles in the historical career of Jesus.

The third incident in this section is the feeding of a crowd, numbered at "about four thousand" (8:9). This is sometimes taken as a doublet of the earlier miraculous feeding pericope (6:30-44); but it is more probably to be regarded as an intentional insertion of a story, set in a non-Jewish milieu, designed to portray Jesus as the bread of life to the Gentiles. This suggestion goes back to Augustine, who noted the striking vocabulary differences between the two accounts.[36] It could hardly be accidental that in each chapter the miraculous provision of food sets in motion a similar cycle of events:

Feeding, crossing the lake	6:45-56	8:10
Controversy with the Pharisees	7:1-23	8:11-13
Incidents in which there is "bread"	7:24-30	8:14-21
Healing miracle	7:31-37	8:22-26

The last mentioned cases of healing are notable for the precise parallels: Vincent Taylor has set down the evidence in some detail.[37] Both stories are also in a class apart in relation to the other healing miracles in the Gospels; e.g., no reference is made to human faith. In the latter case, there are parallels found in hellenistic healing accounts. R. H. Lightfoot offers an elaborate explanation of this, and accounts for its placement here on the ground that it forms a bridge connecting the blindness of the disciples in the earlier part of the Gospel with the illumination that came to them in the second part of the narrative,

[34] *Jesus' Promise to the Nations*, p. 36.

[35] So M. Dibelius, *From Tradition to Gospel*, pp. 83ff. See now J. M. Hull, *Hellenistic Magic and the Synoptic Tradition* (1974).

[36] See A. Richardson, *The Miracle Stories of the Gospels*, p. 98.

[37] *The Gospel according to St Mark* (Macmillan New Testament Commentaries) (1952), pp. 368f.

beginning with the turning-point of the revelation of Caesarea Philippi.[38]

At all events, the subsequent *pericope* (8:27—9:1) marks a major crisis in the ministry, precipitated by Jesus himself, who takes the initiative in both the preliminary (vv. 27, 28) and leading questions (vv. 29, 30). Peter, spokesman for the Twelve, gives his plain answer to the momentous issue, "Who do you say that I am?": "You are the Messiah." In contrast to the Matthean counterpart of this incident (16:13-28), Mark portrays Jesus as accepting the title with little enthusiasm, for it is clear that Peter had no idea of the kind of Messiah Jesus was and would be. For that reason, the accompanying explanation in terms of a humiliated and suffering Son of Man was warmly repudiated by the apostle, and Jesus rejected, with equal animation, all that Peter's rebuke implied. Peter's thought was filled with notions of an all-conquering messianic prince, and Jesus' disclosure of a pathway of suffering was totally unexpected. "What is more, if it is the will of God that the Messiah should suffer, it might well be his will that the Messiah's disciples should suffer a similar fate; from that . . . the natural man shrinks."[39] The retort of Jesus takes up these two issues: his destiny requires, as a divine necessity, an acceptance of a cup of suffering and woe (vs. 31); and discipleship equally requires a close identification with him as corporate Son of Man and servant of God in a similar fate (vv. 34-38; the last verse should probably read, "Whoever is ashamed of me and *mine*," i.e., the disciples).

Chapter 9:1 is a *crux interpretum.* C. H. Dodd gives full force to the perfect participle: "until they have seen that the kingdom of God has come with power."[40] The disciples (he interprets) will soon be aware that the kingdom is already come, i.e., it is a present reality of Jesus' ministry. But this exegesis seems strained.[41] Thus it is better to translate the verse as the RSV does: "before they see the kingdom of God come with power." At some future time the disciples will be aware that the kingdom has come, but no indication is given of the duration of the interval, which is elsewhere envisaged in his eschatological instruction (ch. 13).

The transfiguration is dated with reference to the confession at Caesarea Philippi and is the natural sequel to it. As the disciples have confessed Jesus to be the Messiah, they (or their representatives, the chosen three) are permitted to see his true stature and to share the secret of his filial relationship with the Father. The heavenly voice (vs.

38 *Op. cit.*, pp. 90ff.
39 Nineham, *op. cit.*, *ad loc.*
40 *The Parables of the Kingdom* (1935), p. 53.
41 Cf. W. G. Kümmel, *Promise and Fulfilment*, pp. 25-28. On the whole question of "realized eschatology," note the significant footnote in J. M. Robinson, *The Problem of History in Mark*, p. 24.

7), "This is my Son, the Beloved," combines two messianic titles, coupled with an approbation that, even if men may reject and despise him, he is to be followed by his own. "Hear him" carries the thought "obey him," as in Deuteronomy 6:4.

The snatch of conversation (9:9-13) as the disciples come down from the hill seems to have suffered some disorder in transmission, and C. H. Turner's suggestion that vs. 12b should follow vs. 10 has much to commend it.[42] The disciples are engaged in the resolution of a genuine perplexity. Contemporary expectation of a Messiah associated him with a triumphant reign, and awaited a returning Elijah (Mal. 4:5) to herald his arrival. Jesus had spoken about a rising of the Son of Man, but why was this required? It seemed to imply death and defeat. Yet the Old Testament (they would reason) knows nothing of such a defeat. Jesus points to what has already occurred: Elijah has come back in the person of John the Baptist and met a strange fate (unlike the Old Testament prophet who escaped the wrath of his enemies). The Son of Man can expect no less.

The cure of the epileptic lad directs attention to the central place occupied by faith, defined by J. A. Findlay as "a painstaking and concentrated effort to obtain blessing for oneself or for others, material or spiritual, inspired by a confident belief that God in Jesus can supply all human need."[43] In this regard the present miracle story contrasts with the two earlier accounts from which the emphasis on faith is absent. Jesus' evaluation of the high place of faith in his miracles is classically recorded in vs. 23: "Do you say 'ability'? Everything is within the ability of him who has faith."

A second announcement of the forthcoming rejection and death of the Son of Man (9:30-32) is set within a stereotyped framework observed by R. H. Lightfoot[44] —the sayings are set in a scene in which the disciples have failed to perceive Jesus' ultimate destiny. This setting is clearest at the third prediction of the passion (10:32-34) when "they were on the road going to Jerusalem, with Jesus at the lead; and they were bewildered, and as they followed they were frightened." At no point in the gospel story is the gulf which divided Jesus' understanding of his messianic vocation and the disciples' hopes and fears of what they might expect more vividly portrayed—a vast distinction well described by H. E. W. Turner as the "Messianic cross-purpose."[45] And in both the second and third predictions of the cross, the teaching of Jesus which follows each announcement is occasioned by the disciples' false ambitions and worldly aspirations (9:33-37; 10:35-45).

Chapter 10 removes the public ministry of Jesus from Galilee

[42] *Op. cit., ad loc.*
[43] *Jesus as They Saw Him* (1921), p. 107.
[44] *Op. cit.*, pp. 117ff.
[45] *Op. cit.*, p. 115.

to Judaea and Transjordan. At this point (10:1) the stage is being prepared for the final drama of the crucifixion, although it is likely that considerable time elapsed between the events of chs. 10 and 15. The journey from Galilee may be dated late summer, AD 32, thereby allowing nine months or so before the events of the following year's passover and permitting the five episodes recorded by John's Gospel (the Feast of Tabernacles, an autumn and winter in Jerusalem, an interval beyond the Jordan, a visit to Bethany, and a retreat to Ephraim).

Mark relates the breaking out of a fresh conflict, apparently as soon as Jesus set foot in Judaea. The point at issue was the vexed question of marriage and divorce (10:2-12). Jewish law at that time gave an unshared right of divorce to the husband, a right which could be exercised in a most arbitrary way by serving a written notice of the marriage's dissolution. No redress was possible for the wife, nor did she enjoy any corresponding right. Her sole method of obtaining a divorce was to persuade her husband to take the initiative and offer her release from the marriage vow. Jesus was concerned to challenge this obviously unfair situation, uphold the ideal of the indissolubility of marriage, and base his teaching on God's intention—declared in paradise—that marriage is an equal partnership for all time (vv. 6, 7, 9). Divorce followed by a remarriage with a third party runs counter to the divine purpose (vv. 10-12).

The following conversations and interviews show how clearly the demands of the kingdom of God are based on its character, which is offered to and understood by the childlike spirit, which takes it with simplicity, gratitude, and trustfulness (10:13-16); yet which requires a priority and a full-hearted acceptance which brooks no rival. The riches of the man who was "very wealthy" (vs. 22) proved to be a tragic stumbling-block, not because they were evil *per se* but because they came to hold a place which God alone must have. In wealth ("Mammon" is an Aramaic term signifying "wealth") Jesus found a terrible obstacle to human reliance on God himself; and not surprisingly Paul characterizes (Col. 3:5) "possessiveness" as idolatry. A trust in material possessions virtually excludes a trust in God and therefore an entry into his realm (10:25).

An even greater tragedy, however, is that the professed followers of Jesus have yet to learn the lesson of the kingdom's true nature. They are momentarily startled by the third reminder of what the journey to Jerusalem will entail (10:32); but the deep impression on their minds is clear from their actions and words in these sections. They brush aside the children as though their Master had more important business on hand (10:13); and they deal equally summarily with blind Bartimaeus' request for healing (10:48), possibly on the same score—that Messiah is too busy to attend to such trivia as the cure of a wayside beggar. Moreover, when two of their number, James and John, manage to get in a plea for special places at Jesus' heavenly court, the rest are incensed (10:41) that these two have sought preferential treatment and have "jumped the line." Their minds, no less than the crude, vaulting ambition of James and John, are full of earthly prestige and status symbols to be enjoyed when Jesus enters upon "his glory" (vs. 37), i.e., as messianic prince in Jerusalem in the soon-to-be-established kingdom.

The disciples still need the solemn instruction of 10:42-45, with its climactic prophecy that the Son of Man's title to lordship is to be gained along a road of self-denying service to man and the full and final offering of his life to God as a ransom-price for his people (vs. 45), as the obedient and humiliated Servant of Yahweh (Isa. 53) and martyr-figure (2 Macc. 7; 4 Macc. 6:29; 17:22).[46] If verbal teaching failed to convince them—as it evidently did—they had a second chance to get the message from the acted symbolism of his entry into the holy city (11:1-11), according to the usual interpretation of this passage.

4. The Final Journey to Jerusalem

Jesus came into the city as a king. So the narrative makes plain (with an undertone drawn from 2 Kings 9:13 and—more explicitly in the later synoptics and John—the arrival of the lowly king of Zech. 9:9). Yet, in Mark's account, to insist that he marched on Jerusalem as a king goes beyond the evidence. The acclamation of the entourage (in vv. 9, 10) may be no more than an outburst from enthusiastic pilgrims bound for the festival; and a decisive point against the popular view that he staged a triumphal entry to make a messianic claim apparent is the fact that neither the Jews nor the Romans found it needful to take action against what transpired. It has been argued[47] that he entered the city as Messiah incognito with a chief motive to claim the temple as his rightful possession as the sanctuary of God, but this is doubtful.

The barren fig tree incident (11:12-14, 20-25) poses certain problems. It is obviously intended to make two points: it gives an example of faith and prayer and provides a didactic point, the fate of the fig tree symbolizing the fate that awaited Jerusalem and the Jewish people and religion.[48] This fate overtook them in AD 70 at the fall of Jerusalem. The chief problems are (1) that this "miracle" involves a judgment on an inanimate object, and is thus akin to the wonders related in the apocryphal gospels;[49] and (2) if the event is

46 These texts are discussed by C.K. Barrett, "The Background of Mark 10:45," in *New Testament Essays*, ed. A. J. B. Higgins, pp. 12f.

47 By E. Lohmeyer, *Lord of the Temple* (ET 1961), pp. 34f.

48 See Nineham, *op. cit.*, *ad loc.*

49 For examples see M. R. James, *The Apocryphal New Testament* (1924), pp. 49ff.

dated on the days following the traditional dating of Palm Sunday, i.e., in March/April, no figs would be expected in any case—hence the editorial note added in vs. 13: "for it was not the season of figs."

T. W. Manson offers some explanation of these two difficulties.[50] Vs. 14 may be construed as a statement more than a curse, the tone of voice alone deciding which the speaker originally intended. A hypothetical Aramaic behind the Greek would allow for either, the imperfect and jussive in that language being consonantally identical. Thus what is now rendered as a curse—"May no one ever eat fruit from you again"—may conceivably have been uttered as a statement of fact—"No one will ever again eat"—couched in the form of a prophecy and implying various possibilities. Perhaps the tree was already dead or was in the process of dying; or perhaps Jesus expected the end of the age or the fall of Jerusalem before the next harvest time; or perhaps the indefinite "no one" in vs. 14 veils an allusion to the speaker himself, in which case it is prophecy of his impending death (like Mark 14:25 and parallels).[51]

The second difficulty is that of Gospel chronology. Manson suggests that this event and what follows in the later parts of the Gospel are to be dated at the time of an earlier festival—Tabernacles—six months before Passover. Church calendar sequences are responsible for telescoping the events between the triumphal entry and the cross into one week—a foreshortening explicitly denied in Mark 14:49: "I was *daily* in the temple teaching." The advantage of this reconstruction is that it permits the story of the fig tree to be placed at a season when figs were likely, and so adds likelihood to Jesus' prophetic word and later appeal to the nation.

The sad condition of Judaism is illustrated by his visit to the temple (11:15-19). The outer court was a part of the temple precinct to which everyone, Jew and Gentile alike, was entitled to come for worship. Yet its facilities were effectively denied to the Gentiles by the temple authorities, who were using the area as a market place and a money exchange. Consequently, the area was a convenient thoroughfare for pedestrians (vs. 16). Jesus' reform was designed to restore Gentile privileges and to purify the temple of all that denied its importance as a house of prayer.[52]

Not surprisingly Jesus' action called forth a violent reaction (11:27-33), centering on his authority to interfere in what was a priestly (i.e., Sadducean) preserve. Jesus' retort takes up the broad principle of the legitimacy of all decisions in religious affairs, citing the case of John as a test issue. Clearly the question thrust the temple leaders on the horns of a dilemma. Faced with the unenviable choice

[50] In *BJRL*, 33 (1951), 271ff.
[51] So H.-W. Bartsch, *ZNTW*, 33 (1962), 256-60.
[52] See further J. Jeremias, *Jesus' Promise to the Nations*, pp. 65ff.

of denying John's authority as a recently martyred accredited prophet of God or admitting that they had been wrong to refuse him, they preferred to keep silence. To such men Jesus will not declare himself.

But the question of Jesus' authority is not completely evaded. He does declare himself by a parable, the point of which is taken by those who hear it (12:12). Based on Isaiah 5:1-7, the story builds on a common feature of Palestinian economic life in the first century, the *latifundia* rented out to local peasants to be farmed in return for a share of the produce. This system was much resented, especially by those tenants who had strong nationalist feelings. Moreover, the story as told by Jesus has allegorical features intended to show the identity of the chief actors, and in particular the character of his enemies, who would shortly bring about his death.[53] In spite of a realistic assessment of the situation and his being under no illusion as to how his fate would be decided (vs. 7), Jesus looked beyond rejection to a vindication scene, borrowed from Psalm 118:22-23. There is no valid reason why he should not have quoted this Scripture, which was to figure prominently in the later church's apologetic *vis-à-vis* Judaism (Acts 4:11; cf. Eph. 2:20; 1 Pet. 2:7).

The subsequent *pericopae* exemplify the various efforts made by Jesus' enemies to discredit him in public debate, and may follow naturally from the embarrassment they suffered after the initial encounter of 12:12. The subtle and disingenuous questions challenged him at different levels. On a political plane, the issue of the tribute money was calculated to expose him as either a pro-Roman sympathizer (and so turn the crowds against him as a traitor of Israel's hopes as expressed in the *Psalms of Solomon*) or an anti-imperial nationalist, too dangerous to have his freedom. Either way he seemed to be caught in a trap. But Jesus refused to legislate as though Roman rule and Jewish freedom were mutually exclusive. Both political power and religious freedom are right in their respective spheres (cf. Rom. 13:1ff.; 1 Pet. 2:13-17) and must not be pitted against each other. "They marveled at him" for this simple solution to a vexed question of state and church. When in later centuries the state turned persecutor and the church strove for territorial power, no such simple directive was possible.

Theologically, the question posed by the Sadducees (vv. 18-27) was in character, as the evangelist notes (see Acts 23:6-8). The question they formulated stretched credulity but could not be ruled out as impossible. Jesus replies that if the only hope a person has is in the form of survival in his descendants by proxy, it is ill-founded. But grant a personal God who cares for his own in life and death—and

[53] Cf. C. H. Dodd, *The Parables of the Kingdom*, pp. 124-32; opposed by W. G. Kümmel, in *Aux sources de la tradition chrétienne. Festschrift M. Goguel* (1950), pp. 120ff. See later, pp. 301f.

the Hebrew patriarchs illustrate this *par excellence;* hence, Moses was told that Yahweh is God of these men after their death—and life beyond the grave becomes transformed into personal existence in the love of God, and is not simply a prolongation of earthly conditions. The Scriptures thus speak of an eternal God who enters into a communion with his people which death cannot sever.

A further query, ostensibly and almost certainly serious and sincere, touched on a matter then being debated in Judaism. "Which commandment is first of all?" recalled many Jewish attempts to reduce religion to its basic essentials. Rabbi Simlai sought to reduce all the commandments to the one requirement of Habakkuk 2:4. [54] Jesus concentrated on the prior claims of love, in the order "love to God" issuing in "love to men" (Deut. 6:4f.; Lev. 19:18). Yet a theoretical acceptance of truth never suffices; it brings a person only in sight of the kingdom (vs. 34). Personal attachment to Jesus and the demands of discipleship are needed to bring a person, however well-meaning and sincere, into the kingdom (cf. Luke 9:57-62). In other words, character comes before action in both senses: it is more important and it explains why a person acts as he does.

After a series of interrogations, it is Jesus' turn to raise a problem, apparently one of current rabbinic interest. How can the scribes maintain that the Messiah is a descendant of David?[55] The question is cast in the form of a so-called haggadah question, i.e., one which indicates an apparent contradiction in Scripture, to which the answer is given: both passages are right but they refer to different points.[56] The point at issue is the precise relation of David, the traditional author of Psalm 110, and the Messiah. In Jewish expectation the messianic hope spoke of a coming nationalist leader who would revive the political fortunes and prestige of David's empire (cf. 2 Sam. 7:12; Jer. 30:9; Ezek. 34:23; *Ps. Sol.* 17). Yet—and herein is the embarrassing difficulty of the Pharisaic notion—David not only looked forward to his illustrious successor, the Messiah, but looked up to him as someone infinitely higher than any "second David" could be. David himself called him Lord: how can he be also David's descendant? A solution was eventually reached in Romans 1:3f. (cf. 2 Tim. 2:8), where the qualification "in power" attached to "marked out as Son of God" in reference to David's Son implies that Christ in his post-resurrection glory exercises the functions that belong to the Old Testament Yahweh (for which the LXX uses the Greek *κύριος*, Lord) as in Philippians 2:9-11.

The brief condemnation of the scribes (12:38-40) summarizes

[54] Cited by Loewe and Montefiore, *A Rabbinic Anthology* (1938), p. 199.

[55] T. W. Manson, *The Teaching of Jesus*, p. 266n., has a pertinent comment on this question.

[56] Cf. D. Daube, *The New Testament and Rabbinic Judaism* (1956), pp. 158-63.

the philippic of Matthew 23, and is directed against the worst members of the Pharisee party. Not all Pharisees deserved this verdict, but it is ever a danger with a religious outlook such as Pharisaism that it is more deadly when it succeeds (inducing pride) than when it fails (calling down on it the traditional judgment of "hypocrites"). The Pharisees' love of money (vs. 40)[57] serves as a backdrop for the lovely story of "the widow's mite." As Montefiore observes: "In contrast to the bad Scribes, who 'eat' widows' property, we have now the tale of the good widow and her sacrifice."[58]

The apocalypse (ch. 13) is placed at this point to mark the closing stages of the Lord's activity and to give hint of the final days. It thus forms a species of *discours d'adieu*, patterned on the Old Testament examples of farewell speeches delivered by Jacob (Gen. 48—49), Moses (Deut. 31—32), Joshua (Josh. 23—24), Samuel (1 Sam. 12), and David (1 Chron. 28—29).[59] But this chapter has the more important function of investing the subsequent passion narrative with an aura of glory and suffusing it with the light of the ultimate triumph beyond the darkness of defeat, treachery, and death.[60]

Whether this passage had a prior existence before its incorporation into Mark's Gospel (the Little Apocalypse theory) or not; and whether it represents the substance of Jesus' prophetic teaching or is the work of some Jewish-Christian apocalyptist, expanded by the insertion of dominical sayings by the evangelist, is a matter for debate. G. R. Beasley-Murray examines and is critical of the Little Apocalypse theory,[61] and champions the basic integrity of the chapter. Nineham, on the other hand, supports the latter proposal, arguing that a clear distinction should be made between what Jesus could have foreseen (e.g., vv. 9-13; cf. 8:34ff.) and the use he is reported to have made of an apocalyptic, cosmically oriented genre of language and ideas (vv. 24-27) common in such treatises as Enoch, the Sibylline Oracles, and the Assumption of Moses, which are pseudonymous.[62] The reference to "the desolating sacrilege set up where it [or, he] ought not to be" clearly has the fall of Jerusalem in view (Luke 21:10). It is possible, as many scholars hold, that Mark's recasting of this narrative (assuming the Lukan priority of this apocalyptic section) has taken a prophetic utterance of Jesus, in the spirit of the Hebrew prophets, who foretold the destruction of Zion (Micah 3:12; Jer. 26) and turned it into an apocalyptic prediction-schema, based partly on a reminiscence of events in AD 40 when the mad emperor Caligula

57 Cf. Josephus, *Antiquities* 17.2.4; and I. Abrahams, *Studies in Pharisaism and the Gospels*, I (1917), ch. 10.
58 *The Synoptic Gospels*, I (1927), *ad loc.*
59 On this literary genre see J. Munck, in *Aux sources de la tradition chrétienne*, pp. 155-70.
60 See Nineham, *op. cit.*, p. 341.
61 *Jesus and the Future* (1954).
62 Nineham, *op. cit.*, *ad loc.*

ordered his statue to be set up in the temple,[63] as Antiochus Epiphanes had done with the altar of Zeus in the Maccabean period (1 Macc. 1:54; cf. Dan. 9:27; 11:31; 12:11). But this hypothesis has some doubtful features and seems to credit Mark with overmuch ingenuity and creative skill at the expense of the historical truth of the discourse as delivered by the Lord himself.

A time of fierce testing lies ahead of the disciples and their future representatives, according to vs. 19. But beyond the cosmic upheaval and distress of vv. 24f. the ultimate vindication of the Son of Man (as in Dan. 7:13ff.) is assured, a note struck later when the conflict seems to enter its darkest phase (14:62). The final salvation of the elect is promised. The outbreak of the struggle is imminent (13:28-29), even though the time of the final denouement is a secret locked in the mind of the Father, to which even the Son has no access (vv. 30-32). Yet the disciples' duty is at least clear: faithfulness when bogus messiahs are on the rampage (vv. 5-8, 21-23) and the ruling authority is implacably hostile (vv. 9-13), added to watchfulness (vv. 33-37), lest his coming should find them ill-prepared and irresponsible. So, "what I say to you, I say to all: be watchful" (vs. 37)—a common theme in early Christianity (1 Cor. 16:13; 1 Thess. 5:6; 1 Pet. 5:8; Rev. 3:2, 3; 16:15).

The last three chapters of Mark cover a period between the plot to arrest Jesus (14:1-2) and the events of the crucifixion, burial, and visit of the women to the tomb (16:1-8). As it stands, the record appears to compress all the happenings into a few days, set around the observance of the Jewish festival of Passover (cf. John 12:1, where the anointing occurs six days earlier than Passover). Unfortunately, it is not clear which day of the week coincided with the actual Passover observed in Judaism as Nisan 14 (sunset)/15 (daylight hours). The preceding two days (14:1) are, then, filled with the incidents of ch. 14, including the anointing at Bethany (14:3-9) by an unnamed woman (not to be equated with Mary Magdalene or the woman of Luke 7), who wished by her costly demonstration to show her love and possibly to acknowledge Jesus' messianic status by supplying the consecrating oil (cf. 1 Kings 19:16; 2 Kings 9:3) for his kingly office. Perhaps, too, she glimpsed something of his destiny as one fated to die—at least this is how Jesus is reported to have received the action (vs. 8). R. H. Lightfoot's comment is apposite here: "The passion is the supreme act of the Messiah, and conversely the Messiahship of Jesus is the explanation of the passion."[64] The woman with the anointing oil perceives, as in a mystery, the interrelation between messiahship and passion.

In stark contrast to such a "lovely deed" (vs. 6), the next

[63] Josephus, *Jewish War* 2.10.1.
[64] *Op. cit.*, p. 141.

incident reveals something of the hardness and callousness of the human heart. In exchange for money Judas Iscariot[65] agreed to betray the Lord by revealing something of his movements, so that the authorities could seize him quietly (cf. Luke 22:6).

The intention of the chief priests and scribes, reported in 14:2, was to apprehend Jesus *before* the festal season. There are two problems with 14:12-16: (1) it seems to be at odds with the earlier chronological notice; and (2) it seems to equate the first day of unleavened bread with the time when the Passover lambs were slain in the temple, when in fact the lambs were killed during the hours from 2:30 p.m. to sunset on Nisan 14, and the "first day of unleavened bread" began at 6 p.m. at the commencement of the next day, Nisan 15. Possibly, 14:12 originally read *πρὸ τῆς ἡμέρας*—"before the day of unleavened bread."[66] Or perhaps the Aramaic underlying this verse has been misunderstood and should read: "on the day before the feast of unleavened bread," i.e., Nisan 14.[67]

The following paragraphs represent the last meal of Jesus with his disciples as the Passover celebration (to be dated, from Mark 14:17ff. onwards, Nisan 15 according to the usual view of 14:12). This scheme contrasts with John, who dates the supper one day earlier and therefore regards it as an "anticipatory" Passover (or some other meal, such as Sabbath Qiddush or rabbinic *ḥabûrāh*) and makes the official Jewish Passover celebration on Nisan 14 coincident in time with the death of Jesus, God's paschal lamb (John 1:29), on the cross (cf. John 18:28; 19:29, 36).

Whether the last meal was a regular[68] or an anticipated[69] Passover, it is clear that it must be understood against the background of the Passover ritual and haggadah as a special example of Jewish table fellowship. From the latter come the notions of blessing God as the giver of food and drink (vs. 22) and the common life which binds the participants at the table. The paschal liturgy, drawn from Exodus 12 and interpreted in the haggadah for Passa, explains the use of the bread and the cup as "interpretative symbols," recalling the events of the Exodus and enabling Jewish families to relive the redemptive experience their fathers had known firsthand in Egypt.[70]

After singing the Hallel hymns (taken from Pss. 113—118) the band went out into the darkness of the ominous events which lay

[65] The name probably means "man of Kerioth," thus, unlike the other disciples, a southerner. For other possibilities see R. P. Martin, in *New Bible Dictionary*, *s.v.*

[66] So W.C. Allen, *The Gospel According to Saint Mark* (The Oxford Church Biblical Commentary) (1915), *ad loc.*

[67] So D. Chwolson, *Das letzte Passamahl Christi* (1908), pp. 133ff. See also J. Jeremias, *The Eucharistic Words of Jesus*, pp. 2-4.

[68] J. Jeremias, *op. cit.*

[69] V. Taylor, *The Gospel According to St. Mark*, pp. 664ff.

[70] See A. J. B. Higgins, *The Lord's Supper in the New Testament* (1952); R. P. Martin, *Worship in the Early Church*, pp. 110-18.

ahead, warned by the solemn announcement of desertion, betrayal, and death (14:26-31, 42). The failure of the disciples is typified (and aggravated) by the complete insensibility of the chosen three in Gethsemane (vv. 32-52), with Peter's lack of vigilance receiving special rebuke. Jesus greeted his arrival with "He's got his money" (ἀπέχει, a commercial term used in the papyri for a receipt) and placed himself into the hands of his foes. An attempt was made to defend him and an unnamed bystander lost his ear (possibly by accident). Jesus curtly rejected any such armed defense. He was not a (Zealot?) brigand whose cause needed to be bolstered by violence and hatred. Up to the last, he is seen to be refusing all unworthy notions by which his destiny may be averted.

The tantalizing *pericope* (14:51-52) has been taken as an autobiographical insertion made by John Mark, but had Mark been an eyewitness of these events, it is hard to explain why the dating of the last meal is so imprecise and uncertain. And the "awkward connexion [with the foregoing narrative] proves that he [the evangelist] is dependent on a source for the story."[71]

The trial scenes are divided into two parts.[72] First, the arraignment before the Sanhedrin appears to have as its object fastening some accusation on Jesus which will make a remission to Pilate a necessary next step. It is doubtful, then, if we should speak of the first hearing as a judicial "trial." More likely it was a preliminary investigation, informal and not too careful about legal procedures. The suborning of false witnesses (vv. 55-59), the claim to overthrow the temple (vv. 58ff.) and to be the Messiah (vs. 61) which are not *per se* tantamount to blasphemy, and the fact of holding the session at night and during the Passover season[73]—all these points show that the Sanhedrin "trial" was more in the nature of a preparatory inquiry. Moreover, if the Jewish "trial" were self-contained, why did the authorities not proceed, immediately after the sentence had been passed (vs. 64), to carry it out by stoning, the prescribed penalty for blasphemy and heresy according to the law (Lev. 24)? The answer may be found in John 19:31, 32, which records the Jews' inability to kill any man.[74]

G. D. Kilpatrick has endeavored to show that the earlier investigation was an effort on the part of the Sadducean aristocracy to prove to the Pharisees that Jesus was a public danger, while the Sadducees reserved the charge of treason, the crime of *lèse-majesté* for Pilate's court, thereby intending to implicate the Romans with the

71 Nineham, *op. cit.*, *ad loc.*
72 See R. P. Martin, "Trial of Jesus," in *New Bible Dictionary*, with bibliography there given, to which should be added D. R. Catchpole, *The Trial of Jesus.*
73 See J. Jeremias, *The Eucharistic Words of Jesus*, pp. 52f.
74 See C. K. Barrett's full note, *The Gospel According to St. John* (1955), *ad loc.*

major share of responsibility for his death.[75] In keeping with this charge, the question presented to Pilate was one of politics. Jesus claimed to be a king and thus was guilty of anti-Roman activities (amplified in Luke 23:2). Pilate was faced with an unenviable set of choices: either release Jesus at the expense of incurring the increased enmity of the Jewish leaders, whose tender susceptibilities he had already aroused (Luke 13:1ff.), or bow to the claims of expediency and condemn Jesus in order to quiet the clamor of his enemies. He tried to escape the dilemma by offering the freedom of Jesus in exchange for another Jesus, surnamed Barabbas.[76] But the crowd, incited by the priests, opted for Barabbas, a Zealot leader.

In Mark's account the Roman authorities are presented in a neutral light, and Pilate in particular is viewed as a man caught in a very difficult position. The Jews, on the other hand, are the villains (vv. 11, 13, 15) and the pressure group, exerting a baneful influence on the procurator, who knows full well how they are motivated (vv. 10, 14). In the Matthean version (27:24-25) this placing of the onus on the Jews is clearly emphasized, as P. Winter remarks.[77]

The tragedy moves now to its close, with the chief theme (that Jesus is the Messiah, incriminated by the Jewish leaders and so branded as a rebel against the empire by the Roman officials) picked up in the soldiers' mockery (15:16-20). Along the *via dolorosa* he stumbled and needed the assistance of a passerby, Simon, identified (perhaps because well-known to the Christian community at Rome in Mark's day; cf. Rom. 16:13) as the father of Alexander and Rufus, to carry the *patibulum* or crosspiece of this "most cruel and hideous punishment" (*crudelissimum taeterrimumque supplicium*, in Cicero's onomatopoeic description).[78]

Again at the scene of the cross the same charge is leveled at Jesus as a mocking taunt: "Let the Messiah the king of Israel come down from the cross, that we may see and believe" (vs. 32). The Jews are hostile to the last as the Romans maintain a reserved impartiality, passively accepting an ugly situation. In fact, passivity turns to a more positive attitude when a Roman centurion announced the early Christian confession: "Truly this man was a/the Son of God" (vs. 39). The absence of the definite article in the Greek is no proof that the statement should be understood in an indefinite sense.[79] Mark evidently intended that this confession on his lips should represent the

75 Kilpatrick, *The Trial of Jesus* (1953).

76 Given in some manuscripts in Matt. 27:16f. See Deissmann in *Mysterium Christi* (1930), ed. Bell and Deissmann, pp. 19-21.

77 Winter, *On the Trial of Jesus*; for a look at the difficulties in Winter's reconstruction see A.N. Sherwin-White, *Roman Society and Roman Law in the New Testament* (1963).

78 *In Verrem* 2.5.64.

79 See E. C. Colwell, *JBL*, 52 (1933), 12-21.

firstfruits of Gentile Christianity. The earlier mention of a kindly deed (vs. 36, where "vinegar" refers to the soldiers' *posca*, a mixture of sour wine and egg with water drunk by Roman soldiers on duty) seemed to follow the same tradition of presenting the Romans in a uniformly good light.

The early Christian understanding of Christ's death evidently included an overt reference to his burial (in 1 Cor. 15:4, which is usually taken to be a pre-Pauline *credo*, emanating from some Aramaic-speaking community).[80] The pericope (15:42-47) which relates how Joseph of Arimathaea made himself responsible for this office serves an evidential purpose. It certifies that he who was crucified really tasted the bitterness of mortality. Included here may be the beginnings of Christian speculation about the query, what did the Lord do between Good Friday and Easter (cf. also 1 Pet. 3:18ff.; 4:6)?

In primitive Christianity the validity of the assertion "Christ is alive" rested on a number of different grounds: the personal appearances of the living Lord; the fulfilment of the prophetic Scriptures, notably (apparently) Hosea 6; and the conviction of which Mark 16:1-8 is a witness, that the tomb was open, with the great stone removed, when the women (who had been last at the cross, 15:40-41) were the first to visit it on Nisan 17 (16:4). Open, but not exactly empty, for "a youth sitting on the right side, wearing a white robe" was inside and passed on the message: "He has risen: he is not here: here is the place where they laid him. But go and give this message to his disciples and Peter."

With the women's reaction of startled amazement to this news, the Gospel suddenly breaks off. This abrupt ending may be explained either as accidental (perhaps the last section was lost or destroyed) or by design (perhaps the writer was caught in a pogrom and hurriedly concluded his work or intended in any case to end his Gospel at that exact point). No one knows. But whether by mishap or interruption or deliberate intention, the evangelist expects his readers to be able to complete the story for themselves, for in vs. 7 he records the promise of an appearance in Galilee whither the risen Christ as shepherd will lead his scattered and bewildered sheep (cf. 14:28). In what is the final metaphor of the Gospel, Mark has pointed forward to the parousia, for 14:27—"I will strike the Shepherd, and the sheep shall be dispersed"—uses the eschatological technical term διασκορπισθῆναι to indicate a time of tribulation before the end of the age.[81] Hence the promised gathering of the scattered flock is a symbol of the approaching redemption for all the Gentiles (Matt. 25:31f.; John 11:51f.).

80 So A. M. Hunter, *Paul and His Predecessors*[2] (1961), pp. 117f.; cf. Acts 2:29; 13:29.

81 See J. Jeremias, *Jesus' Promise to the Nations*, p. 64.

In the later synoptic tradition there are divergent emphases in the geographical placing of the risen Christ's appearances. Matthew concentrates on Galilee; Luke confines the appearances to Jerusalem.[82] But all the Synoptics agree in stressing the validity of Jesus' personal presence after death and his reunion with his disciples. What is implicit in Mark (e.g., 13:10; 14:9) becomes an explicit command in Matthew (28:18-20) and Luke (24:47-48): these persons are charged with a commission to proclaim the message in the world (cf. Mark 16:15) as they are assured of the Lord's abiding and validating presence with them.

MARK'S LANGUAGE AND CONTENT

Vincent Taylor, using the important studies of H. B. Swete and C. H. Turner, has the fullest modern discussion of Mark's style.[83] Interest has centered on Mark's supposed Semitic style, about which Taylor concludes:

> We have good reason to speak of an Aramaic background to the Greek of the Gospel: there are grounds for suspecting the existence of Aramaic sources, which may, however, be oral; and we can speak of the Evangelist's use of a tradition which ultimately is Aramaic; but to say more is speculation.[84]

The most obvious features of Mark's Semitic style are the use of the paratactic *καί* to join sentences in preference to the use of subordinate clauses; the use of *ἤρξατο* ("he began") before the verb; the introduction of direct speech by the participle λέγων ("saying")—a common Old Testament feature; the very common genitival pronoun; the habit of using πολλά ("many") with adverbial force;[85] and the way the *pericopae* are arranged in groups of two or (more usually) three.[86]

A second trait of Markan style is his predilection for Latin terms and expressions. The most obvious, in verses where the Greek thinly disguises the underlying Latin word or words, are *modius* (4:21); *legio* (5:9, 15); *speculator* (6:27); *denarius* (6:37); *sextarius* (7:4); *census* (12:14); *quadrans* (12:42); *flagellare* (15:15); *praetorium* (15:16); *centurio* (15:39, 44ff.). Some of these are direct loan words, Latin words written in Greek characters. Significantly, in the case of *centurio*, the parallel verses in Matthew and Luke use the Greek ἑκατοντάρχης in the place of Mark's κεντυρίων.

A particularly striking case of Latinism involves the use of the term Ἡρῳδιανοί in a section (3:6) which contains another Latinism—

82 See A. M. Ramsey, *The Resurrection of Christ* (1946), for the motifs behind these emphases.
83 *The Gospel According to St. Mark* (1952), ch. v and vi.
84 *Ibid.*, p. 56.
85 See Moulton, *Grammar*, II (1919-29), 446.
86 Cf. W. Grundmann, *Kommentar* (1971), p. 18.

the phrase συμβούλιον ἐδίδουν ("they held a council").[87] Other Latin expressions have been found in 14:65 (*verberibus eum acceperunt*); 15:15 (*satisfacere*); 15:19 (*genua ponere*). It is of some importance that Mark has retained the name of Simon's family (15:21) and that these names (Alexander, Rufus) recur in Romans 16:13 as the names of church members at Rome, where presumably Latin was the language used. This evidence of Mark's Latinisms has a direct bearing on the question of the recipients of the Gospel.[88]

Three facets of Mark's characteristic content may be noted.

1. The vivid way in which the stories are told is a feature which impresses all careful readers. The narratives are full of intimate details, unimportant in themselves, yet such as an eyewitness would be likely to recall when, at a later period, he related the incidents. For instance, the attitudes, the expressions and even the gestures of Jesus are reported (7:33; 9:36; 10:16), with special emphasis on his observation (5:32) and his attitude to those who came under his scrutiny (1:41, where the reading ὀργισθείς, "being angry," is to be preferred to the TR; 3:5; 3:34; 10:21; 10:23; 11:11). Similarly, snatches of conversation between the disciples are noted; and the remarks of the onlookers and the crowd are remembered. A good illustration of this is 9:14-29, in which the unusual wealth of detail convinces even the form critic K. L. Schmidt that the story "can only go back to good tradition."[89]

These facts seem clearly to point to the presence of an eyewitness who both remembered the penetrating look of Jesus and recalled that those who heard his voice and saw his mighty works reacted in a decisive way. Perhaps the story of the rich young man (10:17-22) makes this point clear, especially when we compare the absence of detail in the parallel version in Luke (18:18-27). The Third Gospel omits such characteristic details as that the young man ran and knelt; that Jesus looked on him and loved him; and that, faced with the Lord's challenge, his countenance fell. Another realistic detail is preserved in 10:32. On the last journey to Jerusalem, Jesus walked alone, ahead of his disciples, and as they followed, fear gripped them. As B. K. Rattey comments, "Mark alone tells us all this; but who told Mark? It could only have been one of the Twelve."[90]

J. Weiss notices that in some of the stories the action is told from the standpoint of those who see Jesus more than from the standpoint of Jesus himself, especially in the case of the call of the

87 Josephus regards the title "Herodians" as a Latinism; *Jewish War*, 1.16.6. For συμβούλιον ἐδίδουν, see the commentaries *ad loc.*

88 Grundmann, *op. cit.*, p. 19. But see R. P. Martin, *Mark: Evangelist and Theologian*, p. 65.

89 *Der Rahmen der Geschichte Jesu*, p. 227.

90 *The Making of the Synoptic Gospels* (1942), p. 32.

Galilean fishermen (1:16-20).[91] This observation again hints at Mark's dependence on an eyewitness tradition, notably that of Peter himself. Alternatively, many modern scholars use these data to affirm that Mark was a superb literary artist, who added lifelike touches by way of verisimilitude.

2. The attitude of Peter is clearly to be seen. B. W. Bacon pointed out that in the majority of references to Peter in this Gospel he is mentioned in terms of disgrace or rebuke (8:27ff.; 9:5, 6; 10:28ff.; 14:29ff.; 14:66-72). Two explanations are possible to account for this. Rawlinson deduces from these candid appraisals and criticisms that when the Gospel was published, Peter's memory as a martyr was already revered and his character invested with an honor no stain from the record of his earthly life could tarnish.[92] The second possible explanation is that Peter's own confessions of failure and disgrace account for the report of these episodes. This seems to be supported by the way Peter's name is attached to certain parts of the record, where the other Gospels give only a vague reference to "they" or "one of the disciples" (1:36; 11:21; 16:7). Conversely, it becomes difficult to account for the omission of Jesus' encomium (Matt. 16:17-19) if Mark wanted to glorify Peter. Only the humbled apostle who was willing to relate in such detail his denial of the Lord would have left out the words of the Lord's blessing on him. Further, the words "Peter remembered and said to him" (11:21) must have come to the evangelist direct from Peter himself (cf. 14:72).

A further confirmation that Mark depends directly or indirectly on Peter for these details is found in his attitude to the disciples as a body of men. Mark spares no detail when he reports the failures and misunderstandings of the Twelve. The clearest instance of this feature is 4:38: "Teacher, do you not care if we perish?"—a curt reproof on the lips of the disciples in the boat, which has been softened in the corresponding incident in Matthew (8:25) and Luke (8:24).

D. E. Nineham has raised a challenge to this ascription of Mark's material to his dependence on Peter. Nineham's main argument is a form-critical one, namely, that Mark's material "*bears all the signs of having been community tradition* and cannot therefore be derived *directly* from St Peter or any other eye-witness."[93] Community tradition, however, may well include the report of eyewitness testimony in its first stage; after all, *someone* had to set the process in motion, unless these stories are spun out of the fertile imagination of that anonymous entity, the faceless "community." Nineham's subsequent statement that if *some* of the Markan material is a community product (which no one denies), then "all of it, without exception," is

[91] Cited by V. Taylor, *The Four Gospels* (1945), p. 53n.
[92] A.E.J. Rawlinson, *op. cit.*, p. xxix.
[93] *Op. cit.*, p. 27 (ital. in orig.).

so, is exaggeration and false logic. Third, Nineham overlooks the role of Mark as an evangelist and editor—a new emphasis which has come with redaction criticism.

3. The prominence given to the cross is a marked trait of this Gospel, whose *leitmotiv* may be said to be that of suffering and martyrdom. T.A. Burkill cites W. Marxsen's thesis that Mark composed his Gospel backwards, thus giving supreme prominence to the cross: "The passion-story represents the first text of the tradition concerning Jesus to be fixed in writing. This then grew backwards."[94] Almost a third of the record is taken up with the passion story. "Mark devoted three-eighths of the gospel to events immediately leading to his death," J. Bowman comments.[95]

The shadow of the cross falls across the page as early as 2:20 and 3:6. There is a threefold prediction of the passion in precise terms (8:31; 9:31; 10:33ff.), as well as allusions—sometimes veiled (9:12), sometimes explicit (10:45)—to how Jesus expects his ministry will end.[96] Interwoven with the thought that the Lord's life will end in a sacrificial death for sinners is the teaching that those who are his followers must expect to suffer for his sake (8:34ff.; 10:38ff.). Rawlinson proposes that this interest derives from the first audience for the Gospel—the church at Rome, which was undergoing persecution and in which the possibility of martyrdom was a live one.[97]

The emphasis on the cross and the teaching of the disciples' dying for Christ's sake are the two most important supports for the theory, put out by G. Volkmar in 1857 and maintained since by B. W. Bacon, that the entire Gospel was written to undergird, with a narrative in the form of an allegory, the distinctive tenets of Paulinism.[98] The theory has met with little acceptance,[99] but more recent studies have explored another possible link between Paul's bare announcement of the cross and resurrection and Mark's desire to clothe that kerygma with flesh and blood.

THE STRUCTURE OF THE GOSPEL

As we saw in our opening chapter, Mark (like the other evangelists) does not present a biography of Jesus, in the popular sense of that

94 Burkill, *Mysterious Revelation* (1963), pp. 218ff.; cf. Marxsen, *Mark the Evangelist*, p. 31.

95 *The Gospel of Mark: The New Christian Jewish Passover Haggada* (1965), p. 312.

96 On these passion prophecies, cf. R.H. Fuller, *The Mission and Achievement of Jesus* (1954), pp. 55-64.

97 *Op. cit.*, p. xvii. See now W. L. Lane, *Commentary on the Gospel of Mark* (1974), pp. 12-17 for a life-setting in Roman persecution.

98 For the other features of Mark which are supposedly "Pauline," see V. Taylor, *The Gospels*, pp. 56ff.

99 Cf. J. Moffatt, *Introduction to the Literature of the New Testament* (1918), pp. 235ff.; Rawlinson, *op. cit.*, pp. xliii ff. M. Werner wrote his

term.[100] The exordium of the Gospel (1:1) makes it clear that Mark's intention was to write a *gospel*, i.e., a record of the good news which came with Jesus Christ (cf. 1:14, 15; 14:9, and, in the appendix, 16:15). Of this good news Jesus Christ is both the author and the content. His coming into the world constituted the fact of the gospel, while at the same time in his public ministry he proclaimed the gospel. Mark, however, is not concerned to provide a full description of the Lord's personality. He focuses attention on the events of the ministry. This accounts for the obvious omissions in his gospel story (e.g., the birth narratives, accounts of Jesus' boyhood, the factors which shaped his thought and career, and explicit estimates of his personal appearance and the impact of his personality on others). Mark himself is hidden and makes no attempt to pass a personal judgment on the story he narrates. Likewise none of the persons who appear on the stage is mentioned for his or her own sake, but for the Lord's.

1. Even if it be granted that Mark's Gospel was not intended to be in the nature of a biographical picture of the historical Jesus, after the style of Boswell's *Life of Johnson*, it is possible that he does present an intended sequence of events, set in a true historical framework, of Jesus' public ministry and activity. This is the theory known as the Markan hypothesis, and it is the foundation on which the once popular "lives of Christ" were built. Even the more critical scholars were not exempt from this initial conviction. It is an assumption of the integrity of the Markan outline that lies at the heart of T. W. Manson's reconstruction of Jesus' teaching about himself as Son of Man.[101]

The rise of form criticism has meant that this theory has been seriously attacked. The first effects of this opposition to the Markan hypothesis are seen in A.E.J. Rawlinson's commentary, which starts from the premise that "such attempts to treat the Markan arrangement of the Gospel materials as supplying an outline, in chronological order, of the course of events are profoundly mistaken."[102] He proceeds to set forth how the Markan hypothesis "in recent years has been riddled with criticisms of the most damaging kind." The most fundamental difficulty is the intrinsic improbability that anything like a chronological outline of our Lord's ministry, or an itinerary of his movements, would be preserved throughout a whole generation of oral

study *Der Einfluss paulinischer Theologie im Markusevangelium* (1923) expressly to refute this notion.

100 For the influence of contemporary historiography on the understanding of the nature of the Gospels, cf. J. M. Robinson, *The Problem of History in Mark*, ch. 1.

101 See T.W. Manson's *The Teaching of Jesus*, esp. pp. 201ff. This assumption is questioned by J.M. Robinson, *A New Quest of the Historical Jesus*, p. 38n, and Norman Perrin, *The Kingdom of God in the Teaching of Jesus* (1963), pp. 96ff.

102 *Op. cit.*, p. xx.

tradition by a church not primarily interested in such matters. On this view, the Gospel writers themselves provided the framework and the arrangement for the materials which they derived from the tradition. This assumption may be said to be the guiding principle of the form-critical approach to the Gospels and to Mark in particular. And historically, the approach of the form critics was developed as a denial of the Markan hypothesis.

C. H. Dodd has argued that the Markan framework conforms to the pattern of the Acts-kerygma (esp. in Peter's speech in Acts 10:34ff.) and that Mark's "generalizing summaries," placed together, form a continuous piece of narrative. This proposal has bolstered the Markan hypothesis by showing that the author evidently did intend some historical progression in relating the movements of Jesus. [103] Dodd's article has been critically scrutinized by D.E. Nineham, who holds that the order of events was of no significance in the apostolic preaching. [104] But Dodd's thesis has proved very influential, especially in Britain and pre-World War II America, and has checked any large-scale capitulation to the conclusions of the form critics, to whom Dodd's conclusion runs counter: "Markan order does represent a genuine succession of events, within which movement and development can be traced."

The debate over the integrity of the Markan outline as reflecting the actual course of events in Jesus' ministry is still proceeding. [105] In effect, the line-up is decided by this question: Is the story of Jesus a loose assortment of *pericopae* put together in an artificial way and partly the creation of early Christian imagination, or did the first Christians have a real interest in the historical development of Jesus' ministry among men?

2. A view at the opposite end of the scale to that of Dodd is represented by the German form critics Dibelius and Bultmann. [106] On this showing, the Markan material forms an accidental collection of disconnected stories and sayings. An even more devastating attack on Mark's order of events was made by K.L. Schmidt, whose thesis

[103] *ExpT*, 43 (1932), 396-400; repr. in *New Testament Studies*, pp. 1-11, entitled the "Framework of the Gospel Narrative."

[104] "The Order of Events in St. Mark's Gospel—An Examination of Dr. Dodd's hypothesis," in *Studies in the Gospels in Memory of R.H. Lightfoot*, ed. D.E. Nineham, pp. 223-39. See also the introduction to his Pelican commentary on Mark.

[105] Nineham's objections to Dodd have been opposed by H. Sawyerr, "The Marcan Framework," *SJT*, 14 (1961), 279-94, and A.T. Hanson, *Vindications*, pp. 74-102. Nineham has defended his position in a number of essays, including ". . . *Et hoc genus omne*—An Examination of Dr. A.T. Hanson's Strictures on Some Recent Gospel Study," in *Christian History and Interpretation*, pp. 199-222, and "History and the Gospel," *London Quarterly and Holborn Review*, 36 (1967), 93ff.

[106] Their views have been popularized by R.H. Lightfoot, *History and Interpretation in the Gospels*, and F.C. Grant, *The Earliest Gospel* (1943).

may be stated in his own words: "As a whole, there is no life of Jesus in the sense of an evolving biography, no chronological sketch of the story of Jesus, but only single stories, sections (*pericopae*), which are put into a framework."[107] The points of interest which emerge from this treatment are mentioned by V. Taylor, but, as he grants, "Schmidt's views have every appearance of a reaction which has been carried too far."[108] But the reaction has persisted chiefly through the work of Bultmann's disciples in Germany and J.M. Robinson in America.[109]

3. Vincent Taylor begins from the supposition that the evangelist has used a series of what he calls "complexes," which he regards as small groups of narratives or sayings which belong together.[110] Mark, according to Taylor, took over these complexes, which had an independent existence, added his own comments and connected them with some simple literary ligatures. On this view Mark's role is strictly that of editor and compiler.

A modification of this idea is found in the work of H.A. Guy, who harks back to the Gospel's basis document, which consisted of the papyrus leaves on which were written stories of Jesus, which would have proved of inestimable value to the early preachers. An unknown editor, Guy believes, brought these together and added teaching material, but did not arrange the papyrus sheets into any coherent pattern. The latter task, which was the work of the "compiler," was undertaken by John Mark, who was held in high esteem in the churches on account of his association with Peter.[111]

Taylor also describes some older views of Markan sources which scholars have postulated. Of special note in recent discussion are the elaborate attempt at source criticism by W.L. Knox, especially his isolation of a "Twelve-source," showing Jesus' dealings with the disciples and a passion story;[112] B.S. Easton's work on the controversy-stories of chapters 2-3 and 12;[113] and T.W. Manson's development of the views of C.H. Turner who sought to isolate certain passages as "Petrine."[114] Manson seeks to enlarge the scope of this Petrine material and to classify it. Other sources were at Mark's disposal, he adds; and these are of considerable antiquity and conse-

107 *Der Rahmen der Geschichte Jesu*, p. 317.

108 V. Taylor, *The Gospels*, p. 59.

109 See Robinson's *A New Quest of the Historical Jesus*, ch. 2.

110 *The Gospel According to St. Mark*, pp. 90-104; cf. C.H. Dodd, *loc. cit.*, p. 10.

111 H.A. Guy, *The Origin of the Gospel of Mark* (1954).

112 Knox, *The Sources of the Synoptic Gospels*, I (*St. Mark*) (1953).

113 In *Studies in Early Christianity*, ed. S.J. Case. According to Easton, 2:13—3:6 and 12:13-27 were originally a unit which "was formed in pre-Markan times and belonged to the tradition of the Palestinian Christian community" (p. 92).

114 "The Foundation of the Synoptic Tradition: The Gospel of Mark," *BJRL* (1944); repr. in his *Studies in the Gospels and Epistles*, pp. 28-45.

quent worth (such as the "Passion of John" in 6:17-29, which "has all the appearance of being a piece of Palestinian [originally Aramaic] tradition"). The tendency which Manson's work represents leads to an increased confidence in the Gospel record and away from the form-critical ideas that the sections of the Gospel were "manufactured" by preachers in the hellenistic church.

4. There is a group of hypotheses which try to maintain that Mark's structure is governed by considerations of the liturgical and cultic needs of the early churches. Best known are the arguments of P. Carrington and A. Farrer. Carrington begins with the assumption that the church took over a lectionary scheme from the Jewish synagogue worship. The sections of Mark then appear in a sequence dictated by the order of festivals in the Jewish festal lectionary.[115]

Carrington's novel theory has not met with much favor.[116] Its weakness is its implication, *ex hypothesi*, that the Gospel material has been doctored to conform to a supposed liturgical pattern; and that there are some verses which do not fit in and therefore need to be ironed out. Nonetheless, the transmission of the gospel via the worshiping life of the early churches is a presupposition for which recent study has produced some important evidence.

Austin Farrer, in a series of erudite volumes, has supported the view that the governing principle of Mark's composition is conformity to Old Testament typology and prefigurations. On this theory, even the simplest gospel story becomes invested with cryptic significance and esoteric meaning, especially with regard to the employment of numbers. The elaborateness of such a construction does not argue for its cogency; and its oversubtlety is its weakness. Farrer himself revised its construction.[117] Helen Gardner, in a penetrating survey of Farrer's ideas, places her finger on the real point: "I find it hard . . . to believe that the first readers of St. Mark would have been as ingenious in picking up symbolic references as is suggested [by Farrer]."[118] J.M. Robinson faults the methodological assumptions of both Carrington and Farrer, whose "argument is not built upon what Mark clearly and repeatedly has to say, but upon inferences as to the basis of the Markan order, a subject upon which Mark is silent."[119] If the Markan

[115] *The Primitive Christian Calendar* (1952). Later studies appear in "The Calendrical Hypothesis of the Origin of Mark," *ExpT*, 67 (1956), 100-103; and *According to Mark* (1961).

[116] See criticisms by R.P. Casey, "St. Mark's Gospel," *Theology*, 55 (1952), 362ff.; and in great detail by W.D. Davies, "Reflections on Archbishop Carrington's *The Primitive Christian Calendar*," in the Dodd *Festschrift*, repr. in his *Christian Origins and Judaism* (1962), pp. 67ff.

[117] Cf. Farrer's modification of the earlier *A Study in St. Mark* (1951) in his *St. Matthew and St. Mark* (1954).

[118] "The Poetry of St. Mark," in *The Limits of Literary Criticism* (1956), p. 34.

[119] *The Problem of History in Mark*, p. 12.

order is uncertain, then Carrington and Farrer have lost their cases.[120]

5. The catechetical needs of the early Christians are the decisive issue in Mark's structure, according to the theory of G. Schille, who maintains that the entire composition of the Gospel is directed so as to indicate the elaborate parallel between the life of the Lord and the experience of catechumens, who came into the church through the gateway of baptism, instruction, the holy supper, and the prospect of martyrdom.[121] This sequence is reflected in the chapters of the Gospel and in other parts of early Christian literature (esp. Heb. 6:1ff. and the *Didache*).

6. E. Lohmeyer attaches important meaning to the geographical data of the Gospel.[122] Lohmeyer's idea that there were two main centers of early Christianity, quite distinct from each other, located in Galilee and Jerusalem, is examined sympathetically by R.H. Lightfoot and F.C. Grant.[123] As far as Mark is concerned, the dominant motif, according to Lohmeyer, is the importance of Galilee as the locus of divine revelation and the place to which the apocalyptic Son of Man will return as a prelude to the parousia (see 14:28 and 16:7, on which Lohmeyer builds a great deal).

Another writer to attach importance to the geographical settings of Mark is W. Marxsen.[124] He maintains that the shaping of Mark's Gospel has been determined by two ideas—the parousia which was awaited in Galilee, and the orientation of Jesus' ministry to Galilee. These two notions are related, he says, since the parousia was expected in the same place as that at which the first coming took place. Marxsen's deduction is that Mark 13 means that Mark wrote in Galilee for the community which had fled from Jerusalem at the outbreak of the Jewish war. This explains the conclusion that 16:7 is not a reference to the appearance of the risen Christ, but his imminent parousia. Because the parousia has not yet taken place, Mark could not report the fulfilment of the promise in 16:7.[125]

THE AUTHORSHIP OF THE GOSPEL

The earliest witnesses to the Second Gospel—Papias, Irenaeus, Clement of Alexandria, Origen, Jerome, and the Muratorian Canon if we accept

[120] For further criticism of Farrer, see T.A. Roberts, *History and Christian Apologetic* (1960), pp. 114-43. Roberts subjects Farrer's historical methodology and vocabulary to a perceptive criticism.

[121] "Bemerkungen zur Formgeschichte des Evangeliums. Rahmen und Aufbau des Markus-Evangeliums," *NTS*, 4.1 (1957-58), 1-24.

[122] This is the basis of an elaborate theory advanced in *Galiläa und Jerusalem* (1936).

[123] Lightfoot, *Locality and Doctrine in the Gospels* (1938); Grant, *The Earliest Gospel*, ch. 6.

[124] *Mark the Evangelist*.

[125] For a fuller treatment of Marxsen's thesis, see J. Rohde, *Rediscovering the Teaching of the Evangelists*, and Ralph P. Martin, *Mark: Evangelist and Theologian* (1972), pp. 70-75.

the usually allowed textual conjecture[126] —associate the Gospel with Mark and link him with Peter. The Papias tradition (related by Eusebius) has pride of place in the patristic tradition, and runs as follows:

> The Elder said this also: Mark, who has been Peter's interpreter, wrote down carefully as much as he remembered, recording both sayings and doings of Christ, not however in order. For he was not a hearer of the Lord, nor a follower, but later a follower of Peter, as I said. And he [Peter or Mark] adapted his teachings to the needs of his hearers but not as one who is engaged in making a compendium of the Lord's precepts.[127]

Modern discussion has questioned the validity of this ancient *testimonium*, with many points raised in objection.[128]

The important argument is that which attacks the tradition of a connection between the author of the Gospel and Peter. The lack of a strict chronological outline and Mark's dependence on traditional material make it hard to explain the statement that he adapted Peter's teaching to the needs of his hearers (or of the moment). But we should also observe the qualifying remarks—that Mark was not making a compendium of the Lord's precepts and that he did not write the "sayings and doings" of the Lord "in order."[129]

On the positive side, this testimony says three things. First, it traces back one of the sources which Mark used to Peter's teaching. Second, it remarks that Mark himself had no firsthand knowledge of the sayings and deeds of the Lord, but depended on eyewitnesses. Third, the information he picked up was gleaned in the course of his work as ἑρμηνευτής to Peter. This term means something like private secretary or *aide-de-camp.*[130] A similar picture is found in the anti-Marcionite prologue to the Gospel, which describes the evangelist as Peter's *interpres.*[131] The same document declares that Mark composed his Gospel in Italy after Peter's departure (*post excessionem*). There are problems connected with this statement, but T.W. Manson's summing-up seems reasonable. "If Peter had paid a visit to Rome some time between 55 and 60; if Mark had been his interpreter then; if after Peter's departure from the city Mark had taken in hand—at the request of the Roman hearers—a written record of what Peter had said; then the essential points in the evidence would all be satisfied."[132]

126 See Rawlinson, *op. cit.*, p. xxvii.
127 See H.E.W. Turner, "The Tradition of Mark's Dependence upon Peter," *ExpT*, 71 (1960), 260-63.
128 See Austin Farrer, *A Study in St. Mark*, pp. 10ff. Papias is not free from the charge of writing to prove a point: see R. P. Martin, *Mark: Evangelist and Theologian*, pp. 80-83.
129 For the different meanings attached to the use of the term "order" (τάξις)—whether chronological, rhetorical or calendrical—see H.A. Guy, *The Origin of the Gospel of Mark*, ch. 2.
130 So T.W. Manson, *The Teaching of Jesus*, p. 23n.
131 See W.F. Howard, *ExpT*, 47 (1936), 534-38.
132 *Studies in the Gospels and Epistles*, p. 40.

John Mark is known to us from references in the Acts of the Apostles (12:12, 25; 13:5, 13; 15:37, 39) and the Epistles (Col. 4:10; 2 Tim. 4:11; Philemon 24; 1 Pet. 5:13). His close association with apostolic testimony is clearly indicated in these texts. Both his home and his family connections played an important part in early Christian history. His mother (of sufficient importance to be named) was a member of the Jerusalem church and her home was a regular venue for Christian assembly. To her home Peter came after his escape from prison. Then follows a period of intimate contact with Paul and his party; subsequently to be followed by association with his cousin Barnabas and the mission to Cyprus. About twelve years later (we learn from the captivity letters) Mark is reconciled to Paul and is commended to the church at Colossae. Later again Paul asks that Timothy shall bring Mark to him at Rome, for "he is useful to me for ministering." At last, Mark is brought to association once more with Peter, who refers to him as his "son" in a letter written from Rome.[133]

These varied allusions to Mark's acquaintance with early Christian leaders confirm Manson's judgment that "Mark had considerable opportunities of gathering knowledge of the kind that would later be useful in the composition of the gospel."[134] Furthermore, Mark's close contact with Peter, both in Jerusalem and in Rome, would go far to explain the phenomenon in the Second Gospel to which C.H. Turner has drawn attention: that Mark's account of many incidents in the gospel story stands in direct contrast with Matthew and Luke. Mark's version "may be called autobiographical. They [Matthew and Luke] write Lives of Christ, he records the experience of an eye-witness and companion."[135] Turner notes that if Mark's uses of the third person plural are read in the first person plural, as though Peter were speaking, a vivid impression of forceful narration is registered. Commenting on Mark 1:29, he applies this principle: "We came into our house with James and John; and my wife's mother was ill in bed with a fever, and at once we tell him about her." Turner detects this process elsewhere in the Gospel—1:21; 5:1, 38; 6:53, 54; 8:22; 9:14, 30, 33; 10:32, 46; 11:1, 12, 15, 20, 27; 14:18, 22, 26, 32. In Turner's observations we have one of the most cogent proofs of the apostolic testimony (Peter's) behind the Second Gospel, written by John Mark.

Recently, however, there has been a definite swing away from the traditional identification of the author of this Gospel with John Mark of Jerusalem.[135a] Points raised against the acceptance of this

[133] So 1 Peter 5:13, apparently; see Papias in Eusebius, *Church History* 2.25. On this verse, see E.G. Selwyn, *First Epistle of St. Peter* (1947), pp. 60-62.

[134] *Studies in the Gospels and Epistles*, p. 37.

[135] *Op. cit.*, p. 48.

[135a] In particular, K. Niederwimmer, "Johannes Markus und die Frage nach dem Verfasser des zweiten Evangeliums," *ZNTW*, 58 (1967), 172-88.

tradition include the form-critical argument that this Gospel is an assemblage of earlier traditions, which makes no room for eyewitness testimony via Peter; the commonness of the name Mark in the Roman Empire, which means the early church must have had many persons so named on its register; the destruction of any connection between Mark and 1 Peter 5:13 if 1 Peter is a much later, non-apostolic document; the evidences adduced that the evangelist had no firsthand acquaintance with Palestine (5:1; 6:45; 7:24, 31; 8:22; 14:12).

DATING OF THE GOSPEL

1. The external data speak with no decisive voice about the date of Mark's composition. Irenaeus writes that "after their deaths [Peter and Paul] Mark, the disciple and interpreter of Peter, himself also handed down to us in writing the things which Peter had proclaimed."[136] On the other hand, Clement of Alexandria says that Mark was instructed by Peter to write out the things the apostle had said, and that this literary effort was published later, but in Peter's lifetime, for Peter's comment on the composition is recorded.[137] Attempts have been made to discount the interpretation placed on Irenaeus' words by suggesting that he does not mean to give chronological information, but is concerned simply to state the continuity of Mark's writing and Peter's preaching. But this is far from obvious.[138] The accuracy of Irenaeus, however, may be impugned in the light of his earlier remark that Matthew was produced while Peter and Paul were still preaching—a historical notice difficult to maintain. The external evidence is thus divided, and no certain dating is possible from this source.

2. Internal evidence of the date of the Gospel is subject to various interpretations. The reference to persecutions (8:34; 9:31; 10:33f., 45; 13:8, 10)[139] and to the controversies which surrounded the issue of Gentile freedom (in 7:17-23, 26f.; 13:10) are taken to indicate that the Gospel belongs to the decade AD 60-70.[140]

The enigmatic verse, 13:14—"But when you see the desolating sacrilege (τὸ βδέλυγμα τῆς ἐρημώσεως) set up where it ought not to be (let the reader understand), then let those that are in Judaea flee to the mountains"—with its cryptic allusion to the profanation of the temple at Jerusalem, has been used to suggest that Mark must have been written within a few years of the siege of the Holy City in 66-70.[141] Alternatively, C.C. Torrey and T.W. Manson have sought to

136 Irenaeus, *Against Heretics* 3.1.2.
137 Cf. Eusebius, *Church History* 6.14.
138 As V. Taylor grants, *The Gospels*, p. 51.
139 See Rawlinson, *op. cit.*, pp. xvi-xvii.
140 Taylor, *The Gospel According to St. Mark*, p. 31.
141 On this verse see G.R. Beasley-Murray, *Jesus and the Future*, pp. 255ff. and *Commentary on Mark Thirteen* (1957), pp. 59-72.

relate this text to Caligula's attempt to set up his statue in the temple in AD 40.[142] Some scholars see the reference to the desolating scourge as a prophecy after the fact, and thus take it to have no bearing on the question of the Gospel's dating.[143] Against this, in addition to its wrongheaded understanding of the role of Jesus as a prophet, is the objective fact that certain verses (13:1ff.) imply that the temple was still standing when the evangelist wrote.

All in all, a date in the decade AD 60-70 seems certain in spite of some notable attempts to champion an early dating.[144] A more precise dating is offered by Rawlinson and Taylor, both of whom date the publication in the years 65-67, chiefly on the ground that the Jewish war does not appear to have broken out, as the references in chapter 13 are vague and imprecise.[145] On the other hand, S.E. Johnson thinks that the Gospel may have been written after the destruction of the temple (which seems to be hinted at, he says, in certain premonitory signs of ch. 13, esp. vv. 19-22) but before the conclusion of hostilities in Palestine.[146] These hostilities were not finally concluded until April 74, so the Gospel may conceivably fall within a larger period of time.

More recently, one of the most ambitious attempts to place the publication of Mark's Gospel in the frame of historical circumstance has been made by S.G.F. Brandon. He has expressed the view that at the conclusion of the Jewish war in AD 70-71 there was a resultant need for some literary apologetic to make life tolerable for Christians in the Roman Empire by dissociating them from rebellious Jews.[147] Mark's Gospel, with its anti-Jewish bias (says Brandon), provides just that apologetic.

THE ORIGIN AND DESTINATION OF THE GOSPEL

It is impossible to give a final answer to the query of where and for whom the Gospel was written. The external and internal evidence do offer some pointers to the conclusion that Mark wrote in Rome and for some Gentile constituency.

1. There is a statement in Irenaeus, which is endorsed by the otherwise divergent testimony of Clement, that Mark was in Rome

[142] Torrey, *Our Translated Gospels* (n.d.), p. 262; Manson, *The Sayings of Jesus*, p. 329.

[143] For this view, see, e.g., B.W. Bacon, *The Gospel of Mark*, p. 93.

[144] E.g., Harnack, *Date of the Acts and Synoptic Gospels* (1911), 126-33, suggesting a date before AD 60; W.C. Allen, *The Gospel according to Saint Mark*, suggesting a date before 50.

[145] Rawlinson, *op. cit.*, pp. xxix-xxx; Taylor, *The Gospel According to St. Mark*, p. 32.

[146] *The Gospel According to St. Mark* (Harper's NT Commentary) (1960), p. 20.

[147] *Jesus and the Zealots*. See above, pp. 93-97, 126.

when the Gospel was published. The anti-Marcionite Prologue preserves the same tradition in the statement that "after the departure of Peter himself he [Mark] wrote down this same Gospel in the regions of Italy (*in partibus Italiae*)."[148]

This evidence tallies with Papias' witness that Mark was Peter's interpreter; and we know that Peter was martyred at Rome.[149] 2 Timothy 4:11 and 1 Peter 5:13 locate Mark in Rome, if we assume (with most commentators) that in the latter text "Babylon" is a cryptogram for the imperial capital. The earliest attestation of the use of the Gospel comes from 1 Clement 15:2 and Hermas, *Sim.* 5.2, which are both associated with Rome.[150] Interestingly, 1 Clement quotes Isaiah 29:13 in the same form as that used in Mark 7:6.[151]

A Roman provenance would be consonant with the references in the Gospel to persecutions and martyrdom (8:34-38; 10:38f.; 13:9-13). It is claimed that these texts are best understood in the light of Nero's treatment of Christians in Rome in the seventh decade of the first century. But this deduction is not conclusive, although Rawlinson presents an attractive case for it.[152]

Against this consentient witness to the Roman origin of the Gospel is the report of Chrysostom that it originated in Egypt.[153] This statement, as Johnson says, is probably based on a misunderstanding of Eusebius' remark: "They say that Mark set out for Egypt and was first to preach there the gospel which he had composed."[154] Eusebius speaks further of Mark's association with the church at Alexandria. This claim of an Alexandrian connection with Mark should not be lightly dismissed,[154a] but the evidence seems weighted in favor of Rome.

Some modern scholars opine that Antioch was the place of origin,[155] but this is more speculative than substantial. Storr, for instance, tried to show that the father of Alexander and Rufus (mentioned in Mark 15:21) is referred to because his sons were among the men who went to Antioch in the Gentile mission of Acts 11:19f. But this is sheer hypothesis. Nor is there good reason to accept W.C.

[148] See further on this text R.M. Grant, *Anglican Theological Review*, 23 (1941), 231ff.

[149] See O. Cullmann's full treatment, *Peter: Disciple, Apostle, Martyr*^{2} (1962), Part I, ch. 3.

[150] On the latter text, see S.E. Johnson, *op. cit.*, p. 7.

[151] Cf. H. Köster, *Synoptische Überlieferung bei den apostolischen Vätern* (1957), pp. 21f.

[152] *Op. cit.*, pp. xxi-xxii; cf. B.H. Streeter, *op. cit.*, pp. 495ff. and Lane, *op. cit.*, pp. 15-17, 25.

[153] *Homily on Matthew*, 1.

[154] *Church History* 2.16.1; cited by S.E. Johnson, *op. cit.*, p. 15.

[154a] See Manson, *Studies in the Gospels and Epistles*, pp. 38f.

[155] E.g. J.V. Bartlet, *St. Mark* (Century Bible) (1922), pp. 36f., following G.C. Storr.

Allen's theory (following Blass and C.C. Torrey) that the Gospel was first written in Aramaic in Jerusalem and later translated into Greek at Antioch,[156] which was a bilingual center of early Christianity, of which G. Dix writes: "It was a bastion of Hellenism in the Syriac lands . . . the inevitable meeting point of the two worlds."[157] More recently W. Marxsen has sought to uphold the view that the Gospel was published first in Galilee.[158]

2. That Mark wrote for Gentile readers is all but finally proved by the internal evidence of the Gospel itself. In the first place, he explains Jewish customs and practices which may have been unfamiliar to his non-Palestinian readers (e.g., 7:3, 4).

Second, Aramaic expressions which remain in the text in a Greek form are interpreted for the readers; e.g., *'Abbā* (14:36, which receives the same interpretative addition in Rom. 8:15 and Gal. 4:6). But the addition is only approximately correct, as Johnson notes.[159] In other places, however, Mark is content to incorporate a block of teaching in its Aramaic form, which is turned woodenly into Greek (esp. in 14:22ff., the Semitic background of which has been demonstrated by J. Jeremias).[160]

Third, a series of Latinisms (see above, pp. 202f.) betrays both the Gentile milieu in which the author moved and a Gentile audience for whom these expressions would be meaningful.

Finally, some scholars claim that Mark was unacquainted with Palestine because he refers to place-names (such as Dalmanutha, 8:10; Gerasa, 5:1; Bethsaida, 7:26) and mentions the Herodian family (6:17) and Jewish divorce laws (10:12), which show no firsthand knowledge of Palestinian topography and life.[161] But it may be that Mark is simply faithful to the tradition he has received, so that the allegation of inaccuracy is unnecessary. Nevertheless, he writes as one who is more concerned to relate the gospel tradition than to interject his personal reminiscences.

TWO SPECIAL PROBLEMS

1. The abrupt opening of Mark: "The beginning of the gospel of Jesus Christ (Son of God)" (1:1) has often called forth comment. The recent view is that this sentence is the title of the whole book which follows, but it may conceivably be simply the heading of the first paragraphs (up to 1:8 or up to 1:13) as R.H. Lightfoot thinks.[162]

[156] W.C. Allen, *op. cit.*
[157] *Jew and Greek: A Study in the Primitive Church* (1953), p. 33.
[158] *Mark the Evangelist*, pp. 80ff.
[159] See Johnson, *op. cit.*, pp. 15f.
[160] *The Eucharistic Words of Jesus*, pp. 118ff.
[161] E.g. Johnson, *op. cit.*, pp. 15, 18f.
[162] *The Gospel Message of St. Mark* (1950), pp. 15ff.; see also N. B. Stonehouse, *The Witness of Matthew and Mark to Christ* (1944), ch. 1. Marxsen argues against this view, *Mark the Evangelist*, §1.

Allied with the theory that the first verse introduces the opening sections of the Gospel only are two other suggestions. The first proposal is that the verse is syntactically related to what follows in verse 4. Verses 2 and 3 are thus in the nature of a parenthesis, of the Old Testament-Qumran *pesher*-type, citing Malachi and Isaiah as prophetic witnesses to the advent of Christ. If this Old Testament section is omitted, the text reads smoothly: "The beginning of the gospel of Jesus Christ . . . was (ἐγένετο) John, who baptized in the wilderness."

T.W. Manson, following Spitta, argues that Mark's beginning is defective.[163] This notion is built on the observation that it is usual for the event to be referred to *before* the Old Testament prooftext is given. In Mark 1:1 this is not the case, and the "normal order . . . that first the fact is stated, and then the relevant text . . . cited with the formula καθὼς γέγραπται or the like" is not followed. Manson's explanation is that Mark's Gospel became mutilated at the first page. He assumes that it was written in codex form, so that it would be understandable for the first page to be torn or missing. This explanation has been criticized by H.A. Guy on two grounds: first, that if the page was lost through "fair wear and tear" (as Manson claimed), it is difficult to imagine that the autograph became mutilated in this way. (This has a bearing on the cognate question of the so-called lost ending of Mark.) Second, Manson's statement that it was Christian practice first to give the event and then to add the Old Testament corroboration holds for only a certain type of usage; and the Acts of the Apostles contains many instances of Christian apologetic which begins with the Old Testament Scripture and then shows how the fulfilment came about in Jesus.[164]

It seems that there is no need to have recourse to the idea of a lost page. If the Old Testament texts are in the nature of a parenthesis, the subject of verse 1 is picked up at verse 4; and this accords with the early Christian *kerygma* of Acts, in which John the Baptist is made the *terminus a quo* (Acts 1:22; 10:37; 13:24, 25) of the gospel story.

2. Similarly, the concluding 12 verses (16:9-20) of the Second Gospel present a problem. Indeed, they are something of a *cause célèbre* of textual criticism.[165] We may set forth a few facts first:

163 *Studies in the Gospels and Epistles*, pp. 31ff.
164 *The Origin of the Gospel of Mark*, pp. 155ff.
165 Important in the discussion of this matter are Rawlinson, *op. cit.*, pp. 267ff.; F.F. Bruce, "The End of the Second Gospel," *EQ*, 17 (1945), 169ff.; N.B. Stonehouse, "The Conclusion of Mark," *op. cit.*, ch. 4, pp. 86ff. Fresh evaluations of the data, including some new materials, are provided by Eta Linnemann, "Der (wiedergefundene) Markusschluss," *ZThK*, 66 (1969), 255-78. She argues that 16:15-20 is original in Mark's autograph, but 16:9-14 is not. K. Aland has contributed in "Bemerkungen zum Schluss des Markusevangeliums" to the *Festschrift* for Matthew Black, *Neotestamentica et Semitica*, ed. E.E. Ellis and M. Wilcox (1969), pp. 157-80. He asserts that the Gospel ended at 16:8 and the so-called shorter ending (printed as a footnote in the RSV under the

In the first place, verses 9-20 are omitted by ℵ, B, Sin. Syr., and most manuscripts of the Armenian versions; and Eusebius and Jerome are witnesses that the best manuscripts in his day ended at verse 8a.[165a]

Second, a "shorter ending" (printed in RSV and NEB) is attested along with TR in L, Ψ, 579, Sah., Eth., Hark. Syr., and the earliest Boh. manuscripts, while in *k* (Bobbiensis) the shorter text stands alone: "They briefly relate to Peter's companions all that they had been told. Then Jesus himself appeared and from east to west he spread with their help the sacred and indestructible message of eternal salvation."

A third ending is given by W, which adds, in addition to verses 9-20, an extra interpolation after verse 14.

Fourth, a 10th-century Armenian version, which ascribes verses 9-20 to "the presbyter Ariston," is too late to be of any value, although F.C. Conybeare professed great respect for this attribution.[166] This attribution is taken by C.S.C. Williams to be possibly no more than a guess based on the Armenian version of a well-known passage in Eusebius which refers to the presbyters Aristion and John.[167]

The Longer Ending (which is printed in the KJV) was apparently known to Tatian (*c.* 170). It is found in a preponderant number of manuscripts (C, L, Cop.-Sah. and Boh., A, W, D, Old Lat.—except *k*, which represents the African Latin in 4th-5th centuries). It has been suggested that Justin (*c.* 140) is the author of this Longer Recension.[168] Whether this attribution is correct or not, it is clear that the

---

longer ending) has claim to being regarded as an early (i.e. second-century) part of the Gospel transmission. J.K. Elliott, "The Text and Language of the Endings to Mark's Gospel," *ThZ*, 27 (1971), 255-62 surveys the textual data and discusses the non-Markan elements in 16:9-20. Lane, *op. cit.*, has a full note on the textual problem (pp. 601-5). The latest study is that of W.R. Farmer, *The Last Twelve Verses of Mark* (1974). He presents the case for the tentative view (which in our present state of knowledge cannot be proved) that 16:9-20 represents a Markan composition (except possibly 16:10) and was used by the evangelist as traditional material which was written by him at the time earlier than the composition of his Gospel. This conclusion is based on a new examination of the external data (to show that 16:9-20 were known in the manuscripts of the second century) and the linguistic connections of the pericope (arguing that the majority of the verses contain nothing which militates against Markan authorship).

165a But see the evidence of the Mai text assigned to Eusebius; Farmer, *op. cit.*, ch. 1. This would suggest that he knew copies of Mark containing 16:9-20.

166 F.C. Conybeare, "Aristion, the Author of the Last Twelve Verses of Mark's Gospel," *The Expositor*, 4th s., 8 (1893), 241-54; 10 (1894), 219f.

167 *Alterations to the Text of the Synoptic Gospels and Acts* (1951), p. 41. The passage in Eusebius is *Church History* 3.39. Notice the spelling in Armenian E 229—Ariston [sic] eritzu'.

168 Von Soden, *Schriften des Neuen Testaments* (1902-1913), I, 1621ff. Against this view see E. R. Buckley, *JTS*, 36 o.s. (1935), 176.

Longer Ending was written in the first half of the second century.[169] But it is equally clear that it did not come from the pen of Mark. Several minuscules mark it with an asterisk to show that it was suspect. Moreover, the verses are under suspicion on lexical and stylistic grounds, for both their vocabulary and style are noticeably different from the rest of the Gospel. The description of Mary in 16:9 confirms this suspicion, for that verse apparently overlooks the earlier reference to her in 16:1. Verses 9-20 seem to be made up of material taken from the other Gospels; and this fact too endorses the supposition that the Longer Ending is an editorial compilation, added (as were the "shorter" and the third ending) to complete the Gospel by some later scribe or editor who thought that "they were afraid" (16:8) could not conceivably end the chapter and the Gospel.

Did Mark intend to finish here? Was it accidental that he did so? Or was he prevented from completing his task? Or was the ending deliberately suppressed because it was believed to contain a contradictory account of the resurrection out of harmony with the other Gospels?[170]

Recent scholars, following the initial discussion of J. Wellhausen,[171] have argued that Mark intended his work to finish with the cryptic ἐφοβοῦντο γάρ.[172] Many would contend that the unusual style of ending both a sentence and a literary work is not impossible and has certain precedents.[173] Furthermore, such an abrupt ending accords with the note of mystery and the "numinous" which pervades the Gospel as a whole (cf. Dibelius's dictum that Mark is a book of "secret epiphanies").[174]

The major difficulty with this view is trying to imagine a situation in which the evangelist would break off in what looks on the face of it to be the middle of a sentence, leaving the women in great fear. Some interpreters, therefore, propose that "they were afraid" (ἐφοβοῦντο) should be taken to mean "reverential awe or fear,"[175] rather than terrified uncertainty. On this view, the Gospel ends on the

169 So Williams, *op. cit.*, p. 42, and now, Farmer, *op. cit.*, p. 74.

170 For this view see Lake, *The Resurrection of Jesus Christ* (1907), pp. 70f., 88ff., 143ff., 224ff.; Bultmann, *History of the Synoptic Tradition*, p. 285n. For further motives why the Markan ending may have been intentionally suppressed, cf. Williams, *op. cit.*, pp. 44f. and (differently) Farmer, *op. cit.*, pp. 59-74.

171 *Das Evangelium Marci* (1903), p. 146.

172 Cf. J. M. Creed, *JTS*, 31 o.s. (1930), 175ff.; R. R. Ottley, *JTS*, 27 (1926), 407ff.; Lohmeyer, *op. cit.*, pp. 356-60; R. H. Lightfoot, *Locality and Doctrine in the Gospels*, chs. 1, 2; *The Gospel Message of St. Mark*, pp. 80-97, 106-16; A. Farrer, *A Study in St. Mark*, pp. 172-81; N.B. Stonehouse, *op. cit.*, pp. 101ff., and Lane, *op. cit.*, pp. 59f.

173 They are given in Lightfoot, *Locality and Doctrine*, pp. 10-18, in response to the charge of W.L. Knox, *HTR*, 35 (1942), 13ff., that if Mark had ended his Gospel so abruptly he would have violated all the canons of ancient story-telling.

174 *From Tradition to Gospel*, p. 230.

175 So Stonehouse, *op. cit.*, p. 107.

climactic note of the human response to the solemn announcement (vv. 6, 7) that Jesus of Nazareth is risen and will await his followers in Galilee. "The chief impact of the verse [8] is simply to describe the indescribable. . . . The amazement of the women turns into trembling, astonishment, fear, flight, silence. All of these are considered in the Bible to be appropriate and normal human responses to an appearance of God, to a message from God, to an event in which God's power is released."[176] Moreover, it accords with the theology of the Gospel as a whole that the note of mystery in the revelation of the hidden Son of Man should be preserved up to the last verse.

It cannot be said that this reconstruction has persuaded all scholars, though the tide of opinion is running in that direction today.[176a] Perhaps most writers are content to believe that Mark's abrupt ending may be explained in one of a number of coincidental ways. The ending of the Gospel may have been caused by damage (whether accidental or the work of hostile man). The difficulty with this view is the corollary that "this damaged copy should be the sole legitimate ancestor of all existing manuscripts."[177]

The remaining possibility is that the Gospel was never completed by its original author, for reasons at which we can only guess.[178]

MARK'S THEOLOGICAL EMPHASES

At least four theological emphases are detectable in this Gospel.[179]

1. *The humanity of Jesus* is portrayed and is seen in such ways as his refusal to give demonstrable proofs of his claims (8:11-13; 9:30; 14:65); his ready consent to suffer and to taste the bitterness of death (8:31f.; 9:12; 10:32-34, 45); and a frank admission of his true humanity in the limitations imposed on that humanity (6:5, 6; 13:32; 15:31).

2. *The importance of faith* is stressed as the atmosphere in which Jesus' mighty works were performed. This appeal to faith marks him out from pagan wonder-workers (esp. 9:14-29).[180]

3. *The cost of discipleship* entails a following along a road of misunderstanding and rejection. The disciples are closely bound with

[176] P.S. Minear, *Saint Mark* (Layman's Bible Commentaries) (1962), p. 136.
[176a] See H.-W. Bartsch, "Der Schluss des Markus-Evangeliums," *ThZ*, 27 (1971), 242-54.
[177] Vincent Taylor, *The Gospels*, p. 50.
[178] So Rawlinson, *op. cit.*, p. 270; and Zahn, *Introduction to the New Testament*, II (ET 1909), 930ff.
[179] These are discussed in some detail in R. P. Martin, *Mark: Evangelist and Theologian.*
[180] H.D. Betz, "Jesus as Divine Man," in *Jesus and the Historian*, ed. F.T. Trotter, pp. 114-33. For a statement of the case against seeing Jesus as "divine man," see O. Betz in *Studies in New Testament and Early Christian Literature*, ed. D.E. Aune, pp. 229-40.

Jesus as (corporate) Son of Man who comes to his throne via suffering. To be his disciple is no easy vocation, and it is this which forms the stumbling-block in the way of the disciples, who have false notions of a political or military messiah. They are at cross purposes with Jesus throughout the Gospel.

This would have special relevance to Mark's church, which faced the hostility of persecution in Rome in AD 64 and following.

4. *The real messiahship of Jesus is essentially incognito*, misunderstood by official Judaism (3:20-35), hidden from the inattentive onlooker, and unrecognized by the disciples, who fill the term with a political or worldly content (8:27—9:1). But the truth is glimpsed by unlikely characters in the Markan drama (demons; the woman at Bethany, 14:3-9; a pagan centurion at the cross, 15:39). This gives encouragement to the Gentile mission in Mark's day (cf. 7:24-30; 13:9, 10; 14:9; 15:38, 39); and a rebuke is administered to Jewish and Greek notions of power (1 Cor. 1:21-23) in the picture of a suffering Lord (2 Cor. 13:4).

A RECENT THEORY

The present writer has envisaged a situation in the post-Pauline mission churches where Paulinist Gentile Christians had carried the apostle's teaching to the extreme of denying Jesus' true humanity and reposing their confidence in a heavenly Redeemer figure, remote from empirical history.

The occasion for the publication of Mark's Gospel may be traced to this situation, for his Gospel book puts together just those individual sections which emphasize the paradox of Jesus' earthly life in which suffering and vindication form a two-beat rhythm. Moreover, the nature of the Christian life (as Mark understands it) carries the same pattern: the disciple is bidden to take up his cross and then follow the Lord, who entered his glory by way of suffering and outward defeat. The evangelist is thus offering a dramatization in the life of Jesus, by a selective use of the materials at his disposal, of the twin elements which made up the apostolic preaching: the humiliation and enthronement of the church's Lord.

S. Schulz reaches a similar conclusion. He maintains that Mark reinterpreted the Jesus-traditions which he took over in a radically new way by means of an epiphany-Christological pattern of humiliation and exaltation.[181] U. Luz concluded that Mark is an attempt "to make the *theios-aner* ["divine man"] Christology and the epiphany thinking of the hellenistic congregation understandable in terms of the kerygma-of-the-cross rather than to eliminate it," a pattern which is

[181] S. Schulz, "Die Bedeutung des Markus für die Theologiegeschichte des Urchristentums," *Studia Evangelica*, 2 (1964), 135-45.

found in the pre-Pauline formulae (Rom. 1:3, 4; 4:25; 8:34; 1 Cor. 15:3ff.), in the reports of apostolic proclamation in the Acts-kerygma (2:36; 4:10, 11; 5:30, etc.), and in the more developed kerygmatic texts of 1 Tim. 3:16 and 1 Pet. 3:18-22.[182]

This approach to Mark's Gospel may claim to do some degree of justice to the following considerations. It explains how the term "Gospel" came to be transferred from oral preaching to a literary deposit (the striking novelty of this *genus litterarium* is well brought out by Marxsen, who devotes a whole section of his book to the concept of *εὐαγγέλιον* in Mark).[183] It keeps the traditional ascription of authorship within the evidence of Mark's link with both Peter and Paul. It accounts for the way in which the entire Gospel appears to be composed backwards from the passion,[184] and confirms the measure of truth in Kähler's dictum of a passion narrative with an extended introduction,[185] though there is far more in Mark than this dictum would allow if understood literally (as C. F. Evans has pointed out).[186]

There is much of a "biographical" character in Mark's story.[187] Jesus is seen as an authoritative teacher who, unlike a gnostic revealer, centers his teaching on suffering, both his own and as the vocation of his disciples. Above all, this view of Mark catches the characteristic emphasis of Jesus' teaching which his life, death, and victory exemplify, namely, "He who loses his life for my sake and the gospel's will save it" (8:35); "The Son of Man did not come to be waited upon, but to wait upon, and to give his life as a ransom for many" (10:45). A refusal to give demonstrable proofs and a ready consent to suffer rejection and taste the bitterness of death in utter desolation—these are the paths chosen by the Markan Jesus. And they are two emphases which underscore what E. Schweizer has termed the "matter-of-factness" of Mark's account.[188] As immediate knowledge of Jesus' wonderful power leads only to a false faith (such as the demons profess, and so need to be enjoined to silence), God's way lies in hiddenness, ignominy, and humiliation; it leads to the cry of dereliction of the cross. True faith can come only in following Jesus along his road of suffering, a path marked by such "human" features as the blindness of the disciples, the impotence and rejection at Nazareth, a denial of the date of the parousia. And faith is a divine gift, as the confession of a pagan centurion makes clear (15:39). Once

182 "Das Geheimnismotiv und die markinische Christologie," *ZNTW*, 56 (1965), 9-30.
183 See also his remarks in *ThL*, 81 (1956), col. 347.
184 So Marxsen, *Mark the Evangelist*, p. 32.
185 M. Kähler, *The So-Called Historical Jesus and the Historic Biblical Christ*, p. 80.
186 *The Beginning of the Gospel*, pp. 63f.
187 Marxsen even speaks of "*kerygmatic* 'biography,' " in *ThL, loc. cit.*
188 E. Schweizer, *The Good News According to Mark*, pp. 380-86.

the curtain of the temple had been split down the middle, the door is thrown open to Gentiles. Jewish privileges, which in the body of the Gospel have led only to unbelief, are at an end.

The same paths are trodden by the apostle to the Gentiles, the pioneers of the Gentile mission, and not least by the martyr church, which is strengthened by the exalted Christ as it seeks to obey his missionary mandate, and suffers in consequence.[189]

[189] Cf. H. Conzelmann, *An Outline of the Theology of the New Testament* (ET 1969), p. 141. He comments on the question, What is the exalted One doing in the interim between the resurrection and the parousia? He is strengthening the persecuted confessor.

CHAPTER FOURTEEN

The Gospel of Matthew

MATTHEW'S GOSPEL IN THE EARLY CHURCH

Matthew's Gospel was the church's most popular Gospel in the decades up to the time of Irenaeus (AD 180). This conclusion stands at the close of E. Massaux's comprehensive survey.[1] He shows that this Gospel was widely quoted both by later Christian writers, who appealed to the Lord's words as authority (e.g., *Didache*, Justin), and by the rank-and-file of the church. This Gospel, Massaux says, above the other evangelic records, became "normative for the Christian life; it created the climate of ordinary Christianity." Several factors led to this popularity.

1. An early Christian understanding of the gospel of Jesus Christ as a "new law" (*lex nova*) arose at the time of the apostolic fathers.[2] This concern to emphasize the need for the Christian's obedience to God's law expressed in the gospel found encouragement in such verses as Matthew 5:17-20 with their insistence that Jesus had come not to abrogate the law but to establish it. The gospel account which contained this teaching would naturally gain a wide acceptance by Christians, who saw much of the essence of their faith in a life of obedience to and observance of the divine commandments.

2. The rise of the catechumenate came early in the development of the church's responsibility to new converts. The young in the faith needed instruction, and for this purpose collections of Jesus' teaching on how he expected his followers to live would be of great practical value. Such chapters as Matthew 5—7 (the Sermon on the Mount), 13 (the parables of the kingdom), and 24—25 (apocalyptic utterances) seem to be put together with catechetical interest in view. This would give the First Gospel an obvious value to teachers and converts in the early church.

[1] E. Massaux, *Influence de l'évangile de saint Matthieu sur la littérature chrétienne avant saint Irénée* (1950), p. 652.

[2] See T. F. Torrance, *The Doctrine of Grace in the Apostolic Fathers* (1948).

3. Certain interests surfaced in the post-apostolic church. The existence of apocryphal gospels evidence a desire to know as much as possible about the infancy and boyhood of Jesus. Matthew's Gospel is rich in its nativity stories (ch. 1, 2) and its sections would minister to Christian needs. Also, ecclesiastical discipline played an important role in the church's internal life, as questions of sin, confession, restitution, forgiveness, penitence, and corporate decision-making and prayer became live issues. Matthew's Gospel conveniently gathers much of the teaching together into a compact section (18:15-20) to form what has been called "a veritable rule of discipline" similar to the Rule of the Community (1QS) at Qumran.[3] This interest would have his Gospel held in high esteem.

4. Matthew's twelve fulfilment passages show how certain aspects of Jesus' earthly life or events in his ministry were presaged in Old Testament prophecy. This would be useful information for Christians debating with the Jews. Chapter 23 is a sustained attack on the culpable excesses of Pharisaic Judaism, and this too must have provided an arsenal for Christians in critical dialogue with the synagogue even beyond the time of the Fall of Jerusalem in AD 70. The reconstituted Judaism which centered on Jamnia raised questions about Jesus' ancestral lineage which could only be answered by an appeal to the fulfilment motifs such as Matthew's Gospel provides in full measure.

5. The earliest witness to Matthew as the author of the *logia*, which he composed (says Papias)[4] in the Hebrew language, gives him an important place among the evangelists as the author of a collection of "oracles" of the Lord. There is no difficulty in imagining that such a collection of dominical oracles would be highly valued, thus giving to the Gospel which traditionally was associated with Matthew an unrivaled authority. Once Papias had ascribed this dignity to Matthew, it was quickly picked up by later church fathers.

It is perhaps symptomatic of the high place accorded to Matthew's witness to Christ and the use to which his Gospel was put that his book stands first in the canonical listing, even when other evangelical records fluctuate in the sequence according to different sources in which the order is given.

Our conclusion seems inevitable. Early Christians were drawn to this Gospel because of its practical serviceability in showing the intimate connections between Jesus and his Old Testament Jewish heritage and in providing a compendium of his teaching which could be used with obvious convenience in training and teaching young converts. Its apparent comprehensiveness, embodying much of Mark and some of Luke's narrative sections, gave the impression that it was, in Augustine's phrase, the fullest of the Gospels, and when tradition

[3] P. Bonnard, *L'évangile selon saint Matthieu* (1963), p. 267.
[4] In Eusebius, *Church History* 3.39.16.

appended the name Matthew to it or its chief source, the stage was set to ensure its popularity.

SOME FEATURES OF MATTHEW'S GOSPEL

1. Matthew's Jewish interest is seen in many features of his Gospel. Small wonder that Papias concluded that "Matthew composed the *logia* in the Hebrew language," though it is debatable exactly what these words mean, and indeed how they should be translated (see later, p. 238).

The opening verse of Matthew's Gospel stands at the head of a list of this evangelist's salient features. Whether or not he is consciously putting in a bid for his subsequent work to be regarded as "holy scripture,"[5] it is certainly true that the opening verse carries distinct echoes of the Old Testament formula of "enrolment by genealogy" (cf. Gen. 5:1; 37:2; 1 Chron. 9:1; Ezra 8:1).[6] Moreover, the links with prominent Old Testament characters are meant to show the intimate connection in a scheme of promise and fulfilment between the messianic and covenantal aspects of Old Testament faith and expectation and their realization in Jesus, Israel's true king and fulfiller of the covenant.

It is this motif that explains the use of the rabbinical literary device of *gematria* (Matt. 1:17), by which the letters of the Hebrew alphabet are given numerical value and the sum of the values of the letters of a name are believed to produce a significant total. It cannot be accidental that the three radicals of David's name in Hebrew (*daleth*, *waw*, *daleth*) yield a total of fourteen (4+6+4); and this provides the artificial framework of the genealogy of Matthew's account of Jesus' ancestry and his obviously selective division of it into periods.[7] Further, Matthew's initial chapter contains a clear case of Jewish literary devices based on language—the paronomasia in 1:21 based on the phonetic similarity between the name "Jesus" (Ar. *yešûaʿ*, Heb. *yᵉhošûaʿ*) and the Hebrew verb "to save" (*yašaʿ*).

Other issues which betoken a Jewish outlook on the part of the author may be seen. High on the list of the distinctive features

[5] So W. Marxsen, *Introduction to the New Testament* (ET 1968), p. 151. He renders the verse: "the book of the history of Jesus Christ," and comments: "By means of this phrase therefore the work is presented almost as 'Holy Scripture'—by analogy with the Old Testament—to which one can appeal and from which one can take one's bearings if one wishes to observe or teach others to observe what Jesus commanded (xxviii.20)."

[6] See M. D. Johnson, *The Purpose of the Biblical Genealogies* (1969), pp. 146ff., for a consideration of the *Toledoth* passages.

[7] For the problems here, see K. Stendahl, "Matthew," in *Peake's Commentary on the Bible* (1962), pp. 770-71, and the critical discussion in Johnson, *op. cit.*, pp. 223ff. For *gematria*, see G. H. Box, *ZNTW*, 6 (1905), 85.

which mark out this Gospel are the examples of Matthew's interest in fulfilled prophecy. He quotes the Old Testament 41 times, of which about a half are common to Mark and Luke. But of the remaining quotations, about 20 in number, a half are found in no other New Testament book. And of the 41 texts, 37 carry the introductory formula "that it might be fulfilled." There is no uniformity in the language of these citations, nor is there any one method which Matthew has followed. Recent study divides the types of quotations into a liturgical type and an interpretative (*pesher*) type, the latter term being drawn from the method of biblical exegesis practiced at Qumran.[8]

There are several sections in this Gospel whose purport is severely to limit the mission of Jesus to Israel (15:21-28) or to restrict the scope of the apostolic mission to the confines of the Jewish nation (10:5, 6, 23). These passages are problematical, and they will come up for discussion later. Here we may note them as part of this evangelist's concern to concentrate the interest of the earthly Jesus on the Jewish people. In the same vein, Matthew presents the tradition of Jesus' teaching (5:17-20) that he had not come to abolish the law but to make its claims still more binding.

When these verses are taken in isolation from the rest of the Gospel, it is possible to see how it could be maintained that Matthew was a converted rabbi who wished to show his fellow Jews that in Jesus they should recognize their true Messiah and the one to whom the law pointed.[9] Even more adventuresome is B. W. Bacon's proposal that we have in Matthew an heretical Jewish-Christian who labors under the mistaken notion that it is required of believers in Jesus to observe the total requirements of the law and live under its regimen.[10]

2. But there is another side to the picture, which makes the suggestions of von Dobschütz and Bacon virtually untenable; and to this we turn, recognizing that this counterbalancing set of data, which presents Matthew's interest in the Gentile world, raises the question whether after all Matthew was a Gentile Christian whose so-called Jewish interest was purely academic and historical. The possible effect of this conclusion would be that Matthew represents a church in a pagan-Christian culture, and that he is the spokesman for their anti-Jewish sentiments occasioned by the virulent anti-Jewish ethos of the city in which the church was set and which was reacting to the suspicion in which the Jews were regarded in the period after the close of their great rebellion against Rome (*c.* AD 70-74).[11]

[8] See K. Stendahl, *The School of St. Matthew*[2] (1968), pp. 97ff., 203ff.

[9] So E. von Dobschütz, "Matthäus als Rabbi und Katechet," *ZNTW*, 27 (1928), 338-48.

[10] B. W. Bacon, *Studies in Matthew* (1930), ch. 10.

[11] For these views see S. G. F. Brandon, *Jesus and the Zealots*, ch. 6, and S. van Tilborg, *The Jewish Leaders in Matthew* (1972).

One evidence of Gentile interest and anti-Jewish bias on the evangelist's part is the denunciation of the Pharisees and scribes in chapter 23 as "hypocrites" and evil men (in the light of ch. 13). To this evidence may be added the Matthean account of the passion, which places the blame squarely on the Jewish leaders, an indictment equivalent to that of murderer in view of 23:31-35 and 22:7; both descriptions are found only in Matthew.

Second, Matthew's Gospel alone contains such telltale signs of Israel's rejection as are found in 8:12 and 21:43. This seems to indicate a decisive break with the synagogue in the evangelist's day and a consequent understanding of the gospel as universalistic, though the judgment on Israel may conceivably be regarded as penultimate and as a chastening visitation which prepares for a future hope as the gospel is proclaimed to all, both Jews and Gentiles (23:39). The synagogue may be an alien institution (10:17; 23:34), but this is more a judgment on Israel's past than a foreclosing of her future place in God's saving history.

This leads to a third consideration—the missionary motif which runs through the Gospel, stretching from the visit of the Magi (2:1-12), anticipating the wider outreach of the good news and the appearing of Christ's light to the Gentiles (prefigured in Isa. 60:3; cf. 60:6), through such passages as 4:15; 8:5-13; 12:18, 21; 13:38; and, especially, 21:43, to the climactic mission-charge of 28:18-20.

Fourth, at one decisive point it looks as though Matthew's intimate knowledge of and feeling for the Hebrew Bible fails him, and his handling of the Hebrew idiom of synonymous parallelism in Zechariah 9:9—

> Lo, your king comes to you;
> triumphant and victorious is he,
> humble and riding on an ass
> on a colt the foal of an ass

—seems to betray a misunderstanding at 21:7, where Jesus is made to sit on the two animals at the same time.[12] Moreover, the fulfilment quotations are in part guided according to the form in the LXX. It has been a subject of continuing discussion whether Matthew is quoting from the LXX on occasion, as it suits his purpose, or is relying on his memory, or is availing himself of an early Christian handbook containing prooftexts.[13] In any case, Matthew shows familiarity with the Greek Bible, and this acquaintance has confirmed to some scholars

[12] But see the explanation offered by R. H. Gundry, *The Use of the Old Testament in St. Matthew's Gospel* (1967), pp. 197-99.

[13] See discussion by K. Stendahl, R. H. Gundry, and J.-P. Audet, *RB*, 70 (1963), 381-405.

that his Gospel was designed for a predominantly Greek-speaking church, which had broken with the synagogue.[14]

3. Recent study of Matthew's Gospel has exposed the pastoral interest of the author in the problems of the church of which he was a member and a teacher. It is along this line that the solutions to the problems posed by the above-mentioned set of data are most likely to be sought.

It is clear that this Gospel was written with an eye on the church. The internal life of the church is mirrored in the collection of sayings which form the core of 18:10-22. There the twin elements of an individualizing concern for the stray sheep (the defecting church member) in 18:10-14 (in contrast to Luke's account of the parable in 15:3-7), as well as the stress on corporate church life (18:17-20), are both attested. This merging of the personal and the social suggests a developed form of church life in which pastoral questions are very much to the fore.

The sections of 5:31, 32 and 19:3-9 (contrast Mark 10:2-9) contain Jesus' words on marriage and remarriage, but they are set (by the use of the clause "except on the ground of unchastity") in a framework which presupposes a set of questions which could only arise when the church is becoming predominantly Gentile.[15]

The most obvious feature which marks out Matthew's interest in the organized life of the church is that it is his Gospel alone which preserves the word for "church" (ἐκκλησία), in both instances (16:18 and 18:17) in the context of the authority of "church" personnel and "church" ordinances (16:19; 18:18). This would seem to reflect a time when questions of apostolic authority and community ordinances are under discussion.

Matthew's pastoral concern for the church is visible in a number of ways. First, his didactic interest is shown in his adaptation and abridgment of selected passages drawn from Mark. In Mark 5:1-20 the story of the Gerasene demoniac is told in 326 words: Matthew abbreviates this to 134 by some simple expedients, e.g., leaving out descriptive details and concentrating on the main elements of the

[14] K. W. Clark, "The Gentile Bias in Matthew," *JBL*, 66 (1947), 165-72; P. Nepper-Christensen, *Das Matthäusevangelium: ein judenchristliches Evangelium?* (1958); cf. N. A. Dahl, "Die Passionsgeschichte bei Matthäus," *NTS*, 2 (1955-56), 28.

[15] The background of the clause which allows the grounds for divorce is Lev. 18, which proscribes marriage within the limits of affinity. The situation in Matthew's account is that of a Gentile convert who needs guidance from the Lord in respect of his predicament over a wife whom he married before conversion but who stands within the list of prohibited degrees. See Bonnard, *op. cit.*, p. 69, citing the Jewish rubric in Strack-Billerbeck, III, 353-58. Cf. *ibid.*, II, 729f., for the evidence for the meaning of πορνεία as sexual sin resulting from marriages contracted within the forbidden degrees of consanguinity.

narrative succinctly and crisply. This procedure suggests an editoria policy of trimming Mark's narrative in order to produce a compressec teaching model suitable for instructional purposes in his church.

Second, Matthew has, alternatively, expanded certain o Mark's stories by the addition of paraenetic material (e.g., Matt 14:28-31, added to Matt. 14:22-27 = Mark 6:45-52). The incident o Peter's attempted walking on the water underlines the pastoral mes sage: when in distress, a man should look to Jesus.

Third, Matthew's characterization of the twelve disciples i governed by a pedagogical method. He has edited out all suggestior (found in Mark) that the disciples were men of fear, ignorance, anc hardness of heart. The rebuke of Mark 4:13 is omitted in the Mat thean parallel text (13:18). The reproach at the second announcemen of the passion (Mark 9:32) is likewise changed to a statement of thei distress (Matt. 17:23). The lesson seems clear: since the Matthear disciples are not disturbed by bewilderment and lack of faith, there i room for a development of their faith and its growth to maturity.[16] We may pursue this line a step further, and suggest that the role of th disciples in Matthew is that of model believers who advance in th school of Christ. This fits in with Matthew's understanding of th church as a Christianized *beth ha-midrash*, a house of instruction ir which Jesus is the great teacher (11:28-30; 23:8-10), and in whick faith and knowledge go hand in hand.

Perhaps the most acute application of Matthew's pastora concern is seen in the way he has angled the teaching of Jesus. Th Matthean Jesus issues repeated calls to righteousness, sets a lofty standard in perfection, and demands obedience to God's law, which i not abrogated or set aside. These Matthean motifs run consistently through the Gospel, and have been exposed in recent study,[17] witl particular reference to Matthew's special vocabulary and theologica emphasis. To illustrate the point, we shall look at one particular case the dialogue between Jesus and the young ruler (Matt. 19:16-22 = Mark 10:17-22 = Luke 18:18-23).

Matthew has simplified the life setting of Mark's account; h has concentrated on the didactic points of the narrative; and by a least five deliberate "editorial" touches he has made the story serve hi own purpose as a creative theologian.

First, by transferring the adjective "good" from the title o Jesus to the occasion of the question, Matthew has emphasized Jesus role as authoritative teacher and spotlighted the issue of the dialogu as to the nature of "good deeds."

[16] See A. F. J. Klijn, *An Introduction to the New Testament* (1967), pp 30f.

[17] Esp. in the essays of G. Bornkamm and G. Barth in *Tradition an Interpretation in Matthew*, and G. Strecker, *Der Weg der Gerechtigkeit*[2] (1966).

Second, by changing the verb from "you know the commandments" to "keep the commandments," he has stressed the importance of "doing the will of God" (another favorite Matthean phrase) as a call to serious ethical endeavor.

Third, his inclusion of "You shall love your neighbor as yourself" is a compact summary of a Christian's personal ethics found in precisely this context in Romans 13:9, 10, and suggesting an epitome of the Decalogue for Gentile Christians. Matthew gives it as a quiet reminder that the law is still binding on Gentile believers.

Fourth, the reference to deficiency is placed on the inquirer's lips instead of being given as a statement from Jesus. The man's admission, "What do I still come short in?" seems clearly to reflect the catechumen's desire to aspire to the heights of "perfection"; Matthew had added the reference to "being perfect" as part of his summing up of Christian morality (cf. 5:48) and as a warning against any slackness or moral indifference.

Finally, Matthew alone calls him "a young man" by transposing the Markan-Lukan "I have kept all these things (i.e., items in the law) from my youth" into a noun which describes the questioner's age at the time of the interview. Does he do this to make his question a fitting one on the lips of a neophyte, as Bonnard suggests? Or to drive home the application of this pericope to his Gentile readers, who could not be expected to have known the Jewish law before their conversion but on whom the law is now seen to be binding?

In spite of some recent denials of this conclusion,[18] it appears that Matthew's pastoral concern is to rebuke the moral laxity in a church which is facing a temptation to ethical indifference. He stands opposed to this trend as a teacher of rigorist ethics. He calls his constituency, in Jesus' words, to a better righteousness (5:20; 6:33; 13:43, 49; 25:31-46). He sees the disciples' goal as set at no less a standard than "perfection," meaning "the wholeness of consecration to God."[19] So the record of the great sermon includes the rigorous exhortation of 5:48. So it is that Matthew has Jesus insist on the abiding validity of the law in 5:17-20, with a denunciation both of Pharisaic casuistry—which atomized the law's requirements and so denied its spirit (cf. 23:23ff.)—and of an antinomian rejection of the law's binding character (7:15ff.) in the interest of a lip service and a false teaching (24:11). Matthew leaves his readers in no doubt that Jesus' teaching does not abolish the law (3:15; 5:18) and that the test of true discipleship is a fervent and practiced obedience (7:12, 24) which stays close to the spirit of the old Torah (23:3) as well as accepts the new law which Jesus brought (22:40; 28:20).

How then are we to reconcile the two competing interests in

[18] For example, D. Hill, *The Gospel of Matthew* (1972), pp. 66ff.
[19] G. Barth, *loc. cit.*, p. 101.

Matthew's Gospel—particularistic and Jewish flavor (e.g., 10:6; 15:24) with its stress on the serious ethical demands of the gospel; and his outreach to the Gentile world and conscious universalizing of Jesus' message to embrace the non-Jewish community? David Hill's study of the question seeks to draw the strands together into a unity by postulating Matthew's fidelity to earlier traditions, his pastoral responsibility to tell the church how its origin is to be traced to a life-situation in Jesus' ministry, and his theological task as an interpreter of the continuity of salvation history.[20] We accept this analysis, but we would want to take it a stage further.

If we think of the evangelist as a Christian church leader of the Jewish-hellenistic wing of the church,[21] we may further remark that his Gospel shows first of all the strenuous claim of the moral law, symbolized in the Torah but reinterpreted in special reference to the Gentiles (e.g., 5:32; 19:9),[22] and secondly the inalienable place of Israel, represented by messianic prophecy, within the scheme of salvation history. Matthew's church is quickly becoming predominantly Gentile, and the evangelist captures its outlook in his universalistic teaching (e.g., 28:19, 20).[23] But he is aware of two dangers arising from this situation.

First, Gentile Christians may well have been resisting the claims of the moral law by a perverted understanding of the teaching of the apostle to the Gentiles (Rom. 6:1ff.; cf. 3:8, 31). Hence Matthew stresses the importance of righteousness, not in the Pauline sense, but as "the ethical comportment of the disciple, an integrity which is the essential object of Jesus' demand."[24] Secondly, Gentile Christians may also have shown a desire to be rid of the incubus of the church's Jewish "pastness" and to cut loose from the church's historical moorings (which was the policy advocated later by gnosticism). To this tendency Matthew responded with an insistence that "salvation is from the Jews" (as the Fourth Gospel remarked), and showed a corresponding particularistic strain (in such places as 10:5, 6, 23; 15:24) alongside the dominant emphasis on universalism (8:11; 21:43; 24:14; 26:13; 28:18-20). Whatever the truth of the above attempt to suggest a *Sitz im Leben* for this Gospel, we have to reckon with these two puzzling emphases and to hold them in some sort of equipoise. Only then can we do justice to this adaptation of Mark which the church calls κατὰ Ματθαῖον.

20 Hill, *op. cit.*, pp. 71f.
21 As E. P. Blair permits us to describe him, *Jesus in the Gospel of Matthew* (1960), pp. 42, 157ff.
22 See above, n. 15.
23 See N. A. Dahl, *loc. cit.*
24 Strecker, *op. cit.*, p. 157.

THE COMPOSITION OF THE GOSPEL

1. *Matthew as a Community Product.* Source criticism, which sought to analyze and arrange the gospel data into hypothetical components and to construct theories of dependence to explain the interrelation of these components, has given way to a newer method. By its attempt to get behind the written records of the New Testament to the living community of the church which produced them, form criticism had prepared the way for this new understanding of Matthew's Gospel book. An important step in a new direction was taken in 1946 with the publication of G. D. Kilpatrick's *The Origins of the Gospel According to St. Matthew.* This was followed in 1954 by Krister Stendahl's work, which bore the significant title *The School of St. Matthew.*[25] Both writers adhere to a thesis that the Gospel exhibits by its literary arrangement features and influences of the church's liturgical life.

Kilpatrick accepted source criticism to the point of affirming that Mark, Q, and M were read repeatedly in the worship services of Matthew's church and that around these documents a fixed element of exposition grew up, patterned on the way the Hebrew texts were "targumized" in the synagogue liturgy by the addition of explanatory paraphrases. Matthew's Gospel, on this understanding, was the end-product of this process and appeared as "a kind of revised gospel book, conveniently incorporating into one volume the three documents Mark, Q and M."[26]

Stendahl, and more recently G. Schille,[27] have modified Kilpatrick's approach by speaking more of the catechetical purpose of the evangelist's arrangement of his material. In place of the formative influence being sought in the lectionary use to which the Matthean sources were put, these two later authors suggest a setting in the training of teachers and church leaders (Stendahl) or new converts preparing for baptism (Schille). Stendahl broke new ground because he was able to call attention to and use the methods of scriptural exegesis at Qumran. He went on to argue that the form and purpose of Matthew's use of the Old Testament corresponded to similar practices in the scriptorium of the Dead Sea community. As a necessary concomitant of this view (shared by the three scholars mentioned), which sees the Gospel as a liturgical production shaped in the inner life of the evangelist's church and reflecting its attitude to Scripture and church discipline, there goes the virtual suppression of the evan-

[25] Second edition 1968.
[26] Kilpatrick, *The Origins of the Gospel According to St. Matthew* (1946), p. 70.
[27] "Das Evangelium des Matthäus als Katechismus," *NTS*, 4 (1957-58), 101-14.

gelist himself in favor of the community whose worship, traditions, and ecclesiastical practices are embodied in the finished Gospel book.

2. *Matthew as an Editorial Theologian's Work.* The clumsy phrase "editorial theologian's work" is an attempt to express what is meant by *Redaktionsgeschichte*, which offers a method of treatment described by G. Bornkamm, as we have seen above (p. 136). To recapitulate our discussion there, a *redaktionsgeschichtlich* treatment of the Gospels aims at reversing the notion that the evangelists wrote only as historians, not theologians. Tell-tale clues of editorial redaction are sought in the "seams" or connecting links between the *pericopae* and the alterations the evangelists have made to the *pericopae.*

The upshot of this method of study as applied to the First Gospel is to reinstate Matthew as a distinct personality in his own right and as a church theologian whose recounting of the story of Jesus tells us more about what Matthew's church thought concerning the risen Lord than about Jesus' personality and words as these affected his Galilean audiences. This latter point is the main emphasis in H. J. Held's study of the miracle stories in Matthew.[28] The initial question to be raised as we read these stories is: "What does the picture of the Church look like, which is mirrored in the miracle stories of Matthew?"[29] Repeatedly the Jesus of Matthew's Gospel is presented as the Lord and helper of the church, which, conscious of his presence in their midst, is called to share his authority (cf. 9:8b and Peter's walking on water; both references hold a unique place in this Gospel).

The Gospel writer has become an individual author once again; he is "an individual figure of primitive Christian literary history, even though the hunt for names and biographical traces is renounced" (Bornkamm). Certainly on this showing Matthew is not to be dismissed as a purveyor of an anonymous tradition (as in the Gospel studies of both literary and form critics) or the faceless scribe of a school or liturgical tradition (as Stendahl tended to make him). "Matthew" stands rather for the name of the first evangelist who is "the representative of a congregation"; and his Gospel offers a highly personal and distinctive theological treatise, occasioned by a set of specific needs both in his church and in his relations as a church leader with the outside world, notably of the synagogue.

3. *Matthew as Eyewitness Deposit.* In the view of the earlier source critics the statement of Papias recorded by Eusebius[30] posed something of an embarrassment, for on its face value it connected the Gospel with the apostle Matthew: "So then Matthew compiled the oracles (λόγια) in the Hebrew language, but everyone interpreted [or

[28] In *Tradition and Interpretation in Matthew,* pp. 165-299.
[29] *Ibid.,* p. 267.
[30] *Church History* 3.39.16. Cf. later descriptions in 5.10.3 and 6.25.3,4.

translated] them as he was able." If this witness to Matthew's authorship relates to the composition of the entire Gospel, its value seems compromised by the facts that canonical Matthew is clearly a Greek composition and that apostolic authorship seems hard to reconcile with this Gospel's dependence on Mark. Moreover, the earlier critics eyed the M material suspiciously and treated it as reflecting the theology and ecclesiastical polity of a Jewish-Christian church which still clung to its ancestral heritage or else was exposed to a Judaizing influence and had not shaken itself free. A date in the period of 84-90 seemed safest in the light of passages like 11:12; 27:8; 28:15; the developed trinitarian teaching of 28:19, 20; and the historical allusions (as 22:7) which pointed to Jerusalem's fall as an event in the past as God's judgment on Israel.[31]

Later scholars profess to find clear signs within the Gospel of a still continuing struggle with Israel: "The congregation which he [Matthew] represented had not yet separated from Judaism."[32] This conflict, still in progress and with uncertain outcome, has dictated the presentation of Jesus' messiahship (he is shown to be true Messiah of Israel) and the stress laid on the validity of his teaching within the Judaic framework (e.g., 5:17-20). Part of the reason for this Matthean slant is the desire still to appeal to the synagogue in hope of a successful mission to Israel, and partly as a corrective to the threatened moral laxity which the evangelist foresees as a result of a mass influx of Gentiles into the church.[33]

But this placing of the Gospel's message *vis-à-vis* the synagogue, with Israel's conversion still a viable possibility and hope, seems to require a date before relations between Jews and Gentiles became strained to a breaking-point, a time symbolized by the insertion of the "test-clause" (*birkath ha-minim*) in the synagogue liturgy's Eighteen Benedictions (see above, p. 71). There are indications in the Gospel itself which make sense only in a situation before the destruction of Jerusalem.[34] To be sure, the discovery of earlier traditions which the evangelist has incorporated need not mean that his completed work is to be dated in a period before AD 70, and if he is believed to have used Mark, this fact sets a *terminus a quo* for the Gospel's publication.

R. H. Gundry also endeavors to trace the Gospel back to an apostolic source.[35] The bulk of his work is an examination of the

[31] This deduction has been challenged by H. K. Rengstorf, "Die Stadt der Mörder (Mt. 22, 7)," in *Judentum, Urchristentum, Kirche, Festschrift* for J. Jeremias, ed. W. Eltester (1960), pp. 106-29.

[32] Bornkamm, *loc. cit.*, p. 39.

[33] See G. Barth's essay, *ibid.*, pp. 159-64.

[34] Barth quotes M material, 5:23f.; 17:24-27 (*ibid.*, p. 90); and we may include 10:5,6,23; 15:21-28, which seem to be "archaic" logia going back to a time before the mission to the Gentiles. Cf. F. Hahn, *Mission in the New Testament* (ET 1965), pp. 54ff.

[35] *The Use of the Old Testament in St. Matthew's Gospel*, pp. 183ff.

text-forms underlying the Gospel's Old Testament citations. He traces here a triple tradition, based on a combination of LXX, Aramaic, and Hebrew elements. This language phenomenon, he contends, could only have arisen in one area—Palestine. He builds a further argument on the results of his linguistic comparison of how the Old Testament is quoted in the Synoptics, seeking to demonstrate that, apart from the formal quotations in the Markan tradition, which are strongly under LXX influence, the formula citations in Matthew display the same mixed text that appears elsewhere throughout the Synoptic Gospels. He uses this to displace the theories of Stendahl and B. Lindars,[36] as well as the Testimony Book hypothesis, all of which require some *special* data in the Matthew citations to make his usage distinctive and identifiable. This lack forges the strongest link in Gundry's reasoning. He may carry less conviction when he proceeds to maintain that this language phenomenon certifies the existence of an *Ur*-Matthew in Aramaic or Hebrew, written by the apostle, whom he describes as a "note-taker during the earthly ministry of Jesus . . . [whose] notes provided the basis for the bulk of the apostolic gospel tradition."[37] Perhaps the major obstacle for this view to overcome is the unclear reason why the apostle Matthew would submit to a nonapostolic precedent in the way in which the First Gospel is, *ex hypothesi*, content to follow Mark. Gundry's question, "Is it too difficult to think that Mt wished to preserve the unity of the apostolic gospel tradition and therefore utilized Mk?",[38] simply cannot be treated as rhetorical.

4. Having isolated some recent trends, we conclude this survey by listing three matters now at the forefront of Matthean studies for which no certain decision is yet possible.

First, the role of Matthew the evangelist as a theological interpreter of the traditions he put together into a carefully structured Gospel is fast becoming an "assured result." This trend implies a negative attitude to Stendahl's thesis, which has come under fire from B. Gärtner.[39] He argues that the use of the fulfilment-passages reflects the church's missionary preaching in the Jewish synagogues more than the scholastic work of a "study-group."[40] Stendahl's arguments have also been faulted by Gundry for their failure to "take seriously non-Septuagintal quotations outside the formula-quotations."[41] Georg Strecker has further demonstrated against Stendahl that the language of the *Einführungsformel*—"This was done that it might be fulfilled which was spoken by . . ."—is typically Matthean, a fact

[36] *New Testament Apologetic* (1961).
[37] Gundry, *op. cit.*, p. 182.
[38] *Ibid.*, p. 184.
[39] *Studia Theologica*, 8 (1954), 1-24.
[40] Moule's sympathetic term, *The Birth of the New Testament*, p. 88.
[41] Gundry, *op. cit.*, p. 157.

which suggests that the redactor (i.e., Matthew) is not following a written or continuous oral source but is displaying his own creativity as an author.[42]

A second—and much more problematical—case is the question of the theme of Matthew's theology, for with this are bound up questions of dating and provenance. In spite of Bornkamm and his pupils, it appears that the break between church and synagogue was complete by the time of the First Gospel's publication. Suggestions of "in-fighting," a conflict *intra muros*, are offset by two lines of demonstration given by Douglas A. R. Hare that active hostility between the two religions was a thing of the past.[43] These lines are that the persecution-texts look back to predictions fulfilled in the past rather than indications of a contemporary experience; and that Matthew's description of the synagogue as an alien institution means that Christians were no longer in debate with Jews. Less credible is Hare's adjunct theory that Matthew's theology involved the utter and final rejection of Israel and the notion that "the Church is in no sense a continuation of Israel but a different ἔθνος, non-Israel, which replaces Israel in *Heilsgeschichte* (21:43)"[44] —a statement which surely misconceives the meaning of the text he quotes, overlooks a verse like 23:39, and makes nonsense of *Heilsgeschichte*, which necessarily includes the promise-fulfilment motif of Romans 9—11 and Ephesians.

In the third place, the continuity between old Israel and the new people of God, now comprising Jews and Gentiles, is a major theme of W. Trilling.[45] With a later clarification of this point by Strecker,[46] Trilling identified the common factor uniting both Israel's hope and the church's fulfilment as the messiahship of Jesus, which is adumbrated in the Gospel's Mosaic and Davidic typology. An overriding apologetic purpose controls the evangelist's selection and application of Scripture, and is much wider than his explicit references to the Old Testament would indicate. For example, both J. Jeremias and E. Thurneysen, in their studies on the Sermon on the Mount,[47] show its thoroughgoing christological emphasis. This stress is needed to correct R. Hummel's view that it is the Torah which binds together the two Testaments in Matthew's view of salvation-history,[48] and to complement W. D. Davies' comprehensive study, with its conclusion that the

[42] *Der Weg der Gerechtigkeit*^{2}, p. 50.

[43] *The Theme of Jewish Persecution of Christians in the Gospel According to St. Matthew* (1967). See, too, K. Tagawa, "People and Community in the Gospel of Matthew," *NTS*, 16 (1969-70), 149-62.

[44] *Ibid.*, p. 157.

[45] *Das wahre Israel* (1959).

[46] *Op. cit.*, p. 189.

[47] J. Jeremias, *The Sermon on the Mount* (1963); E. Thurneysen, *The Sermon on the Mount* (1965).

[48] *Die Auseinandersetzung zwischen Kirche und Judentum im Matthäusevangelium* (1963), esp. pp. 156-60.

Sermon "is a kind of Christian, mishnaic counterpart to the formulation taking place" at Jamnia when Judaism was reconstituted in the aftermath of the defeat of the AD 66-70 war with Rome.[49]

AUTHORSHIP

This Gospel is handed down as an anonymous piece of writing: Matthew's name nowhere appears in the form of an author's claim. A few scholars regard 13:52 as a cryptic autobiographical statement, but the description "every scribe who has been trained for the kingdom of heaven is like a householder who brings out of his treasure what is new and what is old," though found only in Matthew, is hardly obvious as a self-reference to the author, and the term scribe (γραμματεύς) can be interpreted in several ways. E. von Dobschütz maintained that Matthew was a converted rabbi, on the ground that his Jewish methods of using the Old Testament and his interest in the law showed that he had some connection with the leading rabbi in the reconstructionist period of Jewish life after AD 70, Johanan ben Zakkai (see earlier, pp. 70, 227).[50] B. W. Bacon saw in this verse a self-portrait of Matthew as a Jewish-Christian who was regarded as a heretic in the eyes of his fellow-Jews, but who replies to criticism in his claim to find in the law of Moses hidden truths which his compatriots were ignoring.[51] C. F. D. Moule wishes to interpret the word γραμματεύς in a secular sense, as meaning "clerk."[52] The verse on this reading says nothing about "Matthew's" background except that the author shared Matthew's profession as a scribe who brought over into his Christian service as a Gospel writer a facility with writing materials, which made him an admirable person to transcribe the Matthean traditions.

Church tradition attached the superscription "according to Matthew" (κατὰ Ματθαῖον) to this Gospel, mainly under the impulse of the church father Papias, whose witness is, as we saw above, a nest of controverted terms. The text (from Eusebius), with its variants, reads: "Matthew composed/compiled the oracles/sayings (τὰ λόγια) in the Hebrew/Aramaic language, and everyone translated/interpreted them as best he could." These alternatives suggest the parts of his statement which cry out for elucidation. The key term is τὰ λόγια. Three possible meanings are given.

The term may refer to part of Matthew's Gospel. In this case

49 *The Setting of the Sermon on the Mount*, p. 315.
50 "Matthäus als Rabbi und Katechet," *loc. cit.*
51 *Studies in Matthew*, ch. 10.
52 *The Birth of the New Testament*, pp. 74, 88, 172. See too his essay, "St. Matthew's Gospel: Some Neglected Features," *Studia Evangelica*, II (*TU* 87; ed. F. L. Cross) (1964), 91-99. The verse is seen as a self-defense of Christian scribes in general, who have an honored place in the house (the church?), by N. Walker, *Die Heilsgeschichte im ersten Evangelium* (1967), pp. 27-29.

there are two sets of material which may be considered. One view is that τὰ λόγια refers to oracles drawn from the Old Testament Scriptures which were collected in the early church in order to show that prophecy was fulfilled in Jesus the Messiah. Supporting this view is Eusebius' use of the words λόγια κυριακά to describe "oracles of the Lord," exactly as in the Old Testament prophets.[53] But on this understanding it is difficult to know how to translate the verb ἡρμήνευσε, because it is highly probable that there was already available in Greek a collection of these *testimonia*. We should then need to render the verb as "interpret"—a suggestion which encounters the objection that Papias was more probably referring to translation than to interpretation in the light of his phrase "in the Hebrew language."

So we are drawn to an alternative proposal: that τὰ λόγια relates to the sayings-source Q, which embodied the substance of Jesus' teaching and whose existence may be inferred from a comparison of verbally exact or closely similar passages in Matthew and Luke. This is T. W. Manson's solution. He believes that Q originally was compiled in Aramaic and was later translated in Greek in the Gospel of Matthew. "If we wish to put an author's name on the title-page of Q, Matthew is the only candidate in the field," Manson suggested.[54]

A second theory casts a more ambitious net to account for Papias' τὰ λόγια. This is to make the term refer to an earlier edition of the entire Gospel in Aramaic or Hebrew. For this version—a proto-Matthew—the apostle is seen to be responsible, and later it was turned into Greek as our canonical Gospel. There are several variations of this general idea, ranging from the view that Papias had in mind a document identical with or similar to certain known apocryphal gospels (such as the *Gospel of the Hebrews*)[55] to the postulate of a highly individual version of the Gospel composed *c.* AD 55 as a Judaizing document and labeled "K" by Pierson Parker.[56]

More credible is the supposition that λόγια refers to a proto-Matthew, comprising the Gospel in its entirety, written by Matthew in

53 *Church History* 3.39.14. Cf. F. C. Grant, *The Gospels*, pp. 65, 144.

54 *The Sayings of Jesus*, pp. 18ff., and "The Gospel of St. Matthew," in *Studies in the Gospels and Epistles*, ed. M. Black (1962), pp. 82ff.

55 This is the gospel mentioned by Eusebius (*Church History* 3.27) as used by the sect of Ebionites in Palestine. Irenaeus speaks of the Ebionites, a Jewish-Christian sect, as favoring only the Gospel of Matthew, but it cannot have been our canonical gospel in view of their rejection of the virgin birth of Jesus (see Irenaeus, *Against Heresies* 1.22). W. D. Davies, "Matthew, Gospel According to," *HDB*, p. 631, mentions the existence in Palestine of documents written in Hebrew and apparently closely resembling canonical Matthew. Cf. D. Hill, *Gospel of Matthew*, p. 26. But these primitive versions of Matthew which are claimed to exist on the strength of two *testimonia* in Jerome—see C. F. D. Moule, *Birth of the New Testament*, p. 186—are very doubtful entities. See the critique of Jerome's words in P. Nepper-Christensen, *Das Matthäusevangelium: ein judenchristliches Evangelium?*, pp. 64ff.

56 *The Gospel before Mark* (1953).

Aramaic, which forms the basis of the later translated work which we know as canonical Matthew.[57] But this hypothesis fails to explain the evidence that our canonical Gospel gives every appearance of being a Greek composition and not a translation from a Semitic language.

A final possibility is to accept J. Munck's conclusion that in this context τὰ λόγια can only mean "statements about Jesus."[58] This view has the merit of deflecting the criticism R. M. Grant leveled at T. W. Manson's identification of τὰ λόγια with the source Q, which was, on Manson's showing, essentially made up of sayings of Jesus. Grant notes the distinction to be made between λόγοι (words) and λόγια (sayings).[59] According to Munck, Papias means to say that Matthew is the author of an undefined body of material, treating both Jesus' teaching and activity, later used in the composition of the Gospel. This conclusion is probably as far as the evidence will take us and may be accepted as the best to date. It has been followed by C. F. D. Moule,[60] who is sensitive to the two features which need to be borne in mind in any serious assessment of Papias' worth: that we cannot dismiss him out of hand[61] in view of the persistence of "the tradition of a Semitic and apostolic original," whose origin it is difficult to imagine if there is absolutely nothing behind it; nor can we take him at face value[62] in view of the strong evidence that this Gospel is a Greek composition, written by a hellenistic Christian and indebted to Mark for its framework.

Our conclusion is that Papias' tradition can at best relate only to a collection of material later used in the composition of the entire Gospel. We may express the view that the apostle stands behind the Gospel as the authority on which the later evangelist called as he composed this work in its final form and published it in the name of the "school" or church which venerated Matthew's name and valued his apostolic credentials.

MATTHEW THE TEACHER

We may gain an appreciation of the role of Matthew's Gospel from an exegetical look at three passages. The first is the instructions Jesus

57 Most recently this view is advocated by C. S. Petrie, *NTS*, 14 (1967-68), 15-33. Earlier proponents are B. L. Butler, *The Originality of St. Matthew*, and L. Vaganay, *Le problème synoptique*.

58 "Presbyters and Disciples of the Lord in Papias," *HTR*, 52 (1959), 228. Cf. Munck, "Die Tradition über das Matthäusevangelium bei Papias," in *Neotestamentica et Patristica. O. Cullmann Festschrift* (1962), pp. 249-60.

59 R. M. Grant, *A Historical Introduction to the New Testament*, p. 117.

60 C. F. D. Moule, *The Birth of the New Testament*, p. 89.

61 As W. G. Kümmel, *Introduction to the New Testament*, pp. 44, 85.

62 As R. H. Gundry, *The Use of the Old Testament in St. Matthew's Gospel*, p. 184, does, ascribing to the apostle Matthew the role of a notetaker during the earthly ministry of Jesus.

gave to his disciples (Matt. 10:5-15). These pose some questions about the scope of missionary interest as a feature of Jesus' ministry and of the church's task in Matthew's day. The question is that of *Sitz im Leben*, especially in verses 5 and 6, which are both negative (do not go to the Gentiles) and positive (go rather to the lost sheep of the house of Israel). That is to say, the Twelve are limited to Galilee in their mission; and they are forbidden to undertake the Gentile mission. The issues here are: first, the antiquity of the sayings, attested by the Aramaic basis;[63] second, the independent witness in 10:23 as unfulfilled prediction, a prophecy which did *not* materialize at the return of the Twelve; and, third, the puzzling relation to other parts of Matthew which are universalistic in scope and show Jesus' concern for the non-Jewish world (like 8:5-13; 13:38; 28:18-20).

The second passage records Jesus' words to the disciples in Matthew 18:10-20. The setting here should be compared with Luke 15:3-7 and the *Gospel of Thomas*, Logion 107:

> Jesus said, "The Kingdom is like a shepherd who had a hundred sheep. One of them went astray; it was the largest. He left the ninety-nine [and] sought for the one until he found it. After he had exerted himself, he said to the sheep, I love you more than the ninety-nine."

The setting in the Matthaean passage is one of ecclesiastical discipline—sin, forgiveness, error, restoration, corporate prayer, and public assembly. There is a Jewish background (esp. vv. 14, 17, 19, 20), yet the passage presupposes a developing church life with problems which arose only later.

Probably this pericope reflects the practices of the churches in Syro-Palestine in the 80s, in turn based on the teachings of Jesus about (and his attitude to) "little ones."

A third passage is one of the evangelist's most characteristic—Matthew 5:17-20, with its heavy underlining of such concepts as the permanent validity of the law (vv. 17, 18); its warning that false teachers will seek to relax the law's authority (vs. 19); and, at the same time, its opposition to the Pharisaic interpretation of the law and the Pharisees' claim to a meritorious observance thereof (vs. 20).

The setting in Jesus' lifetime is seen by comparison with Matthew 11:28-30, but the real application is to those who, in the interest of antinomian freedom, had cast off the authority of all law and had carried Paul's teaching to a false extreme (mirrored in Rom. 3:8, 31; 6:1ff.; Gal. 5:13ff.). Against such an abandonment of moral law, this pericope reasserts the binding validity of the law and enters a warning against all who relax it. At the same time it does not fall into the trap of the Judaizers, who sought to impose the law as a way of salvation (vs. 20).

[63] See J. Jeremias, *Jesus' Promise to the Nations*, pp. 26-28.

Some scholars see a violent anti-Pauline over-reaction here, but it is preferable to view the entire section as an adaptation of Jesus' teaching to a post-Pauline excess by his later, misguided detractors.

From these three selected portions it is now possible to notice Matthew's characteristic emphases on:

1. *Missionary interest*, following the principle "to the Jew first" yet suggesting a wider outreach to the Gentile world (cf. Rom. 1:16; 3:29; 15:8, 9).

2. *Church discipline*, especially in chapter 18. We may note, though, the stress on the individual within the fellowship of the church, and the special promise and pledge, which make sense only in the developed situation of the later church (vv. 19, 20). The teaching on forgiveness became a burning issue in the post-apostolic church.[64]

3. *The question of the authority of the law* also took on momentous proportions in the period when the Gentile accessions to the church changed its original Jewish character. Then there was need to reassert the claim of a strict morality, even at the cost of casuistry and incipient legalism.

The major thrusts of Matthew's Gospel add up to the conclusion that the evangelist was preeminently "an educator of Christian people," to use P. Bonnard's phrase.[65] He appeals to the following three descriptions of Matthew's pedagogy:

1. It was scholastic, in the sense that Matthew records such events as the healing miracles and the feeding of the multitude in such a way as to give a crisp, concise version, suitable for didactic use in the church and capable of memorization.

2. It was practical, with a heavy emphasis on the verb "to desire, to wish" (ϑέλω), and concrete action.

3. It was eschatological, set in the framework of the Last Judgment as an ethical incentive. Yet he is opposed to apocalyptic enthusiasm.

Matthew's church situation required from him a recasting of the story of Jesus to emphasize the continuing validity and authority of the law (over against Gentile forgetfulness of the moral demands of the gospel), and at the same time, to promote the extension of the gospel by his universalistic teaching, which clearly opposes any narrowly Pharisaic understanding of the law and its righteousness.

The evangelist is therefore defending the gospel on two opposite fronts. From Gentile antinomianism he is defending it by an assertion that Christ is no iconoclastic destroyer of the law; from Pharisaic Christianity he is defending it from a re-judaizing movement, which set in later in the first century (cf. *Didache*) and against which

64 See W. Telfer, *The Forgiveness of Sins* (1959).

65 "Matthieu Educateur du peuple chrétien," in *Mélanges Bibliques en hommage au B. Rigaux* (1970), pp. 1-7.

Ignatius wrote in AD 115: "It is absurd to talk of Jesus Christ and to practise Judaism. For the Christian faith did not base itself on Judaism but Judaism looks to the Christian faith."[66]

A date of publication in the ninth or final decades of the first century is therefore suitable, as we learn something of Judaism's vigorous reaction to the growing Gentile church at that time; and the place of origin in Syria is a likely possibility in view of the links with the *Didache* and the tensions which were found in an area where Jews and Gentiles met and mingled.

[66] Ignatius, *Epistle to the Magnesians* 10.

CHAPTER FIFTEEN

The Gospel of Luke[1]

LUKE AND HIS PURPOSE

1. Luke prefaces his Gospel with an exordium, a literary device employed by Greek writers of his era (e.g., Josephus, *Against Apion* 1.1; 2.1).[2]

There are several reasons for believing that Luke intended this prologue to cover both the Gospel and the Acts. It was the custom in antiquity to divide long works into volumes and to provide a preface for the entire work and secondary prefaces to later volumes.[3] The πρῶτος λόγος of Acts 1:1 probably refers to the Third Gospel.[4] Both books are dedicated to the same person, Theophilus.[5] And the phrase "the things accomplished among us" (Luke 1:1) is more applicable to the events related in Acts.[6]

The common authorship of Luke-Acts may be proved on the basis of linguistic evidence. A.C. Clark attempted to disprove unity of

[1] In this chapter I have freely drawn on the work of my research assistant, James L. Resseguie, whose help in the writing of this section I am glad to acknowledge.

[2] Henry J. Cadbury, "Commentary on the Preface of Luke," in *The Beginnings of Christianity*, Part 1, *The Acts of the Apostles*, ed. by F.J. Foakes Jackson and Kirsopp Lake (1922), Vol. II, Prolegomena II, pp. 490f.; E. Earle Ellis, *The Gospel of Luke* (New Century Bible), p. 62.

[3] Cadbury, *loc. cit.*, p. 491.

[4] A.J.B. Higgins, "The Preface to Luke and the Kerygma in Acts," in *Apostolic History and the Gospel*, ed. by Gasque and Martin, p. 79; F.F. Bruce, *Commentary on the Book of the Acts* (New International Commentary) (1954), pp. 18, 30; William Neil, *The Acts of the Apostles* (1973), p. 63; Jacques Dupont, *The Sources of the Acts* (ET 1964), p. 110n.

[5] For the question of which statements in the prologue refer to which parts of Luke-Acts, see Higgins, *loc. cit.*

[6] Cadbury, *loc. cit.*, pp. 495f. See also W.G. Kümmel, *Introduction to the New Testament*, p. 90. Contra, see E. Haenchen, *The Acts of the Apostles*, p. 136n.; Hans Conzelmann, *The Theology of St. Luke*, p. 15n.; Helmut Flender, *St. Luke, Theologian of Redemptive History*, p. 64.

authorship,[7] but his arguments were shown to be unsound by W.L. Knox.[8]

The prologue aids in unraveling Luke's purpose if two questions can be answered: Who is Theophilus? What is Luke's intention in using this dedication? Regarding the identity of Theophilus, Cadbury suggests that he was an influential non-Christian, but that the work is addressed to the educated class in general.[9] Streeter proposed that Theophilus was a name invented to cloak the identity of Titus Flavius Clemens, cousin of the Emperor Domitian and a probable inquirer of Christianity, who was put to death on a religious charge. For him Theophilus, meaning "lover of God" or "friend of God," would be an appropriate pseudonym.[10] Bruce's conclusion is that he was a representative of the middle-class public in Rome whom Luke wanted to win over to a more favorable view of Christianity.[11] A fourth explanation is that Theophilus was a recent convert, or at least a catechumen, and thus a representative of Christians.[12] Finally, there are those who argue that, whether or not he was a Christian, Theophilus was Luke's patron, and he defrayed the costs of publishing Luke-Acts.[13]

The intention of the Gospel and Acts, as derived from Luke's statement in this dedication, depends on the explanation given for the identity of Theophilus. Marxsen contends that by the use of a traditional formula Luke is consciously presenting his book to the educated public, but the details of the prologue should not be pressed too far.[14] Others maintain that Luke wants to correct misinformation about Christianity.[15] Still others see his goal as confirming and supplementing Theophilus' knowledge about the historical basis of

[7] *The Acts of the Apostles* (1933).

[8] *The Acts of the Apostles* (1948), pp. 2-15, 100-109.

[9] Cadbury, *loc. cit.*, p. 510; G.B. Caird, *Saint Luke* (Pelican Gospel Commentary), p. 14.

[10] B.H. Streeter, *The Four Gospels: A Study of Origins*, pp. 535-39.

[11] F.F. Bruce, *op. cit.*, pp. 31f.

[12] For this see Alfred Wikenhauser, *New Testament Introduction* (1958), p. 219; Bo Reicke, *The Gospel of Luke*, pp. 46f.; Alfred Plummer, *A Critical and Exegetical Commentary on the Gospel According to St. Luke* (1922), p. xxxiii. Cf. also J.H. Crehan, "The Purpose of Luke in Acts," *Studia Evangelica*, 2 (1964), 366, who believes that Theophilus was a recent convert or a catechumen, but that Luke intended his Gospel to be only for him.

[13] Ellis, *op. cit.*, p. 34; I. Howard Marshall, *Luke: Historian and Theologian*, p. 38; Haenchen, *op. cit.*, p. 136n.; W. Neil, *op. cit.*, p. 63; G.H.P. Thompson, *The Gospel According to Luke in the Revised Standard Version*, p. 45; C. Stuhlmueller, "The Gospel According to Luke," *The Jerome Biblical Commentary*, ed. by R.E. Brown, J.A. Fitzmyer, and R.E. Murphy (1968), p. 119; N. Geldenhuys, *Commentary on the Gospel of Luke* (New International Commentary) (1956), p. 54.

[14] Willi Marxsen, *Introduction to the New Testament*, p. 156.

[15] Cadbury, *loc. cit.*, p. 510; *The Making of Luke-Acts*, p. 315; Caird, *op. cit.*, p. 44; C.H. Talbert, *Luke and the Gnostics, An Examination of the Lucan Purpose* (1966), p. 56n.

Christianity.[16] But the unlikelihood of identifying Theophilus exactly and the ambiguity surrounding certain terms in the prologue[17] require us to examine Luke's work in its entirety in order to determine his purpose.

2. Several suggestions have been offered regarding Luke's theological purpose. One is that he is writing an expressly anti-Gnostic Gospel. C.H. Talbert has set forth the strands of evidence to show "that Luke-Acts was written for the express purpose of serving as a defense against Gnosticism."[18] On this showing, Luke appeals to apostolic authority in three ways to counter Gnosticism. First, the motif of authentic witness—particularly to Jesus' death, burial, resurrection, and ascension—is a protection against a docetic tendency. Second, in the face of Gnostic misinterpretation of Scripture, Luke appealed to the apostles' legitimate exegesis of the Old Testament. Third, the motif of the succession of tradition of eyewitnesses assured "the guarantee of the truth of the church's proclamation in the midst of Gnostic distortions of the gospel."[19]

Talbert has raised a number of new possibilities in the interpretation of Lukan literature, but it is unlikely that the purpose of Luke-Acts can be subsumed under the one category of defending against Gnosticism. For example, Talbert concludes that the motif of the failure to understand Scripture correctly is a theme of the Lukan mind along these three lines: that Jesus was the Christ; that it was necessary for the Christ to suffer and rise from the dead; and that there will be a general resurrection. Gnosis, he claims, denied these three points. But why does he believe that these three points need to fit *one* problem? Luke could have directed his attention against the orthodox Jews, who would have denied that Christ was Jesus and that the Christ should suffer.

Another prominent suggestion is that Luke's aim was to respond to the embarrassing delay of the parousia. Hans Conzelmann's seminal study is the definitive statement of this position.[20] Luke has recast his sources to eliminate the concept of an imminent parousia. Since the imminence of the end was the most important factor in the kerygma, Luke offered a substitution to explain the delay of the parousia—a history of salvation, which unfolds in three distinct stages: the period of Israel, the period of Jesus' ministry (or "the middle of

[16] Crehan, *op. cit.*, p. 366; N.B. Stonehouse, *The Witness of Luke to Christ* (1951), p. 44; Reicke, *op. cit.*, p. 47; Plummer, *op. cit.*, pp. xxxiii-xxxvi; F.J. Foakes Jackson, *The Acts of the Apostles* (1931), p. xviii.

[17] κατηχήθης, for example, may refer either to religious instruction (as in Paul and Christian writers generally) or to false information (as in Acts 21:21, 24). See Cadbury, "Commentary on the Preface of Luke," *loc. cit.*, pp. 508f.; H.W. Beyer, κατηχέω, *TDNT*, III, 638-40.

[18] *Luke and the Gnostics*, p. 15; cf. his essay "An Anti-Gnostic Tendency in Lucan Christology," *NTS*, 14 (1967-68), 259-71.

[19] *Luke and the Gnostics*, p. 56.

[20] *The Theology of St. Luke.*

time," in the title of Conzelmann's German edition), and the age of the church. This Hegelian dialectic of apocalyptic hope (thesis), met by the problem of Jesus' failure to come again (antithesis), and resolved by Luke with a theology of salvation (synthesis) falls short of being convincing because Conzelmann does not show that the delay of the parousia was at the time of Luke a problem which needed resolution. "The motif," Ellis notes, "could hardly have originated as a solution inspired by embarrassment or disappointment about Jesus' continued absence, since it appears before there was time to get embarrassed." The delay motif in Luke more likely serves the purpose "to counter an overeager or false anticipation of the parousia."[21]

A third group of suggestions is that Luke's purpose is to provide a definite apology, for one of three reasons: an apology of Christianity to Rome, a defense of Paul against Jewish Christian charges, or an evangelistic apology.

B.S. Easton argues for the first reason.[22] Luke, writing towards the end of the first century, at a time of impending persecution, wanted to demonstrate that Christianity should be tolerated by the state. His argument was twofold. On the one hand, he showed the political innocence of Paul and others (Acts 13—28); on the other, he sought to demonstrate that Christianity is nothing more nor less than fulfilled Judaism, and as such has a claim to be permitted to exist as a *religio licita*. But Luke's argument failed to convince Rome because the Christians remained unconvinced that they were a Jewish sect. Paul had done his work too well. Easton's thesis applies only for the Acts and the passion story of the Third Gospel. But even for those sections a political motif is too narrow to account for all the material, which would seem irrelevant to a Roman official.

Others have traced the opposite apologetic interest in Luke-Acts: T.W. Manson holds that Luke's purpose is to show that the Christian community is separate from the Jewish community. "From beginning to end Luke-Acts is out to show the width and depth of the breach between Jesus and his Jewish contemporaries, between the Synagogue and the Church."[23] Also Luke was interested in showing that "the Christian Gospel was no seditious propaganda but a message of universal peace and goodwill."[24]

A recent representative among those who see in Luke-Acts an apology for Paul against Jewish Christian charges is A.J. Mattill, Jr. [25]

[21] E. Earle Ellis, *Eschatology in Luke* (1972), p. 18.
[22] *Early Christianity*, ed. by Frederick C. Grant (1954).
[23] "The Work of St. Luke," in *Studies in the Gospels and Epistles*, ed. by M. Black, p. 61. Manson also recognizes with W.L. Knox a missionary motif in Luke's writings.
[24] *Ibid.*, p. 67. This would date the gospel around AD 70.
[25] "The Purpose of Acts: Schneckenburger Reconsidered," in *Apostolic History and the Gospel*, ed. W. Ward Gasque and Ralph P. Martin, pp. 108-22; "The Good Samaritan and the Purpose of Luke-Acts: Halévy

The evidence for this claim is found in several Lukan features such as the centrality of Jerusalem in the Gospel and Acts, the parallels between Paul and Jesus, and the various anticipations in the Gospel of the life, work, and thought of Paul in Acts. An example of this prefiguring is found in the Samaritan *pericopae* of Luke's Gospel. Accepting Halévy's thesis that the parable about the Good Samaritan in Luke was originally the parable of the Good *Israelite*, Mattill sees behind this secondary creation a Pauline apologetic purpose. By prefiguring the Gentile movement through the evangelization of Samaritans and Gentiles in his Gospel and Acts, Luke is able to show that the outreach of the Gospel is grounded in Jesus himself. The Pauline view and practice of evangelization to the Gentiles is, therefore, buttressed by its appearance as a theme in Jesus' teachings.

Mattill's argument is weak at this one point: What evidence is there to show that Jewish Christianity was a major problem at the time of Luke's writings? The parallels between Jesus and Paul may have been constructed for a pastoral purpose. By showing how a model Christian's life conforms to that of his Lord, Luke could effectively demonstrate to his congregation the way a Christian should live.

Finally, there are those who take the definite apologetic motif in Luke-Acts as intended for the evangelization of the non-Christian world. J.C. O'Neill, dating Luke-Acts in the second century (*c.* AD 115-30) chiefly because Acts most obviously resembles a Christian "apology," similar to those of second-century apologists (e.g., Justin, Aristides), suggests that Luke's apology "had the burning inner purpose of bringing men to the faith. . . . The repeated and dramatic demonstration that Christianity was both politically innocent and religiously the true fulfilment of the expectations of Judaism was not a legal but an evangelistic argument."[26] This evangelistic message was directed to the educated reading public of Rome.

Recently, I. Howard Marshall has suggested that Luke's main concern was simply to present salvation to his readers. Luke's work was not written to deal with a particular problem or situation in the church, but rather to aid the church's task of evangelism. Marshall finds no overt polemic against Gnosticism, no stress on the church as an institution developing rigid forms of organization, and no defense of Paul as a primary aim. Nor was Luke motivated by the delay of the parousia. "It was enough that he should compose this record as a means of evangelism."[27] The severely "negative" element in Marshall's conclusion is perhaps a weakness, since it is arguable that no

Reconsidered," *Encounter,* 33 (1972), 359-76; "*Naherwartung, Fernerwartung* and the Purpose of Luke-Acts: Weymouth Reconsidered," *CBQ,* 34 (1972), 276-93.

26 *The Theology of Acts in Its Historical Setting*² (1970), pp. 176, 180.

27 *Luke: Historian and Theologian,* p. 221.

other New Testament book lacks a definite purpose in its composition and publication.

The fourth proposal is that Luke's aim was a combination of historical and theological factors. The tendency recently has been to see Luke as both historian and theologian. Luke wanted to "compile a narrative of the things which have been accomplished," but it was a narrative directed to a specific audience from a particular point of view. Several scholars have thus been reluctant to limit Luke to a single purpose.

E. Earle Ellis makes reference to no fewer than three theological concerns of the church of Luke's day. First, Luke addresses the dehistoricizing of the gospel events by gnosticizing Christians. Second, his eschatology provides a corrective for those who viewed the kingdom of God only in terms of an immediate return of Jesus. Third, the most pervasive motif—and perhaps the principal Lukan purpose—is the relationship of Judaism and Christianity.[28]

Similarly, William Neil, recognizing that Luke is writing history as a theologian and a preacher, suggests that he is writing both for the church and for the world, "and above all for the Church in the world. . . . He is thinking not only of intelligent enquirers outside the Church who want to know what Christianity is all about, but also of intelligent enquirers inside the Church who want to know how it all began."[29]

Searching for some sort of "umbrella" term or terms to label Luke's purpose in Acts, Stephen G. Wilson describes Luke's aim as "a combination of historical and practical elements." Luke wanted to write history, "but history that had a message for his contemporaries."[30] Therefore, he concludes, Luke's primary interest was practical.

Wilson's discussion of Luke's purpose seems to offer the most satisfactory solution. This, we suggest, is to be found in terms of Luke's general interest rather than his attention to some specific circumstance or set of circumstances. A key-word to sum up Luke's role as a Gospel writer and historian might be the term "pastor." Luke's purpose is seen not primarily in his desire to chronicle events of the past (though he does evince some interest in constructing a "life of Jesus"), nor is he above all a theologian, chiefly concerned to use historical records as a polemical vehicle to rebut heresy or to edify the church of his day. His main interest is to aid the church in his lifetime by proclaiming the kerygma and by offering pastoral counsel and encouragement to his fellow believers who, to be sure, may well have needed some corrective teaching and have required a fresh retelling of the earthly life of their Lord. Luke plays the part of a pastor by the

[28] E. Earle Ellis, *op. cit.*, pp. 58f.
[29] *The Acts of the Apostles*, p. 26.
[30] *The Gentiles and the Gentile Mission in Luke-Acts* (1973), p. 266.

way he assembles the traditions at his disposal, the use he makes of liturgical and catechetical elements (in ch. 1, 2, and 7—the sermon on the plain), the prominence he ascribes to the character of the earthly Jesus as man among men, and especially by his emphasis in the Jesus-tradition on those elements which figured so prominently in Paul's kerygmatic message, e.g., the kindness and compassion of God in Christ and his offer of free grace to the undeserving. To these details we may now turn.

CHARACTERISTICS AND THEMES

The third Gospel is the most difficult of the synoptic records to categorize, in spite of the many features which mark it out from the other two. There are two preliminary considerations which need to be borne in mind as we attempt this task. One is analytical: how much of Luke's distinctiveness comes from his special material, called L (see earlier, pp. 151f.) rather than from his editing of Markan material? The other question is one of intent: how far is Luke's selection and style governed by his purpose, as stated in the prologue? Part of that purpose may be judged from his inclusion of three sections which call for special comment.

1:5—2:52. This section is markedly Jewish-Christian in tone and content. The style of writing is based on the Septuagint, and many fragments of Jewish-Christian hymnody and psalmody are incorporated, e.g., the *Magnificat* (1:46-55); *Benedictus* (1:68-79); *Gloria in excelsis* (2:14); *Nunc Dimittis* (2:29-32).[31] Why does Luke include these chapters in his account? About that there can be little doubt. It was evidently to demonstrate the continuity in the drama of redemption between the old and new covenants. "His aim is to show how God made use of the Temple, its worship, and one of its priests, to announce the coming of the precursor of Jesus,"[32] and so to clamp the two testaments together in a scheme of promise and fulfilment. John the Baptist's role as forerunner of Jesus is emphasized and his place in the old covenant is described, both in the birth narratives and later in the Gospel (7:28; 16:16). He sums up in his person and ministry all the anticipations of the old covenant, and stands at the turning point on the road which leads from the old age to the new messianic era. Luke's intention may be stated in a sentence: to demonstrate the continuous line in salvation-history between the two covenants.

[31] Literary and exegetical studies of the Lukan nativity hymns are legion. See especially H.H. Oliver, "The Lucan Birth Stories and the Purpose of Luke-Acts," *NTS*, 10 (1967), 202-26; and P.S. Minear, "Luke's Use of the Birth Stories," in *Studies in Luke-Acts: P. Schubert Festschrift* (1966), pp. 111-30.

[32] B. Reicke, *op. cit.*, p. 58.

6:20—8:3. This portion contains material from Q plus L. Of particular note are the sermon on the plain and the mission charge to the apostles. This has a catechetical interest, encouraging the successors of the apostles in his day to proclaim the gospel. Equally Luke has provided a manual of instruction for leaders in worship and catechesis. B.W. Bacon pointed out many years ago that the structure of the narrative material in 7:1—8:3 serves Luke's pragmatic interests. Luke has constructed groups of anecdotes "for the purpose of contrasting obedient and disobedient 'hearers of the word.' "[33]

9:51—18:14. This is a most important section, forming the backbone of the Gospel. Often called a travel document (9:51; 13:22; 17:11),[34] it fills the gap in the Markan narrative (at Mark 10:1) and utilizes both Q and L. The content is didactic, representing Jesus as teacher of the Twelve and debater with his critics.[35] Even the parables in this section have a didactic-paraenetic flavor.[36] Moreover, Luke's distinctive features in Jesus' teaching shine out here: the world mission of the church, embracing Samaritans, women, outcasts; the joy which attends the coming of the kingdom in human experience; and the new perspective given the parousia hope—it will be realized "speedily but not immediately."[37]

Luke adopts a conscious literary style which has been praised in Renan's verdict that his Gospel is "the most beautiful book in existence." Whether he set out to produce a work of literary merit, however, may be doubted; and his use of a Septuagintal style in ch. 1-2 and the way he incorporates and edits his traditions seem to contradict this assessment. It might be more accurate to say that it is in those passages where little pre-Lukan influence is seen that the evangelist's literary skill shines through—as in such memorable places as 15:11-32 and 24:13-35.

Another feature of Luke's account is emphasis on the universal character of the gospel. Sometimes this is explicit (2:1; 2:32; 3:1, 2, 38); sometimes it is cryptic (as in 10:1, where 70 or 72 disciples are mentioned, which is the number of nations listed in Gen. 10:1-32).[38] Sometimes the emphasis is made by what is said on the surface of the narrative (Jesus' appeal to women, to sinners and outcasts, to Samaritans, to the economically poor); sometimes by

[33] B.W. Bacon, "The Order of Lukan 'Interpolations'," *JBL*, 35-37 (1917), 118.

[34] See Conzelmann, *op. cit.*, pp. 60-65.

[35] See B. Reicke, "Instruction and Discussion in the Travel Narrative," *Studia Evangelica*, 1 (1959), 206-16.

[36] See J. Jeremias, *The Parables of Jesus*, p. 87; J. Schneider, "Zur Analyse des lukanischen Reiseberichtes," in *Synoptische Studien: A. Wikenhauser Festschrift* (1953), pp. 207-29, esp. pp. 222f.

[37] See F.O. Francis, in *Journal of the AAR*, 37 (1969), 62.

[38] See S.G. Wilson, *op. cit.*, pp. 45-47. Wilson prefers to see the allusion to the seventy as pointing to the fulfilment of Num. 11:16f.

what lies just beneath the surface (4:16-30; 5:1-11, which depicts Peter as "catcher-of-men-alive," and as one needing the same reminder he later received in Acts 10—11).[39]

There is emphasis in Luke's Gospel on the Spirit and the fruit of the Spirit in joy and prayer (3:21; 5:16; 6:12; 11:1; 22:32, 41: 23:34). On broader canvas this is related to the present reality of the kingdom of God, which came with Jesus and continues in the life of the church. Hence Luke's "de-eschatologizing" process is in evidence, by which he defuses the impatient and unhealthy preoccupation with the hope of an immediate end of the age. It is worthwhile to examine in greater detail Luke's use of the teaching on the Holy Spirit.

That the Spirit occupies a central concern in Luke's theology is seen first of all by the numerous references to his activity. Luke refers to the Spirit seventeen times, compared with twelve times for Matthew and six times for Mark. Of Luke's seventeen references, seven occur in the first two chapters, and six of them speak of prophetic inspiration.[40] So Luke records that John will be filled with the Holy Spirit (1:15); that Elizabeth was filled with the Spirit and prophesied (1:41); that Zechariah, filled with the Holy Spirit, prophesied (1:67); and that Simeon received the Spirit and prophesied (2:25, 26, 27). The stress on the prophetic activity of the Spirit, particularly in the first two chapters, is, to say the least, striking. This connection between the Spirit and prophecy is by no means accidental, for "ecstatic prophecy provides a recognizable token of the Spirit's presence."[41] The Spirit's role in prophecy is a familiar theme in the Old Testament,[42] and in the later Jewish literature the Holy Spirit is frequently thought of as the Spirit of prophecy.[43] The sudden reappearance of the prophetic Spirit, which had ceased with Haggai, Zechariah, and Malachi,[44] marks the commencement of a new age which dawned with Jesus' birth.[45] As I.H. Marshall says, "From the outset the activity of the Spirit is the characteristic of the new age."[46]

1. *Jesus and the Spirit.* The activity of the Spirit in relation to Jesus gives the impression that Jesus is just a Spirit-filled prophet, like one of the apostles, who are portrayed as inspired teachers and

[39] See Reicke, *The Gospel of Luke*, pp. 66ff.
[40] I. Howard Marshall, *op. cit.*, p. 91.
[41] A.R.C. Leaney, *A Commentary on the Gospel According to St. Luke* (1966), p. 41.
[42] See the excellent discussion by G.W.H. Lampe, "The Holy Spirit in the Writings of St. Luke," in *Studies in the Gospels: Essays in Memory of R.H. Lightfoot*, ed. D.E. Nineham, pp. 159-200, esp. pp. 160-68.
[43] Strack-Billerbeck, II, 127f.
[44] C.K. Barrett, *The Holy Spirit and the Gospel Tradition* (1966), p. 123.
[45] Frederick W. Danker, *Jesus and the New Age According to St. Luke* (1972), p. 22, calls the Holy Spirit "the documentation for God's action in the New Age."
[46] Marshall, *op. cit.*, p. 91.

miracle-workers. Before the temptation Jesus is led in the Spirit into the wilderness (Lk. 4:1); and he returns in the power of the Spirit (4:14). Before making an inspired saying he is filled in the Spirit (10:21), and at his baptism he is endowed with the Spirit.

E. Schweizer has drawn attention to Luke's distinction between Jesus' endowment with the Spirit and that of the community.[47] Jesus is Spirit-conceived; and, unlike John the Baptist, he does not grow in the Spirit. Luke records that John "grew and became strong in Spirit" (1:80), a perfect parallel with Jesus who "grew and became strong, filled with wisdom" (2:40). There is no implication in Luke's Gospel of gradual growth in participation in the Spirit by Jesus. Even though Jesus is endowed with the Spirit at his baptism and is filled with the Spirit before uttering an inspired saying, it does not alter the fact that for Luke Jesus "is from the very first a possessor of the Spirit and not just the Spirit's object, like the pneumatic."

In this connection the relation between *πνεῦμα* and *δύναμις* is an important one. It is well known that the phrase *ἐν τῇ δυνάμει τοῦ πνεύματος* is Lukan. This expression is used explicitly in Luke 4:14 to indicate Jesus' commencement of his ministry in Galilee after the temptations. John the Baptist is spoken of as being in the spirit and power of Elijah, but only Jesus is "in the power of the Spirit." To describe men acting in the power of the Spirit Luke uses other expressions, particularly *πλήρης πνεύματος ἁγίου* (4:1; cf. Acts 6:3; 6:5; 7:55; 11:24).[48] On another occasion Luke links *πνεῦμα* with *δύναμις*. At the close of the Gospel (24:49) Jesus speaks of "power from high" being given to others. Doubtless the events of the Pentecost were in Luke's mind when he wrote this, so that "power from high" would be closely related to "in the power of the Spirit."[49] Therefore, Jesus, who in his lifetime is the unique bearer of the power of the Spirit,[50] becomes the dispenser of the Spirit.

2. *The Spirit and Prayer.* Several times Luke mentions prayer in connection with the activity of the Spirit. Lampe has called attention to the fact that "prayer is . . . complementary to the Spirit's activity since it is the point at which the communication of divine influence becomes effective for its recipients."[51] So Luke is the only one of the evangelists who mentions that Jesus was praying when the Spirit descended on him at baptism (3:21). At crucial points in Jesus' career, when the Spirit's inspiration, guidance, and power are appre-

[47] E. Schweizer, *πνεῦμα*, *TDNT*, VI, 404-15, esp. p. 405.
[48] C.K. Barrett, *op. cit.*, p. 101.
[49] *Ibid.*, p. 76.
[50] W. Grundmann, *δύναμαι/δύναμις*, *TDNT*, II, 301, writes: "Thus Jesus is for Lk. the Bearer of power in the absolute." H. Conzelmann, *op. cit.*, p. 180n., writes: "Jesus is in his time the only bearer of the Spirit."
[51] Lampe, *loc. cit.*, p. 169.

hended, Jesus is found praying. Before choosing the Twelve he prayed "all night" (6:12), and before Peter's confession at Caesarea Philippi he was praying (9:18). At the Transfiguration Luke records that he went up to pray (9:28), and before the arrest while he was in agony "he prayed *more earnestly*"—an intensity not implied in the other Synoptics.[52] Lampe describes this insistence on prayer as "one of the most characteristic features of St. Luke's teaching" and "the means by which the dynamic energy of the Spirit is apprehended."

Prayer, specifically petitionary prayer, is closely connected to moments in *Heilsgeschichte* whereby God guides the course of salvation history through prayer. At the birth of John "the whole multitude of people were praying" (1:10); before the birth of Jesus, Mary offered praises to God (1:46-55); and at important moments in Jesus' ministry (baptism, Caesarea Philippi, Transfiguration), he is found praying. Significantly, prayer and the Spirit are important features for the advancement of Christianity in Acts. Cornelius, for example, is praying when the angel of the Lord appears to him (Acts 10:23, 30). At the beginning of Paul's missionary journeys they prayed and fasted before being sent out by the Holy Spirit (Acts 13:3, 4). These examples parallel Jesus' prayer activity in the Gospel and Luke's paraenesis that men "ought always to pray and not lose heart" (Lk. 18:1).[53]

3. *The Spirit and the Kingdom.* The relation between the Spirit and the kingdom, a much neglected area in New Testament studies, has been examined by J.D.G. Dunn.[54] Dunn concludes that *πνεῦμα* and *βασιλεία* are closely connected in Luke's writings. For instance, the Lukan variant, "let thy Holy Spirit come upon us and cleanse us," may be a possible equivalent for "let thy kingdom come" in the Lord's Prayer.[55] At times the two are almost interchangeable, so that "where the Spirit is there is the kingdom."[56]

Drawing on this observation, S.S. Smalley relates Spirit, kingdom, and prayer to important moments in *Heilsgeschichte* in Luke-Acts.[57] At Luke 10:1-22, for example, the seventy are commissioned and received back. This is an important moment in the progress of Jesus' ministry. Luke records that the apostles were to proclaim the imminence of the kingdom (vs. 9), and that Jesus rejoiced in the Holy Spirit and at the same time he prayed (vs. 21). This triad—Spirit,

[52] *Ibid.;* cf. S.S. Smalley, "Spirit, Kingdom and Prayer in Luke-Acts," *NovT,* 15 (1973), 59-71, esp. 60n.

[53] The examples are taken from Smalley, *loc. cit.* Wilhelm Ott, *Gebet und Heil, Die Bedeutung der Gebetsparänese in der lukanischen Theologie* (1965), p. 123, considers the collection of prayer paraenesis in Luke's writings to be a development of the remark in Lk. 18:1.

[54] "Spirit and Kingdom," *ExpT,* 80 (1970-71), 26-40.

[55] *Ibid.,* p. 38; S.S. Smalley, *loc. cit.*; Cadbury, *The Making of Luke-Acts,* pp. 287f.

[56] Dunn, *loc. cit.,* p. 39.

[57] *Loc. cit.,* pp. 64-66.

kingdom prayer—also appears at the birth of Jesus (Spirit-conceived—head of an unending kingdom—in response to Mary's prayer); at the baptism (Spirit descends—Jesus prays—*baṯ qôl* applied to Jesus as messianic king); at Peter's confession at Caesarea Philippi; at the Transfiguration; at the beginning of the passion narrative in Gethsemane; and at the cross. In the Acts the same triad appears particularly at important moments in the advancement of Christianity.

Petitionary prayer, then, is the means by which the power of the Holy Spirit is effected for purposes of salvation. Further, the activity of the Spirit is directly aligned with the arrival of the kingdom of God in Luke. The active presence of the Spirit is with Jesus from the birth and baptism onwards. After the exaltation the Spirit is given to "the Christian church as a focus and sign of its inauguration (Acts 2), and also as a continuing means of mediating in history the presence of the kingdom."[58] The Spirit, therefore, serves as a link between the age of Jesus and the age of the church. This is important when we consider Luke's achievement as an evangelist who is seeking to interpret the gospel to the church of his day (see below, p. 259).

In addition to Luke's literary style, universal character, and emphasis on the Spirit, a fourth main theme in the Gospel—and here we must include the witness of Acts—is the relationship between Jews and Gentiles. Luke wants above all to justify the Gentile mission. He does this by rooting it in Scripture, and by demonstrating the scriptural authorization for the inclusion of the Gentiles.

1. The position of Jesus' inaugural address in Nazareth (4:16-30)—whether it is a development of Mark's version (Mk. 6:1ff.) or drawn from a special source—makes it clear that the theme of Jewish and Gentile relationships will occupy a prominent position in the Gospel and the Acts. In Luke 4:18f. the words from Isaiah 61:2, "to proclaim the acceptable year of the Lord," are quoted, but the words immediately following in the Isaianic passage—"and a day of vengeance of our God"—are omitted.[59] Jeremias believes that this omission from the Lukan passage accounts for the sudden change in the attitude—from wonder and astonishment to disbelief and criticism—on the part of the listeners.

Although this suggestion is attractive, and does resolve the paradoxical nature surrounding this passage, it has been weakened on several points.[60] It is possible that verses 18 and 19, which are made up of Isaiah 61:1, 58:6, and part of Isaiah 61:2,[61] may have been

58 *Ibid.*, p. 68.
59 Joachim Jeremias, *Jesus' Promise to the Nations*, pp. 44-46.
60 See Hugh Anderson, "Broadening Horizons: The Rejection at Nazareth Pericope of Luke 4:16-30 in Light of Recent Critical Trends," *Interpretation*, 18 (1964), 259-75, esp. 267-69.
61 A.R.C. Leaney, *op. cit.*, p. 53.

drawn from a Jewish lectionary,[62] but more likely they were freely composed from memory by Luke. He inserted the words ἀποστεῖλαι τεθραυσμένους ἐν ἀφέσει (Isa. 58:6) as a substitute for "and a day of vengeance of our God" (Isa. 61:2).[63] The absence of a note of vengeance against the Gentiles harmonizes well with the situation at hand and with Luke's theology as a whole. The gospel was intended for the Gentiles as well as the Jews.[64]

The actions of Elijah and Elisha (cited in 4:24-27) are a prolepsis of the inclusion of the Gentiles. J.M. Creed's comment is typical: "the incidents cited from the careers of Elijah and Elisha provide good precedents for a mission to the Gentiles—and this no doubt was their real significance to the evangelist."[65] L.C. Crockett has seen in the use of the Elijah-Elisha incidents an attempt on Luke's part to justify Jewish-Gentile fellowship.[66] One of the distinctive features of the Elijah narrative in 1 Kings 17 to which Luke alludes (4:26) was that the prophet was sent to a Gentile land by God to be fed there.[67]

2. Other allusions to or use of prophecy in connection with the Gentile mission are found in Simeon's prophecy (2:30-32), in 3:6, and in the command for missionary preaching (24:45ff.). Although this last does not appear to be directly tied to a definite scriptural text,[68] Luke nevertheless bases it on Scripture (24:45ff.). In ch. 3:6 Luke is the only evangelist to extend the quotation of Isaiah 40:3f. to include the phrase "and all flesh shall see the salvation of God." This is significant for Luke's attempt to justify the Gentile mission.[69] S.G. Wilson concludes that "of all the various methods Luke uses to justify the turning to the Gentiles, this appeal to the Old Testament, and, by implication, to the eternal will of God, is the most profound and fundamental."[70]

3. Not only does Luke employ Scripture to justify the Gentile mission, but also to show that the obduracy of the Jews was foretold even in the Old Testament. The Elijah-Elisha motif (4:25-27) no

[62] See David Hill, "The Rejection of Jesus at Nazareth (Lk. 4:16-30)," *NovT*, 13 (1971), 161-80, esp. 172-77, for compelling reasons for excluding this possibility.

[63] H. Anderson, *loc. cit.*, p. 269; cf. M.-J. Lagrange, *Evangile selon Saint Luc* (1948), p. 138.

[64] But see S.G. Wilson, *op. cit.*, pp. 40f.

[65] *The Gospel According to St. Luke* (1930), p. 66; see also R.C. Tannehill, "The Mission of Jesus according to Luke," in *Jesus in Nazareth*, ed. Erich Grässer *et al.* (1972), pp. 51-75, esp. p. 59.

[66] "Luke 4:25-27 and Jewish-Gentile Relations in Luke-Acts," *JBL*, 88 (1969), 177-83.

[67] *Ibid.*, p. 180.

[68] See J. Dupont, "Le Salut des Gentils et la significance théologique du Livre des Actes," *NTS*, 6 (1960), 132-55, esp. 139f.

[69] *Ibid.*, pp. 138-39.

[70] *Op. cit.*, p. 244.

doubt means that "God will pass over a rebellious Israel and give his blessings to Gentiles."[71]

4. In addition to scriptural quotations and allusions Luke justifies the Gentile mission by showing the piety of the Gentiles.

In the Cornelius narrative (Acts 10—11) the centurion is presented as the ideal devout Gentile. Cornelius fears Israel's God, and he liberally gives alms to all the people. Even the Jewish people attest that Cornelius is a pious man (Acts 10:22). Peter reminds the apostles and elders of the church that God has cleansed the hearts of the Gentiles by faith, so that there is no distinction between Jew and Gentile (Acts 15:9).

In the only healing of a Gentile described by Luke (7:1ff.), he takes great pains to present the devoutness of this Gentile's master. In fact Luke furnishes his source with a new introduction to show that from a Jewish point of view this Gentile deserves to be healed: "He is worthy to have you do this for him, for he loves our nation, and he built us our synagogue" (vv. 4, 5).[72] By his emphasis on the piety of the Gentiles, Luke appears to be saying "that an unbiased look at the past and the present shows the Gentiles to be in every way as good as the Jews."[73]

LUKE'S ACHIEVEMENT

At this point in our consideration we must detach the second half of the two-part volume which goes under the title of the "Lukan writings." However artificial the arrangement may seem to be, we shall separate the Gospel of Luke from the Book of Acts, since it is more appropriate here, in dealing with the Gospel, to consider what Luke's aim may have been in directing Theophilus to his presentation of the life and public career of Jesus. In our second volume we shall return to Luke's achievement as the Christian writer who published what look like the early chapters of the first history of the church.

1. Luke spans the gap between the life of Jesus and the church. Even if we leave the Acts of the Apostles out of account, it remains true that Luke the evangelist writes with an eye on the church of his day. This concern for the church of his own day is true of all Gospel writers, not excluding Mark, who (we saw above) was concerned to offer consolation and hope to a persecuted church and probably to counteract some christological errors in the church of his time.[74] But it is a strange phenomenon of Mark's Gospel that, while

[71] E. Earle Ellis, *The Gospel of Luke*, p. 98; but see L.C. Crockett, *loc. cit.*, p. 179.
[72] Jacob Jervell, "James: The Defender of Paul," in his volume *Luke and The People of God* (1972), p. 204n.
[73] S.G. Wilson, *op. cit.*, p. 245.
[74] See p. 221.

he knows that Jesus is a teacher of the Twelve, he is content to pass by the record of his teaching and tell us little about its actual content. Luke, like Matthew, makes good this deficiency, and (as we have seen) some of the characteristic teachings of Jesus are present in the Third Gospel. This may be shown by recalling Jesus' parabolic teaching (found in L); incidents such as Jesus' dealing with women, children, outcasts, and Samaritans, which Luke alone has recorded; and Luke's obvious interest in catechesis (in the section 6:20—8:3).

But the link between Jesus and the later church is even more securely established by Luke. By contrast with Mark and Matthew, he is the evangelist who places great emphasis on the post-resurrection ministry of the Lord (24:41ff.) and carefully paves the way for the ministry of the church in the post-Pentecostal era.

The link-term is the ascension, which is recorded in both the Gospel and the Acts. The story is found in Luke 24:50-51 and Acts 1:1-11. The Gospel account (vs. 51) presents some textual problems which concern mainly the authenticity of the words "and was carried up into heaven." These are found in most textual authorities, but are omitted in the "Western" tradition (ℵ* D a b d e ff l Syr^{sin} and in parts of Augustine's extant texts). F. J. A. Hort insisted that the authentic text lacked this sentence, and that it was later added on the assumption that a separation from the disciples at the close of the Gospel must be the ascension. Further, he argued, the ascension does not belong to the scope of the Gospels, but to the beginning of the history of the church.[75]

Later scholars have defended the longer reading as original, offering various reasons why the Western editor would have omitted the words.[76] The most satisfactory reason is that the Western text purposely omitted the sentence on the ground that it could be taken to imply that Jesus' ascension occurred on the very day of his resurrection (as in *Epistle of Barnabas* 15:9), which would conflict with the account in Acts 1:3ff., according to which the Lord ascended to heaven forty days after the resurrection.[77] Support for this view is found in Acts 1:2 which contains the clause "until the day he was taken up into heaven." As Streeter remarks, this presupposes an account of the ascension in the Gospel. It is also possible that the longer ending of Mark 16:19 was inspired by the phrase in Luke rather than vice versa. This would make Mark's *ἀνελήμφθη εἰς τὸν οὐρανόν* an allusion to Luke's text. Finally, we should not overlook Luke 9:51,

[75] Hort, *The New Testament in the Original Greek*, p. 73.
[76] Cf. J. Jeremias, *The Eucharistic Words of Jesus*^{2}, p. 151; P. Benoit, "L'ascension," *RB*, 56 (1949), 189; and esp. P.A. van Stempvoort, "The Interpretation of the Ascension in Luke and Acts," *NTS*, 5 (1958-59), 30-42.
[77] This is C.S.C. Williams' explanation, *Alterations to the Text of the Synoptic Gospels and Acts*, p. 52. He follows B.H. Streeter, *The Four Gospels*, pp. 142f.

which anticipates the longer ending of the Gospel as much as the ascension narrative in Acts.[78]

The two accounts in Luke's Gospel and in Acts vary in their respective emphases, but the main point seems clearly to be made: the ascension is both the end of the earthly history of Jesus and the beginning of the story of the church.[79] Luke has clamped together the close of Jesus' earthly life and the opening of his risen life in the church, and he has forged the link firmly with his twice repeated story of how one chapter of Jesus' existence ended and how the second chapter began.

2. Luke is interested in Jesus as a historical person. Our study of Mark endeavored to show that the author of the Second Gospel was not composing a biography and was uninterested in painting a portrait of the earthly Jesus to be admired and applauded. Rather, Mark's stress falls on the kerygmatic intention of the sections which make up Jesus' ministry, with a view to showing how his power was displayed and his authority heeded.

With Luke, there is a noticeable shift of emphasis. To that extent, M. Kähler's dictum that the Gospels are kerygmatic and severely theological documents fails to convince as far as Luke is concerned. For Luke there *is* an interest in Jesus' earthly life, and he is interested in details of his antecedents (ch. 1, 2), his historical and cultural setting (3:1f.), his social relationships (e.g., Mary and Martha, 10:38-42) and his demeanor (e.g., the Lukan descriptive sayings in ch. 22—24, which open a window into Jesus "inner life" of prayer in Gethsemane, of deportment on the road to Calvary, of human concern in his words from the cross).

E. Käsemann is thus correct in his assessment:

> His Gospel is indeed the first 'life of Jesus'. In it, consideration is given to the points of view of causality and teleology; and psychological insight, the composition of the historian and the particular slant of the writer who aims at edification are all equally discernible.[80]

3. In terms of Luke's achievement as an edifying writer, concerned to relate the gospel to the needs of his day, we may further remark that his interest is to give guidance for the earthly existence of the church in his time. The full import of this statement will become evident as we inspect the record and teaching in Acts. But even if we look no further than the Gospel and recall its teaching on the Spirit, the place of prayer, and the presence of the kingdom as a spiritualized

[78] See further C.F.D. Moule, "The Ascension—Acts 1:9," *ExpT*, 68 (1957), 205-209.

[79] S.G. Wilson, "The Ascension," *ZNTW*, 59 (1968), 269-81; cf. C.K. Barrett, *Luke the Historian* (1961), pp. 55-57.

[80] E. Käsemann, "The Problem of the Historical Jesus," in *Essays on New Testament Themes*, pp. 28f. Note the use made of this quotation in E. Haenchen, *op. cit.*, p. 97, and C.K. Barrett, *op. cit.*, p. 48.

power in human lives, it seems clear that Luke is essentially a pastor and has the well-being of the church as his first aim.

His pastoral interest dominates in his desire to show that the church lives under the present rule of Christ by his Word and Spirit through apostolic witness, which is in continuity with the past. For Luke the past is not dead. Here we are disposed to take issue with Käsemann's view, which treats Luke's transformation of the kerygma as though it implied "mere history" and Jesus' imprisonment in an epoch to which the later church looked back wistfully.[81] For Luke, we would maintain, the past speaks to the present, which in turn shapes the future. To give one example. Jesus' reported saying at Nazareth (4:21) takes on fresh meaning in the light of Luke's overall understanding of the fulfilment of Old Testament prophecy in the mission to the Gentiles. How could the Gentile church of Luke's own day fail to hear the speaking of the present Lord and to heed his missionary summons to proclaim repentance and forgiveness to all nations (24:47)? True, the apostles needed the Spirit for this task. That power is now available to the later church, this Gospel declares, as it sets about its unfinished tasks, with Christ the Lord present in its midst.

LUKE'S GOSPEL IN RECENT STUDY

1. To the ongoing debate about whether Luke was a historian or theologian or both, S.G. Wilson's book *The Gentiles and the Gentile Mission in Luke-Acts* brings a welcome perspective. He insists that Luke was primarily a pastor concerned with practical problems in the church of his day. He wanted to write history with a message.

The main thrust of Wilson's book deals, as the title suggests, with the Lukan view of the Gentile mission. In the first chapter he concentrates on two questions: what was Jesus' attitude towards the Gentiles? Did Jesus see a historical Gentile mission? Wilson concludes that Jesus, in his earthly ministry, limited his mission to Israel. Although the Gentiles have a place in the kingdom of God, this is limited to a future time when the kingdom will be manifested in all its fulness. In short, "there is no evidence that Jesus either foresaw or intended there to be a mission to the Gentiles such as actually took place in the early Church." The reason for this lies in his eschatological expectation: he believed that the parousia was imminent.[82]

This viewpoint, however, is not shared by the evangelists. Luke, Wilson finds, is a faithful recorder of the tradition about the Gentiles. That is to say, he does not anachronistically place the mission to the Gentiles within the earthly ministry of Jesus. Distinc-

[81] See E. Käsemann, *loc. cit.*, p. 29; cf. H. Conzelmann, *op. cit.*, p. 168.
[82] S.G. Wilson, *The Gentiles and the Gentile-Mission in Luke-Acts*, p. 28.

tively Lukan, though, is the insertion of the theme of the Gentile mission into his scheme of *Heilsgeschichte*. While Jesus viewed the proclamation to the Gentiles as an apocalyptic event, and Mark saw the mission as an eschatological event which must be complete before the end, Luke made the final break by placing it in ongoing history.[83] This explains Luke's eschatology.

The reason Jesus did not expect a historical mission to the Gentiles—because of his imminent expectation—is toned down in Luke. But Luke does not entirely eliminate the strand of imminence from his eschatology. Rather there are two strands in his eschatology, one which allows for the delay in the parousia, and one which affirms that the end will come soon. Through this twofold approach Luke would be able, from a pastoral point of view, to correct the false extremes of his contemporaries (*c.* AD 75-85).[84] On the one hand, there were some with false expectations who claimed that the end was near or already here. The commission given in Acts 1:6-8 would serve as a reminder to them that there is a mission to be accomplished among the Gentiles. On the other hand, the failure of the parousia to materialize caused some to abandon this hope, denying that the end would come at all. The words *οὕτως ἐλεύσεται ὅν τρόπον* (Acts 1:11) would be a reply to any who would deny the parousia at all.

On several occasions Luke appears to be saying in effect that the Gentiles are just as devout and likable as the Jews. This is the case in the discourse with the pious centurion (7:1-10), with the conversion of Cornelius (Acts 10—11), and in Paul's speech at Athens (Acts 17). In each case Luke is saying that "the average Gentile's response to God is no worse, though neither is it any better, than that of the average Jew."[85]

At other times Luke employs several themes to explain and justify the Gentile mission. He wants to ground the Gentile mission in the Old Testament and therefore in the will of God. In Acts 28:26-28 Luke refers to Isaiah 6:9f. for scriptural proof of the Jews' rejection of the gospel. As we saw earlier Luke alone among the evangelists includes the phrase "and all flesh shall see the salvation of God" in his citation of Isaiah 40:3f. (Luke 3:6). The phrase *οὕτως γέγραπται* (24:36f.) emphasizes that the Gentile mission is based not only on Jesus' command but also on the Old Testament prophecy.

Furthermore, the theme of the Holy Spirit in Luke is not an attempt to produce a systematic and logical theology of the Spirit, but "to reconstruct and make intelligible the experience of the early Church. . . ."[86] Throughout Acts the Holy Spirit is seen as a necessary prerequisite for the extension of the church's mission. Therefore, by basing his claim upon the words and actions of Jesus, the concept that

[83] *Ibid.*, p. 57.
[84] *Ibid.*, p. 85.
[85] *Ibid.*, p. 217.
[86] *Ibid.*, p. 241.

God is not partisan, the proof-from-prophecy theme, and the Jews' rejection of the gospel (though not a fundamental motivation of the Gentile mission), Luke attempted to justify the mission to the Gentiles.

Why was there a need to explain and justify the Gentile mission? Probably, concludes Wilson, it was in response both to simple historical curiosity on the part of Gentiles and even Jews and to disputes with Jewish contemporaries. Concerning the latter, Wilson writes:

> It is possible that the Jews accused the Church of being an illegitimate offspring of Judaism, an aberration in the true course of the history of God's people. This kind of accusation was probably accompanied by personal attacks on Paul, the founder of so many Gentile Churches. . . . The emphasis Luke places both on the Old Testament prophecies of the Gentile mission and on the Jews' wilful rejection of the gospel may be his response to Jewish calumny.[87]

Wilson's thoughtful analysis of the practical, pastoral motivation of Luke's writings, a neglected factor in recent Lukan studies, is a needed corrective. At times the difference between pastor and theologian seems strained, a difficulty Wilson is aware of.[88] Perhaps, then, it is best to recognize both Luke and Paul as both pastors and theologians, differing in motivations and in the centering of their interests. In a time when it is fashionable to offer new and original interpretations of Lukan theology, sometimes forcing Luke's theology into a neat mold, Wilson's study is to be commended for eschewing such a tendency.

2. The starting point for Schuyler Brown's monograph on Luke, *Apostasy and Perseverance in the Theology of Luke*, is Conzelmann's assumption that the age of Jesus is marked on the one end by the devil's completion of temptation (4:13) and on the other by the reappearance of Satan with temptation at the start of Jesus' passion (Lk. 23:3). The age of Jesus is thus considered by Conzelmann to be a "Satan-free" period. Brown finds this position untenable. In the first place, most of the Lukan sayings concerning Satan are found in the section from 4:13 to 22:3.[89] Second, Brown argues, Conzelmann's understanding of πειρασμός may be correct for New Testament writers in general, but Luke's understanding does not conform to the common view. While many writers (e.g., James 1:12) consider πειρασμός to be a test of faith for which the faithful Christian will receive the "crown of life," for Luke πειρασμός has a negative connotation.[90] It is something to be avoided, since it is associated with the sin of apostasy.[91] πειρασμός in non-Lukan writings is usually associated with a special vocabulary such as "the flesh" (σάρξ), "weakness" (ἀσθένεια), and "lust" (ἐπιθυμία), or external agents such

[87] *Ibid.*, pp. 248f.
[88] *Ibid.*, pp. 255, 267.
[89] *Apostasy and Perseverance in the Theology of Luke* (1959), p. 6
[90] *Ibid.*, p. 15.
[91] *Ibid.*, p. 21.

as "seduction" (πλανάω), "deception" (ἐξαπατάω), and "enticement" (σκάνδαλον). Further πειρασμός is generally associated with expressions of a negative outcome such as "not standing the test" and with virtues necessary for a positive outcome, such as "faith" (πίστις), "patience" (ὑπομονή), and "hope" (ἐλπίς). In Luke, Brown finds, these words are either entirely missing or take on a different meaning, which falls within Luke's consistent theological conception of apostasy and perseverance.

The Lukan conception of apostasy and perseverance is the topic of a major part of Brown's book. He considers first of all the perseverance of the apostles in the age of Jesus. More than any of the other evangelists, Luke connects apostleship with this age. There are two reasons for this, according to Brown. In the first place Luke needed reliable witnesses.[92] But it was not only the continuity of the apostles' testimony which was necessary but also "their unbroken faith during the Age of Jesus." For Luke both elements were necessary "to secure the ἀσφάλεια [trustworthiness] of the kerygma and the faith of the church, and both are guaranteed by the apostles' continuous following of Jesus from the beginning of his public ministry in Galilee."[93]

Luke alludes to the apostles' fidelity during the passion (22:28-30). The apostles are said to have "stood by" Jesus in his trials.[94] As a reward for this perseverance the apostles are given "royal rule" (βασιλεία) over Israel.[95]

Jesus' promise that Peter's faith will not fail (22:32) and the command that Peter should strengthen his brethren emphasize the importance of the apostles' faith for the future community. Rejecting the normal interpretation, which sees this strengthening as directed to the other apostles, Brown holds that this is a command for Peter and the other disciples to strengthen the future Christian community.[96] Therefore, "the *fides apostolica*, whose perseverance in the moment of stress is the object of Luke's concern in his passion account, will constitute in the Age of the Church the source of strength for the perseverance of the Christian."[97]

The Lukan concept of discipleship takes the form of a journey: Jesus determines the way, and the disciples follow.[98] Whereas the apostles' perseverance in their "standing by" Jesus represents one side of discipleship, the apostasy of Judas represents the other side of the coin. The apostasy of Judas presented Luke with a "theological problem," since perseverance throughout the age of Jesus is "the indispensable prerequisite" for the apostles' conduct. Luke, however, solves this problem, since the continuity of the apostolic college is

[92] *Ibid.*, p. 55.
[93] *Ibid.*, pp. 56f.
[94] *Ibid.*, pp. 62f.
[95] *Ibid.*, p. 64.
[96] *Ibid.*, pp. 72f.
[97] *Ibid.*, p. 74.
[98] *Ibid.*, p. 82.

established by its numerical integrity.[99] The divinely ordained number twelve constitutes the apostolic college, and therefore by substituting a faithful disciple for the traitor, Luke guarantees continuity.[100]

During the age of the church apostasy continues to be a fact, as seen in the episodes of Ananias and Sapphira (Acts 5:1-11) and of Simon Magus (Acts 8:9-24).[101] But just as there is apostasy so too there is perseverance during this age, as shown in Barnabas' exhortation to the Christians in Antioch "to remain attached to the Lord" (Acts 11:23). This phrase is parallel to another formula of inner-church paraenesis, "abiding in the faith" (Acts 14:22), which means persevering in the Christian kerygma.[102]

In the Book of Acts there is a shift from "your faith" to "the faith." Faith is objectified, i.e., identified with the Christian kerygma. This objectification involves an ecclesialization of the concept of faith: "the bearer of the faith is not the individual Christian but the community."[103] In terms of perseverance and apostasy the Christian perseveres "not by proving *his* faith but by remaining in *the* faith," and he apostatizes "not by suffering the loss of *his* faith but by falling away from *the* faith."[104]

This depersonalization of the concept of faith is offset by a positive theological notion: Luke's desire to establish the historical character of faith. The past historical reality of the earthly Jesus is the object of faith; the church is the agent through which this faith is mediated.[105] However, the Lukan conception of apostasy and perseverance is not to be dismissed as an example of "early catholicism." The historical reality of the earthly Jesus guards against this. At the same time the ecclesial dimension of Christian faith "prevents God's gift of salvation from evaporating in sheer subjectivistic mysticism."[106]

There is considerable merit in Brown's orderly development of the πειρασμός vocabulary in Luke in relation to the other New Testament writers. But the limits of apostasy and perseverance are too restrictive. Perhaps it would be better to develop this thought within a more general scope, such as Luke's pastoral approach to problems within the church.

3. From time to time the traditional interpretations commonly accepted by scholars are sharply challenged and the way opened for new interpretations. Such is the case in a recent collection of essays by Jacob Jervell.[107] Among the long cherished assumptions about Luke which Jervell impugns—at times quite successfully—is the

99 *Ibid.*, p. 94.
100 *Ibid.*, pp. 94-96.
101 *Ibid.*, pp. 98-114.
102 *Ibid.*, p. 114.
103 *Ibid.*, p. 146.
104 *Ibid.*
105 *Ibid.*, p. 147.
106 *Ibid.*, p. 148.
107 *Luke and the People of God.*

view that the church is the "new Israel"; that the Gentile mission is directly a result of the Jews' rejection of the gospel; that the Samaritans are Gentiles; and that the law in Luke is of only peripheral concern.

In his essay "The Divided People of God" Jervell questions the popular thesis that the Gentile mission is a direct result of the rejection of the gospel by the Jewish people. Briefly stated, his line of argument is as follows.

First, in Acts Luke relates the great success of the Christian mission to the Jews. This directly conflicts with the popular conception that Luke describes the Jews as a whole rejecting the gospel. Mass conversions of the Jews are reported at 2:41 (47); 4:4; 5:14; 6:1, 7; 9:42; 12:24; 13:43; 14:1; 17:10ff.; (19:20); 21:20. Moreover, the converted Gentiles mentioned by Luke—e.g., Cornelius—are mainly "God-fearers," i.e., men who were already related to Israel and Judaism via the synagogue.

Second, "Israel" for Luke is composed of two groups—the repentant (i.e., the Christian) and the obdurate. Never is the term used to characterize the church;[108] always it refers to the Jewish people.[109] Luke shows that the Jewish Christian church is a part of Israel in a number of ways. The earliest Jerusalem Christians lived as pious Jews. The Christian missionaries are the true representatives of Israel. The believers live in strict observance of the law.[110] The Lukan picture, therefore, is not that "the church has transgressed the boundaries of Judaism, but that a portion of Israel has forfeited its right to belong to the people of God."[111] Usually the presupposition for the Gentile mission is understood to be that only when the Jews have rejected the gospel is the way opened to the Gentiles. It would be more correct to say "that only when Israel has accepted the gospel can the way to Gentiles be opened."[112]

Third, the mission to the Gentiles is a fulfilment of Scripture. It is not because the Jews have rejected the gospel that the missionaries turn to the Gentiles; it is because God has commanded this mission. In Paul's speech at Pisidian Antioch (Acts 13:16ff.) the Gentile mission appears to be a result of Jewish disobedience: "Since you thrust it [God's word] from you, and judge yourselves unworthy of eternal life, behold we turn to the Gentiles" (vs. 46). But, according to Jervell, this cannot be the proper interpretation because verse 47 clearly indicates that the Gentile mission is a result of God's commands. Thus "the partial rejection on the part of the Jews does not provide the basis for preaching to Gentiles because the Gentile mission is already commanded of God."[113]

108 See P. Richardson, *Israel in the Apostolic Church* (1969), p. 161.
109 Jervell, *op. cit.*, p. 49.
110 *Ibid.*, p. 50.
111 *Ibid.*, p. 54.
112 *Ibid.*, p. 55.
113 *Ibid.*, p. 61.

The Cornelius account (Acts 10:1—11:18) appears to contradict the impression that the Gentiles receive salvation via Israel. This event, though, does not serve to show that salvation is now open to the Gentiles, but simply to indicate that Gentiles do not first have to become proselytes to be saved.[114] What stands out as new in relation to the earlier chapters in Acts "is not the 'idea of Gentile mission' or that the Gentiles now come to share in salvation, but that they are admitted as Gentiles, as uncircumcised."[115]

Therefore, the mission to the Gentiles is not a direct result of the Jews' rejection of the gospel, as is commonly thought, but is a result of the Jews' acceptance of the gospel. Only through Israel's acceptance of the gospel has salvation to the Gentiles become a reality.

Luke's understanding of the apostolate is the topic of Jervell's essay "The Twelve on Israel's Thrones." Once again he queries a popular conception: that which would place the twelve apostles in some role in the church as the "new Israel." But if Luke knows only one Israel, the old Israel, what role do the Twelve play? For Luke the number Twelve is constitutive: the function of the apostolic circle can only be carried out by Twelve. The reason why this is important for Luke is that it is linked to the concept of "Israel."[116] The Twelve are appointed as regents in the eschatological Israel.[117]

The Gentile mission does not involve a severing of ties with Israel, but is an affirmation of Israel. Therefore it is unthinkable for Luke that Israel as a people should be rejected along with her leaders. Rather the leaders by their obduracy have relinquished any right to rule over the people, and the Twelve then become the new leaders of Israel (Lk. 22:30).[118]

Are the Samaritans Jews or Gentiles? This is the basic issue in Jervell's essay "The Lost Sheep of the House of Israel." If they are Gentiles, as is often maintained, several references in Luke make no sense. In Luke 17:11ff., for example, if the Samaritan were a Gentile, it is incomprehensible that Jesus could have sent him along with nine Jews to the Jerusalem temple to perform the rites of purification.[119] Luke on several occasions seems to consider Samaritans as Jews. According to Jervell, Acts 8 and 10—11 clearly show that the Samaritans are not considered to be Gentiles. As a Jew Peter is reported to associate with non-Jews in Acts 10—11, an unheard-of thing. Yet in chapter 8 association with Samaritans is not considered in the same manner. Therefore, by placing the Samaritan mission in chapter 8, Luke shows that the Samaritans were not considered Gentiles.

114 *Ibid.*, pp. 65f.
115 *Ibid.*, p. 66. For a criticism of Jervell's position see S. G. Wilson, *The Gentiles and the Gentile Mission in Luke-Acts*, pp. 222-33.
116 Jervell, *op. cit.*, p. 85.
117 *Ibid.*, p. 89.
118 *Ibid.*, p. 94.
119 *Ibid.*, p. 116.

Further evidence for considering the Samaritans to be Jews is found in Luke's geography. He considers Samaria to be a part of Jewish territory. Luke is careful to dissociate Jesus from Gentile territory, but clearly in 9:51-56 Jesus appears in Samaritan territory.[120] The progress of the mission indicates that Galilee, Judaea, and Samaria constitute a unity which is separate from "the nations."[121]

Luke's attitude towards the law concerns Jervell in his essay "The Law in Luke-Acts." Most commentators regard the problem of the law as only peripheral in Acts. Not so, says Jervell. "For Luke the law remains the law given to Israel on Sinai, in the strict meaning of the word, the law of Israel. And Luke is concerned about the law because it is Israel's law."[122] For Luke the law is the mark of distinction between Jews and non-Jews. Luke never spiritualizes the law, as Paul does. In chapters 1 and 2 he takes pains to show that Jesus and his parents were faithful adherents of the law. In another instance, Mark's pericope on divorce (10:1-12), Luke (16:18) upholds the validity of the Mosaic law.[123] In short, Luke adopts a conservative outlook towards the law "because of his concern for the law as Israel's law, the sign of God's people."[124] This conservative outlook is bound up with the fact that Luke knows only one Israel, one people of God. By being zealous for the law the Jewish Christians prove their identity as the people of God, entitled to salvation.[125]

Luke's view of the law, Jervell points out, is closely connected with his ecclesiology. The law is a sign of the church's identity.[126] Jervell attacks Conzelmann's assertion that the law belonged to the old Israel and to the initial period of the church, thereafter to be replaced by the apostolic decree. For after the Jerusalem Council Paul and the other Jewish Christians continued to obey the law.[127] This way of dealing with the law points to a historical situation in the church in which the Jews opposed the Jewish Christians, charging them with apostasy from Israel. "At the time Luke writes the salvation of Gentiles creates no problem; this had been settled long ago. But the question about the law and Israel is still acute, because the Jewish element within the church is still a decisive factor, if not numerically at least theologically."[128]

Jervell devotes his essay "Paul: The Teacher of Israel" to an examination of the apologetic speeches of Paul recorded in Acts. Specifically, he is concerned with the relationship of the speeches in Acts 22—26 to the preceding portions of the book. Some have considered these chapters as a political-apologetic appeal directed to influential heathen in the Roman Empire. If this is the case, according

[120] *Ibid.*, p. 120.
[121] *Ibid.*, p. 122.
[122] *Ibid.*, p. 137.
[123] *Ibid.*, p. 139.
[124] *Ibid.*, p. 141.
[125] *Ibid.*, p. 142.
[126] *Ibid.*, p. 143.
[127] *Ibid.*, p. 145.
[128] *Ibid.*, p. 147.

to Jervell, this section of Acts "is left hanging in the air and appears as an appendage."[129] Furthermore, the Roman officials appear in an unfavorable light in Acts, which would have been awkward had Luke been seeking their understanding or protection.[130] For example, Pilate in 4:27 is described as Jesus' murderer, a tradition which would have been better omitted if Luke wanted to make a favorable impression on the Roman authorities.[131] On the other hand, there is a strong indication that this section is intended to defend Paul against Jewish charges. The speeches are apologetic with a clear biographical character, making them not the defense of the individual Christian or of Christianity, but of Paul's person and activity.[132] Moreover, Luke's summaries on several occasions of the charges directed against Paul by Jews (21:21; 21:28; 28:17) point to his efforts to defend Paul.

The importance of James in Acts is the theme of Jervell's essay "James: The Defender of Paul." Although Acts says nothing of who James is, his importance is apparent. At two pivotal points (15:13ff.; 21:20ff.) James proposes decisive solutions. Luke's silence about James then can mean only one thing: "For Luke's readers James is an undisputed authority, an uncontestable figure so well-known that it is unnecessary for Luke even to make the slightest mention of his credentials."[133] At the Apostolic Council it is James "whose authority tips the scales regarding the practice of the church, justifying it from 'Jewish perspectives.' "[134] James' authority is emphasized in the opening remark of his interpretation of Scripture: διὸ ἐγὼ κρίνω (15:19).[135] On the other hand, Paul plays a very minor role in Acts 15, in spite of his important role elsewhere (as Luke is well aware) in the exemption of the Gentiles from the details of the law. Jervell's explanation for this is that Luke's readers had little confidence in Paul, but through James the decisions were legitimized and made to agree with Israel's law. In this respect James is the defender of Paul.

At the second pivotal point (Acts 21:15-26) Luke demonstrates that the rumors about Paul are false by James' invalidation of them. Apparently, "Luke is writing for readers who view Paul with suspicion and who know rumors of his apostasy from Moses."[136] Therefore, by the presence of James, who needs no defense, at decisive points in the narrative and the apologetic nature of Paul's speeches in the last half of Acts, Luke is able to establish his defense of Paul against Jewish charges.

Jervell's collection of essays provides a provocative and reasonable analysis of some difficult problems in Lukan writings. He provides some useful correctives. The Jews as a whole, for example, do not reject the gospel, as seen by mass conversions in Acts. But in his

[129] *Ibid.*, p. 156.
[130] *Ibid.*, p. 157.
[131] *Ibid.*
[132] *Ibid.*, p. 161.
[133] *Ibid.*, p. 187.
[134] *Ibid.*, p. 189.
[135] *Ibid.*, p. 190.
[136] *Ibid.*, p. 197.

analysis of the mission to the Gentiles ("The Divided People of God") Jervell wants to separate how Luke motivates the Gentile mission theologically from the origin of the mission understood historically.[137] This is something which Luke does not do. As Wilson says, "Luke saw no contradiction between the idea that the Gentile mission was foretold in the Old Testament and that in practical terms the turning to the Gentiles was frequently a result of Jewish obduracy. . . ."[138] Jervell's essays can hardly be ignored; whether they represent a viable "New Look at Luke-Acts" remains an open question.

d. Dating Luke-Acts in the late 70s or early 80s Frederick W. Danker sees Luke's aim as directed towards two fronts. On the one side, Luke wanted to provide instruction and "resources for evaluating especially theological issues" to the Christian community. On the other side, by arranging his material in such a way, Luke could compel Theophilus, probably a Roman official, "to revise certain misunderstandings provoked by members of the Church or by earlier writers or traditions."[139] In this sense Luke "does not write a 'Life of Jesus,' but 'The Things Fulfilled Among Us,' " i.e. a history theologically interpreted.[140]

Among the areas needing clarification were the nature of Jesus' kingship (Jesus as Messiah is not a competitor to Caesar's throne!) and the subject of apocalyptic. Danker selects three apocalyptic problems which needed resolution: If Jesus is the deliverer at the end-time, why does the power of Satan still appear to be in control? why are there not clear signs that the end is near? and why did his own nation reject him?

To answer the first question Luke shows that Jesus overcame Satan at the temptation and thrust the demonic forces out of the demon-possessed. The meaning of the resurrection is seen in the light of the struggle with demonic forces: suffering and death became necessary factors in Jesus' ascent to glory. This "faithful surrender to God's purpose" by Jesus assures "the Christian community that they will not fall victim to demonic devices."[141]

Luke solves the second problem, suggests Danker, by showing that the kingdom comes in two stages. Jesus as the Son of Man comes to usher in the kingdom. Death on the cross is his entry to enthronement. "No spectacular apocalyptic demonstrations," writes Danker, "are therefore necessary to *validate* that Kingship."[142] The church lives in the entire period of the end-time. But the "end of the end-time," or the judgment time, represents the second stage, when

137 *Ibid.*, p. 42.
138 S. G. Wilson, *The Gentiles and the Gentile Mission in Luke-Acts*, p. 223.
139 F.W. Danker, *op. cit.*, p. xiii.
140 *Ibid.*, p. 4.
141 *Ibid.*, p. xiv.
142 *Ibid.*, p. xv.

Jesus will reappear and will fulfil expectations concerning the Son of Man.[143]

Therefore it may be said that "Luke christologizes and historicizes apocalyptic."[144] That is to say, for Luke apocalyptic must not be seen in terms of traditional apocalyptic descriptions. Rather Jesus is "the apocalypse." Apocalyptic thinking should not be directed towards the end of history, but rather towards Jesus who, as the center of the "New Age," embodies apocalyptic hope as "God's present communication."[145] Luke retains traditional apocalyptic language particularly for the consummation of history. But his contribution lies in pointing to the continuity "in terms of divine revelation between the time of Jesus' appearance and the end of history as we know it."[146] By attributing apocalyptic terminology to events which would not be considered apocalyptic from his opponent's viewpoint, Luke "disencumbered the church of the necessity of determining Jesus' messianic credentials through proofs supplied by 'signs.' "[147] In this way he prepared the church for a "functional existence in history."[148]

The third problem—Jesus' rejection by the religious and theological establishment—is answered by Luke's emphasis upon the criteria of the "New Age." The candidates for the kingdom are more likely to be the lowly, the outcasts, women, "tax collectors and sinners," than the high and lofty, particularly the religious establishment.[149] A sinful woman (Lk. 7) is able to see in Jesus forgiveness and thus responds in love. Similarly Zacchaeus' love for Jesus (Lk. 19:9) brings recognition that he is a son of Abraham. The chief characteristic of a follower of Jesus is his "undivided allegiance, marked especially by renunciation of worldly criteria of success, including money and social status."[150]

If Danker is correct in his assumptions, the *Sitz im Leben* in which Luke wrote his work is more complex, involving more than one audience, than is sometimes thought.

[143] *Ibid.*
[144] *Ibid.*, pp. xv-xvi.
[145] *Ibid.*, p. xv.
[146] *Ibid.*, p. xvi.
[147] *Ibid.*
[148] *Ibid.*
[149] *Ibid.*
[150] *Ibid.*

CHAPTER SIXTEEN

John's Gospel

THE SYNOPTICS AND JOHN

The procedure which sees the growth of the gospel tradition according to the three stages of tradition stemming from eyewitness or kerygmatic use, redaction of that tradition in the name of a church "theologian" or "school" in response to a felt need in the community, and the use of the evangelist's finished work in a church situation, comes to its fullest expression in the Fourth Gospel. Before proceeding to our main concern—what was this Gospel saying to the church of the evangelist's day?—we should examine some details of the writing of this book.

How far is the Fourth Gospel dependent on the Synoptics? Although the Synoptics and John both describe in general outline the course of Jesus' life, we should note some distinctions. In the first place are the differences which become obvious the moment we set Mark's narrative alongside that of John. Mark has only one clearly mentioned visit of Jesus to Jerusalem, made at the time of the Triumphal Entry (Mark 11); John's record has five visits (2:13; 5:1; 7:10; 10:22, 23; 12:12). In Mark 1:14 Jesus' ministry begins as John the Baptist is imprisoned; in John 3:24 the two preachers work side by side. According to Mark the temple was cleansed at the close of Jesus' ministry (11:15-19); in John's account it occurs as a frontispiece to the ministry (2:13ff.). The emphasis on the eucharist (John 6) replaces the Last Supper words in Mark (14:17-25). The day of crucifixion differs between the two accounts: in Mark it is Nisan 15 (our Friday); in John Nisan 14, to coincide with the sacrifice of lambs (19:30f.). Finally, there are cases in which what is apparently the same story is given a new twist (e.g., Mt. 8:5ff. = Lk. 7:1ff. *vs.* Jn. 4:46f.).

A second noticeable distinction between the first three Gospels and the fourth is John's specialized vocabulary (ἀγαπ[η/αω] 44 times, ἀλήθεια and cognates 46 times, γινώσκειν 56/57 times, κόσμος

78 times), and conversely the rarity or absence of certain synoptic terms (kingdom, demons, just men, power [δύναμις], pity, gospel, preach, repent, parable, tax collector, and Sadducee).

Third, John has a novel literary style.[1] Schweizer and Ruckstuhl have examined the favorite expressions of this evangelist not found elsewhere. Schweizer found 33 such characteristics, to which Ruckstuhl added 17 more. Examples include the possessive ἐμός with the definite article, beside a noun which also takes a definite article; the phrases "the last day," "to lay down one's life," "he answered and said" (in place of a participial construction—"having answered, he said"—found in the Synoptics).

Fourth, there is John's characteristic use of statements which modify or correct. Compare 3:22 *vs.* 4:2; 7:8f. *vs.* 7:10; 8:15 *vs.* 12:48; 14:16 *vs.* 16:26; 15:15 *vs.* 16:12; along with statements or comments appended in a postscript way, e.g., 1:28, 44; 4:8; 6:7, 59; 11:5, 17; 18:12; 19:14, 23, 26; 21:8, as though the author were editing an already existing text.

Finally, the reader of the Fourth Gospel gets the impression of an artistic work (a trait which is lacking in the Synoptics), especially in long monologues, elaborate dialogues (ch. 4, 9, 10), the use of symbolism, the presence of Semitic parallelism (3:11, 18, 20-21, 31-32) and *inclusio*, as well as rhythm and various rhetorical devices, like parataxis and asyndeton, with an absence of connectives between the sentences (1:40, 42, 45, 47; 2:17; 4:6; 7:30, etc.).

These characteristics have suggested to some that John wrote with a literary scheme in mind (e.g., numerical) or that he was governed by symbolic motifs or a liturgical format.[2] But it is doubtful that such elaborate schemes were envisioned in a Gospel known for its artless and monumental simplicity. The simplest view is best, namely that the Gospel falls into two parts: the Book of Signs (1—12) and the Book of the Passion (13—20/21), with 13:1 as a hinge. The term ὥρα, used in that verse, can be traced throughout the Gospel of John (2:4; 7:30; 8:20; 17:1; 19:25-27), which suggests a literary key to the Gospel.[3] The evangelist pinpoints Jesus' time *before* and *after* his "hour," and the structure of the Gospel conforms to this single idea. "The Evangelist sees the whole public life [of Jesus] through the prism of 'the hour,' as is clear from 7,6.30; 8,20 and 12,23.27."[4]

[1] This has been investigated by E. Schweizer, *Ego Eimi* (1939), and E. Ruckstuhl, *Die literarische Einheit des Johannesevangeliums* (1951).

[2] D. Mollat, in *The Jerusalem Bible* (1953); A. Guilding, *The Fourth Gospel and Jewish Worship* (1960), tries to make the plan of John conform to that set by the Jewish synagogue triennial lectionary. For a critique, see L. Morris, *The New Testament and the Jewish Lectionaries* (1964); and for a reminder that our knowledge of Jewish lections is limited, see M. McNamara, *Targum and Testament*, p. 47.

[3] C. H. Dodd, *The Interpretation of the Fourth Gospel* (1953), pp. 289-91.

[4] Cited in A. Feuillet, "The Fourth Gospel," *Introduction to the New Testament*, ed. A. Robert and A. Feuillet (1965), p. 614.

We may now state some conclusions about the origins of the Fourth Gospel:

1. John has the same basic outline as the Synoptics but shows no *direct* dependence.[5] At best dependence means adherence to the same general traditions.

2. John has recast his understanding of the gospel to display the themes of revelation (1:1-4), rejection (1:5-11), reception (1:12-18) from the prologue as expressing three main divisions: 1:19—6:71, 7—12, and 13—21. The prologue of 1:1-18 is thus "not so much a preface to the gospel as a summary of it."[6]

3. The governing principle is the progression to Christ's glory in the cross and exaltation, which proceeds *pari passu* with the progression of human resistance and opposition. These parallel movements are the *actualité* of the Gospel; i.e., from beginning to end there are incidents in which men have the option of choosing or rejecting Jesus.[7] This gives rise to a tentative suggestion that the entire Gospel picture should be understood as a *trial* where witnesses for the defense are called and testify; and the opposition builds up its case also. In this sense Kähler's dictum may be modified thus: the Synoptics are passion story with extended introduction; John is passion story.[8]

4. More consciously than the Synoptics John writes from the vantage point of the resurrection and with the aid of hindsight as well as the Spirit (see 2:21-22; 7:39; 11:51-52; 12:16; and the Paraclete sayings in ch. 14—16). This is why he does not refrain from adding his own commentary to Jesus' words, and projects onto the Lord's deeds light which comes from the life of the church. He often gives to the miracles (earlier wonder-stories which he has taken over as part of the tradition?) an undeniable sacramental significance. Note also the use of the perfect tense in the *logia* of Jesus, e.g., 6:63—"the words that I *have spoken* to you are spirit and life."[9]

5. Literary problems cry out for solution. These include textual problems (5:3b-4; 7:53—8:11; 21), irregular sequences (14:31; ch. 5 in relation to ch. 6; 7:15-24); the possibility of sources;[10] and

[5] Contra C. K. Barrett, *The Gospel according to St. John*, pp. 14, 34-37, who argues that John read Mark and was influenced by its contents. Cf. his article "John and the Synoptic Gospels," *ExpT*, 85 (1974), 228-33.

[6] E. C. Hoskyns, *The Fourth Gospel* (1947), p. 137.

[7] So X. Léon-Dufour, "L'actualité du quatrième Evangile," *Nouvelle Revue Théologique*, 76 (1954), 449-68.

[8] Forensic language and concepts play a significant role in this Gospel. See T. Preiss, "Justification in Johannine Thought," in *Life in Christ* (1954), pp. 9-31.

[9] Commenting on this saying A. Corell, *Consummatum Est* (1958), p. 149, remarks: "This refers to the word of Christ as administered by the Church. Mention of the Spirit indicates that the Church is already a realized fact, and the perfect tense λελάληκα shows that Jesus' own earthly mission of preaching the word is now something accomplished."

[10] Cf. R. Bultmann, *The Gospel of John* (ET 1971), pp. 6f., who attributes sections of the Gospel to a "signs-source" (*σημεῖα-Quelle*), conveying the

displacement hypotheses.[11] But the best approach is in terms of a threefold stage of editorial work: a core of eyewitness tradition derived from a Palestinian source, perhaps apostolic; theological revision by the evangelist, intended to convince the readers of the messiahship and divine sonship of Jesus; and a later redaction made when the Gospel was released for publication and chapter 21 added.

Schnackenburg remarks that "John no longer appears as the 'single-storeyed' work of an author who wrote it in one piece. It displays a pre-history in tradition, just as it can be seen to have undergone a subsequent redaction."[12] Literary criticism, while it makes clear identification of sources doubtful,[13] has produced some tentative evidence for such sources. The closest literary affinities are with Luke's special material and the possible σημεῖα-source (20:30). The evangelist apparently drew on independent and original oral narratives, ancient and reliable. There is evidence of a Palestinian milieu for these, with the teaching set in rabbinic form. It appears that he also used *logia*-sources, which contain a collection of Jesus' teaching, and incorporated liturgical and kerygmatic matters (e.g., 6:31-58) drawn from the ongoing life and interpretative ministry of the church of his day. A redactor added chapter 21 when the Gospel was published for church use.

THE PURPOSE OF THE FOURTH GOSPEL

More important than the question of John's dependence on the Synoptics and other sources is the question of why the Gospel was written at all. The starting point in answering this question is found in the words of 20:31: "These are written that you may believe that Jesus is the Christ, the Son of God, and that believing you may have life in his name." As straightforward as it seems to be, that statement is, as we shall see below, hampered by textual uncertainty, and thus it is compatible with diverse theories of the situation that called the Gospel of John into existence. We may examine a few of these proposed explanations.[13a]

At face value, the Gospel would seem to be addressed to Jews, appealing to them with the messianic figure of Jesus. Robinson has

---

teaching on miracles, and a revelation-source (*Offenbarungsreden*), containing the discourses.

11 See A. Wikenhauser, *Evangelium nach Johannes* (1957), pp. 34-37. For an account of this theory in English, see R. Schnackenburg, *The Gospel according to St. John*, I (ET 1968), 33ff.

12 *Op. cit.*, pp. 73f.

13 Cf. P. Parker, *JBL*, 75 (1956), 304: "It looks as though, if St. John used written sources, he wrote them all himself"; and D. M. Smith, "The Sources of the Gospel of John," *NTS*, 10 (1963-64), 336-51.

13a For a survey, see A. Wind, "Destination and Purpose of the Gospel of John," *NovT*, 14 (1972), 26-69.

modified this view to see it as an evangelistic tract appealing to the Jews of the Diaspora.[14] This thesis envisages a revision of the apostle's teaching by a follower who was a Greek-speaking Christian living in the Diaspora. The final edition of the Gospel, on his view, serves to plead with the Asia Minor Jews that they not repeat the mistake of refusing the Messiah, which has been made in Judaea. In contrast, John is thought to be a hellenistic Gospel by B. W. Bacon and E. F. Scott, i.e., one aimed at general audiences both Gentile and Jewish in the Greek world (so C. H. Dodd and C. F. D. Moule).[15]

Kümmel argues—with partial agreement from C. K. Barrett—that a Jewish gnostic background explains the Gospel's setting and appeal, thus making John consciously directed to a situation of religious syncretism.[16] Related to this is the view that John wrote his work to strengthen the faith of Christians in a pagan environment.[17]

Stauffer proposes that, as a message to Baptist communities, John's Gospel is consciously slanted to oppose John the Baptist.[18] Grant sees the Fourth Gospel's real meaning as a refutation of Jewish charges against Christianity.[19]

Recent study of the theological purpose of John has isolated several other key ideas and themes. W. A. Meeks and J. L. Martyn consider "Jewish polemics" the key to the Gospel.[20] Martyn's latest statement of this hypothesis is given in the light of R. T. Fortna's discussion.[21] Fortna separates a *Sitz im Leben* for a signs-source from the final edition of the Gospel. This document is a christological statement in which Jesus' messianic claims are legitimized by his miracles. The presentation is thus one of a divine-man figure, but it contained a passion story. It may be seen as a handbook for potential Jewish converts.

Martyn then asks what developments might have taken place after the publication of this "proto-John" to warrant revision and adaptation of it by the evangelist. He suggests three possibilities: the need to supply proof of Jesus' claim of messiahship (5:39; 6:30ff.;

14 J.A.T. Robinson, "The Destination and Purpose of St. John's Gospel," *NTS*, 6 (1960), 130f.; now reprinted in *Twelve New Testament Studies* (1962), 107-25.

15 Bacon, *The Gospel of the Hellenists* (1933); Scott, *The Fourth Gospel, Its Purpose and Theology* (1920); Dodd, *op. cit.;* Moule, *The Birth of the New Testament*, p. 94.

16 Kümmel, *Introduction to the New Testament*, p. 161; C. K. Barrett, *op. cit.*, pp. 32f.

17 C. K. Barrett, *op. cit.*, pp. 114ff.; A. J. B. Higgins, *The Historicity of the Fourth Gospel* (1960), pp. 13f., 21; Kümmel, *op. cit.*, p. 162.

18 E. Stauffer, *ThZ* (1956), col. 146.

19 R. M. Grant, *JBL*, 69 (1950), 305-22.

20 Meeks, *The Prophet-King* (1967); Martyn, *History and Theology in the Fourth Gospel* (1968).

21 Cf. Martyn, in *Jesus and Man's Hope* (1970), pp. 247-73; R. T. Fortna, *The Gospel of Signs: A Reconstruction of the Chief Narrative Source Underlying the Fourth Gospel* (1969).

7:17); an anti-Moses polemic, in response to Jewish claims that it was Moses who ascended and received heavenly secrets (1:17f.; 3:13; 9:28; cf. 5:45); the need to answer the standard Jewish allegation that the Christians were ditheists, worshiping two Gods (God and Jesus) (cf. 5:19ff. with 5:18).

Käsemann has advanced the thesis that the Fourth Gospel emanates from a left-wing Christian group which is protesting against incipient catholic Christianity.[22] On this showing the Gospel is heterodox in its docetic Christology and offers a cluster of *anti*-positions: it is anti-sacramental, anti-institutional, and anti-historical (because it is enthusiastic and Spirit-inspired; e.g., 16:12-15).

Accepting a multiform development of the Gospel, Schnackenburg finds the key to the message in the work of the "beloved disciple," i.e., a Jerusalem disciple (cf. esp. 18:15), who was later to become the source and authority for the "Ephesus-tradition," which rivaled that of Palestine and took concrete shape as Jewish Christians in the Diaspora faced the prospect of expulsion from the synagogue.[23]

R. E. Brown finds the key in the Paraclete passages.[24] These promises of the Spirit are addressed to three situations in particular. First, with the passage of the apostolic generation, especially with the death of the "beloved disciple" (ch. 21), the question arose how the church was to survive. Second, why the delay of the parousia? The answer is that Jesus *is* present in the Spirit. Third, the persecution being faced by the church needed a rationale. The Spirit's ministry was one of consolation and defense in the face of inquiry and opposition.

Taking all these views into consideration, we may perhaps best approach the questions of the authority and canonicity of the Fourth Gospel along the lines of the first view traced above; namely, that the New Testament book now called John was addressed to hellenistic Jews, confronting them with the messianic figure of Jesus.

AUTHORSHIP, BACKGROUND, AND DATE

R. Schnackenburg correctly remarks on the subject of the authorship of the Fourth Gospel that any hypothesis set forth must seek to do justice both to ancient church tradition and what we know from the Gospel itself.[25]

1. The external evidence for authorship might be thought to begin in the text of the Gospel as we now have it, with the suggestion

[22] E. Käsemann, *The Testament of Jesus* (ET 1968).
[23] Schnackenburg, in *Jesus and Man's Hope* (1970), pp. 223-46.
[24] Brown, "The Paraclete in the Fourth Gospel," *NTS*, 13 (1966-67), 113-32.
[25] *The Gospel According to St. John*, I, 100ff.

in 21:24 of an unidentified group who certify that the beloved disciple (21:20) is the one who wrote and bore witness. More properly, the history of external witness begins with the anti-Marcionite prologue (*c.* AD 170), which in turn depends on Papias (*c.* AD 135), who is called "a dear disciple of John." Papias is not too explicit, as we shall see, since he speaks of two groups of persons, each containing a John. The link between Papias and the apostles is as follows: "apostles" are succeeded by the elders (Aristion, John), who in turn are followed by "any who followed them," and then comes the generation of Papias.

More decisive information comes from Irenaeus (*c.* AD 180), who first reports the tradition that it was John the son of Zebedee who wrote the Gospel at Ephesus. Bishop Victor received a letter from Polycrates of Ephesus (*c.* AD 190) with an endorsement of the same Asia Minor tradition. From the end of the second century on, apostolic authorship is undisputed. But Irenaeus has another line, reflecting the same ambiguity as to two Johns as in Papias. There are two sections in Irenaeus which merit our attention.

First, in a letter to the gnostic Florinus,[26] Irenaeus speaks of his contact with Polycarp, who in turn "told about his familiar intercourse with John and with the others who had seen the Lord." But was this John the apostle? Polycarp, in his letter to the Philippians, does not refer to his relations with the apostle, so perhaps Irenaeus was deceived when he regarded Polycarp's reference to "John" as implying the apostle. However, on this matter H. P. V. Nunn observes:

> If the rest of the people in Asia knew perfectly well that John the Evangelist was not the Apostle and could have corrected the childish mistake of Irenaeus [who calls himself παῖς, and Harnack calculated his age as no more than fifteen years], had an opportunity been given them to do so, how was it that when Irenaeus, in his later life, promulgated his quite unfounded statement that the Apostle wrote the Gospel, everyone believed him both in the East and in the West?[27]

Irenaeus' second reference is more problematic. Here he appeals for his knowledge of John the apostle to "all the presbyters who had met in Asia with John, the disciple of the Lord."[28] Who were these "presbyters"? Some scholars (like Harnack) place Papias among them; others think Papias was involved in the corrupt anti-Marcionite prologue. We do not know for certain that Papias was acquainted with the Gospel.[29] On the other hand, Irenaeus clearly maintains that Papias was a hearer of John (Ἰωάννου ἀκουστής).[30]

26 Eusebius, *Church History* 5.20.4.
27 *The Authorship of the Fourth Gospel* (1952), p. 36.
28 Irenaeus, *Against Heresies* 2.33.3; Eusebius, *Church History* 3.23.3.
29 The case for this is stated by R. Heard, in *NTS*, 1 (1954-55), 131.
30 *Against Heresies* 5.33.4; Eusebius, *Church History* 3.39.1.

The complication arises from Papias' own witness, in which he refers twice to "John":

> I was accustomed to inquire about the sayings of the presbyters, what Andrew or what Peter had said (εἶπεν) or Philip or Thomas or James or John or Matthew or any other of the Lord's disciples; and what Aristion and the presbyter John, the disciples of the Lord, say (οἱ τοῦ κυρίου μαθηταὶ λέγουσιν).[31]

Two persons seem involved in this statement, both surnamed "John." One stands in the circle of the Twelve and is plainly no longer living. He is certainly to be equated with John, son of Zebedee. The other is known as "the elder/presbyter John" (ὁ πρεσβύτερος Ἰωάννης) and is still alive. Yet, Papias had heard of both groups, apostles and presbyters, only through their followers—"if anyone came who had followed the presbyters"—so there is no proof that Papias was a "hearer of John."

A conclusion drawn by a considerable body of scholars, though the question is still an open one, is that if the equating of John the presbyter with the son of Zebedee is not attested before Irenaeus and, on other grounds, is not possible or likely, then there is every probability that the author of the Gospel is the presbyter John, with whom Papias was connected. And this probability is confirmed if the Johannine epistles stem from the same source, for the author of those calls himself ὁ πρεσβύτερος.

Some scholars back away from this conclusion on the basis of a different understanding of Eusebius' motive in alluding to two "Johns." He seems to have a special reason for bringing in this character, to whom he attributes the authorship of the Apocalypse, apparently because of his Alexandrian attitude of antipathy to the Book of Revelation, on the ground of its chiliastic teaching of a millennium on earth. He dissociates that teaching from the Gospel by bringing in a second John. Perhaps, therefore, this presbyter never existed at all, or else the same person is intended in both places, but seen under two aspects: first, as associated with the other apostles and presumably working in Palestine; then, as accessible to Papias along with Aristion at a time when the other apostles had passed away. No barrier to this view is presented by the fact that in the second instance John is called the presbyter, seeing that the apostles have been called "presbyters" earlier in the sentence. The expression "the Lord's disciples" is used in connection with both groups.

The real issue is whether the Gospel which carries John's name is the work of a single individual[32] or whether the existing Gospel is an aggregate resulting from a long process of literary formation and

[31] Eusebius, *Church History* 3.39.3f.

[32] So the tradition enunciated in Eusebius, *Church History* 6.14.7: "John, urged by friends and enlightened by the Spirit, composed a spiritual gospel" (a dictum associated with Clement of Alexandria).

development, comprising strata of diverse age and origin.[33] If the latter is a preferable hypothesis, it becomes more feasible that a later John put together the earlier traditions which are traditionally linked with the name of the apostle—and this view is finding increasing favor. Moreover, there are some grounds for doubting this Zebedean tradition,[34] but these are decidedly shaky.

2. Evidence about authorship drawn from the contents of the Gospel itself is ambiguous. The internal case against apostolic authorship argues that the use of gnostic language in the Johannine discourses militates against the belief that John is an eyewitness reporting the *ipsissima verba* of Jesus at first hand.[35] Furthermore, if the apostolic authorship had been recognized by internal evidence from the Gospel itself, why did the Gospel make such slow progress in gaining recognition in the early church?[36] If John's Gospel depends literarily on Mark, it is also difficult to affirm its composition by a member of the original apostolic band.

Events in the synoptic records which mention the presence of John, son of Zebedee, are carefully omitted in the Fourth Gospel, so as to obliterate the mention of John. This is hard to square with the presence of the author. Among these are the calling of the sons of Zebedee (Mark 1:9f.); the healing of Peter's mother-in-law (Mark 1:29); the choice of the Twelve (Mark 3:13f.); the petition of John's mother (Mark 10:35ff.); Gethsemane (Mark 14:22ff.). In Acts 4:13, John along with his co-apostle are called *ἄνθρωποι ἀγράμματοι καὶ ἰδιῶται*. If this translates the rabbinic Hebrew *bôr wᵉhedᵉyôt*,[37] it marks them as men ignorant of the Torah and so incapable of producing good Greek and being able to enter into the subtleties of rabbinic debate (as in John 7, 8, and 9).

Against all these arguments, and in support of the Johannine tradition, we may set the following considerations:

First, the use of gnostic revealer language in the discourses is not proved, in spite of R. Bultmann's argument for this, and the parallels adduced are somewhat strained. In the case of John 10 recent discussion has shown that this chapter does contain a parabolic story-form (both *παροιμία* and *παραβολή* deriving from the Hebrew *māšāl*) and this brings the Good Shepherd discussion within the orbit of the synoptic parables.[38]

Second, the question of the interdependence of John and the

[33] So R. Schnackenburg, *The Gospel According to St. John*, I, 59-74.
[34] E.g., Mark 10:39, and the de Boor fragment of John's martyrdom, which records a tradition that "John the theologian and his brother James were killed by the Jews."
[35] So W. G. Kümmel, *Introduction to the New Testament*, p. 174.
[36] See C. K. Barrett, *op. cit.*, p. 97; J. N. Sanders, *The Fourth Gospel in the Early Church* (1943).
[37] C. H. Dodd, *op. cit.*, p. 82n.
[38] See J. A. T. Robinson, *op. cit.*, ch. 5.

Synoptics is difficult to solve. Many possibilities are canvassed, and their range is indicated by questions like these: Did John often deliberately avoid covering ground which had already been traversed by the earlier synoptists? Did he set out consciously to correct them? Did he use synoptic material for his own purpose? P. Gardner-Smith has argued for John's independence of the synoptic tradition.[39] This view, if convincing, would make John an independent authority for the life of Jesus, though it raises problems at crucial points where he and the Synoptics differ in historical detail (e.g., the date of the crucifixion). However, recent studies have strengthened the case for independence, though suggesting that both traditions draw from an "unformed tradition of Jesus' teaching" behind the Johannine dialogues, which have no parallel in the synoptic tradition though it can be integrated with it.[40]

While the evidence that John used the Synoptics is hardly persuasive, it is remarkable that John introduces at least some incidents of the synoptic tradition in a roundabout fashion, as though to give an understanding of the "simple" event at a deeper level. For example, 1:14 may be a theologizing interpretation of the transfiguration, and chapter 6 may be a conscious reevaluation of the synoptic Last Supper narrative. Also the Gethsemane incident is concealed in 18:1, 11, and perhaps put back into an earlier phase (12:27), like the cleansing of the temple. The revelation of messiahship follows the same pattern. Whereas Jesus' messiahship is unfolded only gradually in the Synoptics, in John it is boldly announced almost at the beginning of the ministry (1:41; cf. 4:26). The explanation of the transposition must lie in John's purpose as he collects witnesses to Christ in the earlier sections of the Gospel.

Third, the Fourth Gospel's use of Semitic literary style and thought-forms needs to be reckoned with, especially the employment of rabbinic terminology in debate, the knowledge of Palestinic customs and liturgical patterns drawn from the synagogue, the topographical allusions (e.g., John 19:13) which are shown to reflect an intimate acquaintance with Jerusalem and its environs and, now recently, a possible link with the Qumran scrolls.[41] Yet, strictly speaking, the most that this corpus of evidence can *prove* is that underlying the completed Gospel are traditions which go back to or make use of early Palestinian materials, which the final Johannine editor has woven into his work.

[39] P. Gardner-Smith, *St. John and the Synoptic Gospels* (1938).

[40] Cf. A.J.B. Higgins, *op. cit.;* C.H. Dodd, "The Portrait of Jesus in John and in the Synoptics," in *Christian History and Interpretation* (1967), ch. 9; *idem, More New Testament Studies* (1969).

[41] Of the many recent accounts of the relation between John and the Dead Sea scrolls, we may cite L. Morris, *Studies in the Fourth Gospel* (1969), ch. 6.

3. Our solution to the question of the authorship of the Fourth Gospel has to account for the amalgam of early Palestinian references and later theological editing and adaptation. It is this fusion which poses the enigma of the Fourth Gospel. R. Schnackenburg's treatment would seem to do justice to all the phenomena.[42] The theory is that the Gospel grew in defined stages: first, the Palestinian tradition stems from the apostolic source; then this tradition was redacted by the elder/presbyter who also had access to the *logia*-source, which he utilized by including those formulas which were already fixed along with units of discourse (e.g., ch. 3 and 5). He also incorporated liturgical and kerygmatic matter (e.g., the eucharistic homily in 6:31-58). Possibly, he also had the use of a σημεῖα-source (inferentially known from 20:30). Finally, the publication of the Gospel required the backing of an important church, to give it authority as a (friendly?) "rival" to the three existing Gospel books. This points to a place of origin such as Ephesus, and we may trace the authorization of the Gospel by the church at Ephesus in ch. 21, which would have been added at the time of its publication and release (see esp. 21:24).

Schnackenburg's scheme thus does justice to the tradition incorporating a Zebedean eyewitness deposit; to the interpretative work of the evangelist, who gave existing materials their theological shaping in order to convince the readers of Jesus' messiahship and divine sonship (20:31); and to the authorization by the church at Ephesus.

Our conclusion is thus framed like this: John the presbyter sets out in a polemic and evangelistic tract the authentic teaching of John the apostle as the former confronts a new situation in the Dispersion in the light of the old Palestinian debate in which the apostle had been engaged. This interpretation follows J. A. T. Robinson's line of reasoning:

> It [the Gospel] is composed, no doubt, of material which took shape as teaching *within* a Christian community *in Judaea* and under the pressure of controversy with "the Jews" of that area. But in its present form it is, I believe, an appeal to those *outside* the Church, to win to the faith that Greek-speaking *Diaspora Judaism* to which the author now finds himself belonging as a result (we may surmise) of the greatest dispersion of all, which has swept from Judaea Church and Synagogue alike. His overmastering concern is that "the great refusal" made by his countrymen at home should not be repeated by those other sheep of God's flock among whom he has now found refuge.[43]

4. If we accept the view of this Gospel as multi-layered, we have to reckon with at least two sets of milieux: first, a Palestinian

[42] *The Gospel According to St. John*, I, 72ff.

[43] *Op. cit.*, pp. 107ff. The view that the final edition of the Gospel picks up and reflects on Palestinian material forged in debates with the synagogue is, as we saw above, also Martyn's thesis, *History and Theology in the Fourth Gospel* (1968).

Judaism, possibly a heterodox wing such as would be represented by the Jewish beliefs and practices of the people of the Dead Sea scrolls; second, a hellenistic Judaism, coming under influences from the Greek world of contemporary religious thought and culture. In particular, the ideas of mediation and revelation were familiar religious interests also found in this Gospel (cf. the term λόγος).

We may conclude that the original Johannine tradition originated in Palestine and was modified by Syrian influence (because of a kinship with Ignatius of Antioch and the importance of Antioch as a cultural meeting-point of Judaism and Hellenism) before it reached Asia Minor, where it was fixed and edited, possibly at Ephesus. This conclusion would account for some features in the composition of the Gospel—its Judaic coloring, its incorporation of material which points to a setting in Diaspora Judaism and the larger world of Hellenism, and the tradition of Ephesus as its place of origin. The date of publication would be around the turn of the century (AD 100).

THE THEOLOGY OF JOHN

One of the most vexatious questions of New Testament introduction is to find a suitable *Sitz im Leben* for the publication and message of this Gospel. We shall now seek to gather together some fragments of our discussion about the Gospel of John, and to direct an inquiry to this important issue. What theological accomplishment did the evangelist intend in assembling, composing, and publishing his Gospel-book? As we saw above, a correct exegesis of 20:31 would help to decide the answer to this question. But, although it is clear that the author intended the Gospel to end on this climactic note, two textual questions arise.

The textual crux comes in the verb. *πιστεύητε* (present subjunctive) is read by ℵ* B Θ; *πιστεύσητε* (aorist subjunctive) is read by the rest. The meanings would be, respectively: "that you may continue to believe" (in other words, be confirmed in your faith) and "that you may here and now believe" (in other words, become Christians). On the choice between the two rests the question whether John's purpose is confirmatory or evangelistic.

A second question is how to construe the *ὅτι* clause following the verb. Is it an intellectual response that John is seeking? Or is he seeking to lead to a deepening or awakening of personal, "existential" commitment? If it is the former, the Gospel's purpose may be primarily polemical, i.e., offering a true knowledge of God over against a spurious or defective gnosis.

We also noted that there is current focus on a so-called signs-source, the materials of which John is regarded as having taken over intact, treating them in a redactional way, similar to Mark's use of an earlier collection of "wonder-stories" to dispose of the idea of a magical Jesus, or Matthew's use of the miracle-stories to accentuate the teaching on Jesus as Lord of the congregation.[44] John's treatment becomes visible at certain points, e.g., 4:46-54, if we are prepared to accept a redaction-critical assessment of this narrative.[45]

John's theological purpose is also seen in his conscious use of cosmic and dualistic terms and concepts to depict the meaning of the incarnation. Clearly in the prologue but seen elsewhere (e.g., 3:13, 31; 6:33, 38, 58), this motif is a theological reflection on the synoptic tradition, extrapolating from the historical ministry of Jesus the divine truth that he who came as man was none other than the incarnate Logos and saving revealer of God.

In its eschatology, the Fourth Gospel offers a curious blend of realized and futurist. While the parousia-hope is still retained and future judgment is assured (e.g., 5:25-29), the center of gravity shifts to the present possession of eternal life and the foreshortening of the end (5:24; 14:3, 4, 22, 23). This gives rise to a mystical strain in John, based on the intimate union between the believer and his Lord. In 14—17 there is a sustained commentary on the Pauline "in Christ" (ἐν Χριστῷ). An anti-docetic Christology shows that John is also combating any refusal to assert that the Logos became man (1:14; cf. 19:34).[46]

Admittedly, the preaching values of the Gospel of John are not dependent on having a prior answer to the question of its *Sitz im Leben*. A reasonable sermon can be preached on, say, John 3:16 or 10:11 without entering into the background of the Gospel as a whole. This gives John a timeless relevance as a "spiritual Gospel" (Clement of Alexandria). But certain parts of the Gospel yield their deepest meaning only when we have tried to comprehend its overall message, which in turn arises out of a historical situation. We can best attack that problem by considering the interrelation between three of John's key words: λόγος (Word), Jesus of Nazareth, and παράκλητος (Paraclete).

1. On its Old Testament background λόγος stands for the creative and revelatory Word of God, now incarnate (1:14) in Jesus. There is anti-Judaic polemic here (1:17), but John's prologue is more than preface. It is also an epitome, explaining all that follows. Indeed, world history from creation to Jesus is summed up, and the prologue

44 See H. J. Held, in *Tradition and Interpretation in Matthew*, pp. 165ff.

45 See E. Haenchen, "Johanneische Probleme," *ZThK*, 56 (1959), 19-22, and more fully in *Gott und Mensch* (1965), pp. 78-113; and R. T. Fortna, *The Gospel of Signs*, pp. 38-48, 237.

46 Against the view of E. Käsemann, *The Testament of Jesus*, who charges the evangelist with "naive docetism," and sees this Gospel as a protest in the name of a sectarian conventicle with gnosticizing tendencies against orthodox catholic Christianity, see R. P. Martin, in *TSF Bulletin*, 55 (1969), 15.

declares that that final revelation is now here in Jesus. This theme is continued in the dialogues and debates. This is why the Jews become confused: they think they are talking with Jesus of Nazareth, son of Joseph, when in fact they are listening to the incarnate Word of God.

Concerning the use of the term λόγος in John 1:1-18, there are two related questions to be faced: where does the λόγος idea come from and what use does John make of it? Greek philosophy—especially Stoicism, where λόγος stands for a metaphysical principle of the cosmos and is another name for God—is a possible source, but John's interest is obviously not metaphysical but historical (1:14); and whereas the Stoics equated λόγος and θεός as synonymous terms, John does not (1:1). Philo represents a cross-fertilization between Old Testament and Stoic ideas. He speaks of λόγος as a mediator between θεός and ὕλη (the raw material of creation), but in contrast to John he has no clear concept of a personal λόγος.

Another possible source is the Old Testament and rabbinic wisdom literature (Prov. 8:22-31; Sir. 24; Wisd. of Sol. 7). Here λόγος is wisdom in its creative and revelatory capacities and its use as a guide for practical affairs. But, contrary to John, who sets λόγος in antithesis to Torah (1:17), the two are linked in these passages.

A much more promising line of investigation begins with the concept of the divine Word in the Old Testament, both in creation (Gen. 1:1; Ps. 33:6, 9; cf. 4 Ezra 6:38; *Apoc. Baruch* 14:17) and revelation through the prophets (Isa. 55:11).[47]

These two ideas of creation and revelation through God's word are picked up in the prologue and given a christological sense (1:3, 10, 14, 18). But Manson observes a vital distinction. The prophets and wise men of Israel came with a revelation from God and it was by its very nature fragmentary and incomplete (Heb. 1:1). The incarnate λόγος embodies the full and final disclosure of God, and the revelation comes in the person who claims ultimacy (14:9). It is this claim to being God's last word to man and the perfect mirror of his very self that unites the synoptic and Johannine testimony to the person of Jesus Christ.

2. Jesus of Nazareth is for John a real man, hence the anti-docetic features of this Gospel. But he is not only such. The confusion in the minds of his hearers reflects the Jewish-Christian synagogue debates in John's lifetime. Now the evangelist recasts this (esp. ch. 9) onto a Diaspora canvas to meet this situation.[48] And in Jesus there is given a full and final revelation of God to man, which is John's superlative theme: λόγος *in toto*, i.e., in Jesus all we can know of God is given (1:18).

[47] See T. W. Manson, *On Paul and John*, pp. 144ff. We may compare too the common rabbinic description of God as "he who spoke and the world came into being" (Heb. *mî še'āmar wᵉhāyāh hā'ôlām*).

[48] See J. L. Martyn, *History and Theology in the Fourth Gospel.*

3. The παράκλητος, the Holy Spirit, completes the revelation and fills in for the church once the link with eyewitness testimony is broken. In the memorable description given by William Temple: the coming of the Paraclete is the "gain of loss."[48a] The Paraclete offers a message of hope, that Jesus is still with his church (14:16), guiding (16:13) and enabling it to face new problems arising from new situations, especially when historical connections with the apostolic era are severed. The delay of the parousia (2 Pet. 3) is one such issue. To this dilemma the answer is that the Son of Man will eventually return (5:21-29). But meanwhile, Christians ought not to spend time in impatient expectation. Persecution is another issue, and the Paraclete is the defense counsel for believers.[49]

We encounter the term παράκλητος in John 14:15-17, 26; 15: 26, 27; 16:7-11, 13-14. H. Windisch[50] has maintained that these verses form no part of the Farewell Discourses, but belong to a "doctrine concerning the Paraclete" composed of short sayings which the evangelist has taken over and interpreted by identifying the Paraclete with the Holy Spirit and by thus applying his testimony to Jesus as he bids farewell to his disciples. This theory has justly been criticized by Barrett and Johnston,[51] but we may agree with W. F. Howard's verdict that "Windisch's special service has been to show that there are five Paraclete sayings which form a unity."[52]

As with the term λόγος we need to ask two interrelated questions here: what is the origin and background of the term παράκλητος and to what use does the evangelist put it in the Upper Room discourses? It is generally agreed that the setting of the term is forensic. In intertestamental Judaism, however, the legal work of a παράκλητος ("intercessor") is in terms of a counsel for the defense (e.g., *Test. Judah* 20:1, 5). In the rabbinic understanding of the Holy Spirit's work for Israel, it is the function of the Spirit to intercede with God for Israel.[53] It is equally apparent that the rabbis and hellenistic Judaism knew of the Spirit of the Lord as a prosecuting agent and an accuser of wrong (e.g., Wisdom 1:7-9). On balance, however, the emphasis on the Spirit as advocate is predominant, and the Targum on Job 33:21-25 underscores the nation's hope that an Israelite with merit will have an angel (Heb. *mēlîṣ;* Aramaic uses the loan-word *p^eraqlît*) to come forward to show his righteousness before God.[54]

48a William Temple, *Readings in St. John's Gospel* (First and Second Series, 1940), ch. 16.
49 See R. E. Brown, "The Paraclete in the Fourth Gospel," *loc. cit.*
50 H. Windisch, *The Spirit-Paraclete in the Fourth Gospel* (ET 1968).
51 Barrett, *op. cit.*, pp. 75f., 385f.; cf. *JTS*, n.s. 1 (1950), 7-15; G. Johnston, *The Spirit-Paraclete in the Gospel of John* (1970), ch. 6.
52 *Christianity according to St John* (1943), p. 74.
53 Strack-Billerbeck, II, 243, 571; cf. Loewe and Montefiore, *A. Rabbinic Anthology*, p. 677.
54 See S. Mowinckel. *ZNTW*, 32 (1933), 97-130; J. Behm, in *TDNT*, V, 812f.

This sense of "counsel for the defense" certainly is to be seen in 1 John 2:1 where παράκλητος is used of Jesus (cf. John 14:16: "*another* παράκλητος"), but it looks as though John's usage of the term requires some special sense—for example, a helper or friend who gives strength in time of trial, or the spirit behind the apostolic preaching (παράκλησις).[55]

The evangelist's use of the term has been widely canvassed in recent discussion. One view is that John intended to portray the Spirit as Jesus' *alter ego*, bearing the same relationship to the disciples as Jesus does (16:28), teaching what Jesus taught (16:13), reminding the disciples of Jesus' acts and words (14:26; 16:14). He leads them into truth, which is embodied in Jesus (16:13; 14:6). He announces the future (16:13) as Jesus does (4:25f.). He will convict the world (16:8) as Jesus will (7:7). He comes when Jesus has gone (16:7), so in that sense the Paraclete is the presence of Jesus while Jesus is absent. The important implication of John's teaching on the Paraclete lies in the fact that the Spirit is the Spirit of Jesus (7:38, 39; 19:30; 20:22) and stands in a tandem relationship to the risen, unseen Lord.[56]

In this description of the Holy Spirit as Jesus' "other presence," the evangelist is meeting head-on the problems caused by the passing of the apostolic generation (21:20-25) and also conceivably by the deferment of the parousia hope. His answer to both issues is that it is Jesus' gift of the Spirit which provides the continuity with the apostolic age for later Christians and that by the Spirit's abiding presence with the church believers have already a part fulfilment of the promise of Jesus' return to be with them (see clearly 14:18, 19, 23, 28; 16:16, 22).

The other direction in which we should look for an understanding of the Johannine παράκλητος is in terms of a polemical interest on the part of the evangelist. This is the thesis of George Johnston,[57] who places emphasis on John's teaching on the church, which is a society of men that makes the Spirit known to the world. The church is "staffed" by outstanding leaders who embody the spiritual gifts and powers which Jesus promised as the direct result of the Spirit's coming: they are exegetes of Scripture, teachers, evangelists, prophets, consolers, and witnesses in time of persecution. These charismatic figures represent the catholic church in its struggle with false teaching, and so the preeminent role of the Spirit is to empower the church leaders so that they may rebut the claims of heretics who were current in John's day.

Johnston's is an interesting suggestion, but it lacks the persuasiveness of the first line of inquiry.

[55] See C. K. Barrett, *op. cit.*, p. 386; G. Johnston, *op. cit.*, p. 123.
[56] See R. E. Brown, *The Gospel according to John (XIII-XXI)* (Anchor Bible) (1970), *ad loc.*, and the discussion in Johnston, *op. cit.*, pp. 92ff., 123ff.
[57] See Johnston, *op. cit.*, pp. 119ff.

In light of the above, the following theological themes of the Fourth Gospel may be stated:

First, Christ as λόγος is God's answer to man's religious quest. The revelation he embodies is love.

Second, a real incarnation opposes incipient docetism and Greek ideas.

Third, serious consequences result from unbelief.

Fourth, the Holy Spirit is the church's link with the past, and his work is to contemporize Christ.

PART FIVE

The Sum of the Matter

We may now try to sum up some results which have emerged from our studies. The way to do this is by seeking to apply to selected passages of the Gospel records the principles and methods we have learned in the light of the historical and technical data which have been set before us. The scriptural passages which form the basis of the following three chapters are chosen with some care in order to put into practice certain critical principles, which are needed if these sections of Scripture are to yield their fullest import and significance. In particular, the passages are interesting for three reasons: they offer to the student an exercise in form-critical procedures; they yield their fullest sense if set in the framework of their cultural and religious settings; and, above all, they present the christological or kerygmatic motif which runs through all the Gospels, but which is most apparent in texts such as these. By examining these passages we may be in a position better to understand what it is that makes these books entitled to the general description "Gospels," i.e., records of good news which came with Jesus, Israel's Messiah and the church's Lord.

In each case, the treatment of the passage that forms the subject of the chapter is followed by more detailed exegetical notes relating to the Greek text.

CHAPTER SEVENTEEN

The Great Thanksgiving and Invitation

(Matthew 11:25-30)

"These are perhaps the most important verses in the Synoptic Gospels," A. M. Hunter writes.[1] But three preliminary textual questions must be faced before considering the problems and challenges of this passage.

In the first place, all the Greek manuscripts read πάτερ, κύριε τοῦ οὐρανοῦ καὶ τῆς γῆς (vs. 25) in Jesus' address to God: "Father, Lord of heaven and earth." The Old Latin texts, however, show considerable differences; and this divergence in many ways is repeated in the Old Latin of the parallel text in Luke (10:21f.). Birdsall concludes that the text has been subjected to a series of honorific embellishments upon the original form, which was "Heavenly Father" or "Father in the heavens."[2] This is the reading of Tatian's *Diatessaron*, as reported by Ephraem, a Syrian commentator on Tatian's harmony. The shorter form would have the merit of exactly matching Jesus' favorite name for God, "Father" or "Father in heaven."

Second, Harnack maintained that the present ἐπιγινώσκει (vs. 27) is a change from an original past tense (ἔγνω), which is the reading of Clement of Alexandria and Origen.[3] Moreover, Harnack believed that the evidence from patristic quotations shows that the form of the saying in Luke is to be preferred, and that the original version ran: "All things have been delivered to me by the Father, and no one knew the Father but the Son, and anyone to whom the Son revealed him."

Third, this suggestion also requires that the clause concerning the Father's knowledge of the Son be regarded as a later insertion,

[1] *NTS*, 8 (1961/62), 241-49; repr. in *Teaching and Preaching the New Testament* (1963), pp. 41-50.

[2] J. N. Birdsall in *The Cambridge History of the Bible*, I, 337ff. Cf. P. Winter, *NovT*, 1 (1956), 112-48.

[3] A. Harnack, *The Sayings of Jesus* (ET 1908), pp. 272-310.

added to bring the whole passage into line with Johannine Christology. Arguments to the contrary are offered by J. Chapman and A. M. Hunter, on the grounds that the usual order of the clauses in verse 27 presents a "harder reading" which late scribes found difficult and omitted, or that the church fathers were relying on their memory, or that theological sense demands that only as the Father knows the Son does the claim hold up that the Son knows the Father and is able to communicate that knowledge.[4] However, the textual evidence is confused,[5] and no certain verdict is possible on that ground alone. More convincing is the argument advanced by Jeremias that the two lines which express the Father's knowledge and the Son's knowledge are complementary and are needed to express in a Semitic circumlocution the reciprocity of the relationship.

On the question of form-analysis, all commentators agree that this is a poetic piece, full of Semitic turns of phrase and probably reflecting a Palestinian origin.[6] Its claim to authenticity, therefore, ranks high; and this claim rests on the double ground of the attested Aramaic form and language, which is discernible behind the Greek text, and the content of the logion, which is full of Semitic ideas characteristic of Jesus' teaching.

The verses fall into three strophes (I: vv. 25, 26; II: vs. 27; III: vv. 28-30). With this division, we may now proceed to look at the content and try to reconstruct the "life-setting" of the teaching in Jesus' ministry.

STROPHE I

I thank thee, O Father, Lord of heaven and earth,
That thou hast hidden these things from the wise and clever,
And hast revealed them to babes;
Indeed, Father, such was thy gracious will.

The introductory "I thank thee" corresponds to the formula used in the Qumran Thanksgiving Hymns (1QH): *'odᵉkā ᵃdōnāy*. The character of God as Father (*'Abbā*) is distinctive in Jesus' teaching. The amplifying phrase "Lord of heaven and earth" is drawn from the invocation of God expressed in the *tᵉphilla* or liturgical prayer, said at the 3 p.m. service of worship at the temple:

Blessed art thou, O Lord
God of Abraham, God of Israel, and God of Jacob
The most high God, Lord of heaven and earth.

4 J. Chapman, *JTS*, o.s. 10 (1909), 552ff.; Hunter, *op. cit.*, pp. 41f.
5 J.N. Birdsall, *loc. cit.*, has a lucid summary.
6 See the discussions in C. F. Burney, *The Poetry of our Lord*, pp. 133, 171f.; T. W. Manson, *The Sayings of Jesus*, p. 79, and *The Teaching of Jesus*, pp. 109-12; and esp. J. Jeremias, *New Testament Theology*, I, 24, 57f.

Jesus' prayer in this logion contains some hard features characteristic of the Old Testament way of putting a matter.[7] For example, he thanks God for unbelief, which is used as a contrast to a revelation accorded to unlikely persons. In this case the recipients of the inner knowledge of "these things"—possibly the report of success which has attended the mission of the seventy (so Luke)—are the disciples. If there is no immediate connection with the foregoing, and the logion is better placed as a sequel to the incident at Caesarea Philippi, then "these things" refers to Jesus' secret, which the Father has made known to Peter (Matt. 16:17). But it is still the disciples who receive the illumination. They are called *νήπιοι* (Heb. *petī*, Aram. *šabrā*), i.e., men who have no formal religious training and so were treated by the authorities as both backward and irreligious.

In the prayer Jesus realistically faces both the failure of his work to capture the support of the religious leaders in Palestine and the recognition that at least *some* people have responded, even if they are the men whom the authorities dismissed as worthless. This is the mystery of God's inscrutable will and choice (*εὐδοκία*, Heb. *rāṣôn*), expressed in terms of divine election. "Instead of criticizing this will, he offers thanks."[8]

STROPHE II

All things have been delivered to me by my Father;
And no one knows the Son but the Father;
Neither does any man know the Father but the Son,
And anyone to whom the Son is willing to reveal him.

At this point in the section the thought moves on from Jesus' thanksgiving for the revelation of the Father and its recipients to an expression of the medium of that saving knowledge. It is transmitted through the Son and by him it is made available to a company of men. Not surprisingly this claim has been challenged in view of its high-sounding and exclusive nature, and doubt has been cast on whether this part of the text contains the actual words of Jesus. Yet the value of this logion is considerable, for here if anywhere is, in Jeremias' words, "a central statement about the mission of Jesus."

Several questions have been raised against the authenticity of this saying. It appears to be set in the mold of Johannine Christology, which in turn is taken by some interpreters to reflect a dependence on hellenistic mysticism. The parallel given in the London Magical papyrus—"I know you, Hermes, and you know me. I am you and you are I"—is no real parallel, since the types of knowledge involved are quite different. The same verdict must be rendered on attempts to

[7] See J. Jeremias, *op. cit.*, p. 190n.
[8] *Ibid.*, p. 191.

find in the Fourth Gospel a meaning of "knowing God" which is akin to hellenistic and gnostic mysticism.[9] Recent discussion emphasizes that in both Matthew 11:27 and John's Christology (e.g., 5:19-20a) the mutual knowledge of Father and Son is set against an Old Testament background; and the double expression "No one knows the Son except the Father, and no one knows the Father except the Son" is a Semitic periphrasis for conveying the thought of mutual and reciprocal relationship. Only Father and Son really know each other. The effect would be to lift the statement out of the realm of metaphysical relationships and to set it in the context of personal knowledge and family intimacy. This latter view is supported by the characteristic term for God as "Father," which runs through Jesus' teaching. Because of this Jeremias argues that the address of God as *'Abbā*, dear Father, is decisively in favor of the genuineness of the logion.

The lines express the unique claim of Jesus to be both the receiver and the hander-on of divine truth. "All things" (πάντα) refers to the revelation which the Father has committed to his hands: my Father, he is saying, has given me a full revelation.

Then follows the parallelism which unites the Father and the Son in a bond of reciprocal relationship. They are one in mutual recognition and in the intention declared in the claim that only through Jesus does the saving message reach men. Because of the unique place Jesus holds in both his knowledge of God and God's recognition and acknowledgment of him,[10] he alone stands forth as the one true transmitter of the knowledge of God. The ones to whom this secret and saving message comes are the disciples, chosen and called by his ministry and service for the kingdom of God.[11] Jesus is known as a teacher come from God (Mark 10:17; cf. John 3:2) and, in the Johannine idiom, the living way to God (John 14:6). It is therefore eminently fitting that the absolute title of "Son" should be on his lips and should form a central part of the Johannine Christology, which so emphasizes the exclusive role of Jesus as the one access to God.[12]

STROPHE III

Come to me, all who labor and are burdened,
And I will give you relief.

[9] So described by G. P. Wetter, "*Der Sohn Gottes*" (1916), p. 127; cf. the critique in B. Gärtner, "The Pauline and Johannine Idea of 'To Know God' Against the Hellenistic Background," *NTS*, 14 (1967-68), 209-31.

[10] For the verb "to know" (based on the Hebrew *y-d-'*) meaning "to acknowledge," see Amos 3:2; Matt. 7:23, etc.

[11] Cf. Mark 4:11—the mystery of the kingdom is made known to the disciples; Matt. 13:16f.=Luke 10:23f.—the disciples are permitted to see and hear what prophets and righteous men in Israel yearned for.

[12] Cf. I. H. Marshall, "The Divine Sonship of Jesus," *Interpretation*, 21 (1967), 87-103.

Take my yoke upon you, and learn from me,
For I am gentle and humble in heart;
And you will find relief for your lives,
For my yoke is easy to bear, and my burden is light.

This section is not represented in Luke. That is not decisive, however, in rejecting the authenticity of this so-called Great Invitation. The verses must be allowed to stand on their own and their genuineness should be decided on their own merits. It is fitting *a priori* that Jesus' claim to be a revealer of divine secrets and to sustain an intimate relationship to the Father should be followed by a call addressed to others. The fourth line of the previous strophe contained the thought that the secret is made known to "any to whom the Son chooses to reveal him," and that choice implies a summons sent out to Jesus' contemporaries.

The parallels between Jesus' call and Wisdom's appeal in Sirach 6 and 51 have often been observed.[13] The parallels or allusions in the text of the latter read as follows:

Come to her (6:19)
Draw near to me (51:23)

You will toil (*κοπιάσεις*) (6:19b)
I have labored little (*ἐκοπίασα*) (51:27a)

You will find the rest (*εὑρήσεις τὴν ἀνάπαυσιν αὐτης*) she gives (6:28)
I found for myself much rest (*εὗρον ἐμαυτῷ πολλὴν ἀνάπαυσιν*) (51:27)

Her yoke (Heb. *'ôl*) (6:30)
Put your neck under the yoke (51:26)

Let your souls receive instruction (51:26).

The chief elements of common word usage are seen in the verbs "to labor" (*κοπιᾶν*), "to find relief/rest" (*εὑρίσκειν ἀνάπαυσιν*) and in the noun "yoke" (*ζυγός*). But we may also see a parallel in Jeremiah 6:16 (MT).

Some scholars take these parallels to mean that Jesus is identifying himself with a personification of Wisdom.[14] That is probably going too far; and, in any case, the teaching in Jesus' word stands in direct contrast with the intent of Sirach's praise of Wisdom. For the latter, what is being advocated is the study of the Torah, which is promised as a way to gain acceptance and understanding through its study and obedience. Jesus in effect says the opposite. The Torah

[13] See F. Christ, *Jesus Sophia. Die Sophia-Christologie bei den Synoptikern* (1970), pp. 110-19; also M.J. Suggs, *Wisdom, Christology, and Law in Matthew's Gospel* (1970), pp. 77ff.

[14] See R. Otto, *The Kingdom of God and the Son of Man* (ET 1943), pp. 137ff.

proved a heavy burden for the common people (*'ammē hā-'āreṣ*), who were regarded as uneducated and ignorant by the Jewish scholars, who dismissed their "*religious* ignorance and *moral* behavior" as impeding their access to salvation.[15] To such as felt the weight of this burden Jesus offered his relief and comfort, chiefly in the message of God's care and his concern for his children.

Yet the life of discipleship has another side to it. It involves the acceptance of discipline and obedience. This is expressed in Jesus' "yoke" and "burden," which are acceptable since they represent a new relationship to God and a new moral power which flows out of the confidence that God is *'Abbā* and we are his children. In the setting of Matthew's church this demand for the acceptance of Jesus' yoke may well have played a significant part, since it would stress that following Christ is at the same time a commitment to costly discipleship. It then became a feature of Matthew's polemic against an easy-going libertinistic strain on the part of converted Gentiles as they enter the church.

We may sum up the chief elements in this paragraph by remarking how it calls attention to Jesus' self-understanding of his mission and purpose in his life and ministry, which is based directly on his filial relationship to the God whose secret he conveys to those who are willing to receive it and how it sees the people who are most open to Jesus' call. They are those who stand outside the circle of Judaism's religious leaders; they are the disciples and the masses in Galilee who find Pharisaic legalism a heavy burden. The evangelist's inclusion and adaptation of this logion serve a pastoral purpose. He is directing attention to Jesus as a giver of a new discipline of obedience (cf. Matt. 5:17-20). As a church teacher in what we may believe to be a predominantly Gentile congregation, Matthew is entering a warm polemic against a false libertinism which rejects the ethical demands of the gospel.[16]

EXEGETICAL NOTES

vs. 25 *'Εν ἐκείνῳ τῷ καιρῷ*. Note that this follows the condemnation of the Galilean towns. Luke (10:21) has *ἐν αὐτῇ τῇ ὥρᾳ*, the occasion for him being the return of the seventy (-two).

ἀποκριθεὶς . . . εἶπεν. This does not indicate that Jesus was answering a question; instead, this is a Semitism from the Hebrew *wayyo'mer lē'mor*.

'Εξομολογοῦμαί σοι. Lit. "I confess to you," but here with the meaning "I thank you." Cf. Sir. 51:1, *'Εξομολογήσομαι σοι*,

15 J. Jeremias, *op. cit.*, p. 112.
16 See W. D. Davies, *The Setting of the Sermon on the Mount*, p. 435; Suggs, *op. cit.*, pp. 99ff.; and above, pp. 242-43.

κύριε βασιλευ. In Luke this is a "cry of delight" from Jesus at the success of his mission.

κύριε τοῦ οὐρανοῦ καὶ τῆς γῆς. This phrase has links with Matt. 28:18, where Jesus declares that he has been given all authority *ἐν οὐρανῷ καὶ ἐπὶ γῆς*.

ὅτι ἔκρυψας ταῦτα. For the use of *ὅτι* here cf. LaSor, *HNTG* 37.5321. *κρύπτω* = "to hide"; *AG* 455. The question of what *ταῦτα* refers to is difficult, and the context gives no help, because the setting is different in Matt. and Luke. McNeile, *The Gospel According to St. Matthew* (1915), p. 161, speculates that "if *vv.* 20-24 are not in their original position, *ταῦτα* may refer to the methods of the divine Wisdom, which were understood only by the true 'children of Wisdom.' " One possible view takes *ταῦτα* to refer to the recognition of Jesus as Messiah and Lord, but McNeile concludes "Mt. has preserved an isolated saying, so that the antecedents of *ταῦτα* are lost."

συνετῶν. "Intelligent"; *AG* 796.

ἀπεκάλυψας αὐτὰ νηπίοις. *νήπιος* = "childlike"; *AG* 539. "Jesus was thankful, not that the *σοφοί* were ignorant, but that the *νήπιοι* knew"; McNeile, *op. cit.*, p. 161.

. 26 *ὅτι οὕτως*. An elliptical "Yes, I thank you" must be read before this phrase.

εὐδοκία ἐγένετο ἔμπροσθέν σου. This expression "was a common periphrasis to avoid the anthropomorphism involved in God's volition"; McNeile, *op. cit.*, p. 162.

ὁ πατήρ. This is a nominative used for vocative case; Blass-Debrunner-Funk 147.3.

. 27 *πάντα μοι παρεδόθη*. *πάντα* here does not refer to the *πᾶσα ἐξουσία* given after the resurrection (Matt. 28:18). Here *πάντα* must refer to all knowledge of the Father. Jesus is saying that he is the only way to the Father and the only sure knowledge of God is committed to him.

καὶ οὐδεὶς ἐπιγινώσκει . . . ἀποκαλύψαι. This sentence is a "bolt from the Johannine blue"; cf. John 3:35; 5:20; 10:15; 14:9. Statements of close linkage between Father and Son are unusual in the Synoptics. Here we have an insight into Jesus' self-understanding as Son.

ᾧ ἐὰν βούληται ὁ υἱὸς. This is a conditional relative clause, formed with the relative pronoun *ᾧ* + *ἐὰν* (= "whoever").

vs. 28 Verses 28-30 are not in Luke or Q; and there is no equivalent sense in Sirach 51. But see Sirach 6:23-37.

ἀναπαύσω ὑμᾶς. *ἀναπαύω* = "to cause to rest"; *AG* 58. This verse begins the second part of this passage. The first part is the cry of delight; the second the gospel invitation addressed to the *'am hā-'āreṣ* of Jesus' audience.

vs. 29 *τὸν ζυγόν μου ἐφ' ὑμᾶς*. Jesus has a yoke for his people. They are not released from all law, but the law of Jesus is easy to obey. This is not legalism but discipline—a yoke of obedience. If Matthew's purpose in writing this Gospel is to give help to a church, it may be that he is reemphasizing the law in a church that has antinomian tendencies.

μάθετε ἀπ' ἐμοῦ. The yoke of obedience is a pre-condition to learning from Jesus.

ὅτι πραΰς εἰμι. *ὅτι* may be introducing a noun clause ("learn from me *that* I am humble") or a causal clause ("learn from me because I am humble"). *πραΰς* = "humble, meek"; *AG* 705.

καὶ ταπεινὸς τῇ καρδίᾳ. For the dative, cf. LaSor, *HNTG* 35.3231.

ἀνάπαυσιν ταῖς ψυχαῖς ὑμῶν. For the dative, cf. LaSor, *HNTG* 35.3233.

vs. 30 *χρηστὸς*. "Good" in the sense of valuable; *AG* 894. *χρηστός* was later often confused with *χριστός*.

τὸ φορτίον μου ἐλαφρόν. *φορτίον* = "load"; *AG* 873. *ἐλαφρόν* = "light"; *AG* 248. In contrast to the Jewish law, which was impossible to keep, Jesus' yoke is valuable and simple, for he gives the strength to carry it. Cf. Thomas à Kempis: "If you bear the cross, it will bear you."

HNTG is an abbreviation for W. S. LaSor, *Handbook of New Testament Greek*, 2 vols. (1973).

AG is W. Bauer, *A Greek-English Lexicon of New Testament and Other Early Christian Literature*, tr. by W. F. Arndt and F. W. Gingrich (1957).

Blass-Debrunner-Funk is *A Greek Grammar of the New Testament*, tr. and ed. by R. W. Funk (1961).

CHAPTER EIGHTEEN

The Parable of the Owner's Son

(Mark 12:1-12)

This story of Jesus is traditionally referred to as the Parable of the Wicked Tenants of the Vineyard. But, as the following discussion will show, it is better to keep the focus on the chief point of the parable—the son's destiny as the one whom the vineyard's owner sent as a final gesture, and his exalted position as "the head of the corner" (vs. 10). The title "The Parable of the Owner's Son," suggested by A. M. Hunter, is therefore much to be preferred.[1]

THE SETTING

The theme of the story is both a typical piece of history in first-century Palestinian life and Jesus' own picture of Israel's history. Our understanding of the relation between the two levels at which the story may be seen will be decided by an answer to a much debated prior question—whether Jesus' parables were meant to enforce one point, and only one point, or whether his parabolic teaching included the use of allegorical elements. The insistence that a parable has only one point of comparison goes back to A. Jülicher at the end of the last century, and has more recently been championed by C. H. Dodd and E. Linnemann.[2]

If this method is rigorously applied to the parable in Mark 12:1-12, it becomes almost impossible to avoid introducing the element of allegorizing, as critics of Dodd have observed.[3] Almost unconsciously, Dodd has recourse to ideas which can only be treated

[1] A. M. Hunter, *The Parables Then and Now* (1971), p. 104.

[2] A. Jülicher, *Die Gleichnisreden Jesu*, I (1899), 59, 74; C. H. Dodd, *The Parables of the Kingdom;* E. Linnemann, *Parables of Jesus* (ET 1966), ch. 1, pp. 5-8.

[3] M. Black, "The Parables as Allegory," *BJRL*, 42 (1960), 282f.; D. O. Via, *The Parables* (1967), p. 3; J. D. Crossan, "The Parable of the Wicked Husbandmen," *JBL*, 90 (1971), 463.

as allegorizing when he sees in the story the climax of God's dealing with his people, Israel, and his judgment on the nation which follows the death of the Messiah-Son.[4]

Recent discussion has dealt more realistically with the issues provoked by this parable, and it is now conceded that the elements of allegory cannot be denied in the extant version of the story. The focus of attention has switched to the debate on the authenticity of the various parts which go to make up the completed "whole" of the story. Specifically, the question turns on whether the allusions to Isaiah's prophecy and the question-and-answer conclusion are to be regarded as secondary. Support for the conclusion that these elements are secondary is found in the version of the parable given in the Gospel of Thomas (logion 65 and 66) which contains no reference to Isaiah or to the punishment of the tenants.[5] On this theory, the original version of the story contained no vindication of the son, and has no other point save the direct teaching that even evil men will grasp an opportunity when it is presented to them. This is enforced by the recommendation in logion 65: "He that hath ears, let him hear." The function of this hypothetical original version then corresponds to that of the Parable of the Unjust Steward (Luke 16:1-8).[6]

But this method is so severely restricted to the "one point" principle that it cannot tolerate the inclusion of those elements which, on the surface, seem to be allegorizing. It is safer, therefore, to admit the presence of these elements as potentially allegorical.[7]

The historical context of the story is realistically true to life. This raises the matter of possible allegorizing features from another angle.

> Taking into account the amazing patience of the owner, the absurd expectation of the tenants that by killing the son they would obtain the title to the property (Mark 12.7), the killing of the son, one is bound to ask whether things really could happen like that.[8]

The answer can be supplied in the affirmative, since there is evidence that the parable's details yield a realistic description of the Galilean peasants' attitude towards foreign landlords, "an attitude," comments Jeremias, "that had been aroused by the Zealot movement whose headquarters were in Galilee."[9]

The Jews at the time of Jesus' ministry lived in an occupied land which—paradoxically—the more patriotic of them still regarded as sacred soil. The presence of Roman soldiers and foreign mercenaries

4 C. H. Dodd, *op. cit.*, pp. 96-102.
5 For the text, see *New Testament Apocrypha*, I, *Gospels and Related Writings*, ed. R. McL. Wilson (ET 1963), 518.
6 So Crossan, *loc. cit.*, pp. 464f.
7 J. Jeremias' phrase, *Rediscovering the Parables* (1966), 63.
8 *Ibid.*, p. 61. Cf. C. H. Dodd, *op. cit.*, pp. 145ff.
9 Jeremias, *Rediscovering the Parables*, p. 61.

was an affront to their religious convictions and especially to the belief they cherished that the land was Yahweh's land and so their inalienable possession as his people.[10] Zealot protests from the Maccabean days to the time of Judas of Galilee in AD 6 proclaimed that God was the rightful landowner; and so as a natural corollary these nationalistic spirits held that they were the rightful tenants. The situation envisaged in the parable denies this, and the note of grim realism is continued in the inordinate desire, on the part of the tenants, not only to do away with the messengers and the son, but then to lay claim to the possession of the vineyard. In Jewish law, ownerless property could be taken over by those who were first on the scene and took possession of it.[11] This explains the murderous design stated in verse 7: "This is the heir; come, let us kill him, and the inheritance will be ours."

The enormity of the crime is seen further in the sequence recorded in the following verse. The tenants kill the son and cast his body out of the vineyard. This is the final indignity—exposing a corpse without burial (compare Sophocles' *Antigone*); and the sequence of the action in Mark has been modified in both Matthew (21:39) and Luke (20:15).[12] Mark's account, while it vividly portrays the rejection of Jesus, does not give the appearance of having been constructed *ex post facto*, since the passion of the historical Jesus did not occur precisely in this way, as Jeremias observes.[13] But the christological coloring, as he terms it, is clear in this verse, and it is this feature which claims our attention.

THE MEANING OF THE PARABLE

Whatever the problems surrounding the details of the parable are, it seems evident that Mark's redaction (and probably the pre-Markan tradition as well[14]) intended to draw greater attention to the mission, rejection, and destiny of the owner's son. The preparatory mission of the servants (to be taken allegorically in vs. 5 as representing Israel's prophets) conforms to the "rule of end stress," which is familiar in Jesus' other parables.[15] That device serves to emphasize the last item

10 See S. G. F. Brandon, *Jesus and the Zealots*, pp. 67ff. "The first act of the Roman administration, namely, the census, struck at the very roots of Yahweh's sovereignty over Israel—the holy land of his ancient promise was now regarded as the property of the Roman emperor. Every pious Jew must have felt the insult to his ancestral faith that the Roman suzerainty constituted" (p. 63).

11 J. Jeremias, *Jerusalem in the Time of Jesus*, p. 328.

12 Mark's verse seems also intended to emphasize that the murder took place *within* the vineyard, as though to accentuate the guilt of the Jewish leaders, who were blind to the son's presence within the holy community of Israel. See R. P. Martin, *Mark: Evangelist and Theologian*, p. 201.

13 *The Parables of Jesus*, p. 57.

14 So Jeremias; *ibid.*, p. 60.

15 A. M. Hunter, *op. cit.*, p. 36.

in the series. After "another . . . another . . . many others," we are prepared for the crowning overture of the property owner who "had still one other" (vs. 6), whom he sent "finally." This is Jesus' telling of the story of Israel. The servants are the prophets from Elijah to John the Baptist. Now, at the end of the line, he veils the allusion to himself as God's son and heir. This seems clear from several indications. First of all, the language of verse 6, especially with the description "beloved son" (υἱὸν ἀγαπητόν), can only refer to Jesus in Mark's Gospel, in view of the wording in 1:11 and 9:7. Secondly, the allusion to the resurrection in verses 10f., in the form of the rejected stone which God makes the keystone of the arch, points to Jesus. Third, since this was a favorite proof-text (drawn from Ps. 118:22f.), we may raise the question of the propriety of this Old Testament *testimonium*, which says no more than that the rejected servant-son will be acknowledged and acclaimed by God. There is evidence that this Psalm (117, in LXX) was interpreted messianically by the rabbis,[16] and it may further be argued that we are here in touch with a primitive tradition which saw the passion of Jesus in terms of his rejection and vindication.[17] Whether this means that such a passage says nothing about Jesus' own self-understanding and at most gives evidence of the kerygma of the earliest Palestinian church (as Fuller maintains) is a debated issue; and our view is to follow the impressive lines of reasoning given by Jeremias[18] to the effect that Jesus foresaw the possibility of a violent end to his ministry. Implicit in that preview, we seem to be required to hold that he did so because he was conscious of a self-awareness as God's unique son and final messenger and that beyond the inevitable humiliation and rejection he would suffer at the hands of the "tenants," he could look ahead to a vindication scene and to an exaltation by God himself.[19] Thus, this parable which conceivably was told originally to justify the preaching of the gospel to the "poor" (referred to as "others" in vs. 9)[20] takes on a deeper significance in Mark's hands as a way of access to the self-understand-

[16] For the reference to B. Gärtner's discussion, *Studia Theologica*, 8 (1955), 23ff., cf. R. P. Martin, *Mark, Evangelist and Theologian*, p. 194.

[17] H. E. Tödt, *The Son of Man in the Synoptic Tradition*, p. 165; R. H. Fuller, *The Foundations of New Testament Christology* (1965), pp. 118, 152-55.

[18] J. Jeremias, *New Testament Theology*, I, 278ff.

[19] W. G. Kümmel's verdict, "Das Gleichnis von den bösen Weingärtnern," in *Aux sources de la tradition chrétienne* (1950), pp. 120-31 that "no Jew, on hearing the story of the mission and death of the 'son' in our parable, could have imagined that it should be applied to the sending of the Messiah" (p. 130) now seems excessively negative in its denial. We must grant that the title "Son" was not so foreign-sounding in the ears of first-century Jews in regard to the Messiah as Kümmel claims. See R. H. Fuller, *op. cit.*, p. 32: "We may . . . conclude that . . . son of God *was just coming into use* as a Messianic title in pre-Christian Judaism," and O. Betz, *What Do We Know about Jesus?*, ch. 3.

[20] So Jeremias, *The Parables of Jesus*, p. 60.

ing of Jesus and his place within the economy of God's salvation history.

EXEGETICAL NOTES

vs. 1 αὐτοῖς. For the antecedent, cf. Mark 11:27.

ἐν παραβολαῖς. "Mark is referring not to a series of parables, but to the manner of the teaching"; Taylor, *Commentary*, p. 473.

Ἀμπελῶνα ἄνθρωπος ἐφύτευσεν. The details of this parable are taken from Isa. 5:1ff., which is a prophecy of judgment on Israel. ἀμπελών = "vineyards"; *AG* 46. φυτεύω = "to plant"; *AG* 878.

περιέθηκεν φραγμὸν. φραγμός = "fence"; *AG* 873. The φραγμός was raised to provide protection against wild animals.

ὤρυξεν ὑπολήνιον. ὑπολήνιον = "vat"; *AG* 853. The ὑπολήνιον was a vessel or trough into which the juice ran after the grapes had been squeezed.

ᾠκοδόμησεν πύργον. πύργος = "tower"; *AG* 738. The πύργος was a shelter for the husbandman and was also used for watching against thieves or animals. These details have no allegorical significance but simply belong to the total picture. Yet "it is the only parable in the Synoptics which strongly resembles an allegory. The whole becomes meaningful when the tenants are seen as representative of Israel, the servants representative of the prophets, the son representative of Jesus, etc."; Schweizer, *Commentary*, p. 239.

γεωργοῖς. "Tenants, farmers, husbandmen"; *AG* 156. "The reference to the departure of the owner is necessary to the situation and there is no need to interpret it allegorically"; Taylor, *op. cit.*, p. 473. Origen, however, interpreted this to be the withdrawal of the divine presence after God had led the people of Israel through the wilderness by means of a cloud and a fire.

ἀπεδήμησεν. ἀποδημέω = "to go on a journey" (lit. "be away [ἀπό] from home [δόμος]"); *AG* 89.

vs. 2 τῷ καιρῷ. "At the right time," which (according to Lev. 19:23-25) was the fifth year, because in the first three years no fruit could be taken by the husbandmen, and the fruit of the fourth year was given to God.

vs. 4 κἀκεῖνον. Note the crasis; cf. LaSor, *HNTG* 15.52.

ἐκεφαλίωσαν. Most manuscripts have *ἐκεφαλαίωσαν*, which means "to sum up" or "smite on the head" = "slay," while *κεφαλιόω* is not otherwise known. In any case the meaning here is probably "wounded in the head," in the sense of "strike a mortal blow." A conjecture, to read *ἐκολάφισαν*, "they buffeted" (as in 14:65) has been suggested.

vs. 5 *ἀπέκτειναν*. "A marked gradation is manifest in the fortunes of the slaves"; Taylor, *op. cit.*, p. 474.

καὶ πολλοὺς ἄλλους. Nineham, *Saint Mark*, p. 312, says "it is generally agreed that 5b is an embellishment added at a time when the story was beginning to be understood allegorically." Is there any objective evidence for this statement? "Although the action of Israel is difficult to comprehend, the action of the owner is far more incomprehensible—that is, the gracious action of God"; Schweizer, *op. cit.*, p. 241.

ἀποκτέννοντες. *ἀποκτέννω* is a late form of *ἀποκτείνω*.

υἱὸν ἀγαπητόν. *ἀγαπητός* here means "only," as in LXX Gen. 22:2. See J. A. Robinson, *Ephesians* (1904), pp. 229-33. See above, pp. 114, 179, in reference to *Ps. Sol.* 18:4.

ἐντραπήσονται. *ἐντρέπω* = "to respect"; *AG* 269.

vs. 7 *καὶ ἡμῶν ἔσται ἡ κληρονομία*. The Jews thought of themselves as tenants on God's land, and the Roman occupation was an affront to this conviction. But this parable points out that the purposes of the Jews were not so noble. In Jewish law, ownerless property could be claimed by those who first claimed the right of possession. The tenants had forgotten that the owner still lives.

vs. 8 *ἐξέβαλον αὐτὸν ἔξω τοῦ ἀμπελῶνος*. "Left him unburied. A supreme outrage in contemporary eyes"; Nineham, *op. cit.*, p. 312. Matthew and Luke have him cast out *before* he is killed, possibly to point out that Jesus was crucified outside of Jerusalem (but see Luke 13:33).

vs. 9 *ἐλεύσεται καὶ ἀπολέσει τοὺς γεωργούς*. In this parable Jesus saw himself as the "only son" sent by God as a last appeal to Israel (vs. 6); saw his rejection and death (vs. 8); and was assured of ultimate vindication.

δώσει τὸν ἀμπελῶνα ἄλλοις. "The 'other tenants' to whom the vineyard will ultimately be given are of course the Gentiles"; Schweizer, *op. cit.*, p. 241. But Nineham, *op. cit.*, p. 313, says "How St Mark understood the words it is not easy to be certain."

. 10 *Λίθον*. The relative pronoun attracts the noun from the nominative to the accusative. The quotation from Psalm 118:22-23 agrees verbatim with the LXX.

ἀπεδοκίμασαν. *ἀποδοκιμάζω* = "to declare useless"; *AG* 90. According to Nineham, *op. cit.*, p. 313, the passage "makes sense in this context only if the parable is understood as being about the 'rejection' of Jesus, and, on the assumption that that was at most a secondary implication of the original parable, most commentators regard these verses as an addition made when the story was already interpreted allegorically." Do you agree with this judgment? Why or why not?

κεφαλὴν γωνίας. "Head of the corner." "Either the cornerstone which holds the walls of the building together or the keystone of the arch or gateway"; Taylor, *op. cit.*, p. 476.

. 11 *θαυμαστή*. "Wonderful"; *AG* 353.

. 12 *κρατῆσαι*. For the infinitive cf. LaSor, *HNTG* 34.422. The hostility of the priests and scribes here is reminiscent of Mark 11:18.

καὶ ἐφοβήθησαν. RSV translates the *καὶ* as "but." Is this a good translation?

πρὸς αὐτοὺς. Here the meaning is "with reference to" rather than "to," though the sense "against them" (*πρός* + acc. in classical Greek) does commend itself.

CHAPTER NINETEEN

The Footwashing of the Disciples

(John 13:1-20)

This narrative-dialogue in the Fourth Gospel illustrates the close interrelation between soteriology, Christology, and ethics. The New Testament writers never set these elements in watertight compartments. They moved easily from statements about salvation and the person and work of the Lord into considerations of how all this affects the life of the Christian, whether personal or corporate.

The value of John's account of the footwashing of the disciples is that it illustrates the intimate and necessary connections between Jesus' own reported self-admission (vs. 14a) and his call to the disciples to act in the spirit he has just exemplified (vv. 14b, 15). In fact, the word in verse 15 is "example" (ὑπόδειγμα). We are thus encouraged to trace in this passage both a soteriological message (found in vs. 10) and an ethical summons, which arises from the fact that Jesus' action in washing the disciples' feet is paradigmatic in character and intent. What explains and gives point to both elements is the christological grounding of Jesus' recorded self-witness. He is Lord (κύριος) who chooses to play the role of a slave (δοῦλος; cf. Phil. 2:6-11); and by this humiliation and lowly service he both makes cleansing possible to his followers and sets them a pattern for their life of fellowship and service within the church (vs. 16). The call to discipleship is the call to share his spirit and to accept a way of life which conforms to the way he chose for himself.[1] In choosing them to be his followers and friends (vs. 18), Jesus set before them this model. In accepting it and patterning one's life on its diaconal and cruciform structure lies the secret of true Christian joy (vs. 17: "blessed are you, if you do" what I command and exemplify). In any case, there is no other way to understand who Jesus is (vs. 19).

[1] For the notion of "ethical conformity" as the way which relates Jesus' acts and the Christian's response in obedience and following—but not imitation—see N. A. Dahl, "Formgeschichtliche Beobachtungen zur Christusverkündigung in der Gemeindepredigt," in *Neutestamentliche Studien für Rudolf Bultmann* (1954), p. 7.

SOME EXEGETICAL ISSUES

A recent survey article has drawn attention to some of the chief issues which need to be resolved as we attempt to understand the passage.[2] The areas of study are contextual, text-critical, and interpretative; and we shall cover them in that sequence.

1. The contextual question faces a fact which all commentators have observed, namely, that the section has a clear break at the end of verse 11. Verses 1-11 set the scene and include an account of the footwashing incident, which is then followed by a conversation between Jesus and Peter. At verse 12, a discourse of Jesus opens which explains, at least in part, the significance of the incident (vs. 12b). This is given in terms of a paradigm (vs. 15) and a call to follow in the path of service.

R. Bultmann questions whether the two parts of the account belong together, since, he claims, it would be grotesque for Jesus' warning in verse 7—that the disciples do not understand what has taken place but that they will understand later on—to refer to an explanation given only minutes afterward in verses 12ff.[3] But we should not overlook the different audiences involved. Verse 7 is spoken to Peter as part of a private dialogue. In verse 12 Jesus addresses the disciples as a group, and the nature of his discussion necessarily includes a wider reference than to one man (vs. 14: "one another's feet").

Moreover, verse 7 contains phrases ("now"—ἄρτι, "afterward"—μετὰ ταῦτα) which pick up a constant theme in the Fourth Gospel. The disciples do not comprehend what is taking place before their eyes, but at a later time they will come to realize the deeper significance of these events (cf. 2:22; 7:39; 12:16; 14:26; 16:13). What lies between the series of historical events and their perceived meaning is the cluster of saving events which John calls Jesus' glorification (cf. 13:1-3). For this evangelist, these events form a watershed and divide the disciples' limited perception from their full realization. At the supper table they saw only an enigmatic occurrence: Jesus washed their feet as a servant who would attend to the guests prior to a meal. After the cross and resurrection and Jesus' return to the Father—all of which made possible the coming of the Spirit—they will understand the inner meaning of the footwashing, namely that it is an acted parable, a Johannine "sign" (σημεῖον) which powerfully illustrates the nature of what he did on the cross. He surrendered himself in lowly service and obedience as a δοῦλος, and he released a cleansing

[2] J. D. G. Dunn, "The Washing of the Disciples' Feet in John 13.1-20," *ZNTW*, 61 (1970), 247-52. The fullest survey of the history of interpretation from the church fathers to the modern period is G. Richter, *Die Fusswaschung im Johannesevangelium. Geschichte ihrer Deutung* (1967).

[3] *The Gospel of John*, p. 462.

power by which his disciples can find a full renewal ("clean over all," vs. 10).

If this train of thought is near the truth of John's writing, the promise of a fuller revelation—μετὰ ταῦτα in verse 7—is not made good in verses 12ff. but awaits the new age of the Spirit. How then are we to relate verses 12-20 to the foregoing? G. Richter is the latest exegete to conclude that verses 12-20 are redactional.[4] In fact, he traces two sets of redaction (the first, in vv. 12-17, concerned with the need for brotherly love; the second, in vs. 20, related to hospitality and other ministries of assistance). But his arguments are not conclusive, since it is always problematical to call in a redactor to smooth out alleged stylistic differences. Nor is there any compulsion to see verses 12-20 as saying something different from the earlier section. Rather, Jesus' words to the disciples as a group reinforce what has just taken place. There is little force in Richter's argument that the christological-soteriological significance of verses 5-11 cannot be harmonized with the ethical connotation of verses 12-20.

The most profitable line of inquiry which seeks to investigate the connection between these two parts is to ask whether there is a saying in the synoptic tradition which underlies the Johannine account. Bultmann suggests Luke 22:27; and J. A. T. Robinson makes an even better suggestion by remarking that in this passage we should see "the Johannine equivalent of Mark x. 32-45."[5]

As Dunn comments, the great merit of seeing the Johannine passage in the light of a possible synoptic parallel is that it opens the way to relate the teaching on Jesus' passion to his call to his followers to act in the same spirit as he exemplified in his humble service and obedience to death. In Mark 10, Jesus gave his disciples a lesson in what the life of service would be for them and ended on the climactic note of his own unique self-giving (10:45). In John, the same pattern is there in reverse order. Jesus performs his lowly task as a parabolic action, perhaps in a way similar to the Old Testament prophets' recourse to a "sign" (Heb. *'ôṯ*); and then he proceeds to apply this teaching in action by his words, which explicate and enforce the message of his deed. "Later on" (vs. 7), as the disciples recall the acts and the words from the standpoint of their post-Easter experience, they will enter into the deeper meaning of what was done and said in the upper room.

[4] *Op. cit.*, pp. 305-20, following M. E. Boismard, "Le lavement des pieds," *RB*, 71 (1964), pp. 5-24.

[5] R. Bultmann, *op. cit.*, p. 462n.; J. A. T. Robinson, "The Significance of the Foot-Washing," *Neotestamentica et Patristica*, O. Cullmann *Festschrift* (1962), p. 145. For the wider implications, see C. H. Dodd's essay, "The Portrait of Jesus in John and in the Synoptics," *Christian History and Interpretation: John Knox Festschrift*, eds. W. R. Farmer, C. F. D. Moule, R. R. Niebuhr (1967), pp. 183-98.

2. The exact nature of what Jesus did in the footwashing is to be determined by looking at verse 10. Here there is a delicate textual problem.

The text-critical issue is posed by a long and a short form of the tradition. The long text, supported by the majority of the manuscripts, including B W (D Θ) and now P^{66}, and most versions, has "He who has been bathed has no need but to wash his feet." The shorter version, given by ℵ and the Vulgate together with some old Latin texts and Origen, reads "he who has been bathed has no need to wash." The evidence is not so clear-cut as to demand a decision on that basis alone, and it is generally conceded that "the textual question cannot be settled apart from the interpretation of the verse as a whole."[6]

That interpretation is best reached by inquiring what the Johannine Jesus most likely had in view in his use of the verb "to take a bath" (λούεσθαι). Of the several possibilities, the most appropriate one in the context of the whole passage is that Jesus was referring to the cleansing to be made by his death on the cross. The necessity for this cleansing is given in verse 8 where Jesus rebukes Peter with the strong reminder: "If I do not wash you, you have no part in me." Peter adds confusion to his refusal that Jesus should wash his feet by supposing that a more complete cleansing on his whole body is needed (vs. 9), to which Jesus responds by way of clarifying the issue: the person who has been cleansed by my death—of which the footwashing is a symbol—has no need to receive any further cleansing, because there is no further provision other than the cross. Bultmann's comment is exactly to the point: "The λελ. [the man who has received the footwashing referred to in vs. 8] who is not satisifed with what he has received is reprimanded in v. 10; it is Peter, who has received the footwashing, and wanted still more."[7]

This line of interpretation means that the shorter text is the authentic one, and that the addition of "except for his feet" is a mistaken expansion of scribal copyists and editors who failed to see the logic of John's thought, which makes the verbs "to bathe" and "to wash" synonymous and places all the emphasis on the suffering of Christ's redemptive action on the cross. Jesus, in this passage, makes the emphatic Christian declaration that "once one has received the benefit of his love and death . . . he is 'entirely clean' (καθαρὸς ὅλος); further washings are pointless."[8]

3. What is in the evangelist's mind? What purpose is served by including this incident? If we accept the shorter text as original, it practically excludes any reference to the Lord's Supper, as suggested

[6] C. K. Barrett, *The Gospel According to St John*, p. 368.
[7] *Op. cit.*, p. 469n.
[8] C. K. Barrett, *op. cit.*, p. 368.

by O. Cullmann and others.[9] His argument is that John's intention is to bring together in this *pericope* the two sacraments of the church. Baptism is once-for-all as the cleansing of which Jesus speaks in verse 8; but Peter is thought to express a community desire for "a sacrament which is meant to be repeated, the Sacrament of the fellowship of love, the Lord's Supper. That is the meaning of the words *εἰ μὴ τοὺς πόδας* in v. 10." But this is to misread the nature of Peter's request in verse 9. He is asking, not for a repeated cleansing, but for a more complete cleansing to be applied to his whole body. And that, in our view, is the nub of his error. The forgiven Christian, cleansed by Jesus' blood, has all his need met. There is no hint of a repetitive cleansing in Peter's words.

Much more arguable is the suggestion that John is thinking of baptism in water, since early Christian teaching is clear at the point of its insistence that baptism into Christ and his death effectively secures a participation in Christ once-for-all.[10]

The question is not to debate this teaching, but to ask whether the teaching can rightly be discerned in the drift of John's thought, as Barrett, for example, maintains. J. D. G. Dunn, following Bultmann and Richter, has recently offered some grounds for believing that "sacraments and ritual washings are far from John's mind in this passage."[11] His strongest line of argument is that John is consistent through both the Gospel and the epistles that the cleansing effected by Jesus' death and exaltation (for John, this is a single thought) is all-sufficient and once-for-all (cf. 1 John 1:7). John, therefore, is entering a polemic against the gnostics' claim to a perfection which they believed to lie in a post-conversion experience. The evangelist repels this claim by a firm insistence that the cleansing of the cross is complete and final—it can be neither supplemented nor superseded.

What needs to be added to this conclusion is the reminder that, while John's theology requires a once-for-all salvation wrought by Jesus in his uplifting (on the cross and then to the Father's presence), it equally has an exemplary and revelatory character.[12] The unique salvation-event procures a complete cleansing, of which the footwashing is a powerfully acted sermon in advance. The spirit of Jesus which led him to the cross sets a pattern which remains for all later disciples to catch and transmute into their acts of humble service for their brothers. The best commentary is seen in 1 John 3:16 and 4:11.

[9] O. Cullmann, *Early Christian Worship*, pp. 108f. Even further from John's mind is the sacrament of penance, as suggested by A. Corell, *Consummatum Est*, p. 72.

[10] See R. P. Martin, *Worship in the Early Church*, pp. 102-109.

[11] Dunn, *loc. cit.*, p. 252. Cf. R. Bultmann, *op. cit.*, pp. 471f.; G. Richter, *op. cit.*, pp. 287ff. See also E. C. Hoskyns, *The Fourth Gospel*, p. 439; S. S. Smalley, "Liturgy and Sacrament in the Fourth Gospel," *EQ*, 29 (1957), 167.

[12] To use Barrett's terms, *op. cit.*, p. 367.

EXEGETICAL NOTES

s. 1 *πρὸ δὲ τῆς ἑορτῆς τοῦ πάσχα*. If this passage is taken to refer to the Last Supper, John's account is at odds with the Markan story, which has the supper on the day of the Passover (though it should be noted that the Markan account, 14:1, 14:12, is not self-consistent except by recourse to special interpretation of 14:12). See commentaries *ad loc.* Barrett, *op. cit.*, pp. 39ff., argues that Mark is correct and points out that by indicating that the Last Supper was before the Passover, "John emphasizes that the eucharist was not simply a Christian, or Christianized, Passover" (p. 364). J. N. Sanders, *The Gospel according to St. John* (1968), says that Jesus may have had the Passover supper the day before "because he knew that by the proper time he would be dead" (p. 303). There has been much debate over the timing of these last events.

ἦλθεν αὐτοῦ ἡ ὥρα. The hour of his death and exaltation. This is an important Johannine distinctive running throughout the Gospel (see ch. 16, p. 272), with the hinge coming at 13:1.

ἵνα μεταβῇ . *μεταβαίνω* "is equally applicable to the thought of death as a departure, and to ascension into heaven"; Barrett, *op. cit.*, p. 364.

ἀγαπήσας τοὺς ἰδίους τοὺς ἐν τῷ κόσμῳ. *ὁ κόσμος* occurs 40 times in the last discourses of John. "The emphasis lies on the distinction between the world and the disciples"; Barrett, *op. cit.*, p. 365. "This world" is virtually the equivalent of "this age" in the Synoptics.

εἰς τέλος ἠγάπησεν αὐτούς. *εἰς τέλος* may mean "unto the end" (of his life) or "completely" or "finally." Which fits best in this context?

s. 2 *δείπνου γινομένου*. *δεῖπνον* = "dinner"; *AG* 172. The textual authorities are divided over the reading of the verb: *γινομενου* or *γενομενου*. What decision would you make in the light of the evidence and the context?

βεβληκότος. For the genitive absolute see LaSor, *HNTG* 34.5.

ἵνα παραδοῖ. *παραδοῖ* is a vernacular form of *παραδῷ*. A *ἵνα*-clause dependent on a participial clause is extremely rare.

vs. 3 *πάντα ἔδωκεν αὐτῷ ὁ πατήρ*. Cf. Matt. 11:27 and exegetical notes to ch. 17 above for a discussion of *πάντα*. "Jesus washes their feet in full knowledge that he is the Son of God and the heavenly Man"; Barrett, *op. cit.*, p. 366.

πρὸς τὸν θεὸν ὑπάγει. For the present tense cf. LaSor, *HNTG*

31.521. The present tense may also indicate that Jesus knew that the hour of departure was at hand.

vs. 4 τίθησιν τὰ ἱμάτια. "That this action is also a symbolic representation of his death is suggested by the use of the word τίθησιν, which is used in 10:15ff. for Jesus' laying down of his life"; Sanders, *op. cit.*, p. 306.

λέντιον. "Towel"; *AG* 472.

vs. 5 τὸν νιπτῆρα. "Basin"; *AG* 542; only here in the New Testament.

νίπτειν τοὺς πόδας τῶν μαθητῶν. νίπτω = "wash"; *AG* 542. "The washing of the master's feet was a menial task which was not required of the Jewish slave (in distinction from slaves of other nationalities)"; Barrett, *op. cit.*, p. 366. Thus the act was despised by Jews. Here Jesus acts out his role as the Christ: the Lord (vs. 13) of the world becomes the despised servant.

ἐκμάσσειν. "Wipe"; *AG* 242.

vs. 6 σύ μου νίπτεις τοὺς πόδας. Note the use of the pronoun for emphasis: "Do *you* wash my feet?"

vs. 7 ὅ ἐγὼ . . . ταῦτα. Again, note the use of the pronouns for emphasis: "What *I* do, *you* do not yet know."

οἶδας . . . γνώσῃ. Here it is evident that these two words are synonymous. For the form of γνώσῃ cf. LaSor, *HNTG* 24.4151.

μετὰ ταῦτα. This must refer to the death and resurrection of Jesus and the coming of the Holy Spirit. Only by the Spirit can men understand the actions of Jesus.

vs. 8 Οὐ μὴ νίψῃς . . . εἰς τὸν αἰῶνα. The addition of εἰς τὸν αἰῶνα makes the negation (οὐ μή + subjunctive; cf. LaSor, *HNTG* 31.334) even stronger.

Ἐὰν μὴ νίψω . . . ἐμοῦ. Peter's "objection to receiving Jesus' love and service is in fact Satanic pride"; Barrett, *op. cit.*, p. 367. Sanders, *op. cit.*, p. 307, says "Here it becomes evident that the washing of the disciples' feet is a symbol of baptism, which is necessary to salvation. It is in fact the institution of the sacrament." Is this a reasonable interpretation of this verse? See J. D. G. Dunn, *loc. cit.*

vs. 10 ὁ λελουμένος . . . καθαρὸς ὅλος. Barrett, *op. cit.*, p. 368, takes λούω to be synonymous with νίπτω and prefers the shorter reading: οὐκ ἔχει χρείαν νίψασθαι. Thus he understands the meaning to be "whoever has been washed has no need to be washed again." In other words, "you are already with me, you need not be washed again to be initiated." However, J. A. T. Robinson, *loc. cit.*, paraphrases Jesus: "I am not asking you to follow me to death, for where I am going you cannot follow me now—though you shall follow afterwards. I am asking only that you should all identify yourselves with me in the cup I must drink and the baptism I must undergo" (pp. 146f.).

ἀλλ' οὐχὶ πάντες. "Judas has been washed with the other disciples; all possibility therefore of a merely mechanical operation of salvation, whether by baptism or otherwise, is excluded"; Barrett, *op. cit.*, p. 369.

vs. 12 *ἀναπέσεν. αναπίπτω* = "recline." The apostles were reclining on couches; cf. 6:10. But at Passover this posture was mandatory.

Γινώσκετε τί πεποίηκα ὑμῖν. Here the act becomes an example of humility.

vs. 13 *ὑμεῖς φωνεῖτε με' Ὁ διδάσκαλος καὶ ὁ κύριος. διδάσκαλος* and *κύριος* are in the nominative (rather than accusative objects of *φωνεῖτε*); thus they are articular nominative used for vocative. *κύριος* here stands in stark contrast to the act of the *δοῦλος* which Jesus has just performed; cf. Phil. 2:5-11.

vs. 14 *καὶ ὑμεῖς ὀφείλετε . . . πόδας*. J. A. T. Robinson, *loc. cit.*, takes this whole passage to be parallel to Mark 10:35-45. The point of the passage, then, lies in this verse. "If they are to have any part with him it can only be as they are prepared to drink the cup he drinks and be baptized with his baptism. The disciple cannot be greater than his master; he must follow in his path of humiliation; only so can he hope to share in the blessedness of the coming age. For Jesus' glory means the glory of the servant" (p. 145).

vs. 15 *ὑπόδειγμα γὰρ ἔδωκα ὑμῖν. ὑπόδειγμα* = "example, pattern"; *AG* 851. Jesus' action is thus a paradigm for his disciples.

vs. 16 *οὐκ ἔστιν δοῦλος . . . αὐτόν*. Cf. Mt. 10:24. "The disciples are not to expect better treatment than their Lord received, nor are they to think themselves too important to perform the acts of service which he performed"; Barrett, *op. cit.*, p. 370. In fact, only by service can their Lord be glorified.

ἀπόστολος. John never refers to the disciples as apostles, thus it is better to translate this "emissary."

vs. 17 *εἰ ταῦτα οἴδατε, μακάριοί ἐστε ἐὰν ποιῆτε αὐτά*. "The form of this sentence, with two conditional clauses and the main clause between them, is designed to bring out that to know these things is necessary for salvation, but insufficient unless we actually put it into practice"; Sanders, *op. cit.*, p. 310.

vs. 18 *οὐ περὶ πάντων ὑμῶν λέγω*. The exception is of course Judas. Does it include the "beloved disciple" as a man not included in the Twelve? For the "beloved disciple," see John 13:23; 19:26; 20:2ff.; 21:7, 15-23.

ἐγὼ οἶδα τίνας ἐξελεξάμην. ἐκλέγομαι = "to choose." There are two possible interpretations: "I know whom I have really chosen, and of course I have not really chosen Judas"; or "I knew those whom I have chosen, and therefore know that Judas, though I have chosen him, will betray me." The correspondence with 6:70 suggests the second; however, the *ἀλλ' ἵνα* following suggests the former.

Ὁ *τρώγων . . . αὐτοῦ. τρώγω* = "to eat"; *AG* 836. *ἐπαίρω* = "raise up"; *AG* 281. *πτέρναν* = "heel"; *AG* 734. The quotation comes from Ps. 41:9.

vs. 19 *ἀπ' ἄρτι*. "Now."

πρὸ τοῦ γενέσθαι. πρό + inf. = antecedent time; cf. LaSor, *HNTG* 34.4211. "Before [it] happens" refers to the betrayal.

ἵνα πιστεύσητε. "Jesus' foreknowledge, even if it cannot help Judas, can be turned to some account in reassuring the faithful when the disaster happens"; Sanders, *op. cit.*, p. 311.

ὅτι ἐγώ εἰμι. Cf. 8:24. "I am" or "I am he" is used quite often to refer to God. Cf. especially Isaiah 43:10: "in order that you might know and believe and understand that I am." But in John it is an overt claim to deity, corresponding to the Heb. *'ᵃnî hû'*. See E. Stauffer, *Jesus and His Story*, pp. 142ff.; and Barrett on 8:24 (p. 283).

vs. 20 *ὁ λαμβάνων . . . τὸν πέμψαντά με*. Cf. vs. 16. "As verse 16 has prepared us to expect, Jesus now speaks of his sending out his disciples"; Sanders, *op. cit.*, p. 311. The apostles here are made absolute representatives of God, and they are to act the part by being servants even as their master was a servant.

Select Bibliography

Barrett, C. K., *New Testament Background: Selected Documents* (London, 1956).
——, *The Gospel According to St. John* (London, 1956).
——, *Luke the Historian in Recent Study* (Philadelphia/London, 1961).
Bornkamm, G., *Jesus of Nazareth* (London, ET 1960).
Bornkamm, G., Barth, G., and Held, H. J., *Tradition and Interpretation in Matthew* (Philadelphia/London, ET 1963).
Brandon, S. G. F., *Jesus and the Zealots* (New York/Manchester, 1967).
Brown, R. E., *The Gospel According to John*, 2 vols. (New York/London, 1966, 1971).
Bruce, F. F., *New Testament History* (New York/London, 1969).
Bultmann, R., *The History of the Synoptic Tradition* (Oxford, ET 1963).
——, *The Gospel of John* (Philadelphia/Oxford, ET 1971).
Caird, G. B., *Saint Luke* (London, 1963).
Conzelmann, H., *The Theology of St. Luke* (London, ET 1960).
Cullmann, O., *Jesus and the Revolutionaries* (New York, ET 1970).
Davies, W. D., *Paul and Rabbinic Judaism* (London, 1955).
Dodd, C. H., *According to the Scriptures* (London, 1952).
——, *The Interpretation of the Fourth Gospel* (Cambridge, 1953).
——, *Historical Tradition in the Fourth Gospel* (Cambridge, 1963).
Ellis, E. E., *The Gospel of Luke* (London, 1966).
Evans, C. F., *The Beginning of the Gospel . . .* (London, 1968).
Farmer, W. R., *The Synoptic Problem* (New York, 1964).
Gasque, W. W., and Martin, R. P. (ed.), *Apostolic History and the Gospel* (Grand Rapids/Exeter, 1970).
Gundry, R. H., *The Use of the Old Testament in St. Matthew's Gospel* (Leiden, 1967).
Guthrie, D., *New Testament Introduction* (London, 1970).

Hill, D., *The Gospel of Matthew* (London, 1972).
Hoskyns, E. C., and Davey, F. N., *The Riddle of the New Testament*[3] (London, 1947).
Jeremias, J., *Jesus' Promise to the Nations* (London/Naperville, ET 1958).
_____, *The Eucharistic Words of Jesus*[2] (Philadelphia/London, ET 1966).
_____, *Jerusalem in the Time of Jesus* (Philadelphia/London, ET 1969).
_____, *New Testament Theology*, Vol. 1 (Philadelphia/London, ET 1971).
Jervell, J., *Luke and the People of God* (Philadelphia, 1972).
Kümmel, W. G., *Introduction to the New Testament* (Nashville/London, ET 1965).
Leaney, A. R. C., *The Gospel According to St. Luke* (New York/London, 1958).
Manson, T. W., *The Teaching of Jesus*[2] (Cambridge, 1935).
_____, *The Sayings of Jesus* (London, 1949).
_____, *The Servant Messiah* (Cambridge, 1953).
_____, *Studies in the Gospels and Epistles*, ed. M. Black (Philadelphia/Manchester, 1962).
_____, *On Paul and John* (Naperville/London, 1963).
Marshall, I. H., *Luke: Historian and Theologian* (Grand Rapids/Exeter, 1970).
Martin, R. P., *Mark: Evangelist and Theologian* (Grand Rapids/Exeter, 1972).
Metzger, B. M., *The Text of the New Testament*[3] (Oxford, 1968).
Moule, C. F. D., *The Birth of the New Testament* (New York/London, 1962).
Nineham, D. E., *Saint Mark* (London, 1963).
_____ (ed.), *Studies in the Gospels* (Oxford, 1955).
Russell, D. S., *The Method and Message of Jewish Apocalyptic* (London, 1964).
Schnackenburg, R., *The Gospel According to St. John*, Vol. 1 (London, 1968).
Schweitzer, A., *The Quest of the Historical Jesus* (London, 1910).
Stendahl, K., *The School of St. Matthew*[2] (Philadelphia/Lund, 1968).
Stonehouse, N. B., *Origins of the Synoptic Gospels* (Grand Rapids/London, 1963).
Streeter, B. H., *The Four Gospels* (London, 1924).
Taylor, V., *The Formation of the Gospel Tradition* (London, 1935).
_____, *The Gospel According to St. Mark* (London, 1959).
_____, *The Passion Narrative of St. Luke*, ed. O. E. Evans (Cambridge, 1972).
Wilson, S. G., *The Gentiles and the Gentile Mission in Luke-Acts* (Cambridge, 1973).

Index of Principal Subjects

Index of Modern Authors

Index of Main Scripture References